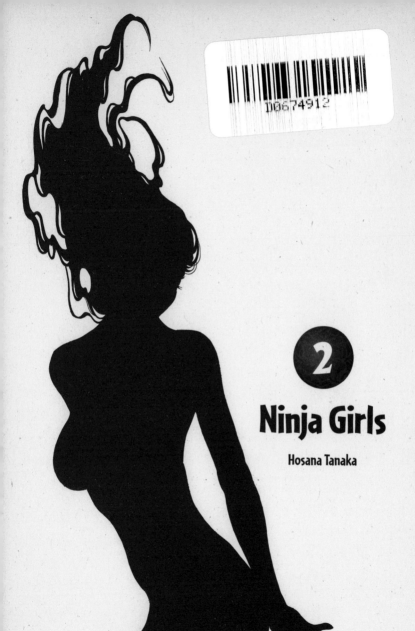

2

Ninja Girls

Hosana Tanaka

Ninja Girls
Volume 2

Contents

The Rebellion So Far:

The only surviving member of the Katana family, Raizo, set off on a journey with the Katana shinobi: Kagari, whose special technique is Shintaigo; Kisarabi, a clairvoyant sniper; and Himemaru, a rope-master and master of disguise. Raizo's life is thrown into chaos by these three beautiful yet dangerous shinobi.

The goal of the journey is to restore the Katana family. Their plan is for Raizo to marry into a noble family, and to then use their influence and power to strengthen the Katana name. Throughout their journey together, Raizo senses his bonds with the shinobi deepening.

Meanwhile, Seigan is planning his attacks. He wants to make Kagari's Shintaigo technique his own—by any means necessary. Their journey keeps becoming more and more chaotic!

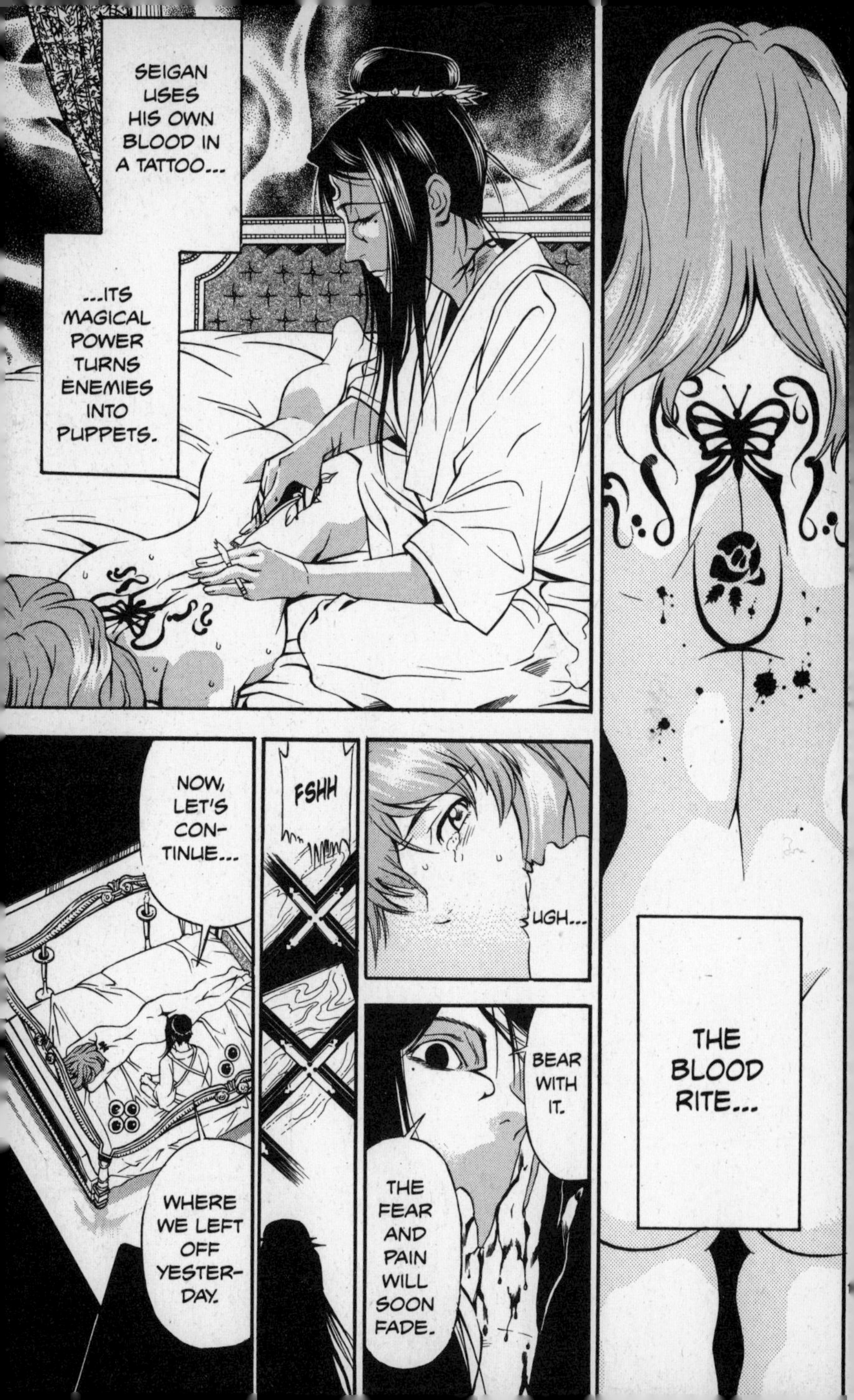
THE BLOOD RITE...
SEIGAN USES HIS OWN BLOOD IN A TATTOO...
...ITS MAGICAL POWER TURNS ENEMIES INTO PUPPETS.
UGH...
BEAR WITH IT.
THE FEAR AND PAIN WILL SOON FADE.
FSHH
NOW, LET'S CONTINUE...
WHERE WE LEFT OFF YESTERDAY.

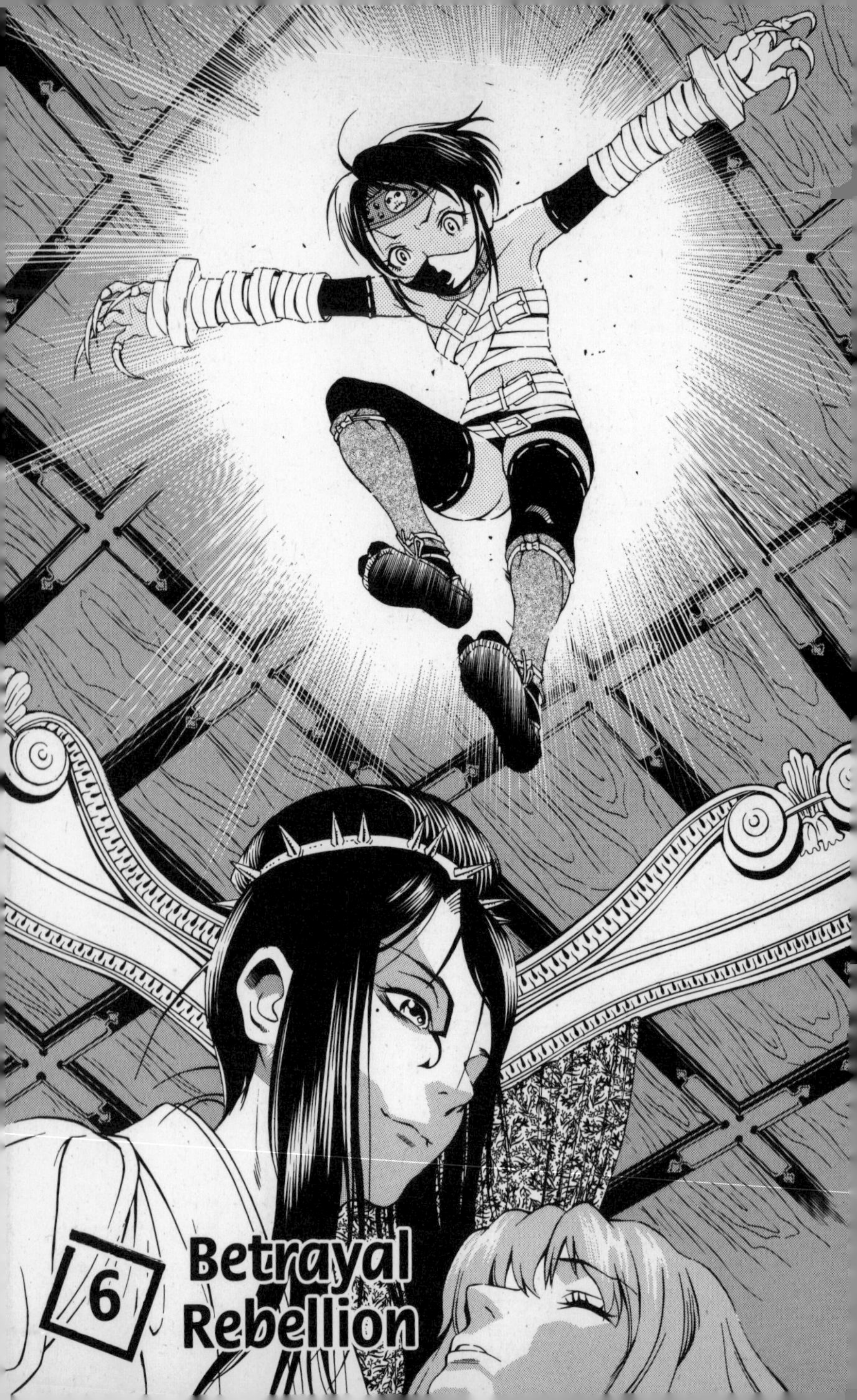
6
Betrayal Rebellion

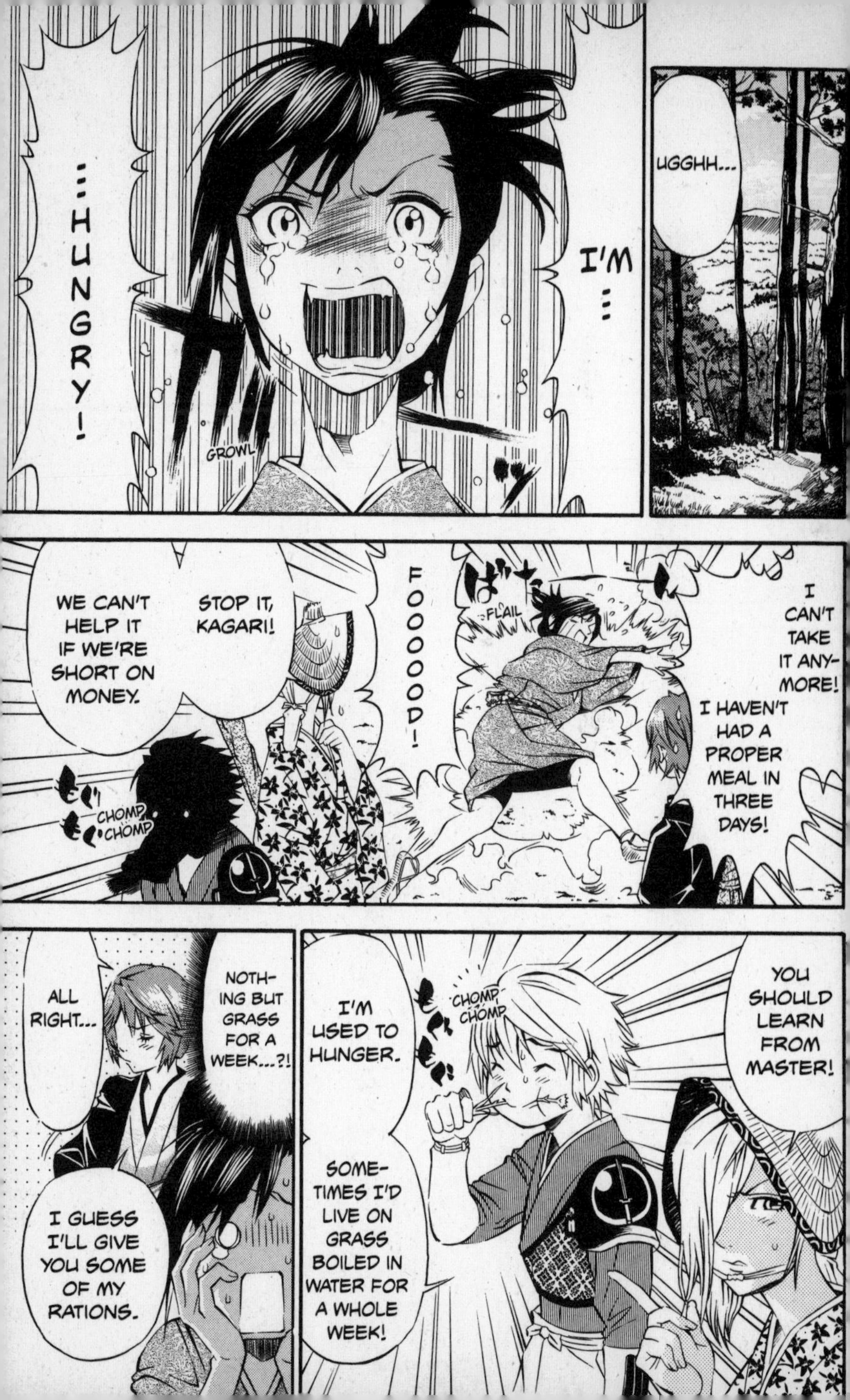
UGGHH...
I'M...
...HUNGRY!
GROWL
I CAN'T TAKE IT ANY-MORE!
I HAVEN'T HAD A PROPER MEAL IN THREE DAYS!
FLAIL
FOOOOOOD!
STOP IT, KAGARI!
WE CAN'T HELP IT IF WE'RE SHORT ON MONEY.
CHOMP CHOMP
YOU SHOULD LEARN FROM MASTER!
CHOMP CHOMP
I'M USED TO HUNGER.
SOME-TIMES I'D LIVE ON GRASS BOILED IN WATER FOR A WHOLE WEEK!
NOTH-ING BUT GRASS FOR A WEEK...?!
ALL RIGHT...
I GUESS I'LL GIVE YOU SOME OF MY RATIONS.

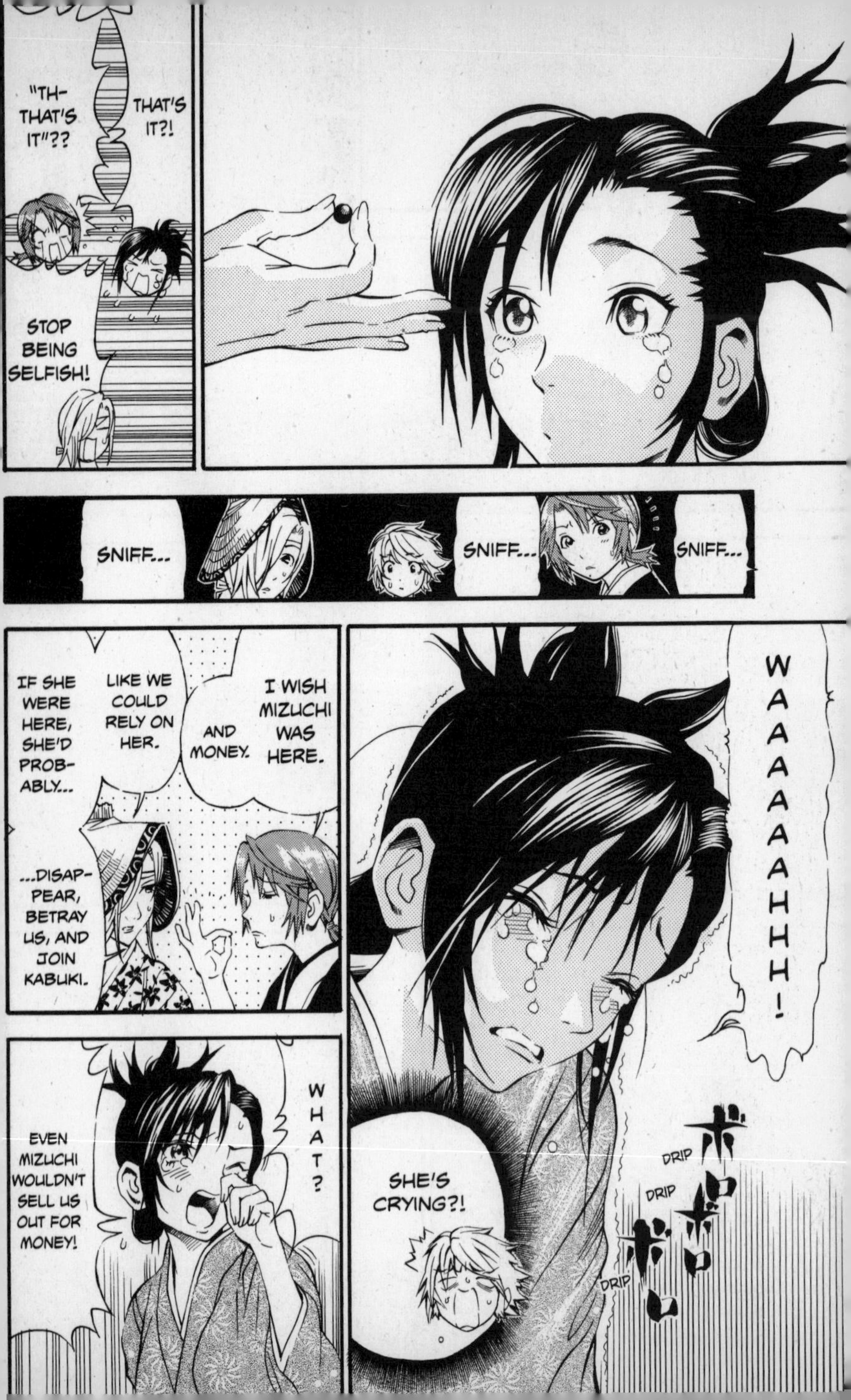
THAT'S IT?!
"TH- THAT'S IT"??
STOP BEING SELFISH!
SNIFF...
SNIFF...
SNIFF...
WAAAAAAHHH!
DRIP
DRIP
DRIP
SHE'S CRYING?!
I WISH MIZUCHI WAS HERE.
AND MONEY.
LIKE WE COULD RELY ON HER.
IF SHE WERE HERE, SHE'D PROBABLY...
...DISAPPEAR, BETRAY US, AND JOIN KABUKI.
WHAT?
EVEN MIZUCHI WOULDN'T SELL US OUT FOR MONEY!

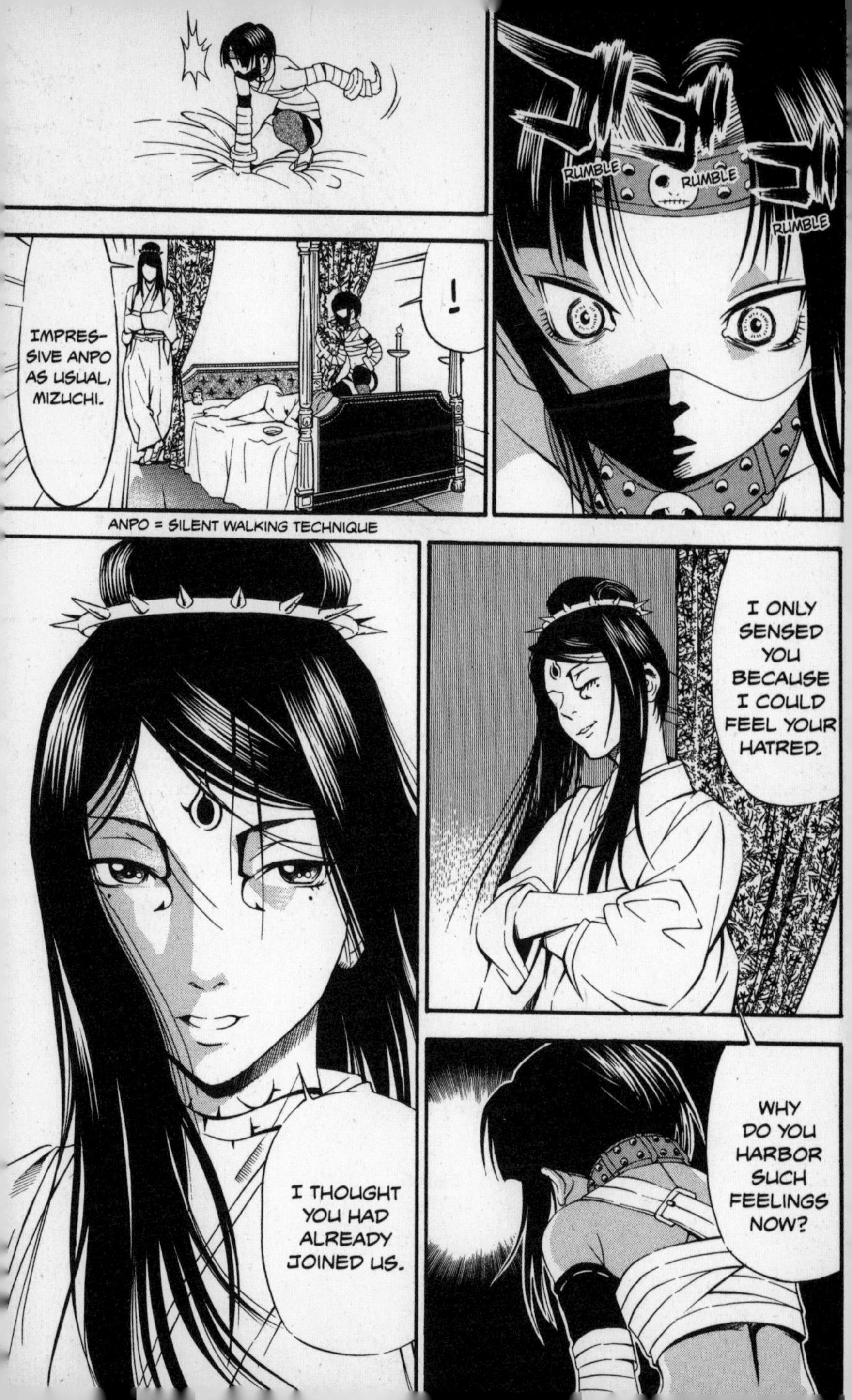
RUMBLE
RUMBLE
RUMBLE
!
IMPRESSIVE ANPO AS USUAL, MIZUCHI.
ANPO = SILENT WALKING TECHNIQUE
I ONLY SENSED YOU BECAUSE I COULD FEEL YOUR HATRED.
WHY DO YOU HARBOR SUCH FEELINGS NOW?
I THOUGHT YOU HAD ALREADY JOINED US.

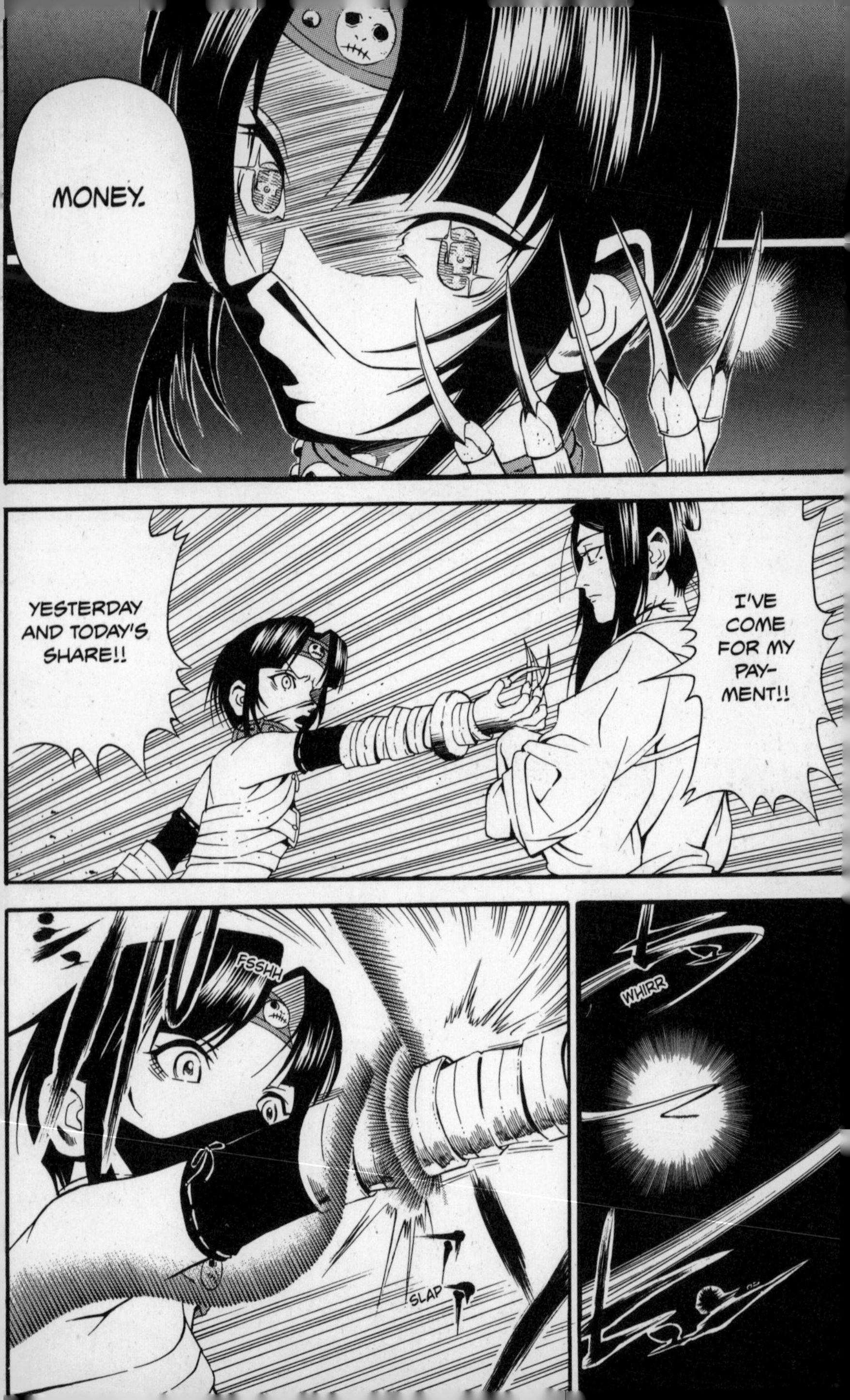
MONEY.
I'VE COME FOR MY PAY-MENT!!
YESTERDAY AND TODAY'S SHARE!!
WHIRR
FSSHH
SLAP

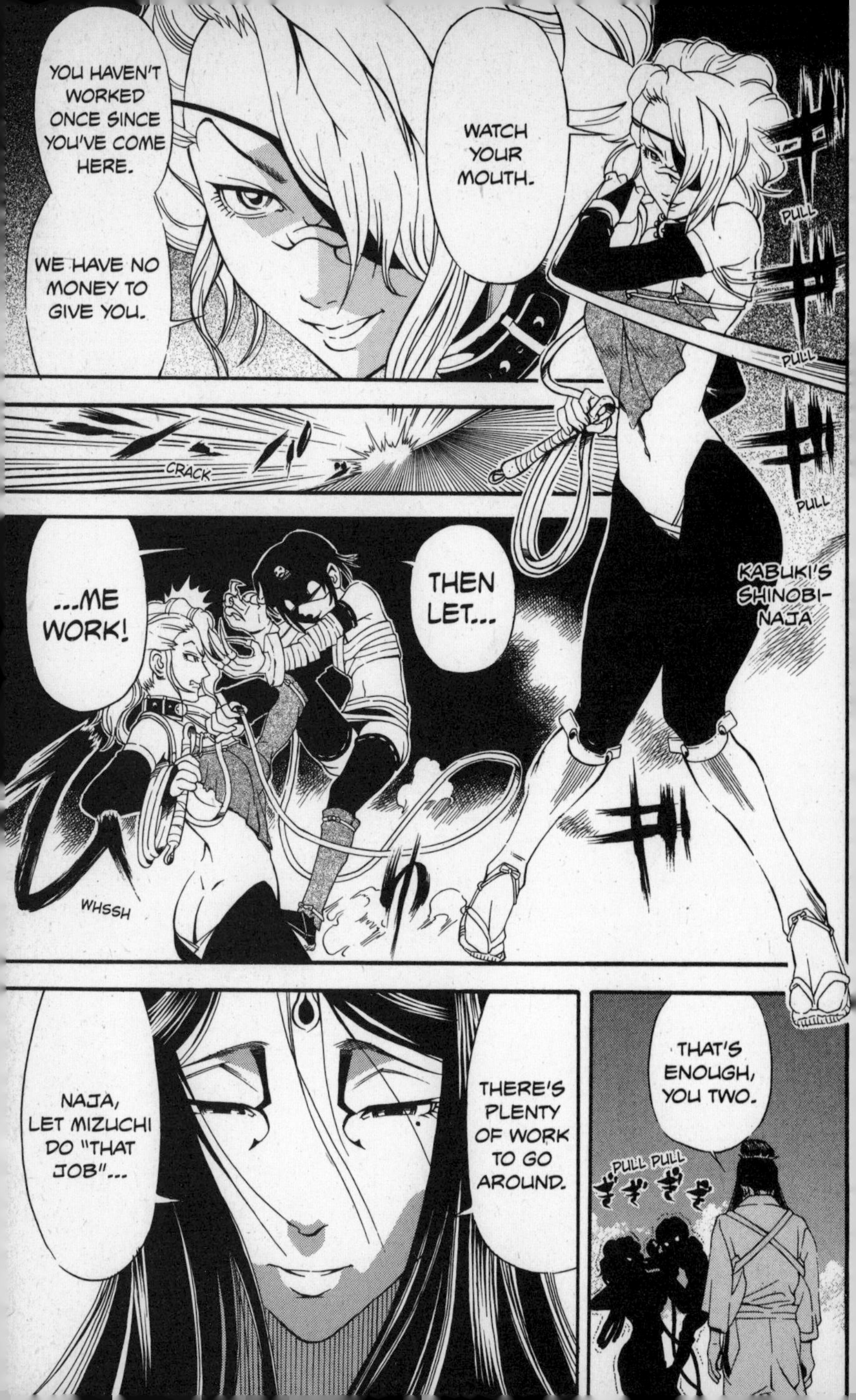
WATCH YOUR MOUTH.
PULL
PULL
PULL
KABUKI'S SHINOBI-NAJA
YOU HAVEN'T WORKED ONCE SINCE YOU'VE COME HERE.
WE HAVE NO MONEY TO GIVE YOU.
CRACK
THEN LET...
...ME WORK!
WHSSH
THAT'S ENOUGH, YOU TWO.
PULL PULL
THERE'S PLENTY OF WORK TO GO AROUND.
NAJA, LET MIZUCHI DO "THAT JOB"...

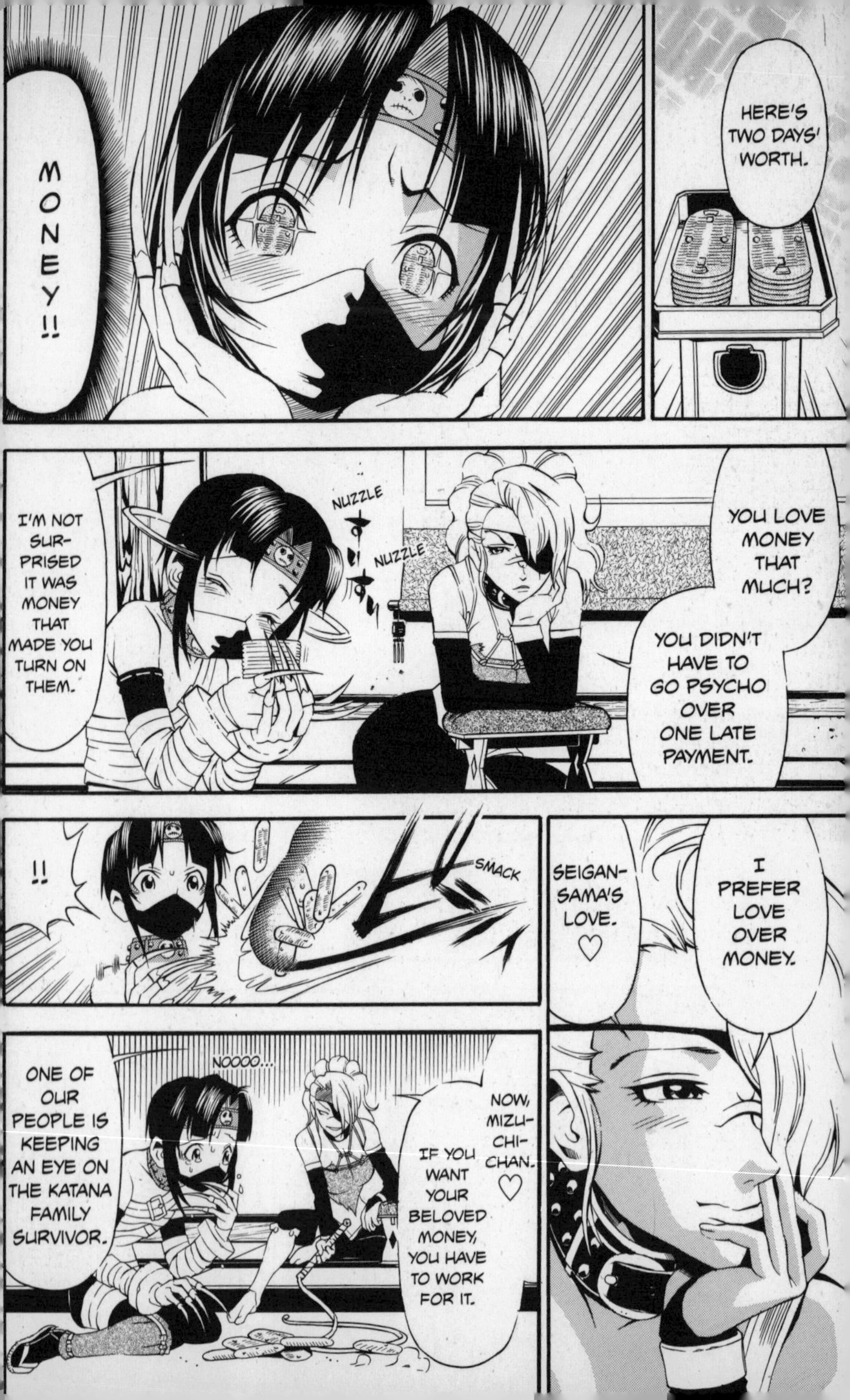

HERE'S TWO DAYS' WORTH.
MONEY!!
YOU LOVE MONEY THAT MUCH?
YOU DIDN'T HAVE TO GO PSYCHO OVER ONE LATE PAYMENT.
NUZZLE
NUZZLE
I'M NOT SURPRISED IT WAS MONEY THAT MADE YOU TURN ON THEM.
I PREFER LOVE OVER MONEY.
SEIGAN-SAMA'S LOVE. ♡
SMACK
!!
NOW, MIZUCHI-CHAN. ♡
IF YOU WANT YOUR BELOVED MONEY, YOU HAVE TO WORK FOR IT.
NOOOO...
ONE OF OUR PEOPLE IS KEEPING AN EYE ON THE KATANA FAMILY SURVIVOR.

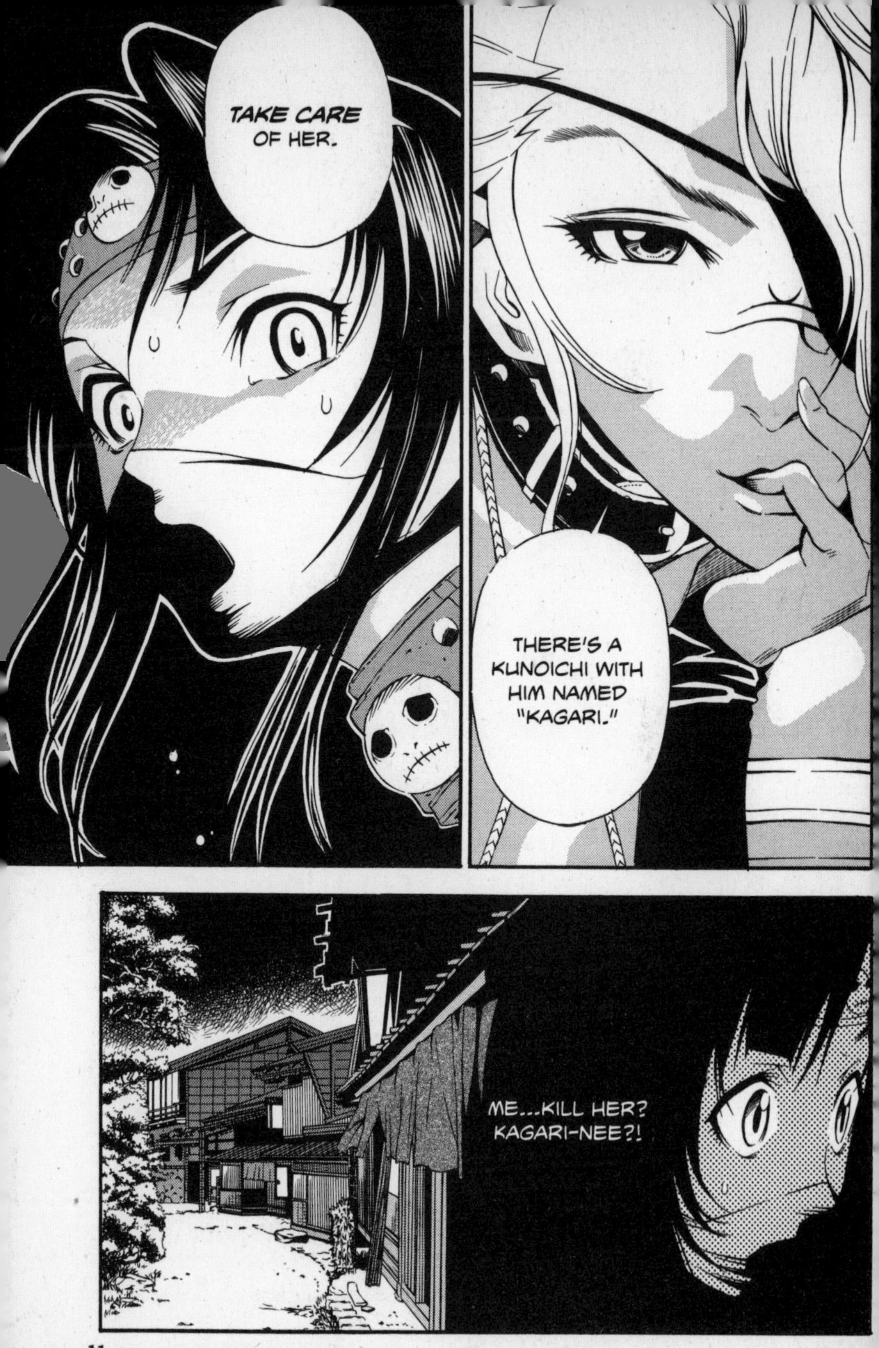
THERE'S A KUNOICHI WITH HIM NAMED "KAGARI."
TAKE CARE OF HER.
ME...KILL HER? KAGARI-NEE?!

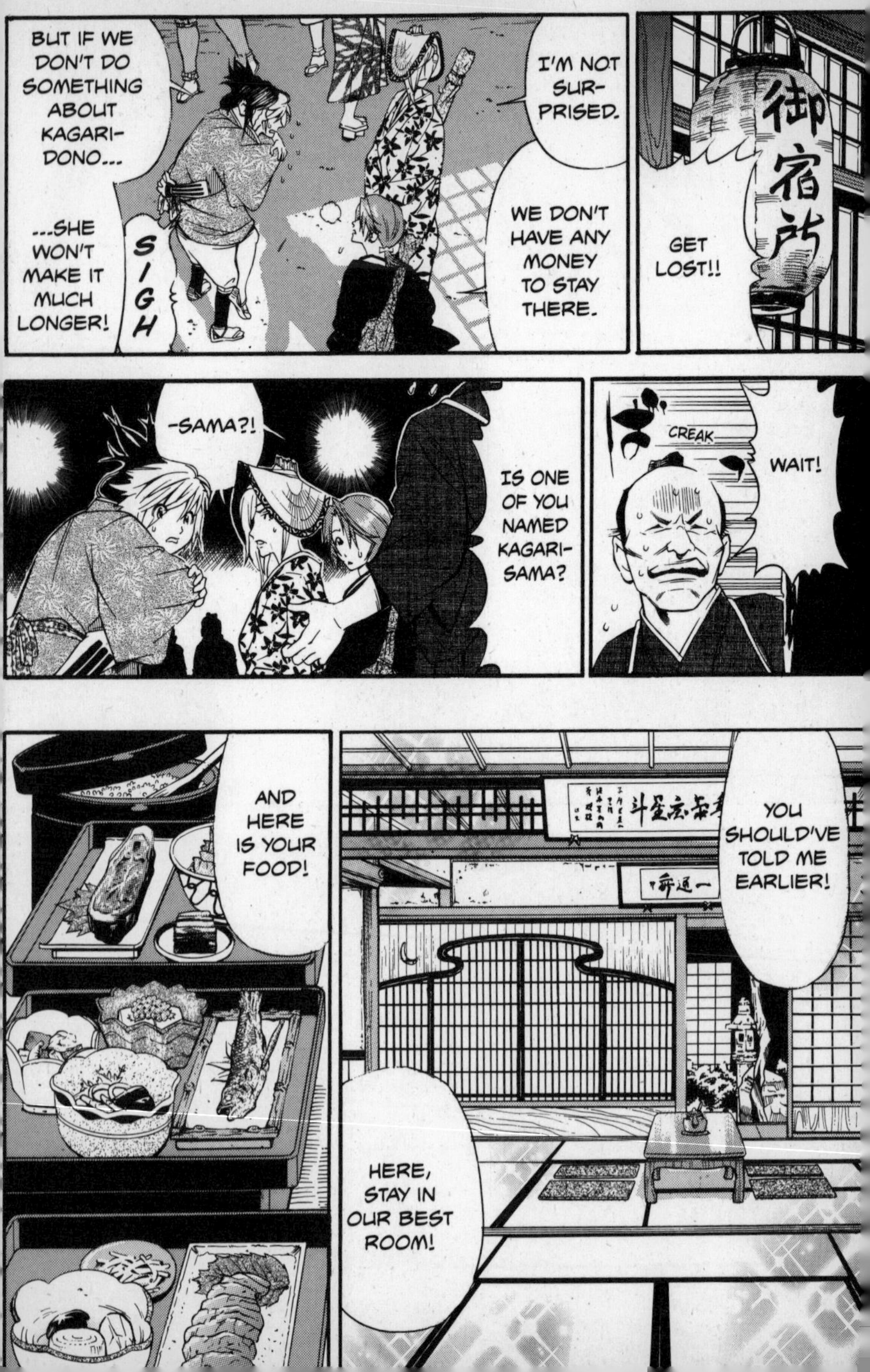
御宿所
GET LOST!!
I'M NOT SURPRISED.
WE DON'T HAVE ANY MONEY TO STAY THERE.
SIGH
BUT IF WE DON'T DO SOMETHING ABOUT KAGARI-DONO...
...SHE WON'T MAKE IT MUCH LONGER!
CREAK
WAIT!
IS ONE OF YOU NAMED KAGARI-SAMA?
-SAMA?!
YOU SHOULD'VE TOLD ME EARLIER!
HERE, STAY IN OUR BEST ROOM!
AND HERE IS YOUR FOOD!

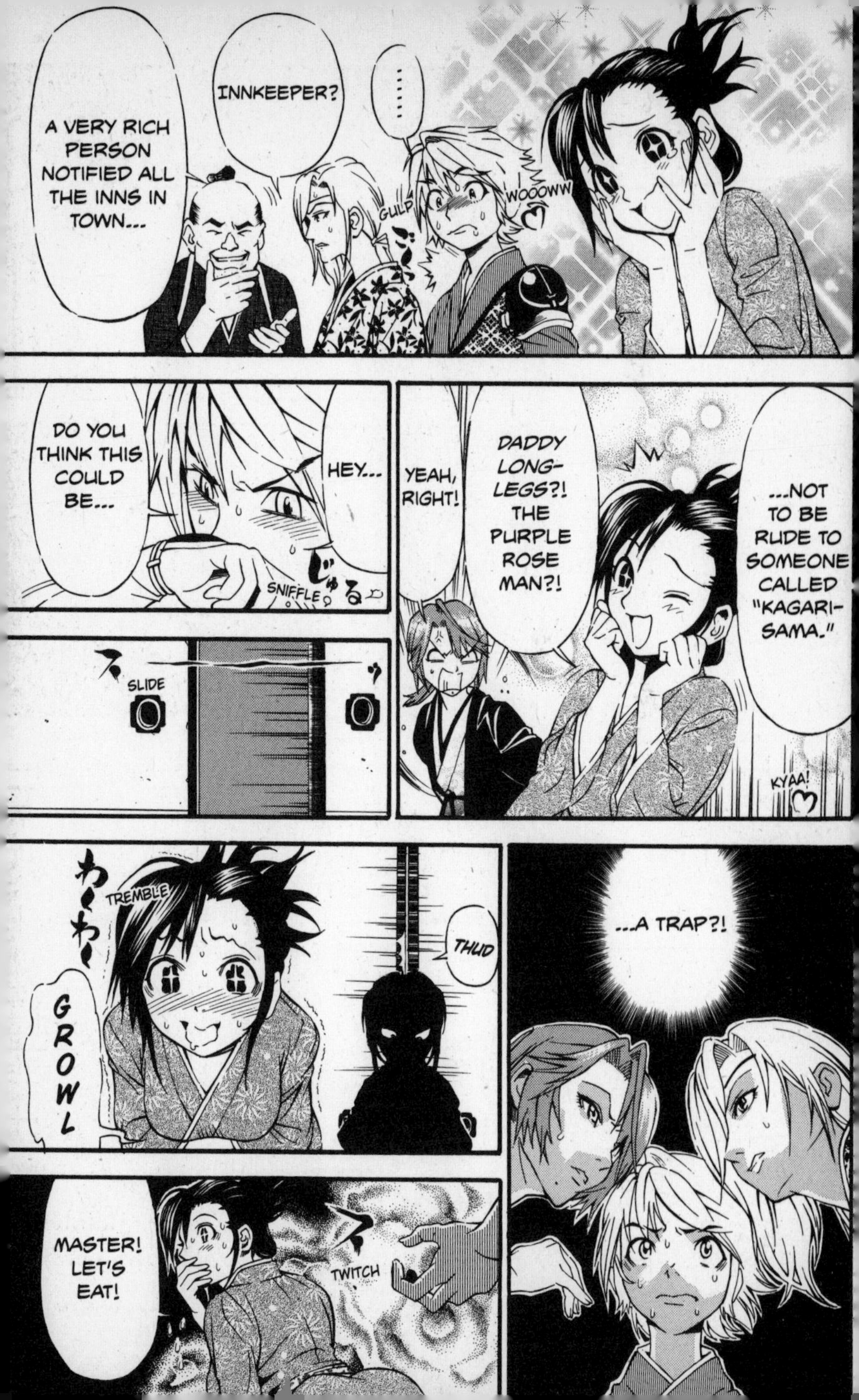
WOOOWW
......
GULP
INNKEEPER?
A VERY RICH PERSON NOTIFIED ALL THE INNS IN TOWN...
...NOT TO BE RUDE TO SOMEONE CALLED "KAGARI-SAMA."
KYAA!
DADDY LONG-LEGS?! THE PURPLE ROSE MAN?!
YEAH, RIGHT!
HEY...
DO YOU THINK THIS COULD BE...
SNIFFLE
SLIDE
...A TRAP?!
THUD
TREMBLE
GROWL
TWITCH
MASTER! LET'S EAT!

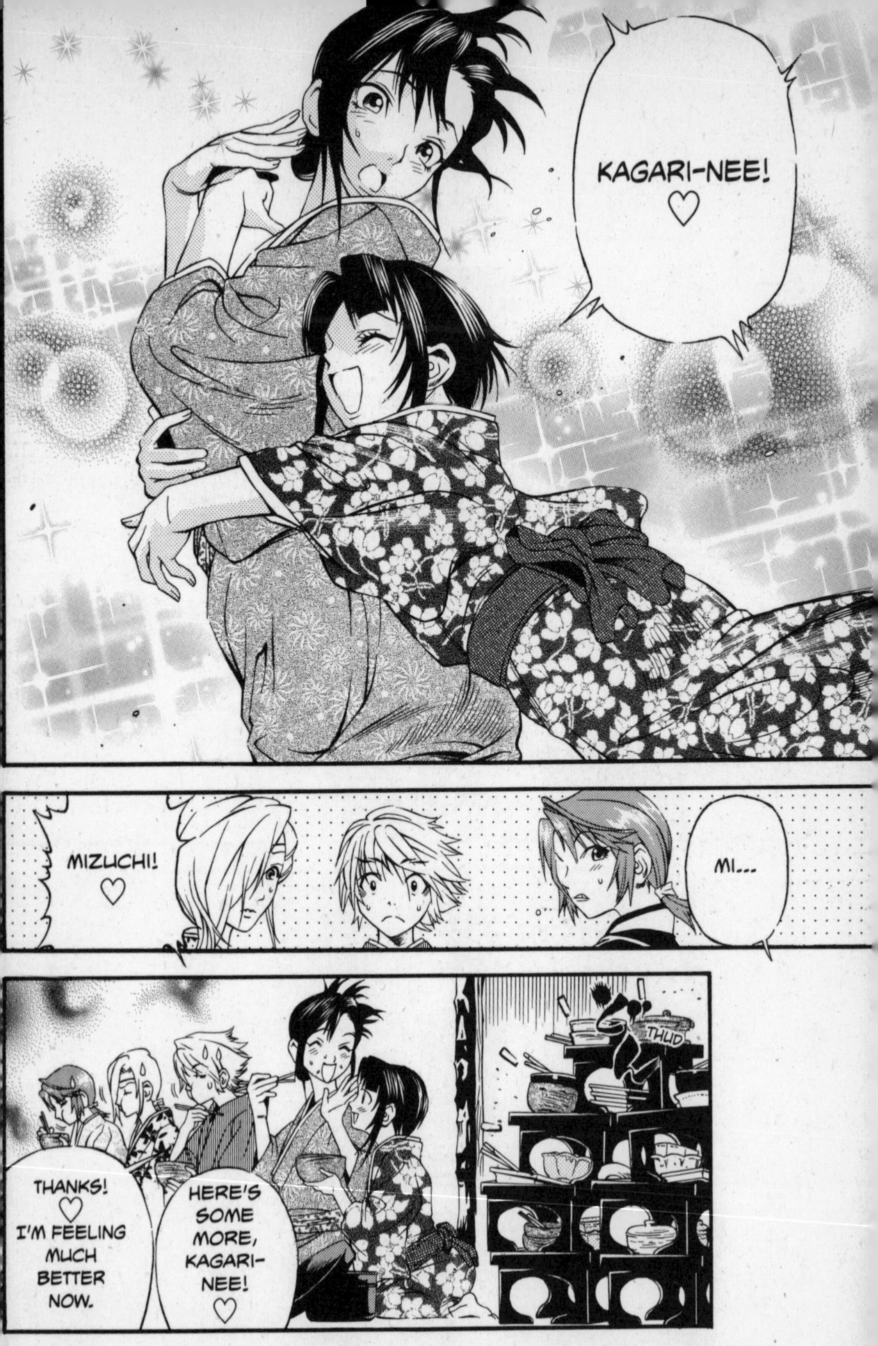
KAGARI-NEE! ♡
MI...
MIZUCHI! ♡
THUD
HERE'S SOME MORE, KAGARI-NEE! ♡
THANKS! ♡ I'M FEELING MUCH BETTER NOW.

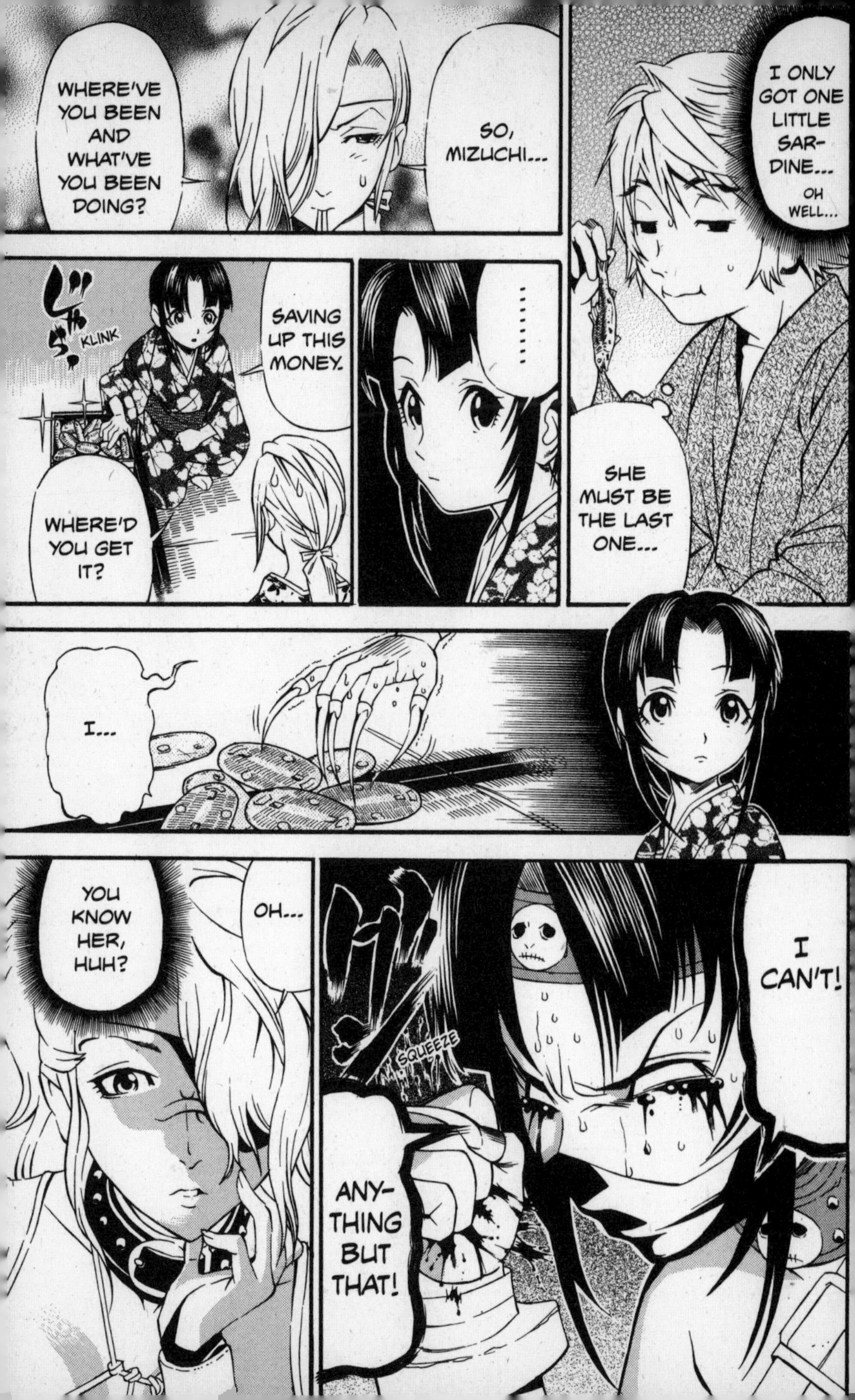
I ONLY GOT ONE LITTLE SARDINE...
OH WELL...
SHE MUST BE THE LAST ONE...
SO, MIZUCHI...
WHERE'VE YOU BEEN AND WHAT'VE YOU BEEN DOING?
......
SAVING UP THIS MONEY.
KLINK
WHERE'D YOU GET IT?
I...
I CAN'T!
SQUEEZE
ANYTHING BUT THAT!
OH...
YOU KNOW HER, HUH?

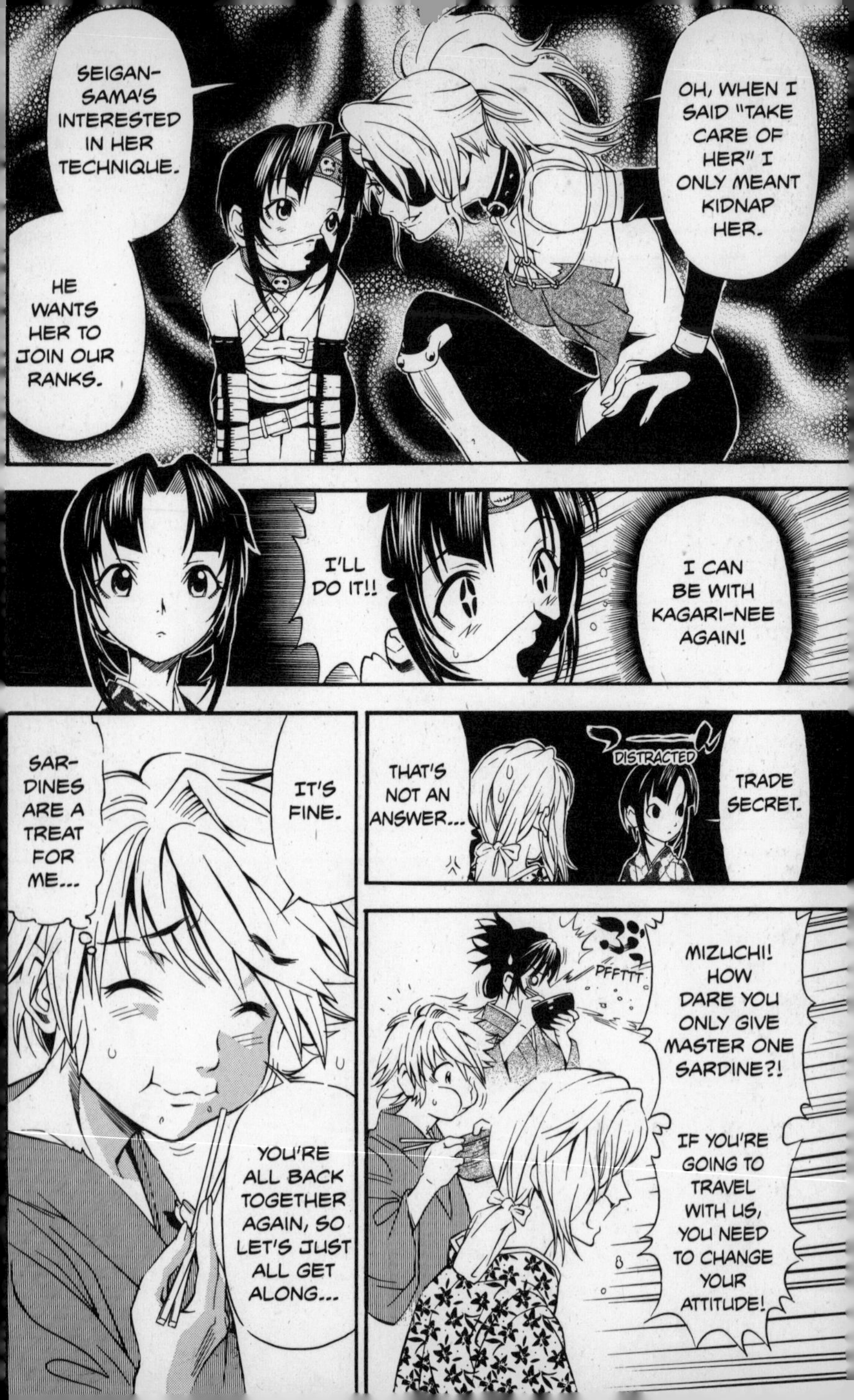
OH, WHEN I SAID "TAKE CARE OF HER" I ONLY MEANT KIDNAP HER.
SEIGAN-SAMA'S INTERESTED IN HER TECHNIQUE.
HE WANTS HER TO JOIN OUR RANKS.
I CAN BE WITH KAGARI-NEE AGAIN!
I'LL DO IT!!
TRADE SECRET.
DISTRACTED
THAT'S NOT AN ANSWER...
MIZUCHI! HOW DARE YOU ONLY GIVE MASTER ONE SARDINE?!
PFFTTT
IF YOU'RE GOING TO TRAVEL WITH US, YOU NEED TO CHANGE YOUR ATTITUDE!
IT'S FINE.
SARDINES ARE A TREAT FOR ME...
YOU'RE ALL BACK TOGETHER AGAIN, SO LET'S JUST ALL GET ALONG...

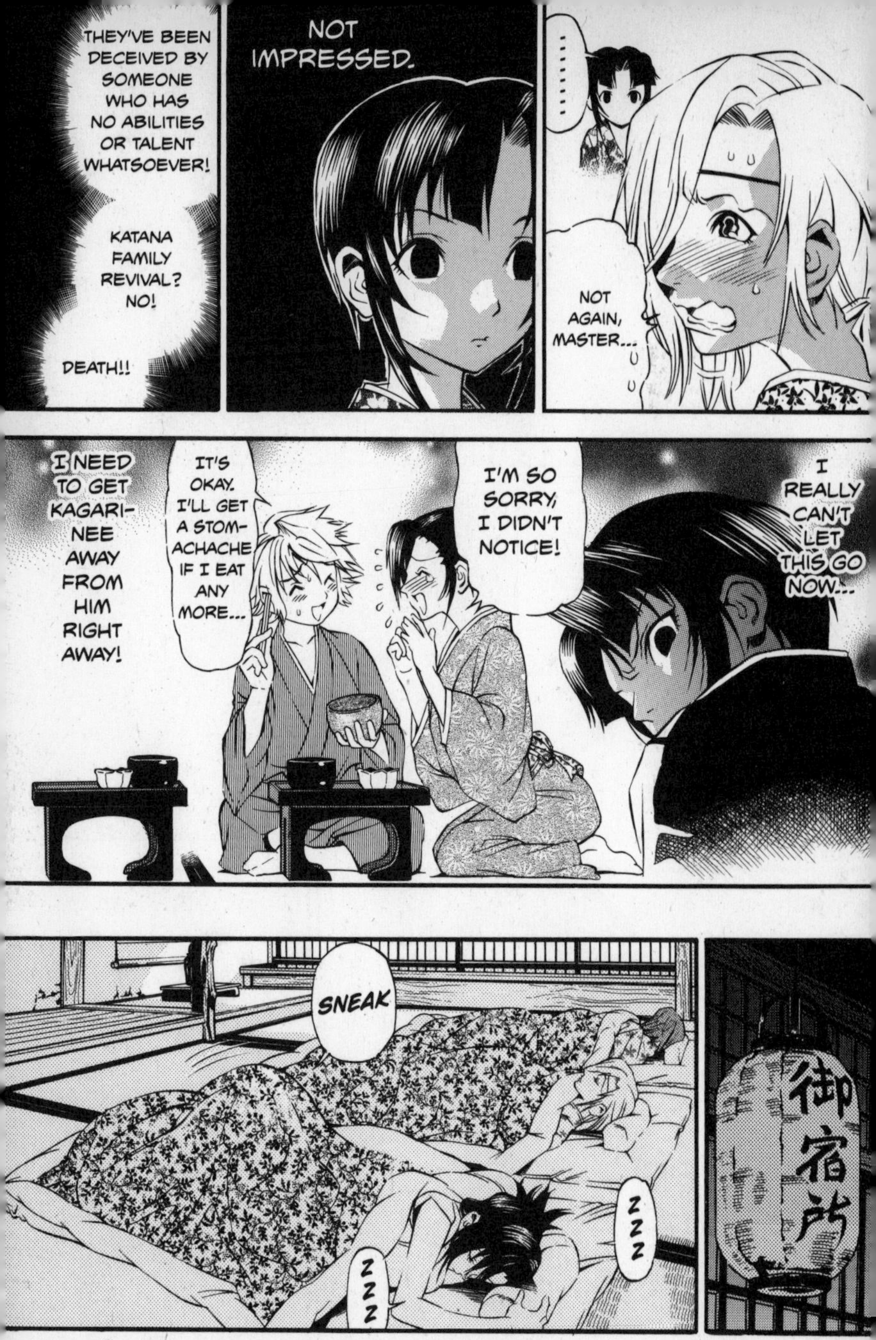

......
NOT AGAIN, MASTER...
NOT IMPRESSED.
THEY'VE BEEN DECEIVED BY SOMEONE WHO HAS NO ABILITIES OR TALENT WHATSOEVER!
KATANA FAMILY REVIVAL? NO!
DEATH!!
I REALLY CAN'T LET THIS GO NOW...
I'M SO SORRY, I DIDN'T NOTICE!
IT'S OKAY. I'LL GET A STOM-ACHACHE IF I EAT ANY MORE...
I NEED TO GET KAGARI-NEE AWAY FROM HIM RIGHT AWAY!
御宿所
SNEAK
ZZZ
ZZZ

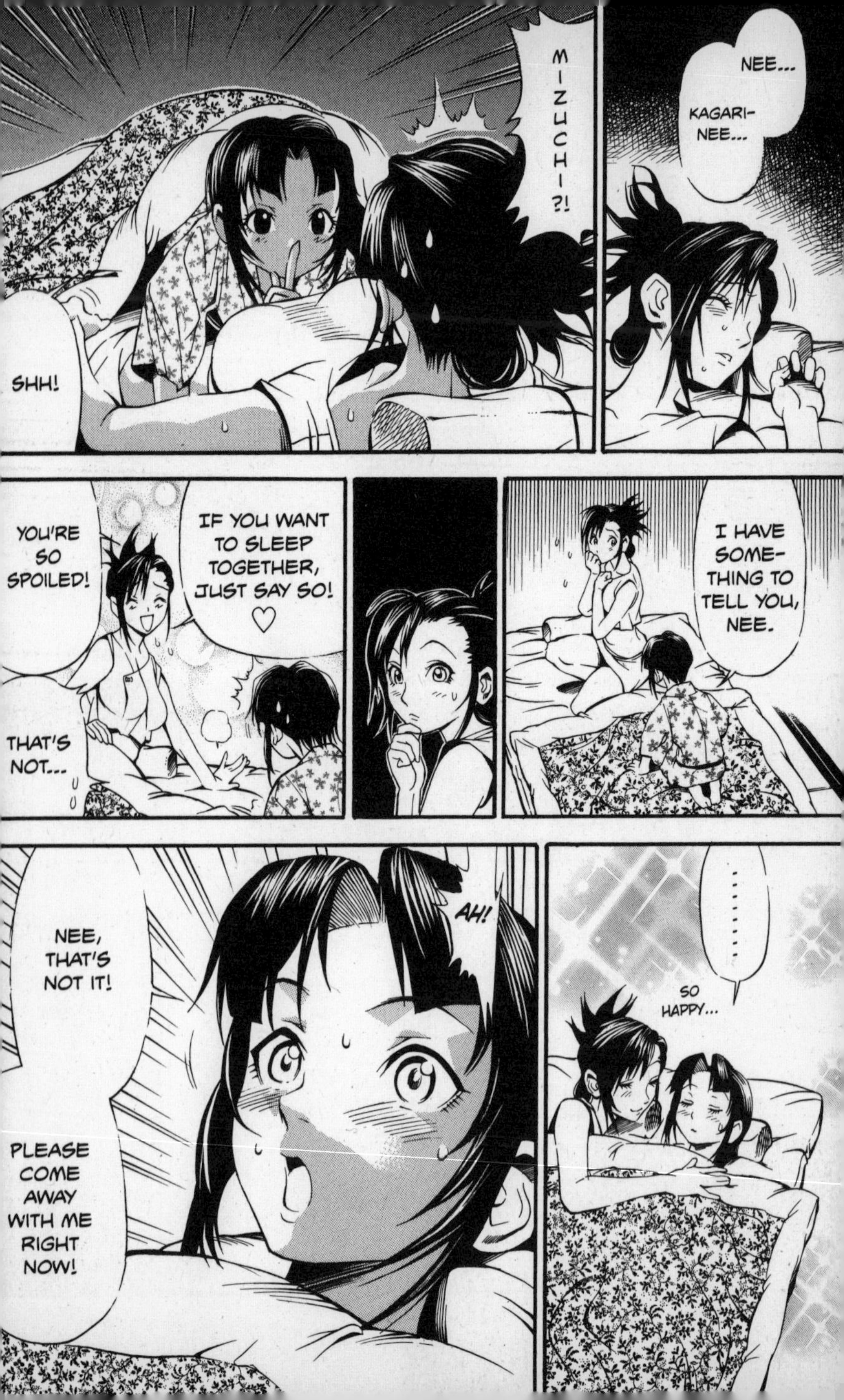

NEE...
KAGARI-NEE...
MIZUCHI?!
SHH!
I HAVE SOMETHING TO TELL YOU, NEE.
IF YOU WANT TO SLEEP TOGETHER, JUST SAY SO! ♡
YOU'RE SO SPOILED!
THAT'S NOT...
......
SO HAPPY...
AH!
NEE, THAT'S NOT IT!
PLEASE COME AWAY WITH ME RIGHT NOW!

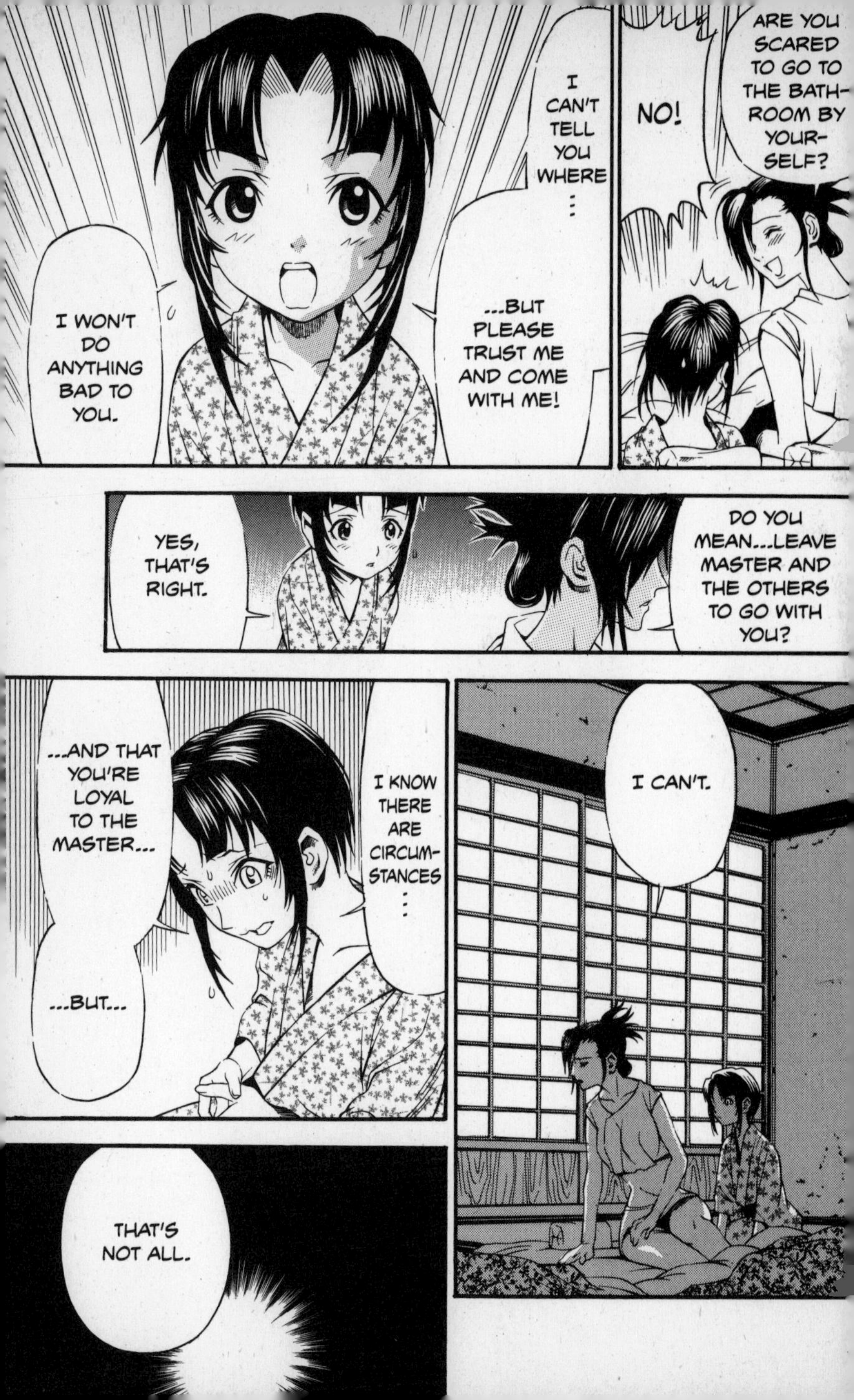
ARE YOU SCARED TO GO TO THE BATH-ROOM BY YOUR-SELF?
NO!
I CAN'T TELL YOU WHERE...
...BUT PLEASE TRUST ME AND COME WITH ME!
I WON'T DO ANYTHING BAD TO YOU.
DO YOU MEAN...LEAVE MASTER AND THE OTHERS TO GO WITH YOU?
YES, THAT'S RIGHT.
I CAN'T.
I KNOW THERE ARE CIRCUM-STANCES...
...AND THAT YOU'RE LOYAL TO THE MASTER...
...BUT...
THAT'S NOT ALL.

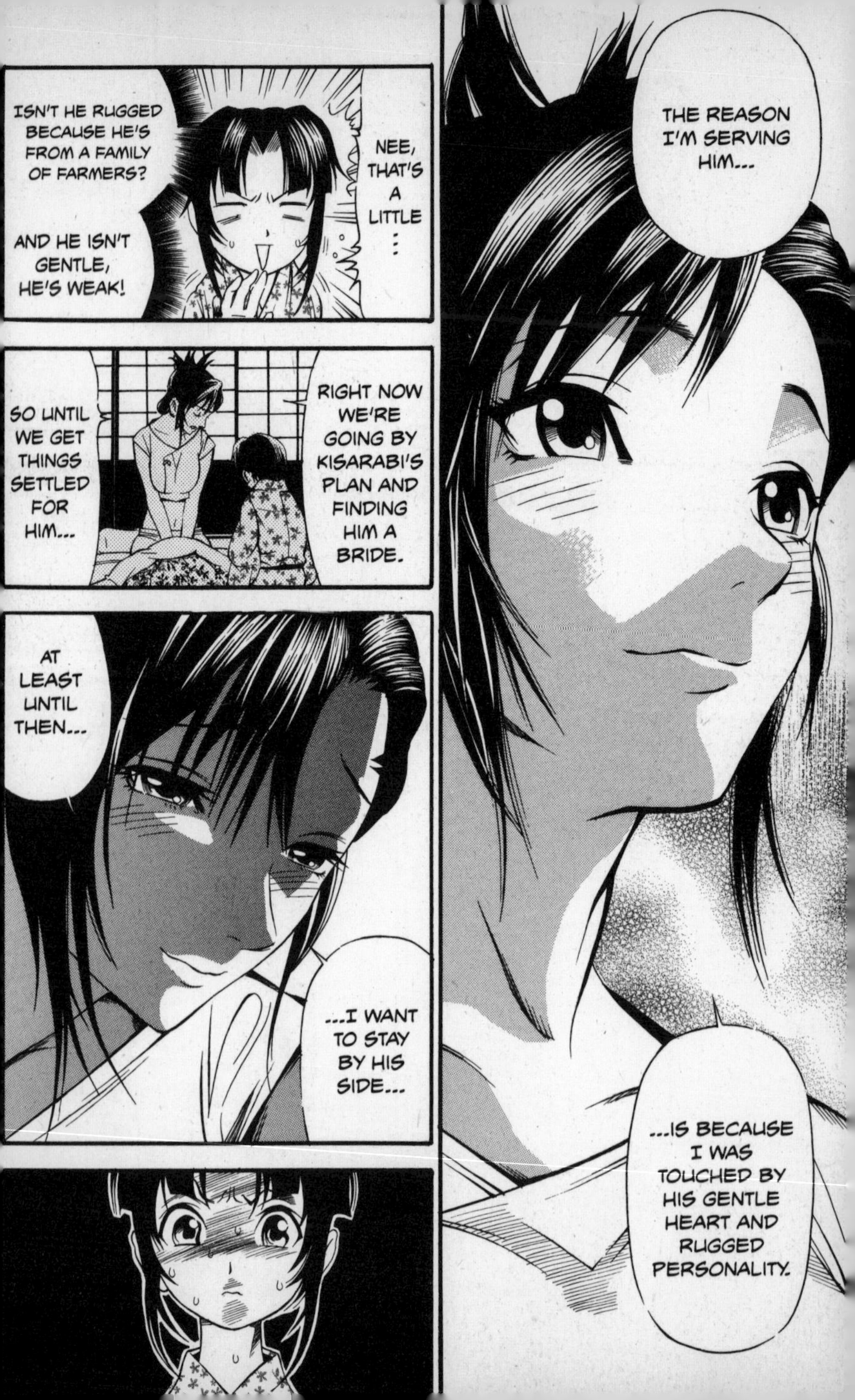
THE REASON I'M SERVING HIM...
...IS BECAUSE I WAS TOUCHED BY HIS GENTLE HEART AND RUGGED PERSONALITY.
NEE, THAT'S A LITTLE...
ISN'T HE RUGGED BECAUSE HE'S FROM A FAMILY OF FARMERS?
AND HE ISN'T GENTLE, HE'S WEAK!
RIGHT NOW WE'RE GOING BY KISARABI'S PLAN AND FINDING HIM A BRIDE.
SO UNTIL WE GET THINGS SETTLED FOR HIM...
AT LEAST UNTIL THEN...
...I WANT TO STAY BY HIS SIDE...

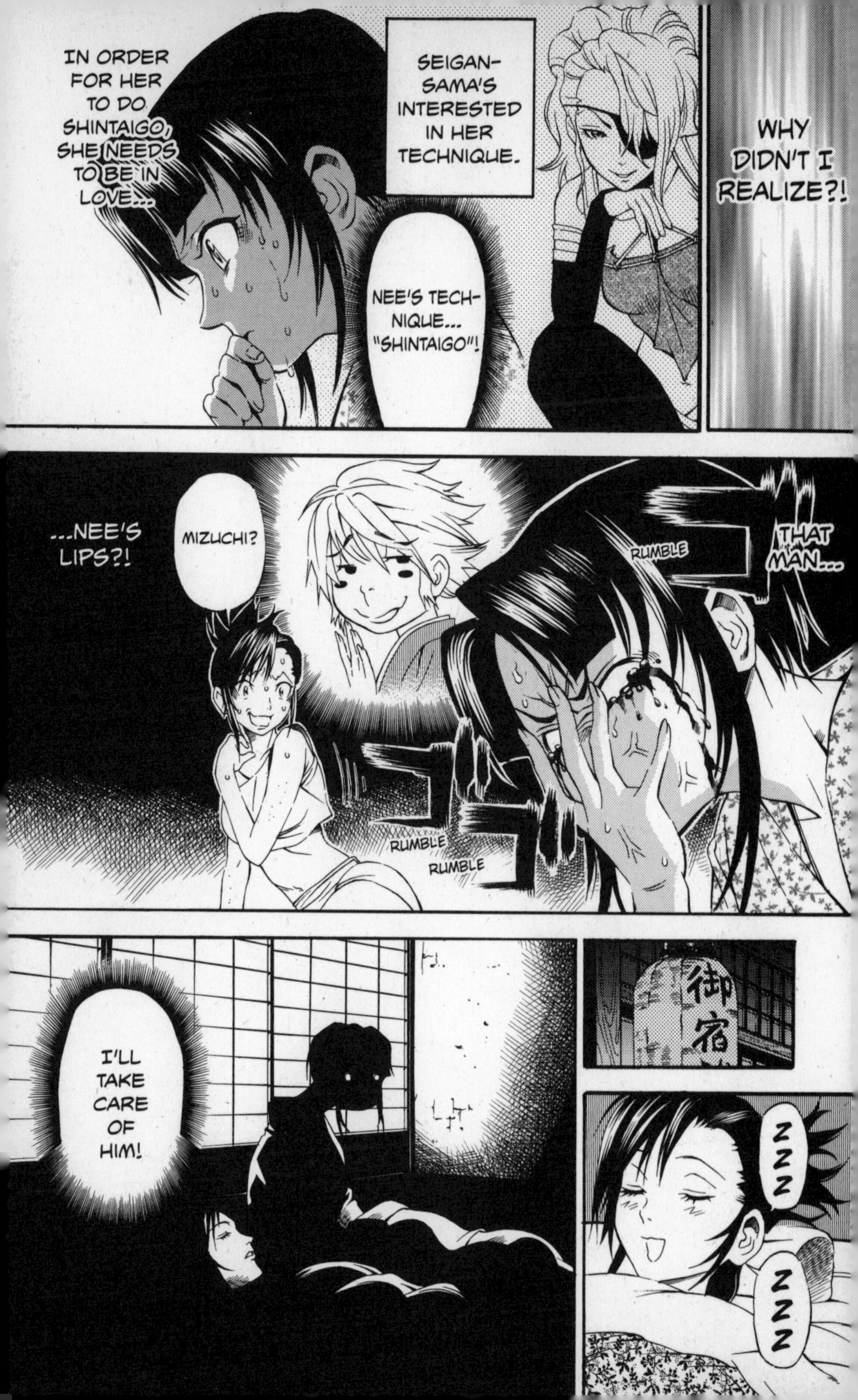

WHY DIDN'T I REALIZE?!
SEIGAN-SAMA'S INTERESTED IN HER TECHNIQUE.
IN ORDER FOR HER TO DO SHINTAIGO, SHE NEEDS TO BE IN LOVE...
NEE'S TECH-NIQUE... "SHINTAIGO"!
THAT MAN...
RUMBLE
MIZUCHI?
...NEE'S LIPS?!
RUMBLE
RUMBLE
御宿
ZZZ
ZZZ
I'LL TAKE CARE OF HIM!

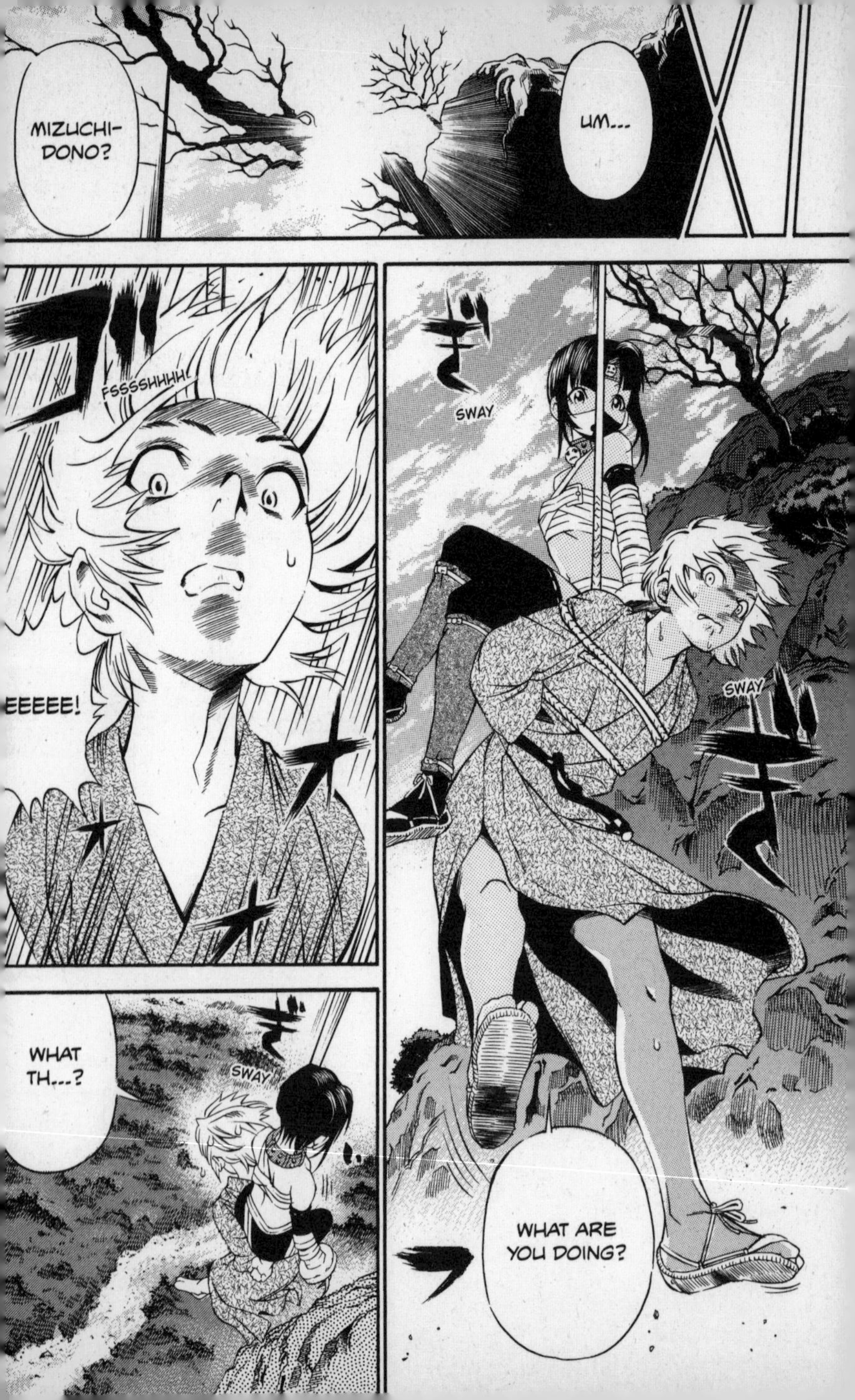
UM...
MIZUCHI-DONO?
SWAY
SWAY
WHAT ARE YOU DOING?
FSSSSHHHH
EEEEE!
WHAT TH...?
SWAY

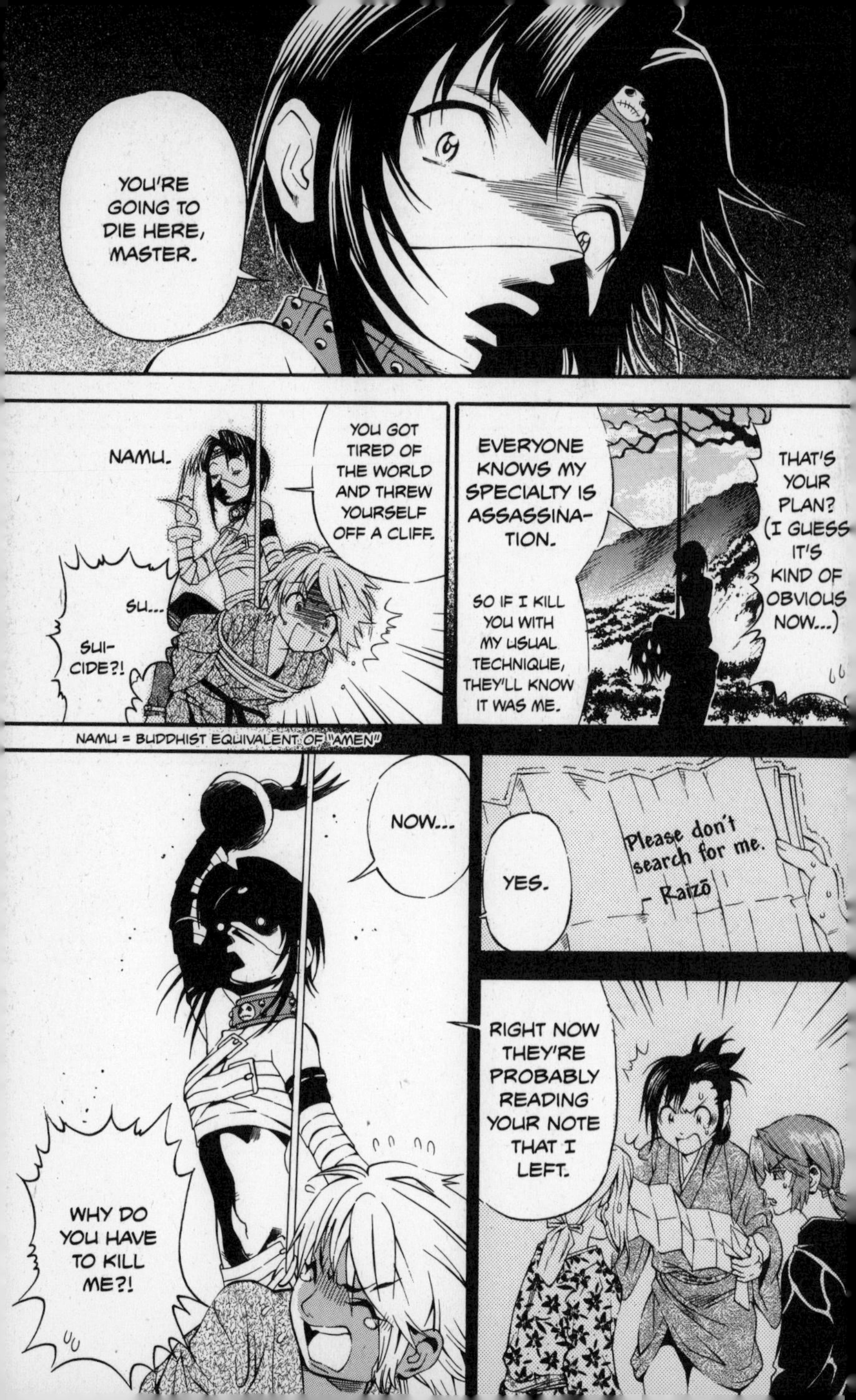
YOU'RE GOING TO DIE HERE, MASTER.
EVERYONE KNOWS MY SPECIALTY IS ASSASSINATION.
SO IF I KILL YOU WITH MY USUAL TECHNIQUE, THEY'LL KNOW IT WAS ME.
THAT'S YOUR PLAN? (I GUESS IT'S KIND OF OBVIOUS NOW...)
YOU GOT TIRED OF THE WORLD AND THREW YOURSELF OFF A CLIFF.
NAMU.
SU...
SUI-CIDE?!
NAMU = BUDDHIST EQUIVALENT OF "AMEN"
Please don't search for me. – Raizō
YES.
RIGHT NOW THEY'RE PROBABLY READING YOUR NOTE THAT I LEFT.
NOW...
WHY DO YOU HAVE TO KILL ME?!

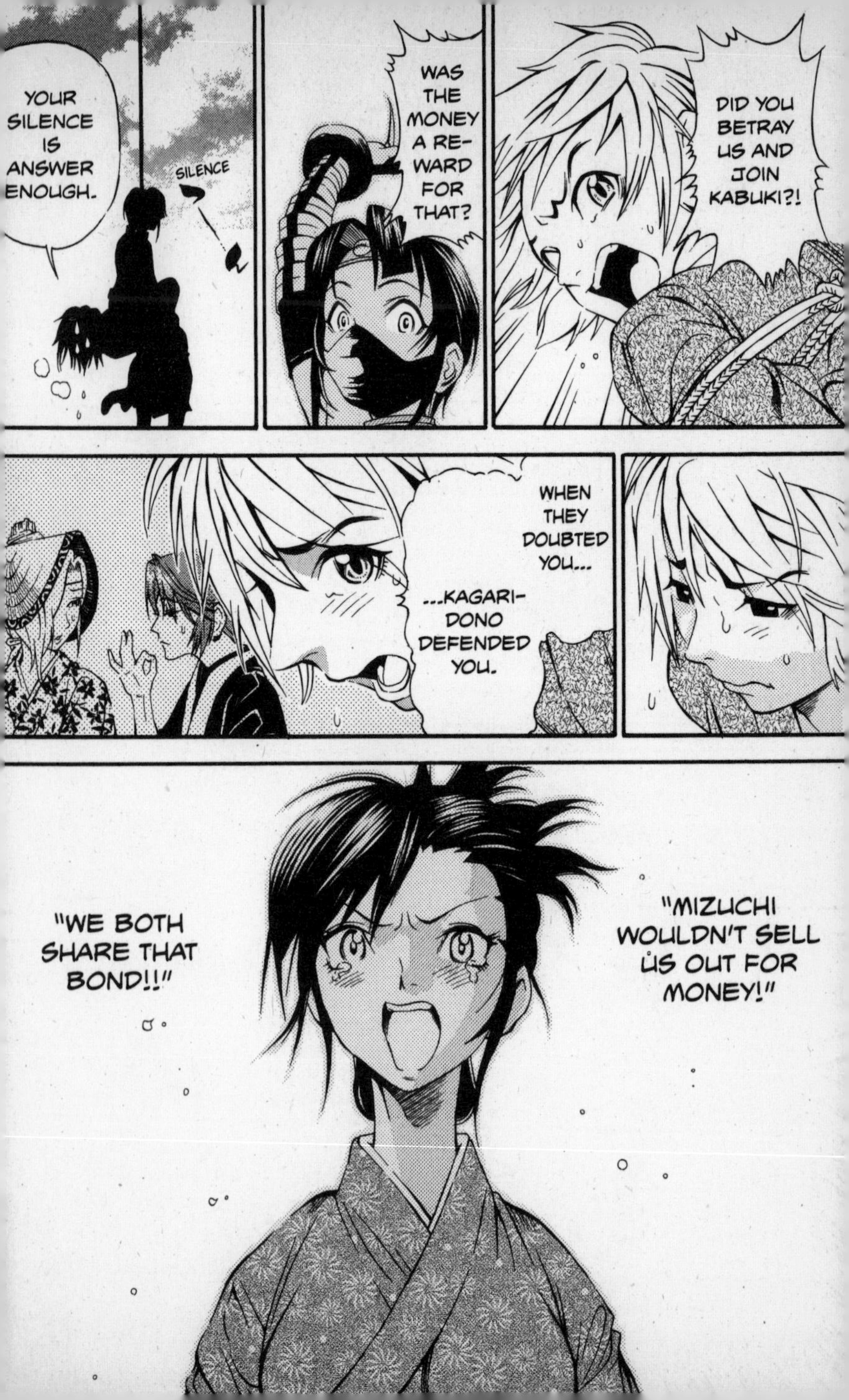
DID YOU BETRAY US AND JOIN KABUKI?!
WAS THE MONEY A RE-WARD FOR THAT?
SILENCE
YOUR SILENCE IS ANSWER ENOUGH.
WHEN THEY DOUBTED YOU...
...KAGARI-DONO DEFENDED YOU.
"MIZUCHI WOULDN'T SELL US OUT FOR MONEY!"
"WE BOTH SHARE THAT BOND!!"

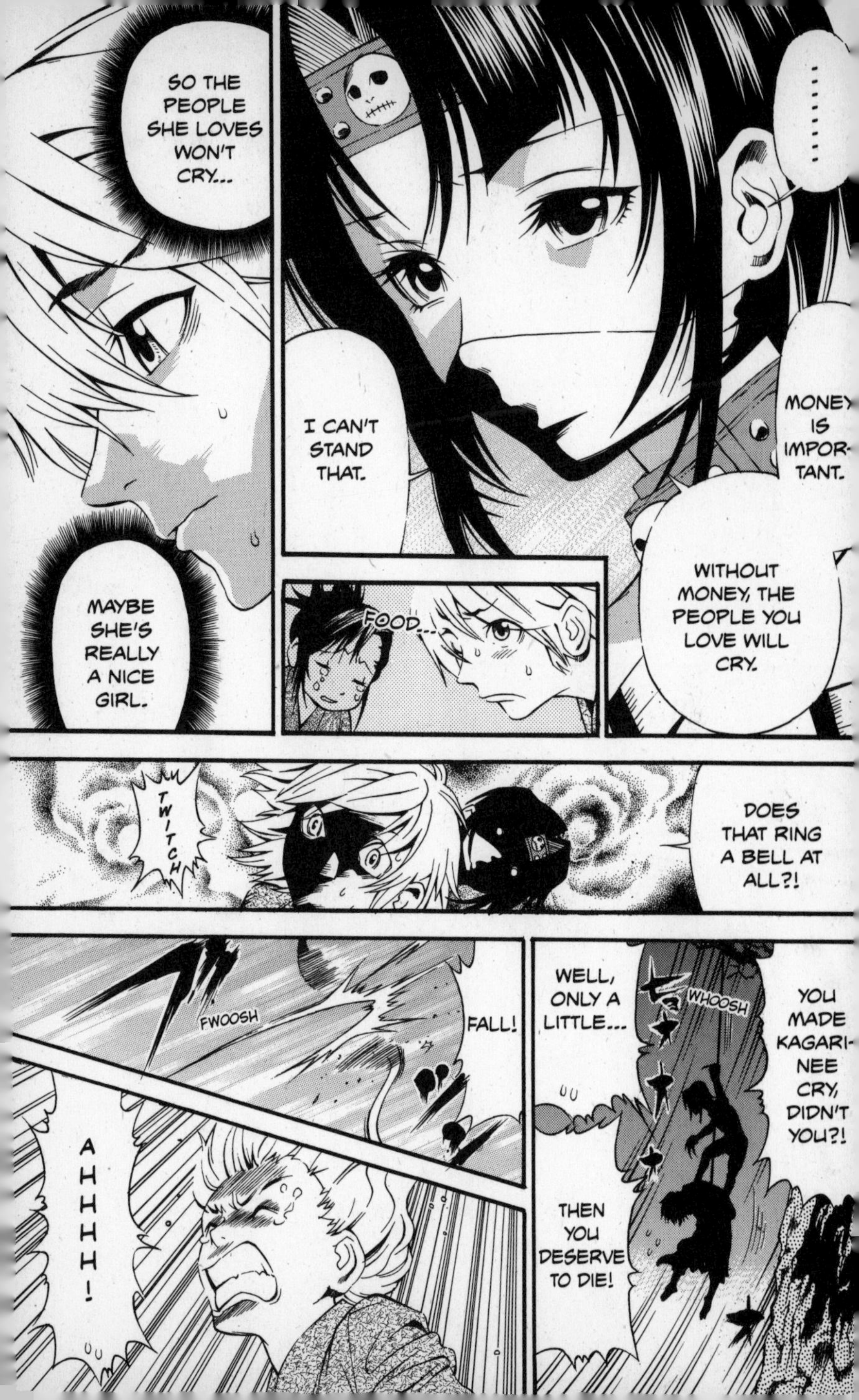
......
MONEY IS IMPORTANT.
WITHOUT MONEY, THE PEOPLE YOU LOVE WILL CRY.
I CAN'T STAND THAT.
FOOD...
SO THE PEOPLE SHE LOVES WON'T CRY...
MAYBE SHE'S REALLY A NICE GIRL.
DOES THAT RING A BELL AT ALL?!
TWITCH
YOU MADE KAGARI-NEE CRY, DIDN'T YOU?!
WHOOSH
WELL, ONLY A LITTLE...
THEN YOU DESERVE TO DIE!
FALL!
FWOOSH
AHHHH!

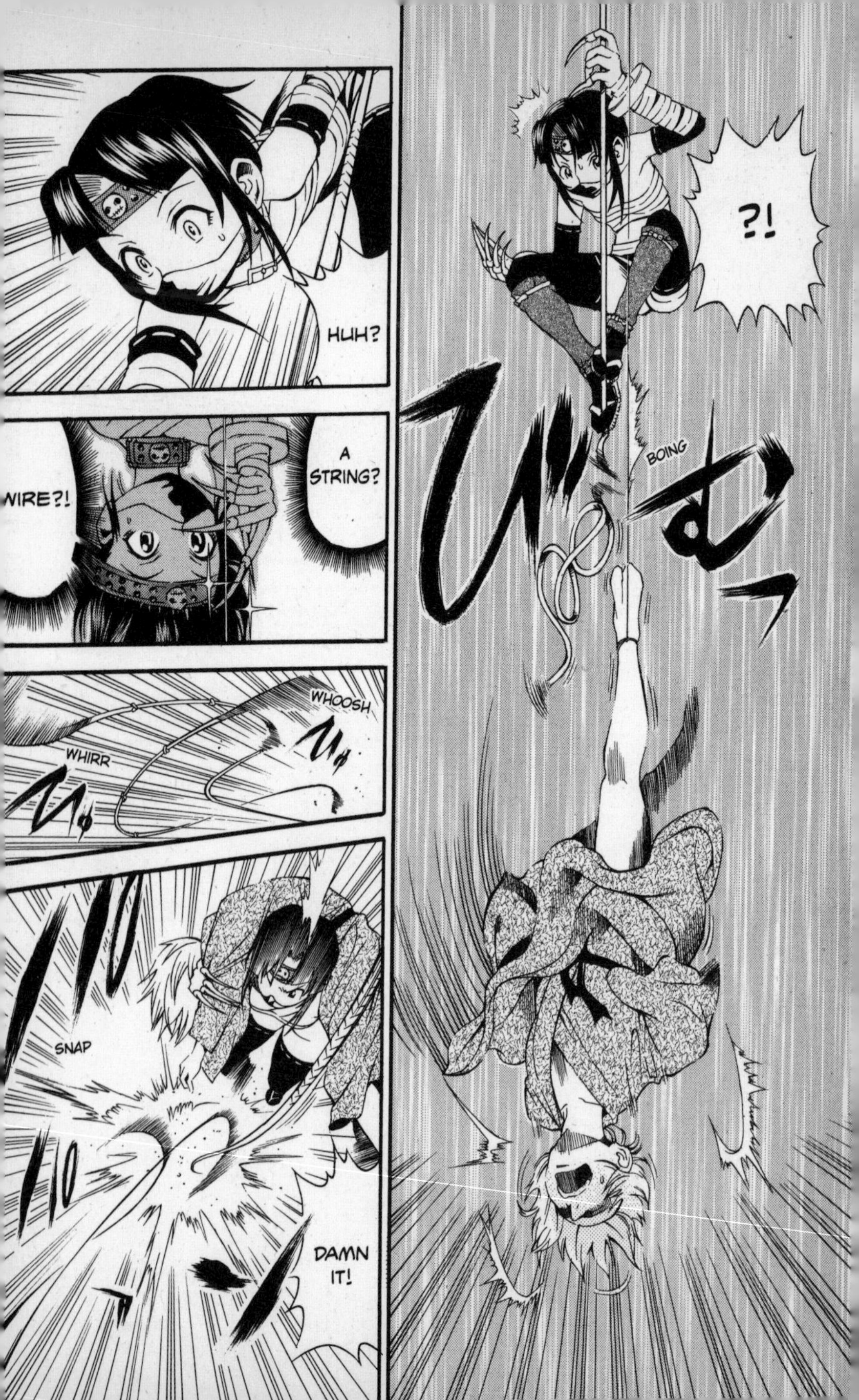
?!
BOING
HUH?
A STRING?
WIRE?!
WHOOSH
WHIRR
SNAP
DAMN IT!

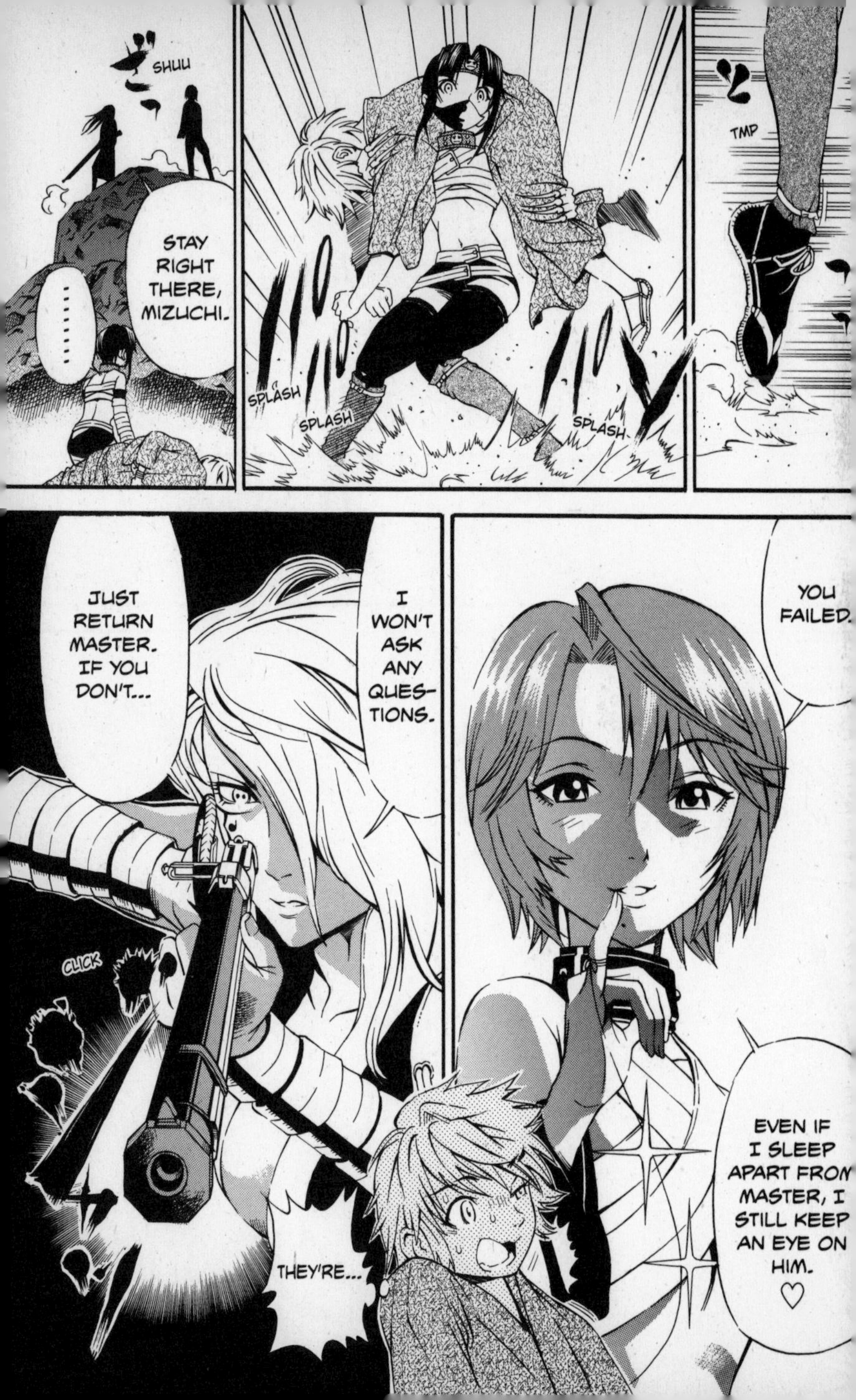
TMP
SPLASH
SPLASH
SPLASH
SHUU
STAY RIGHT THERE, MIZUCHI.
......
YOU FAILED.
EVEN IF I SLEEP APART FROM MASTER, I STILL KEEP AN EYE ON HIM. ♡
THEY'RE...
I WON'T ASK ANY QUESTIONS.
JUST RETURN MASTER. IF YOU DON'T...
CLICK

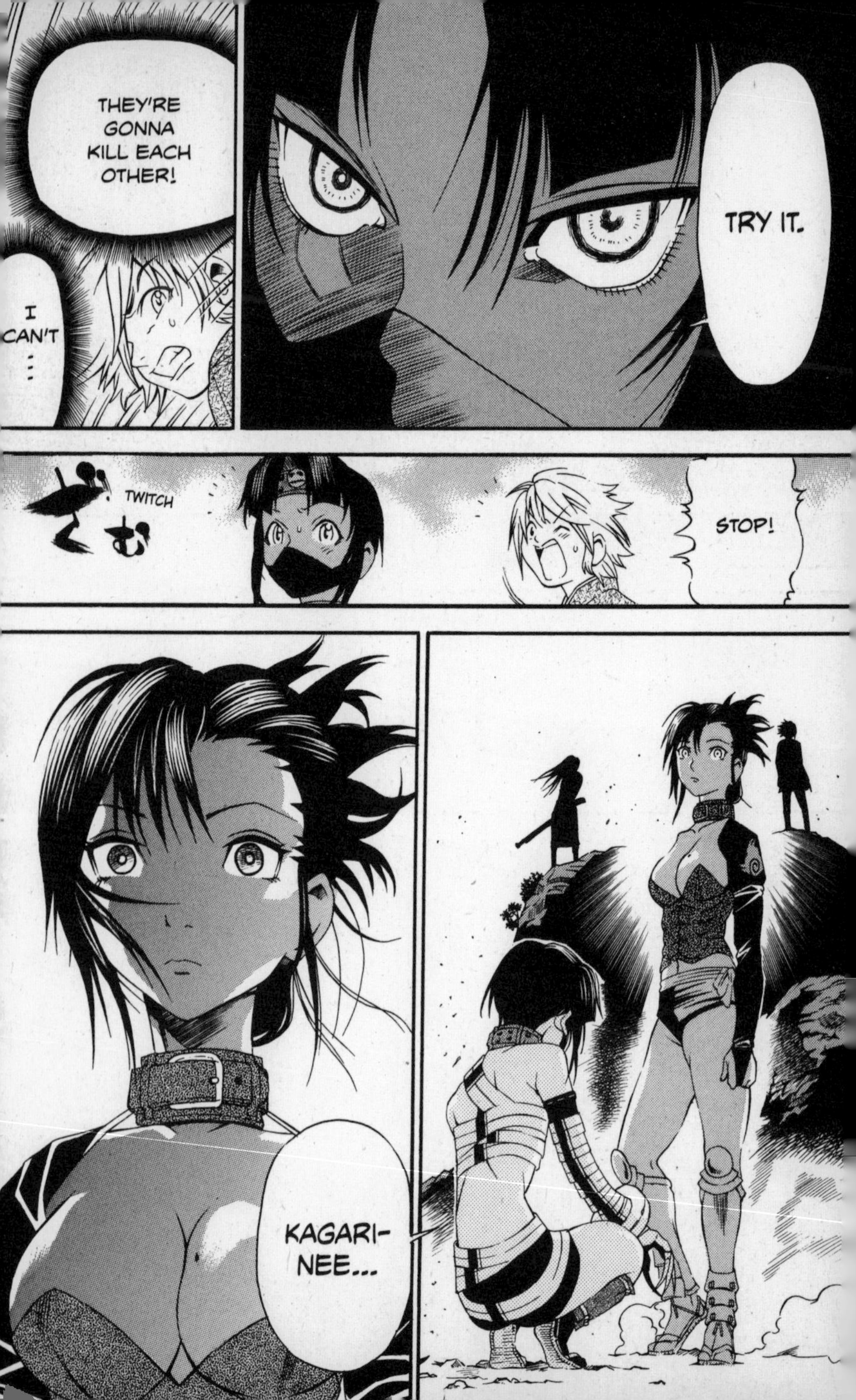
TRY IT.
THEY'RE GONNA KILL EACH OTHER!
I CAN'T...
STOP!
TWITCH
KAGARI-NEE...

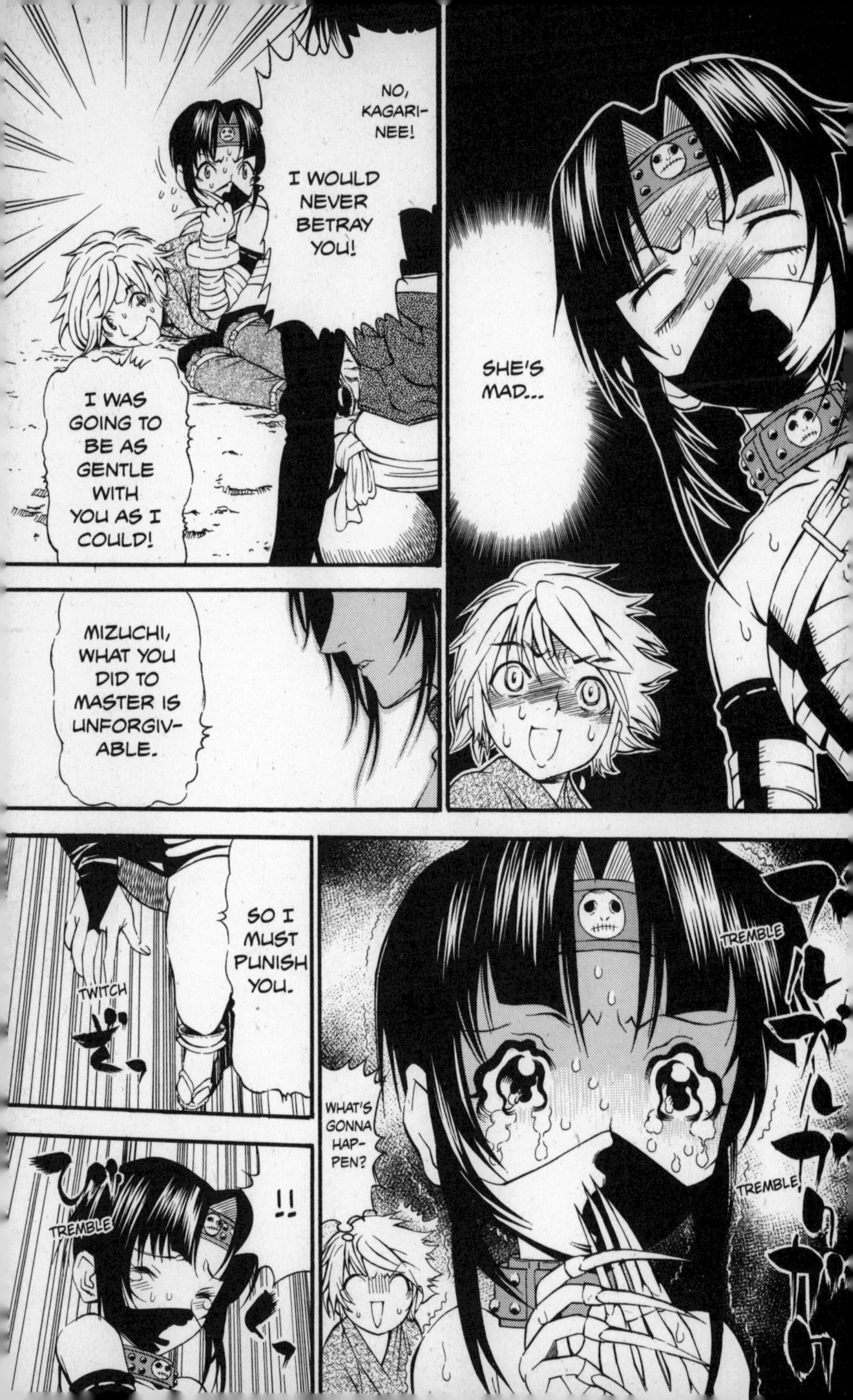
SHE'S MAD...
NO, KAGARI-NEE!
I WOULD NEVER BETRAY YOU!
I WAS GOING TO BE AS GENTLE WITH YOU AS I COULD!
MIZUCHI, WHAT YOU DID TO MASTER IS UNFORGIV-ABLE.
TREMBLE
WHAT'S GONNA HAP-PEN?
TREMBLE
SO I MUST PUNISH YOU.
TWITCH
!!
TREMBLE

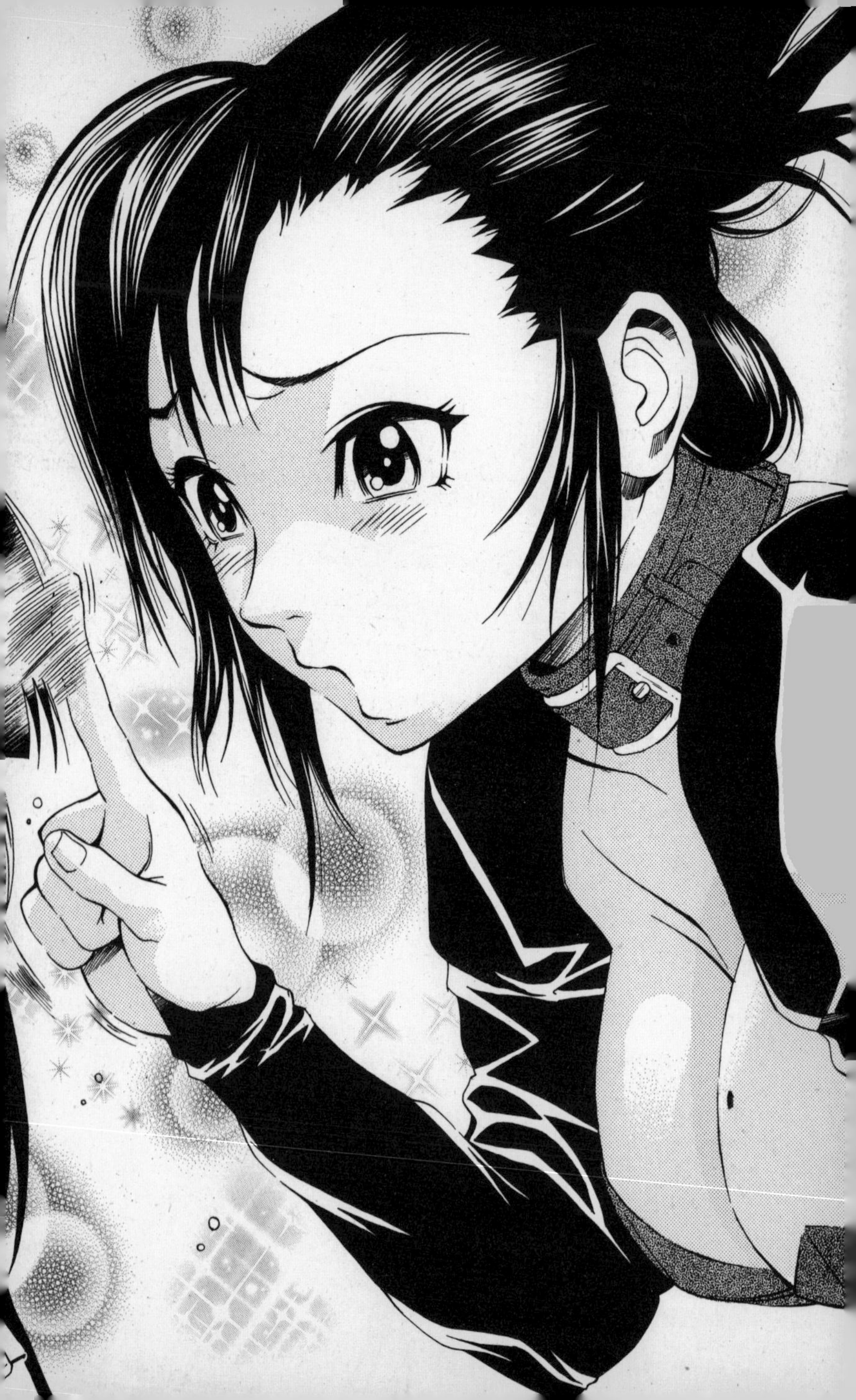

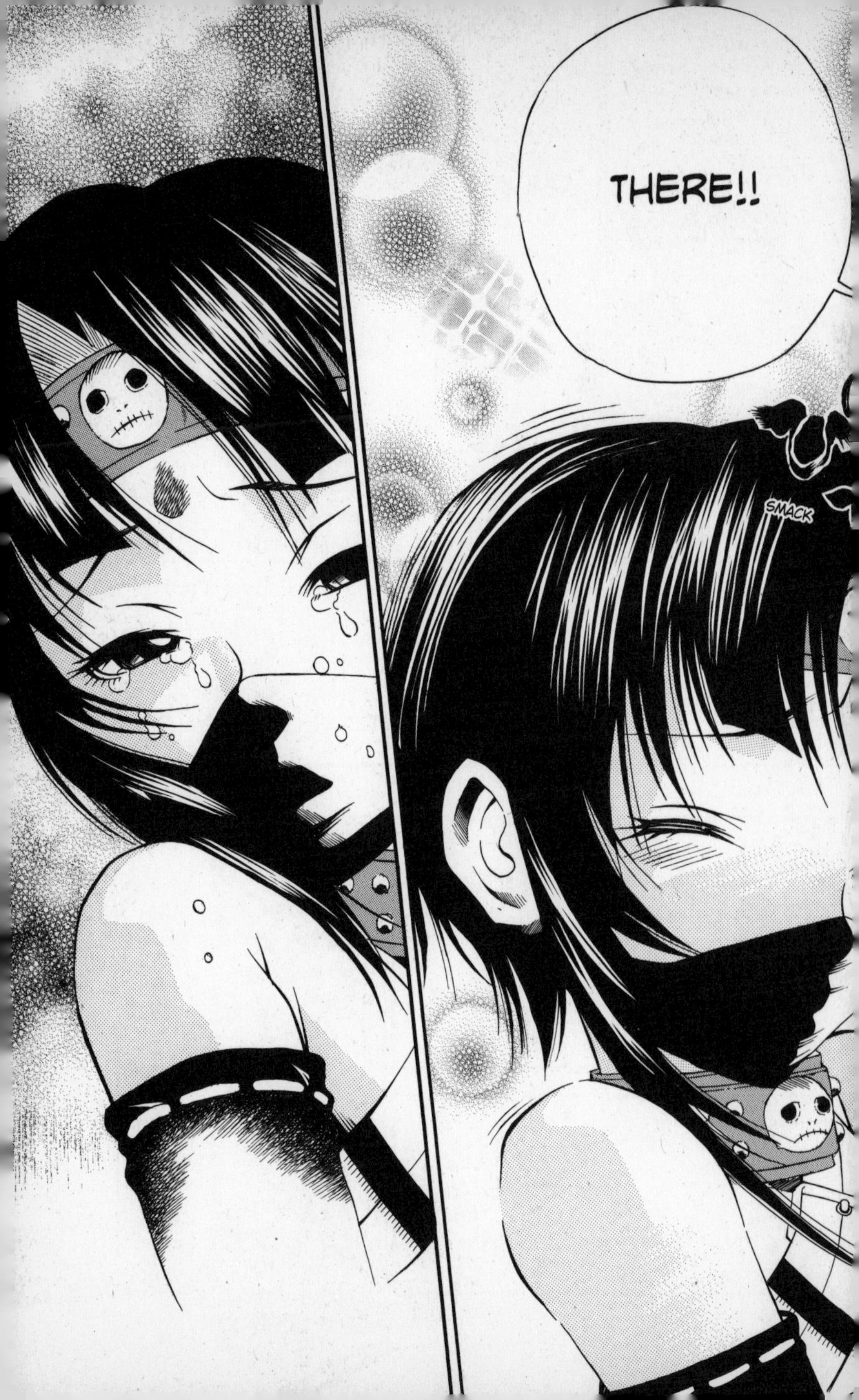
THERE!!
SMACK

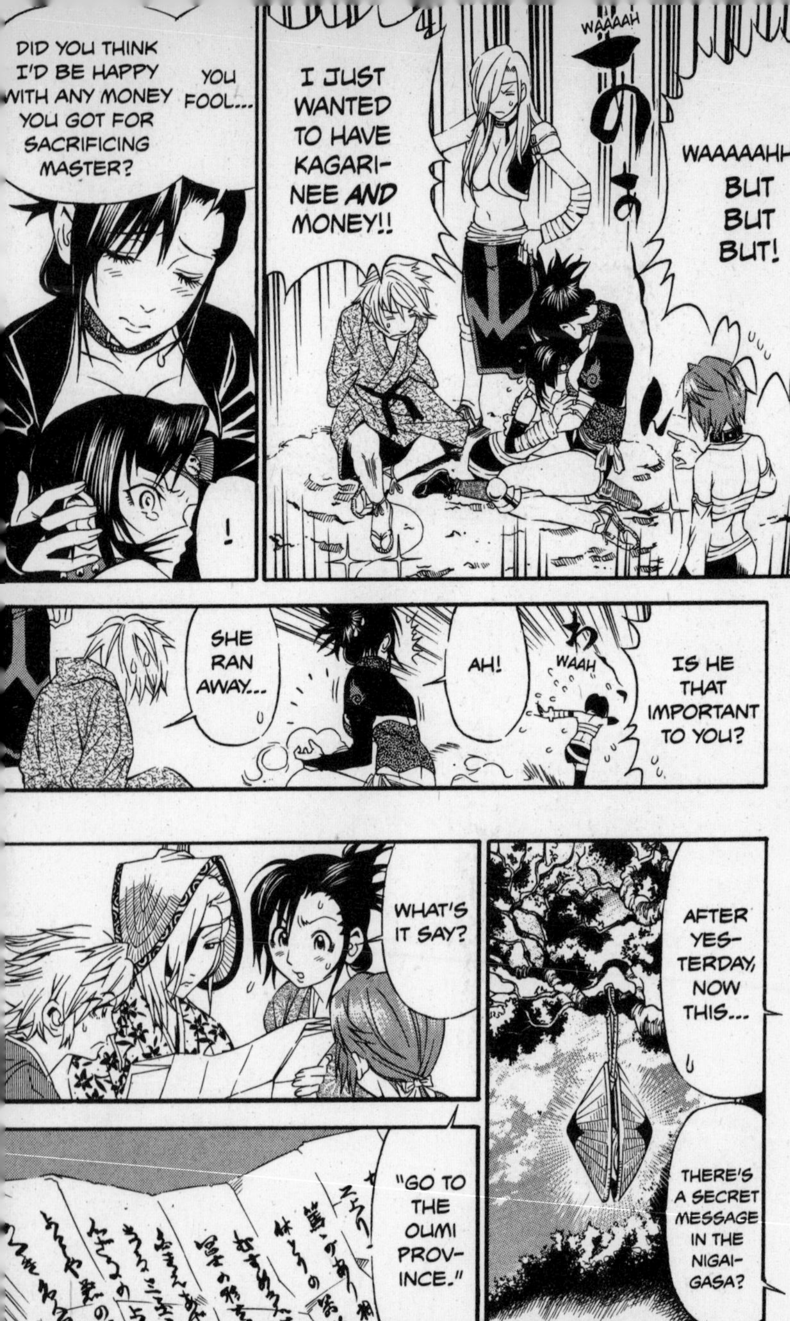
WAAAAH
WAAAAAHHH! BUT BUT BUT!
I JUST WANTED TO HAVE KAGARI-NEE AND MONEY!!
YOU FOOL...
DID YOU THINK I'D BE HAPPY WITH ANY MONEY YOU GOT FOR SACRIFICING MASTER?
!
IS HE THAT IMPORTANT TO YOU?
WAAH
AH!
SHE RAN AWAY...
AFTER YES-TERDAY, NOW THIS...
THERE'S A SECRET MESSAGE IN THE NIGAI-GASA?
WHAT'S IT SAY?
"GO TO THE OUMI PROV-INCE."

NIGAIGASA- SECRET METHOD OF SHINOBI COMMUNICATION

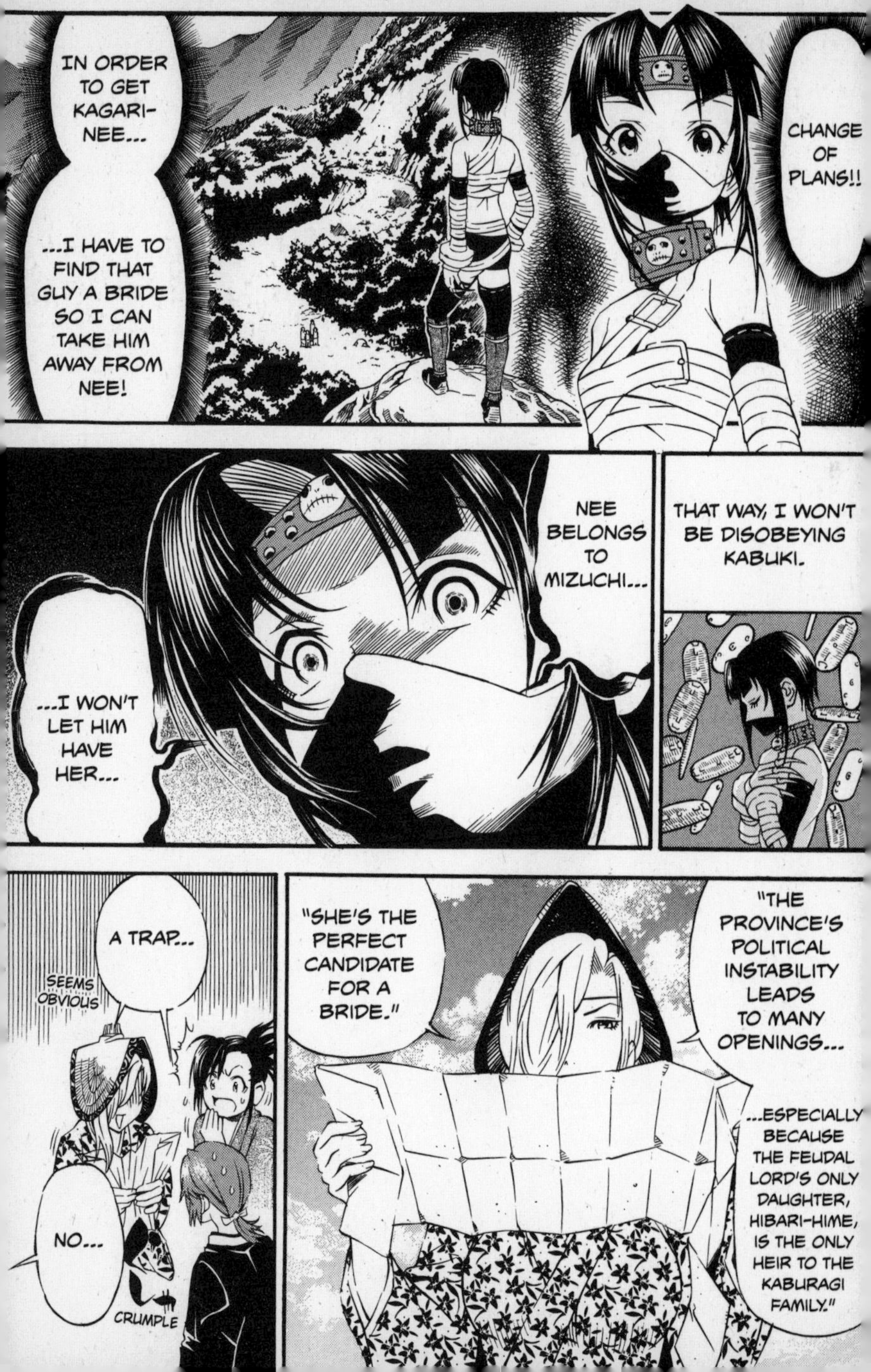
CHANGE OF PLANS!!
IN ORDER TO GET KAGARI-NEE...
...I HAVE TO FIND THAT GUY A BRIDE SO I CAN TAKE HIM AWAY FROM NEE!
THAT WAY, I WON'T BE DISOBEYING KABUKI.
NEE BELONGS TO MIZUCHI...
...I WON'T LET HIM HAVE HER...
"THE PROVINCE'S POLITICAL INSTABILITY LEADS TO MANY OPENINGS...
...ESPECIALLY BECAUSE THE FEUDAL LORD'S ONLY DAUGHTER, HIBARI-HIME, IS THE ONLY HEIR TO THE KABURAGI FAMILY."
"SHE'S THE PERFECT CANDIDATE FOR A BRIDE."
A TRAP...
SEEMS OBVIOUS
NO...
CRUMPLE

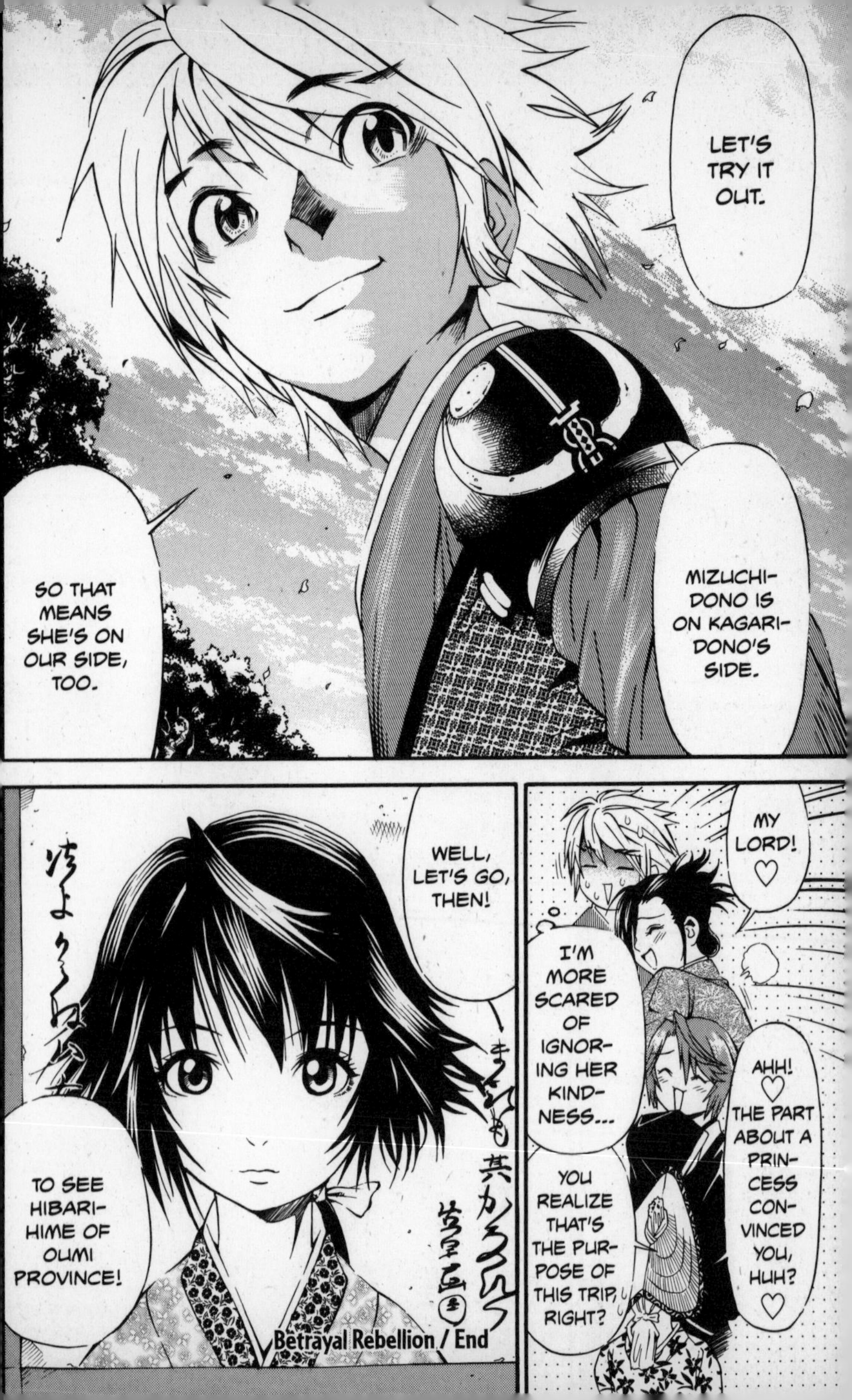
LET'S TRY IT OUT.
MIZUCHI-DONO IS ON KAGARI-DONO'S SIDE.
SO THAT MEANS SHE'S ON OUR SIDE, TOO.
MY LORD! ♡
I'M MORE SCARED OF IGNORING HER KINDNESS...
AHH! ♡ THE PART ABOUT A PRINCESS CONVINCED YOU, HUH? ♡
YOU REALIZE THAT'S THE PURPOSE OF THIS TRIP, RIGHT?
WELL, LET'S GO, THEN!
TO SEE HIBARI-HIME OF OUMI PROVINCE!
Betrayal Rebellion / End

Bonus *Ninja Girls* Manga

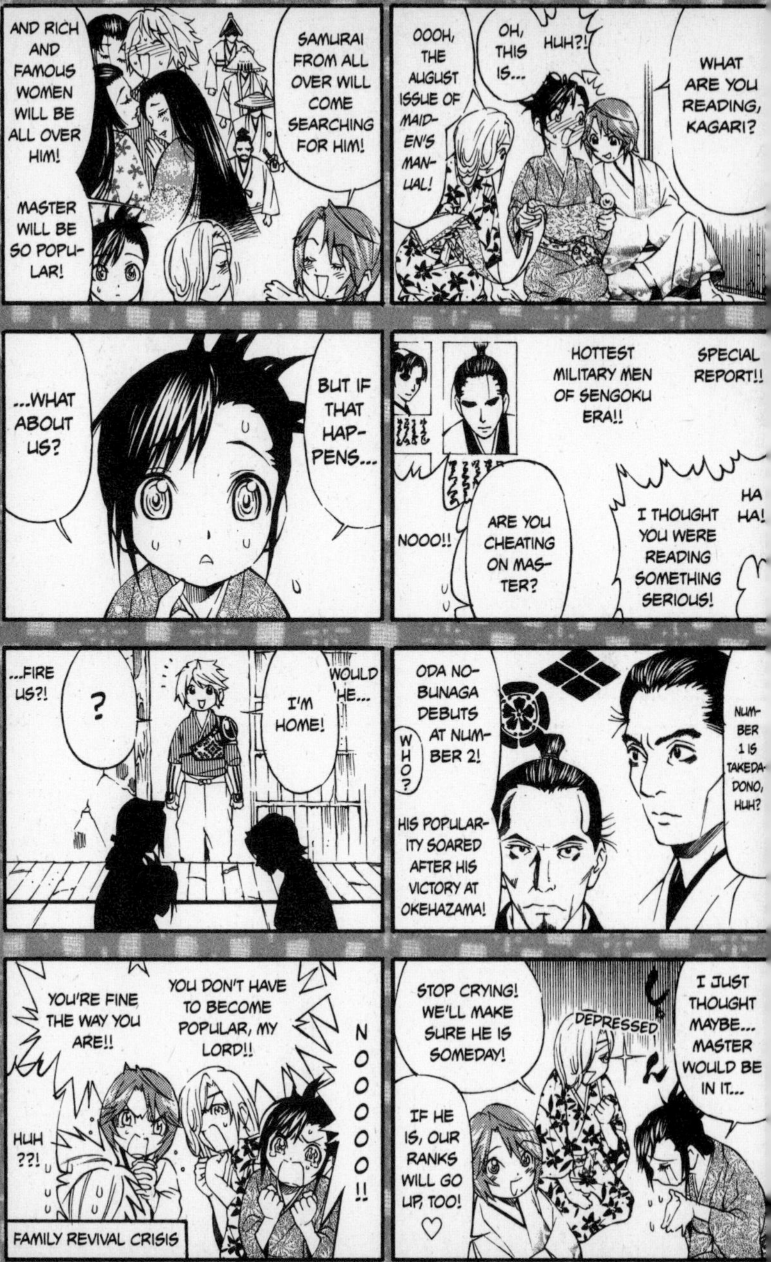
WHAT ARE YOU READING, KAGARI?
HUH?!
OH, THIS IS...
OOOH, THE AUGUST ISSUE OF MAIDEN'S MANUAL!
SPECIAL REPORT!!
HOTTEST MILITARY MEN OF SENGOKU ERA!!
HA HA
I THOUGHT YOU WERE READING SOMETHING SERIOUS!
ARE YOU CHEATING ON MASTER?
NOOO!!
NUMBER 1 IS TAKEDA-DONO, HUH?
ODA NOBUNAGA DEBUTS AT NUMBER 2!
WHO?
HIS POPULARITY SOARED AFTER HIS VICTORY AT OKEHAZAMA!
I JUST THOUGHT MAYBE... MASTER WOULD BE IN IT...
DEPRESSED
STOP CRYING! WE'LL MAKE SURE HE IS SOMEDAY!
IF HE IS, OUR RANKS WILL GO UP, TOO! ♡
SAMURAI FROM ALL OVER WILL COME SEARCHING FOR HIM!
AND RICH AND FAMOUS WOMEN WILL BE ALL OVER HIM!
MASTER WILL BE SO POPULAR!
BUT IF THAT HAPPENS...
...WHAT ABOUT US?
WOULD HE...
I'M HOME!
?
...FIRE US?!
NOOOOOO!!
YOU DON'T HAVE TO BECOME POPULAR, MY LORD!!
YOU'RE FINE THE WAY YOU ARE!!
HUH ??!
FAMILY REVIVAL CRISIS

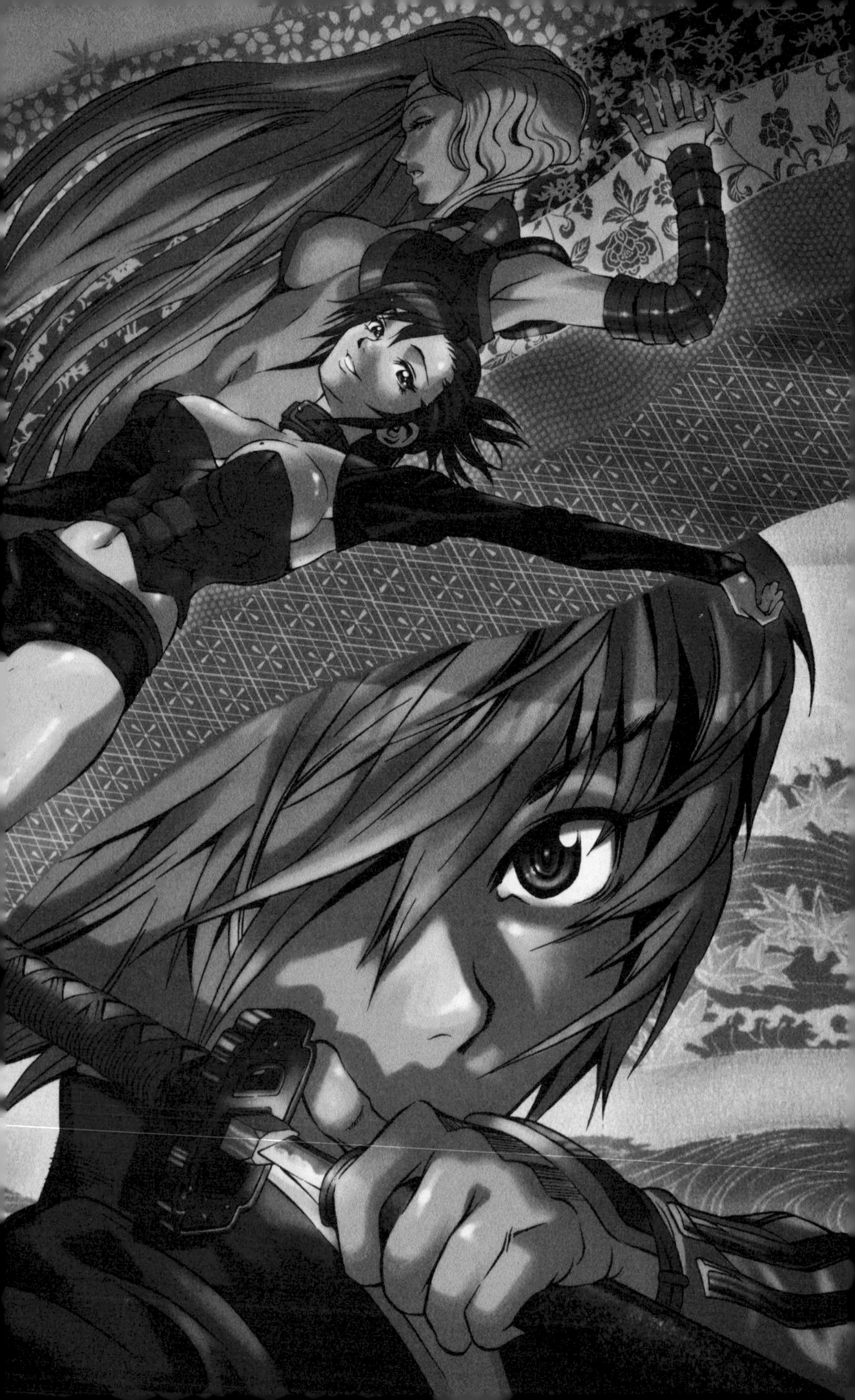

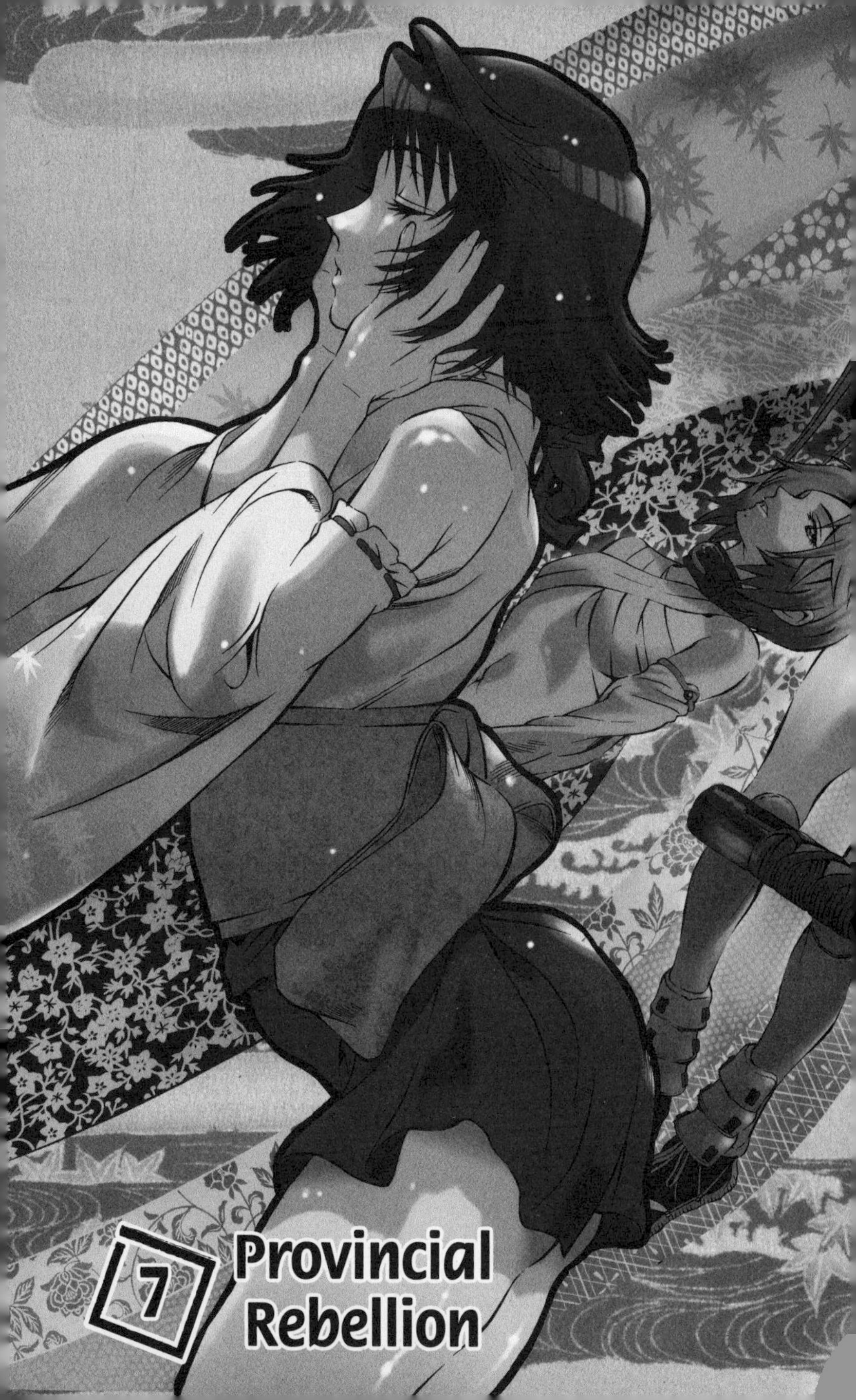
7
Provincial
Rebellion

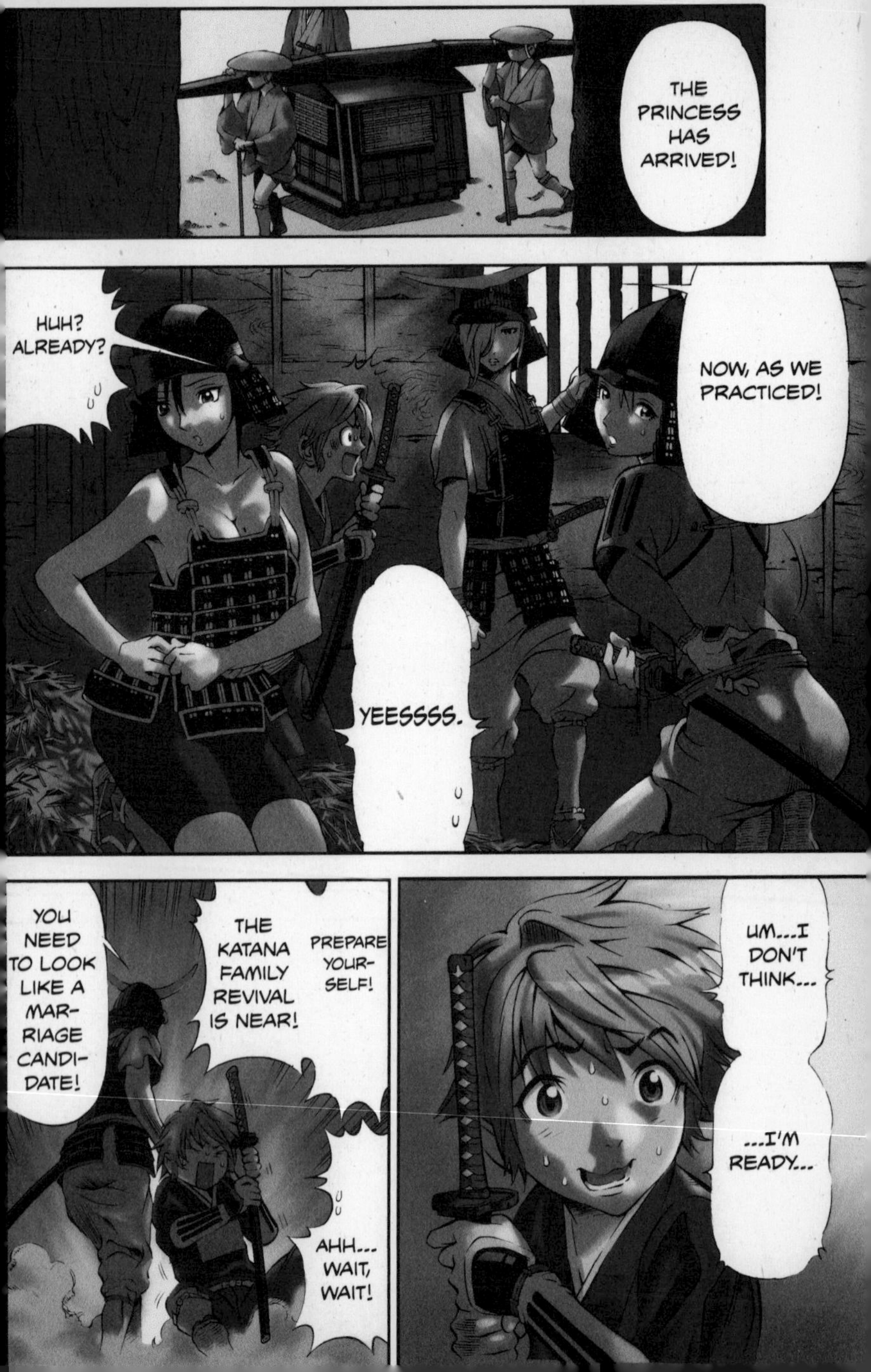
THE PRINCESS HAS ARRIVED!
NOW, AS WE PRACTICED!
HUH? ALREADY?
YEESSSS.
UM...I DON'T THINK...
...I'M READY...
PREPARE YOUR-SELF!
THE KATANA FAMILY REVIVAL IS NEAR!
YOU NEED TO LOOK LIKE A MAR-RIAGE CANDI-DATE!
AHH... WAIT, WAIT!

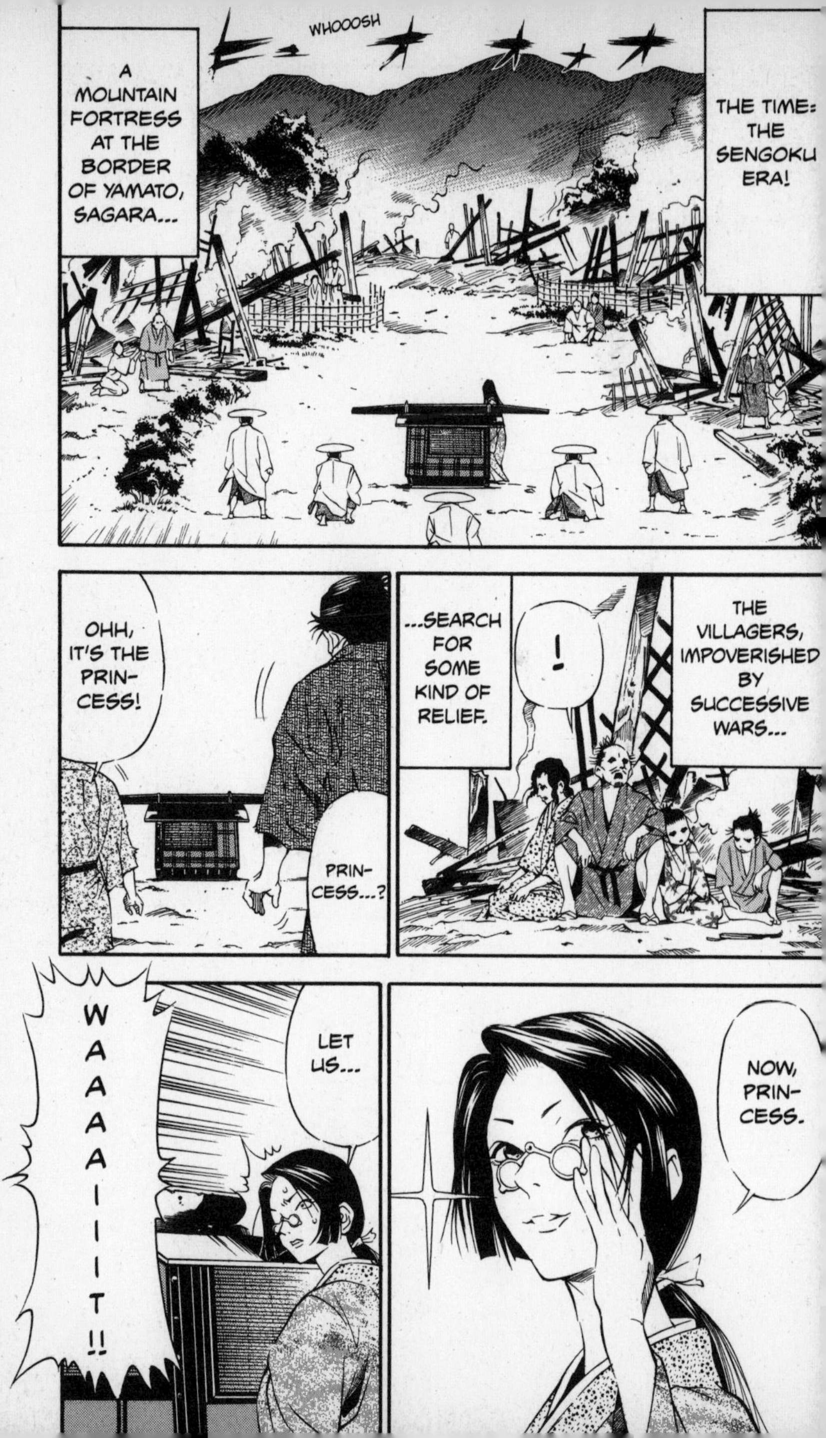
THE TIME: THE SENGOKU ERA!
WHOOOSH
A MOUNTAIN FORTRESS AT THE BORDER OF YAMATO, SAGARA...
THE VILLAGERS, IMPOVERISHED BY SUCCESSIVE WARS...
...SEARCH FOR SOME KIND OF RELIEF.
!
OHH, IT'S THE PRINCESS!
PRINCESS...?
NOW, PRINCESS.
LET US...
WAAAAIIIIT!!

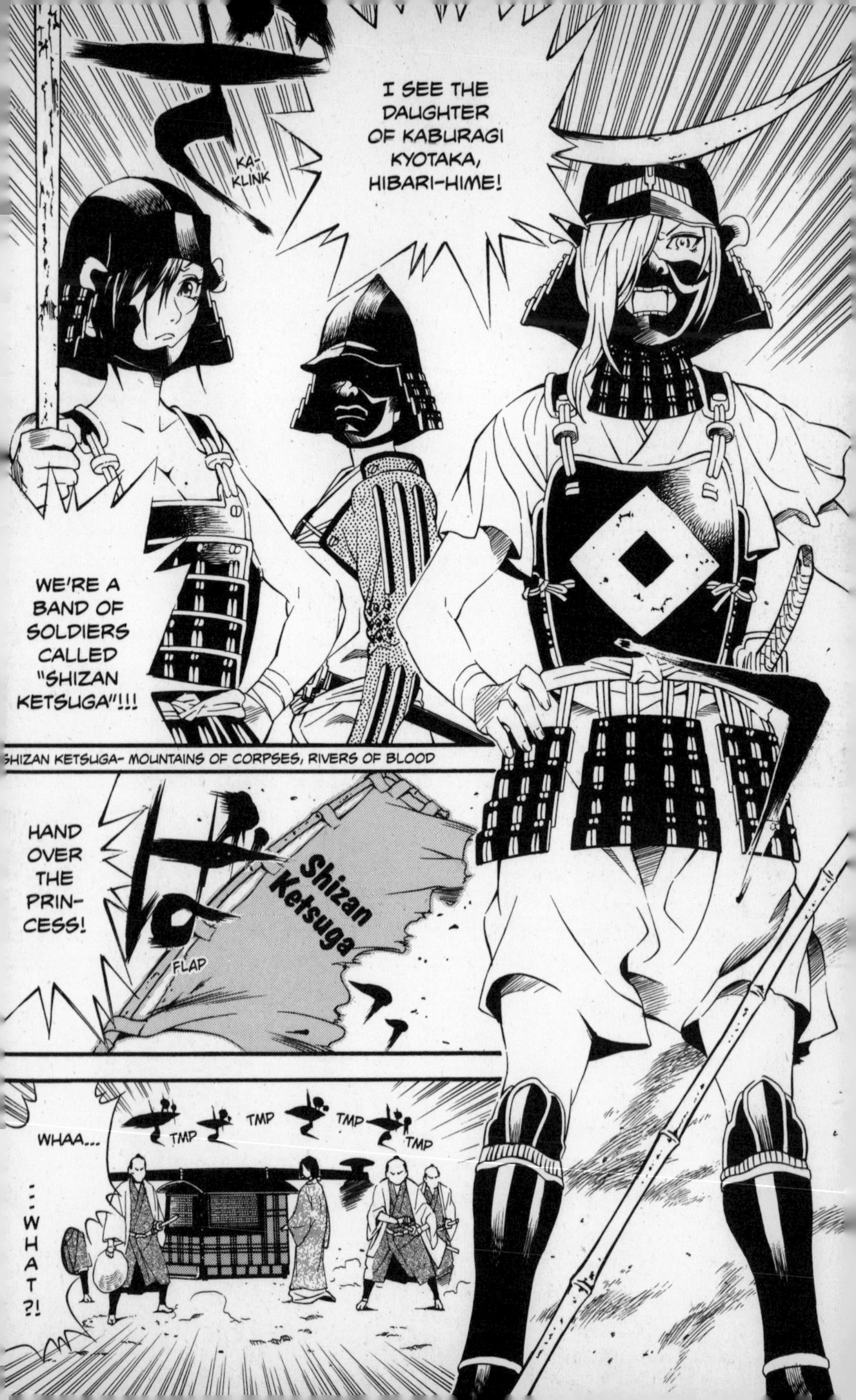
I SEE THE DAUGHTER OF KABURAGI KYOTAKA, HIBARI-HIME!
KA-KLINK
WE'RE A BAND OF SOLDIERS CALLED "SHIZAN KETSUGA"!!!
SHIZAN KETSUGA- MOUNTAINS OF CORPSES, RIVERS OF BLOOD
HAND OVER THE PRIN-CESS!
Shizan Ketsuga
FLAP
TMP TMP TMP TMP
WHAA...
...WHAT?!

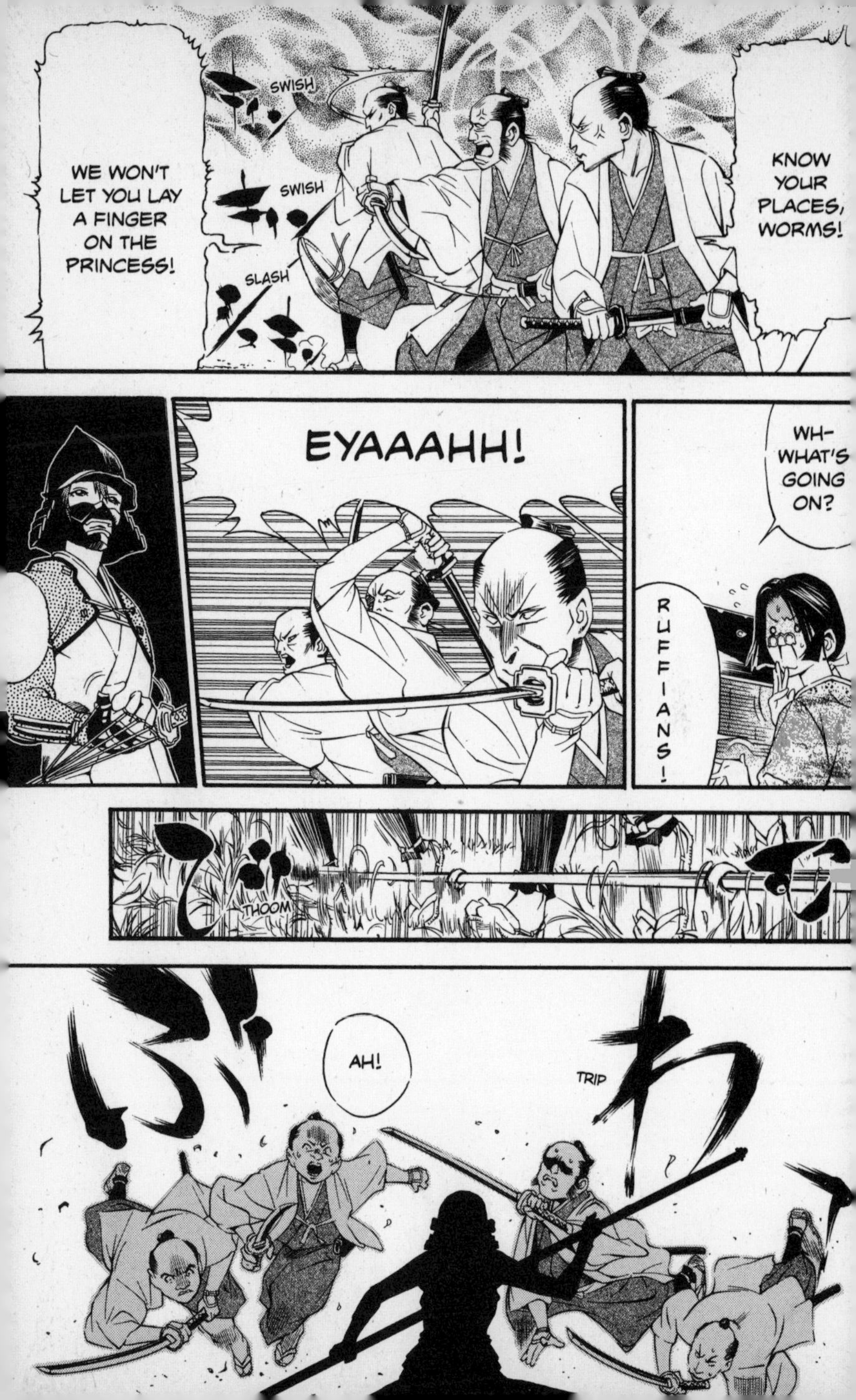
KNOW YOUR PLACES, WORMS!
SWISH
SWISH
WE WON'T LET YOU LAY A FINGER ON THE PRINCESS!
SLASH
WH- WHAT'S GOING ON?
RUFFIANS!
EYAAAHH!
THOOM
TRIP
AH!

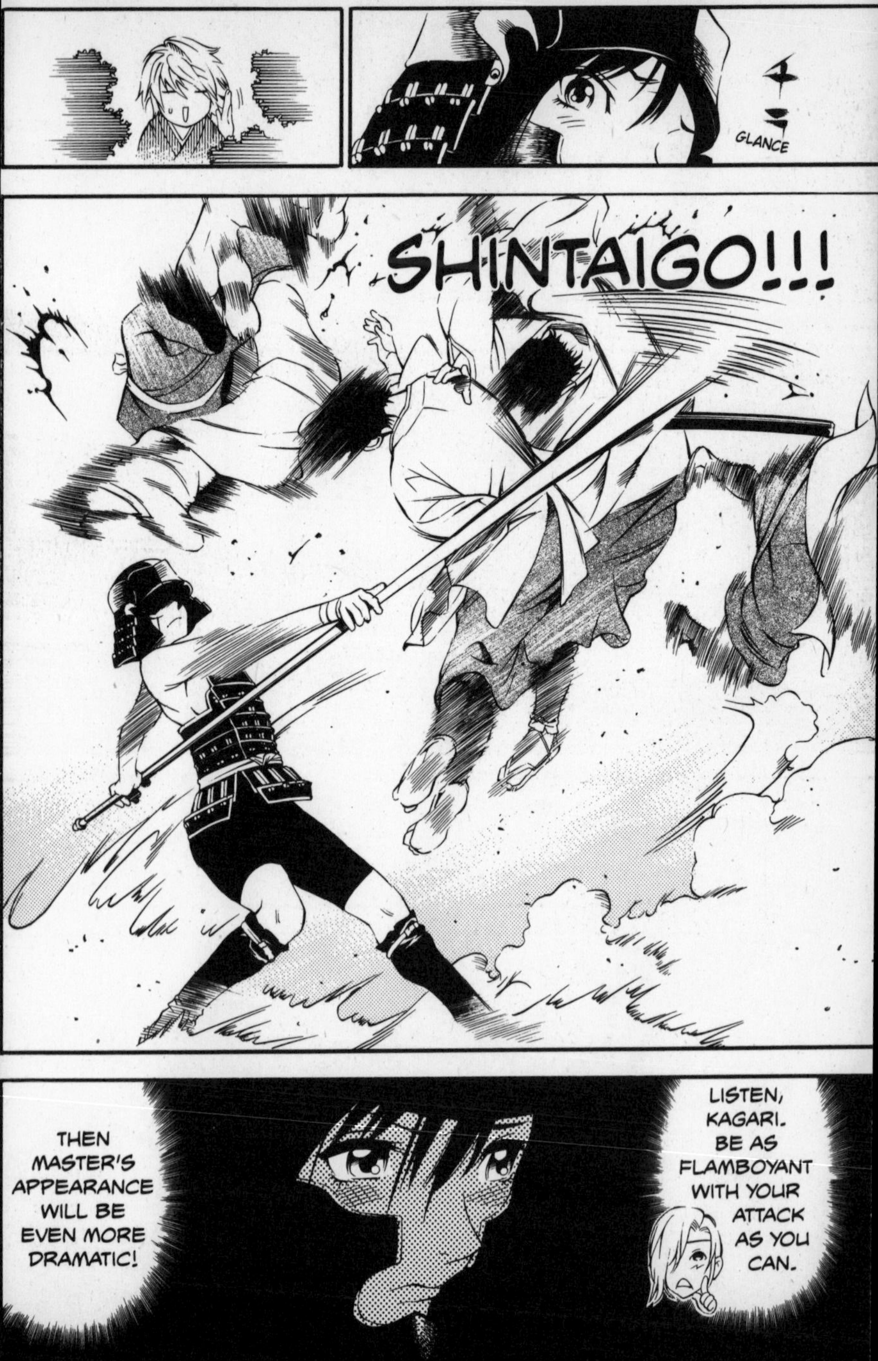
GLANCE
SHINTAIGO!!!
LISTEN, KAGARI. BE AS FLAMBOYANT WITH YOUR ATTACK AS YOU CAN.
THEN MASTER'S APPEARANCE WILL BE EVEN MORE DRAMATIC!

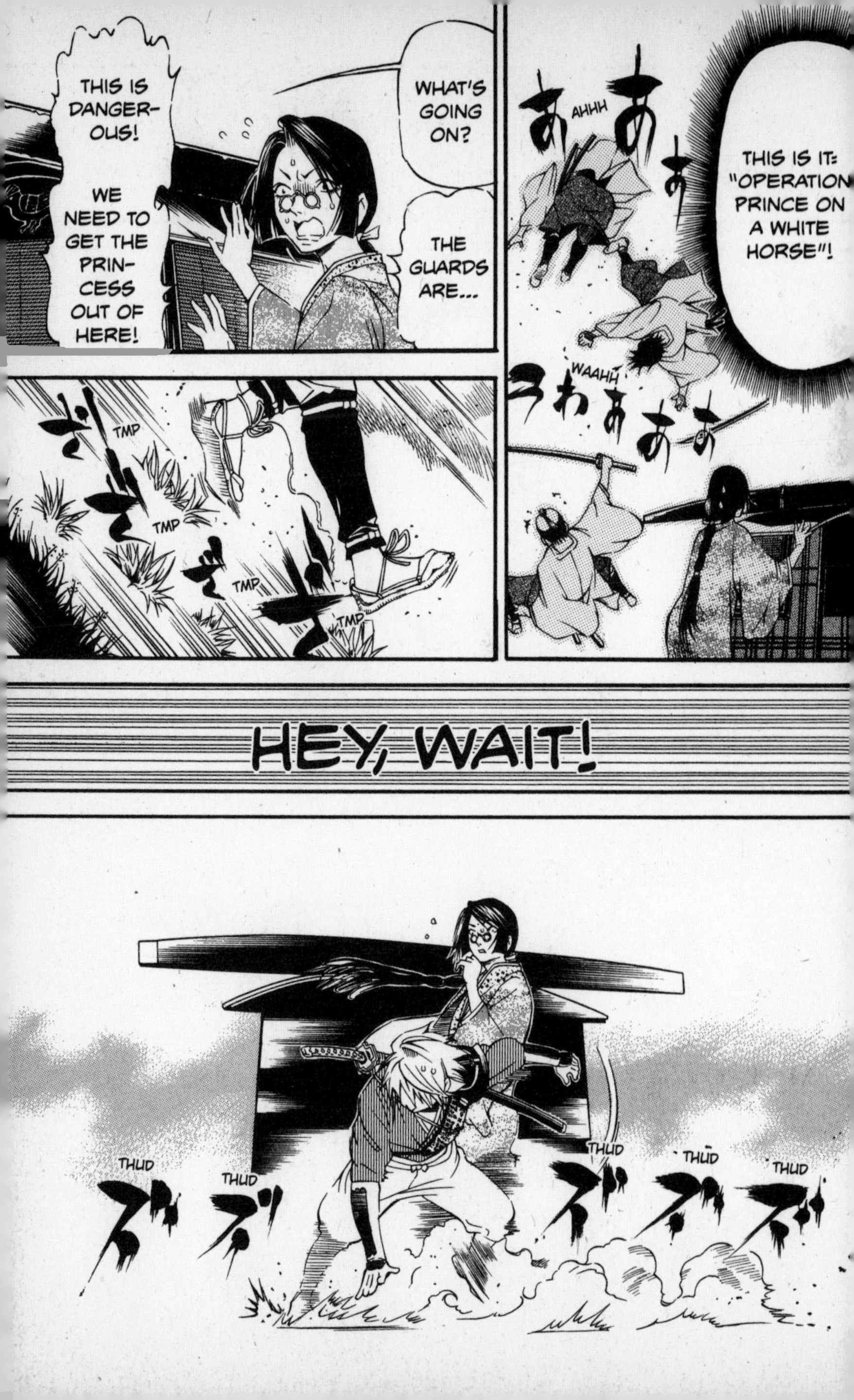
THIS IS IT: "OPERATION PRINCE ON A WHITE HORSE"!
AHHH
WAAHH
WHAT'S GOING ON?
THE GUARDS ARE...
THIS IS DANGER-OUS!
WE NEED TO GET THE PRIN-CESS OUT OF HERE!
TMP
TMP
TMP
TMP
HEY, WAIT!
THUD
THUD
THUD
THUD
THUD

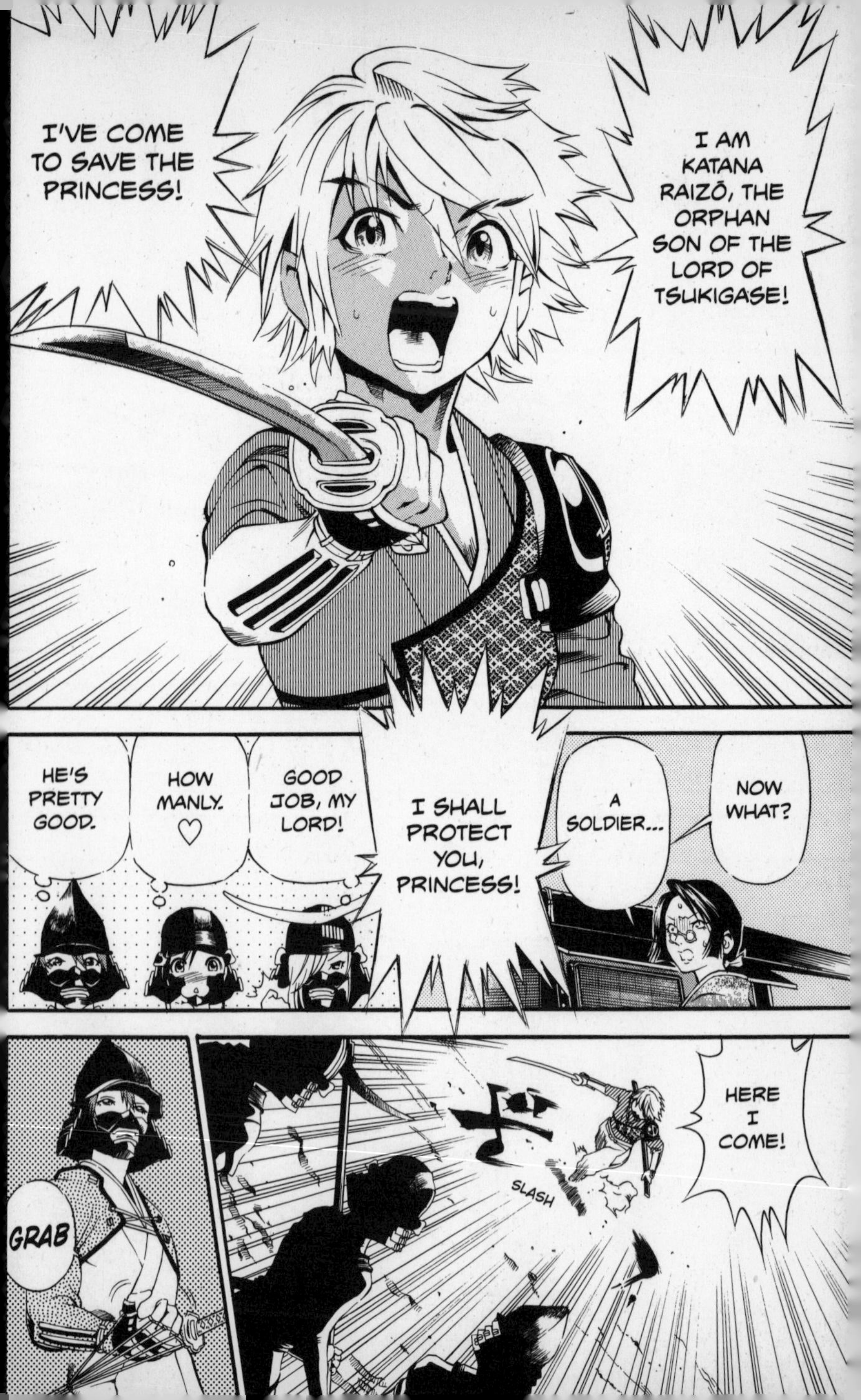
I AM KATANA RAIZŌ, THE ORPHAN SON OF THE LORD OF TSUKIGASE!
I'VE COME TO SAVE THE PRINCESS!
NOW WHAT?
A SOLDIER...
I SHALL PROTECT YOU, PRINCESS!
GOOD JOB, MY LORD!
HOW MANLY. ♡
HE'S PRETTY GOOD.
HERE I COME!
SLASH
GRAB

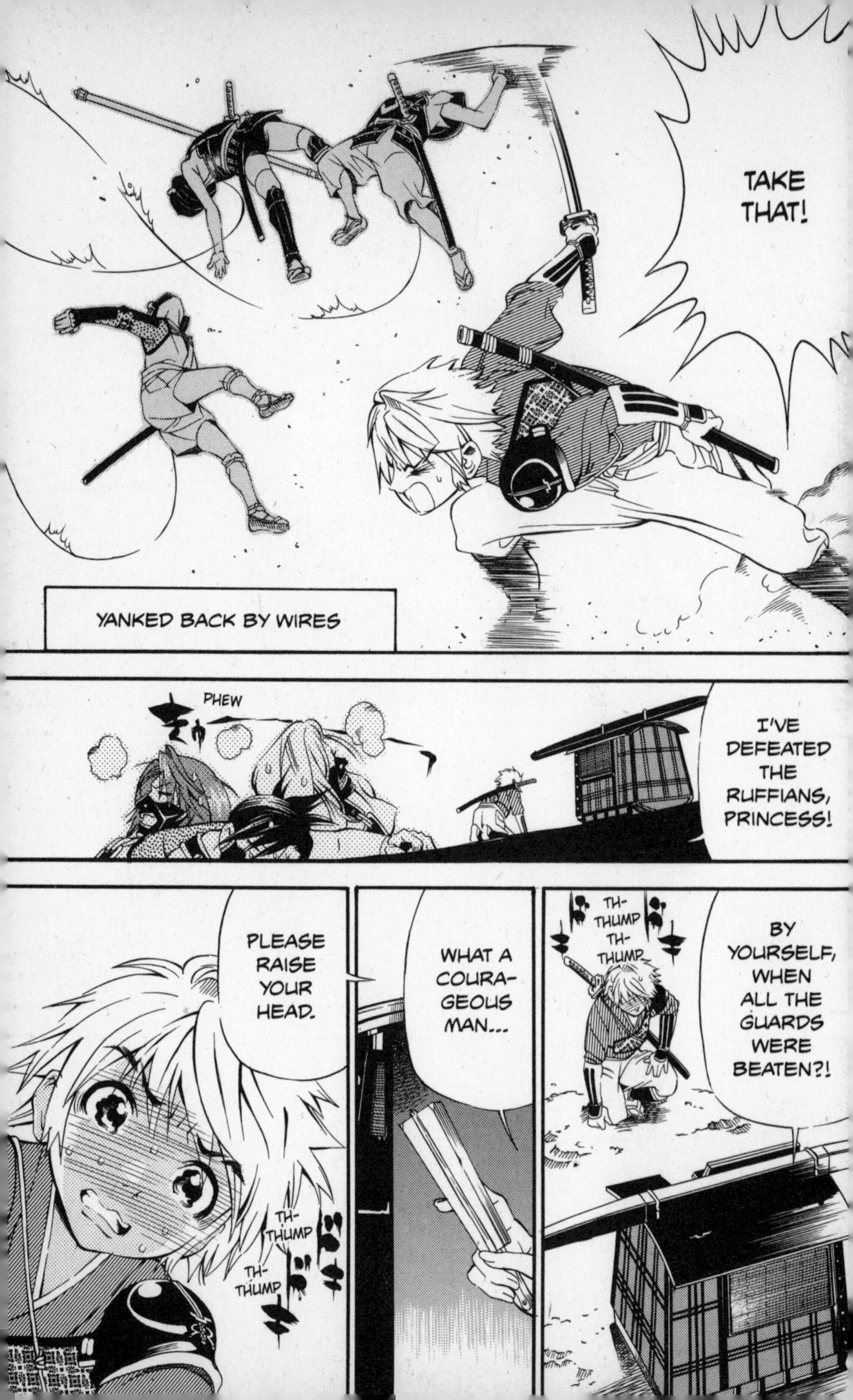
TAKE THAT!
YANKED BACK BY WIRES
I'VE DEFEATED THE RUFFIANS, PRINCESS!
PHEW
BY YOURSELF, WHEN ALL THE GUARDS WERE BEATEN?!
TH-THUMP TH-THUMP
WHAT A COURA-GEOUS MAN...
PLEASE RAISE YOUR HEAD.
TH-THUMP
TH-THUMP

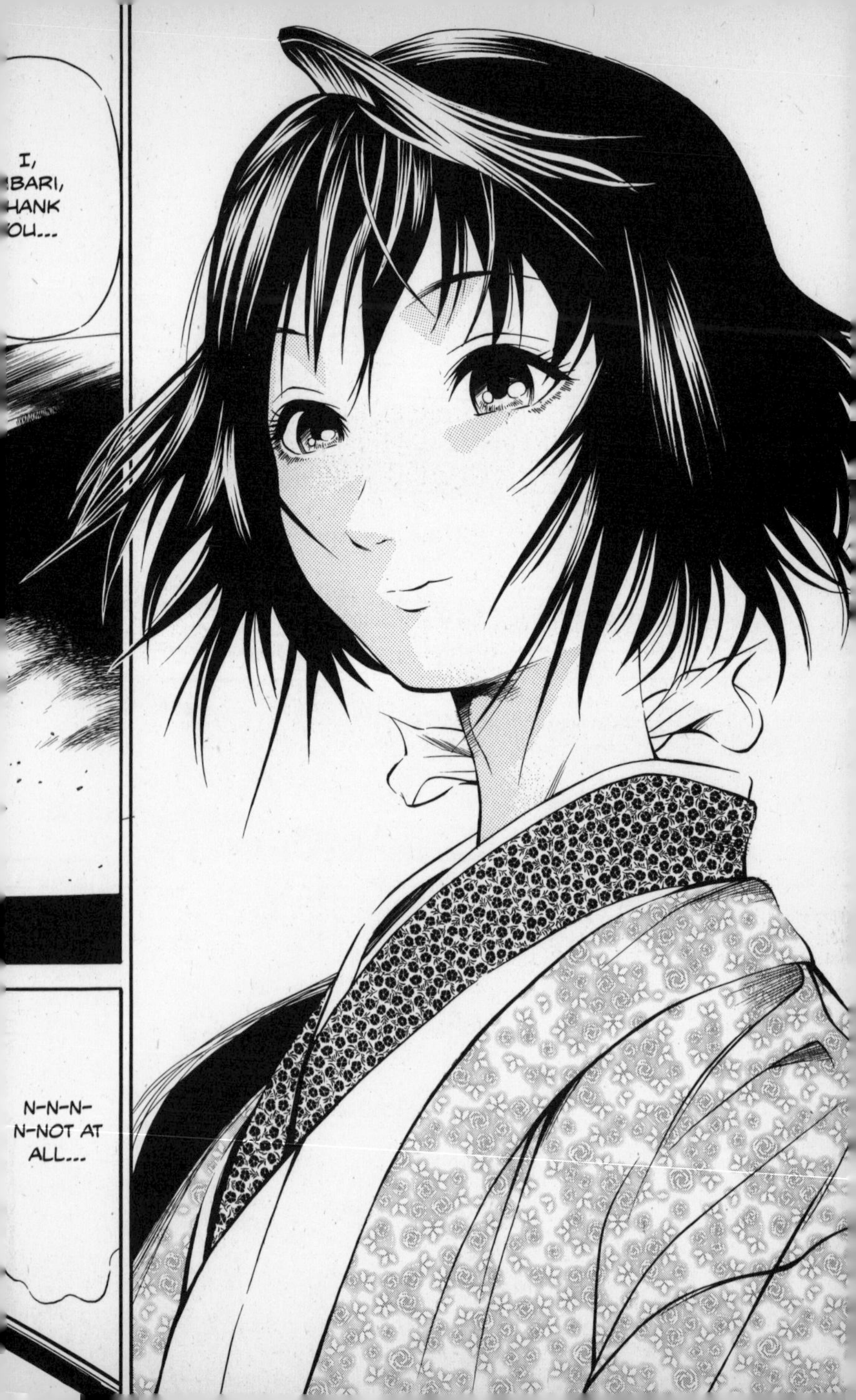

I, BARI, HANK OU...
N-N-N-N-NOT AT ALL...

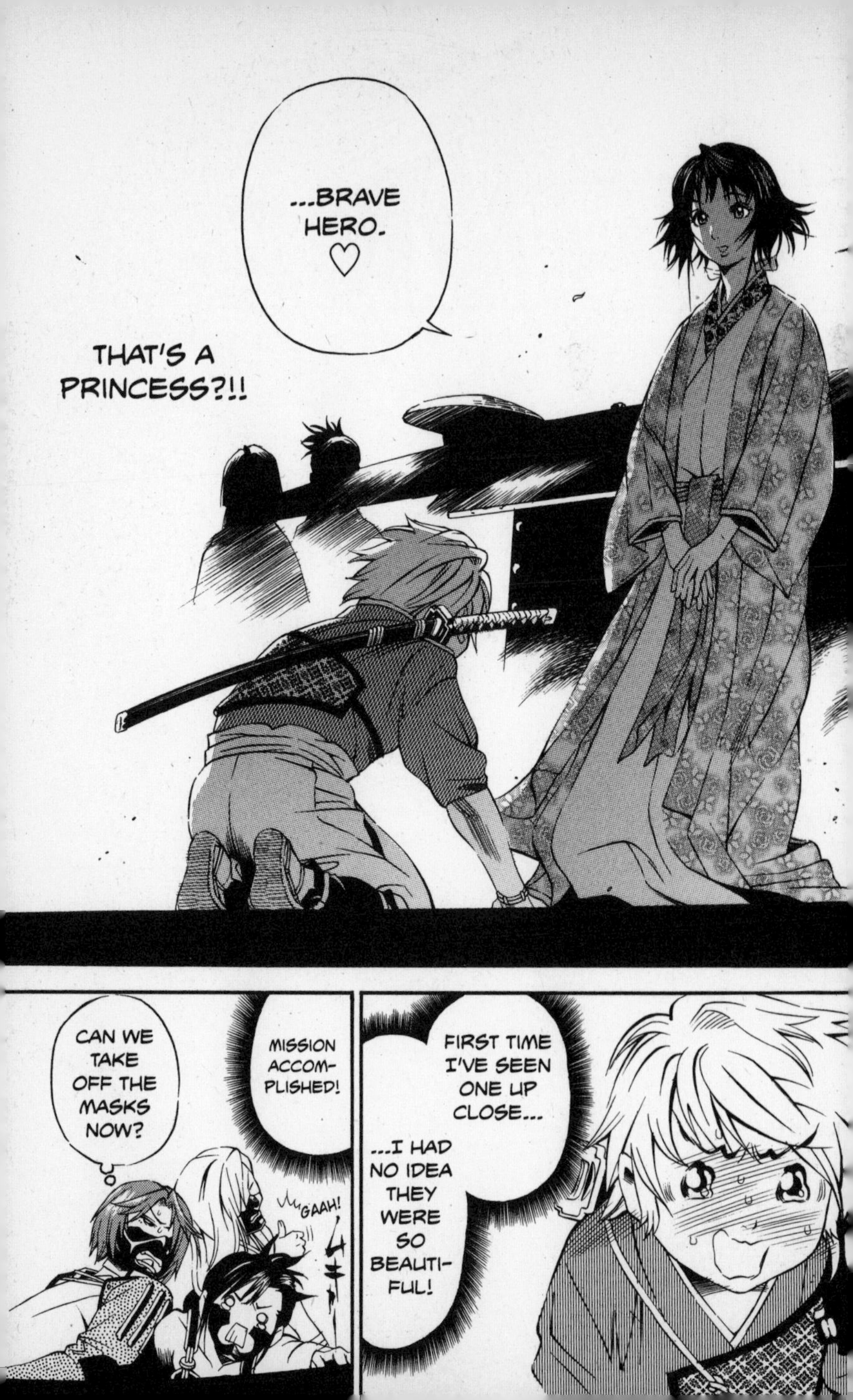
...BRAVE HERO. ♡
THAT'S A PRINCESS?!!
FIRST TIME I'VE SEEN ONE UP CLOSE...
...I HAD NO IDEA THEY WERE SO BEAUTIFUL!
MISSION ACCOMPLISHED!
CAN WE TAKE OFF THE MASKS NOW?
GAAH!

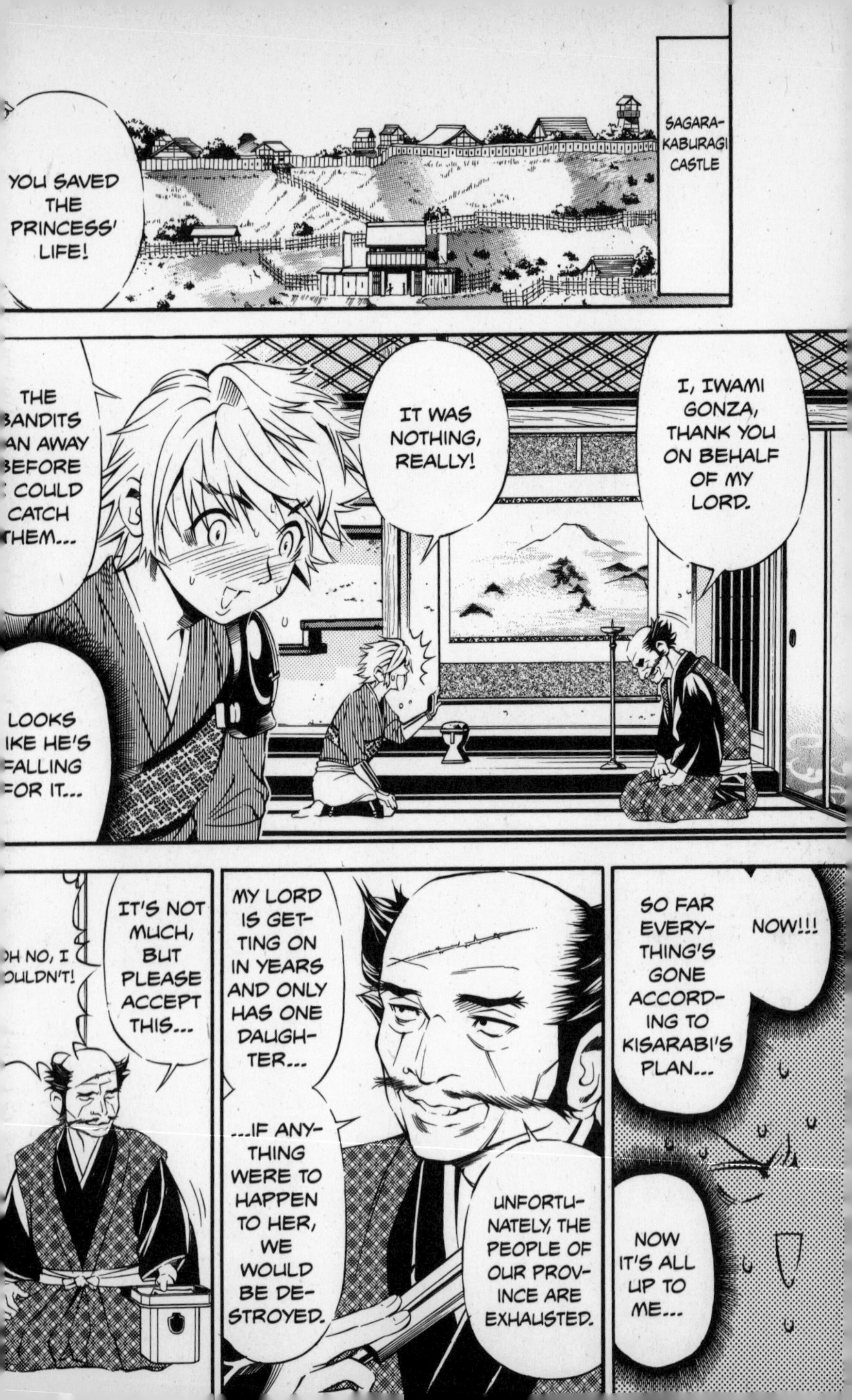
SAGARA-KABURAGI CASTLE
YOU SAVED THE PRINCESS' LIFE!
I, IWAMI GONZA, THANK YOU ON BEHALF OF MY LORD.
IT WAS NOTHING, REALLY!
THE BANDITS AN AWAY BEFORE COULD CATCH THEM...
LOOKS IKE HE'S FALLING FOR IT...
NOW!!!
SO FAR EVERYTHING'S GONE ACCORDING TO KISARABI'S PLAN...
NOW IT'S ALL UP TO ME...
MY LORD IS GETTING ON IN YEARS AND ONLY HAS ONE DAUGHTER...
...IF ANYTHING WERE TO HAPPEN TO HER, WE WOULD BE DESTROYED.
UNFORTUNATELY, THE PEOPLE OF OUR PROVINCE ARE EXHAUSTED.
IT'S NOT MUCH, BUT PLEASE ACCEPT THIS...
H NO, I OULDN'T!

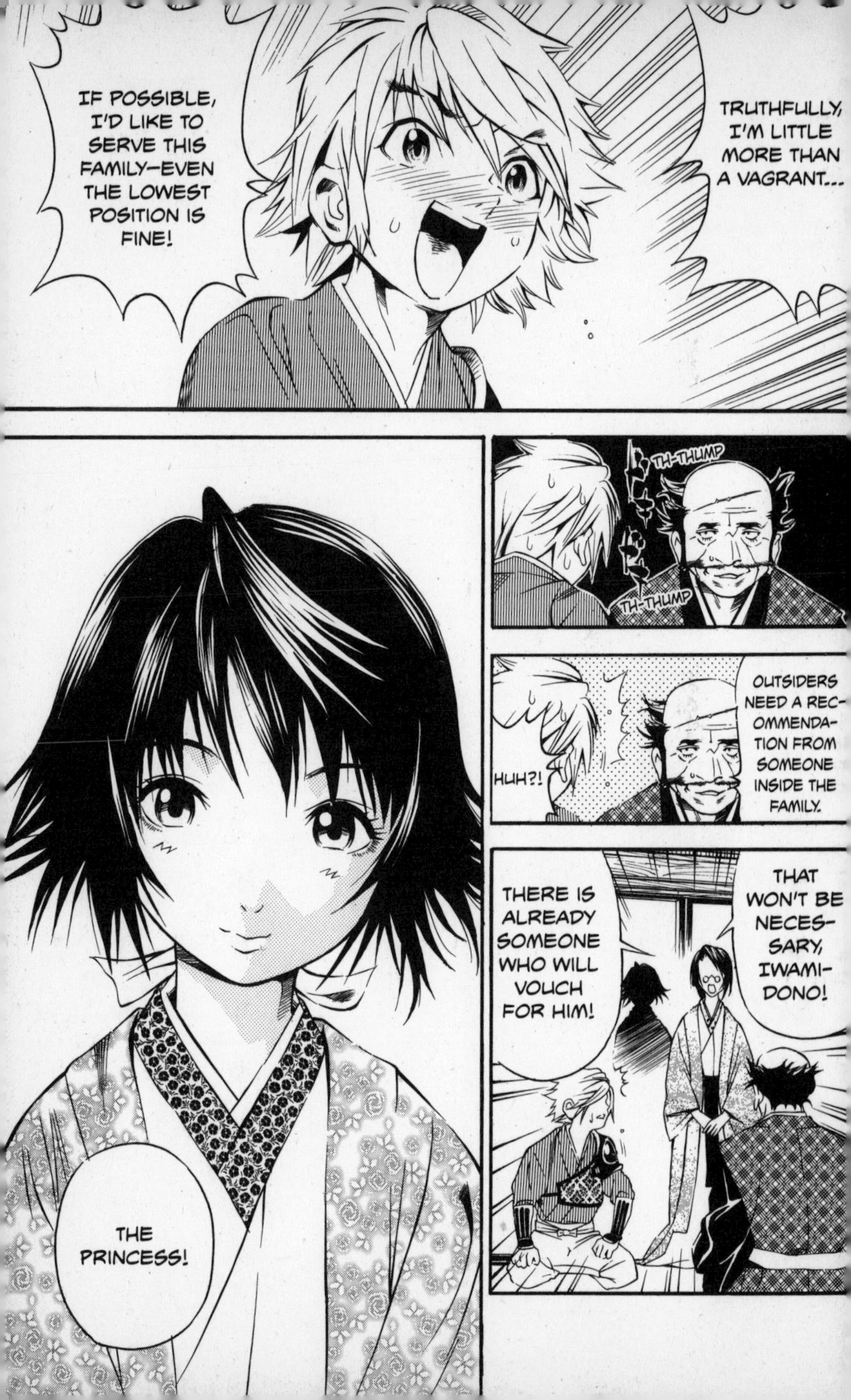
TRUTHFULLY, I'M LITTLE MORE THAN A VAGRANT...
IF POSSIBLE, I'D LIKE TO SERVE THIS FAMILY—EVEN THE LOWEST POSITION IS FINE!
TH-THUMP
TH-THUMP
OUTSIDERS NEED A RECOMMENDATION FROM SOMEONE INSIDE THE FAMILY.
HUH?!
THAT WON'T BE NECESSARY, IWAMI-DONO!
THERE IS ALREADY SOMEONE WHO WILL VOUCH FOR HIM!
THE PRINCESS!

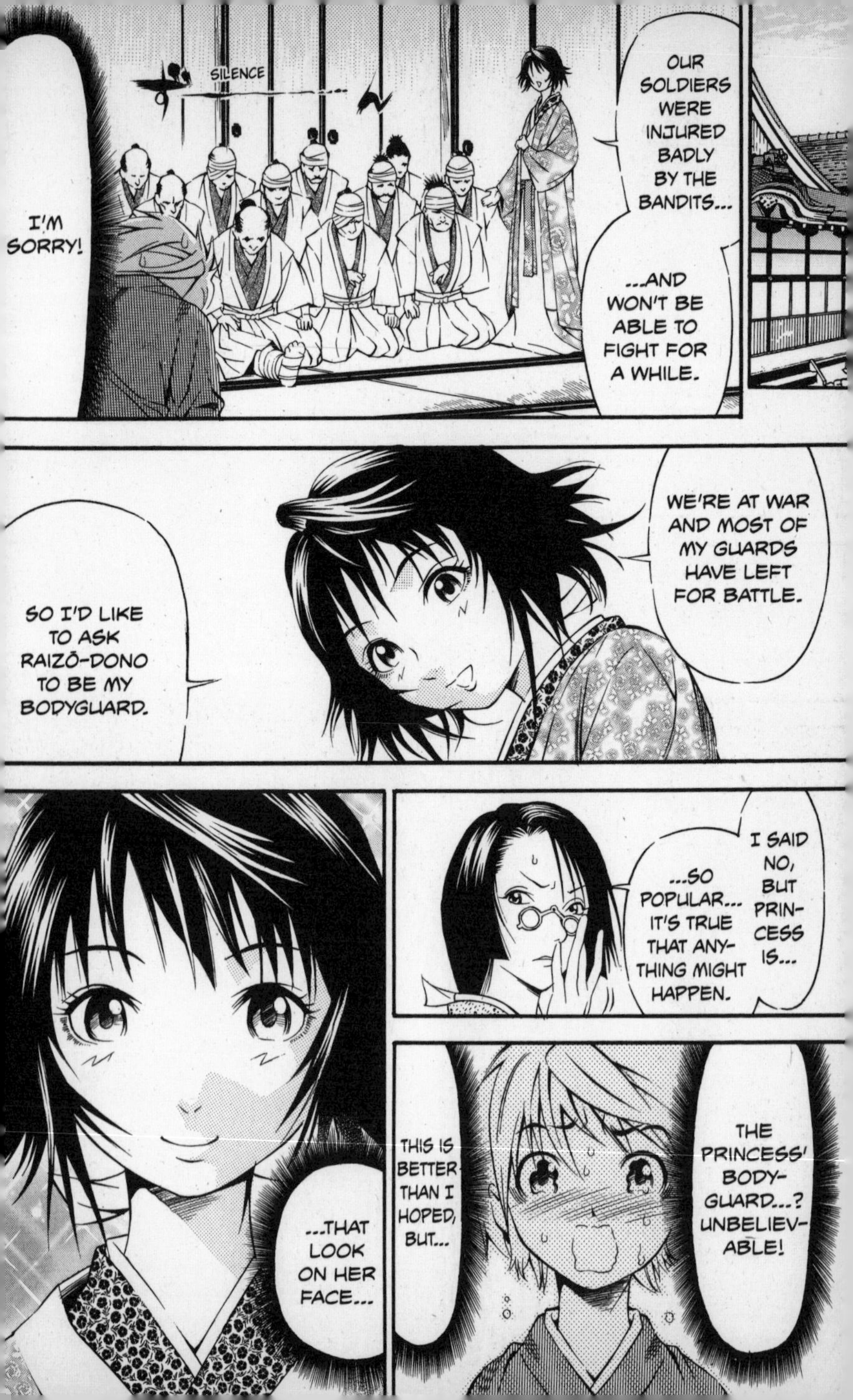
OUR SOLDIERS WERE INJURED BADLY BY THE BANDITS...
...AND WON'T BE ABLE TO FIGHT FOR A WHILE.
SILENCE
I'M SORRY!
WE'RE AT WAR AND MOST OF MY GUARDS HAVE LEFT FOR BATTLE.
SO I'D LIKE TO ASK RAIZŌ-DONO TO BE MY BODYGUARD.
I SAID NO, BUT PRIN-CESS IS...
...SO POPULAR... IT'S TRUE THAT ANY-THING MIGHT HAPPEN.
THE PRINCESS' BODY-GUARD...? UNBELIEV-ABLE!
THIS IS BETTER THAN I HOPED, BUT...
...THAT LOOK ON HER FACE...

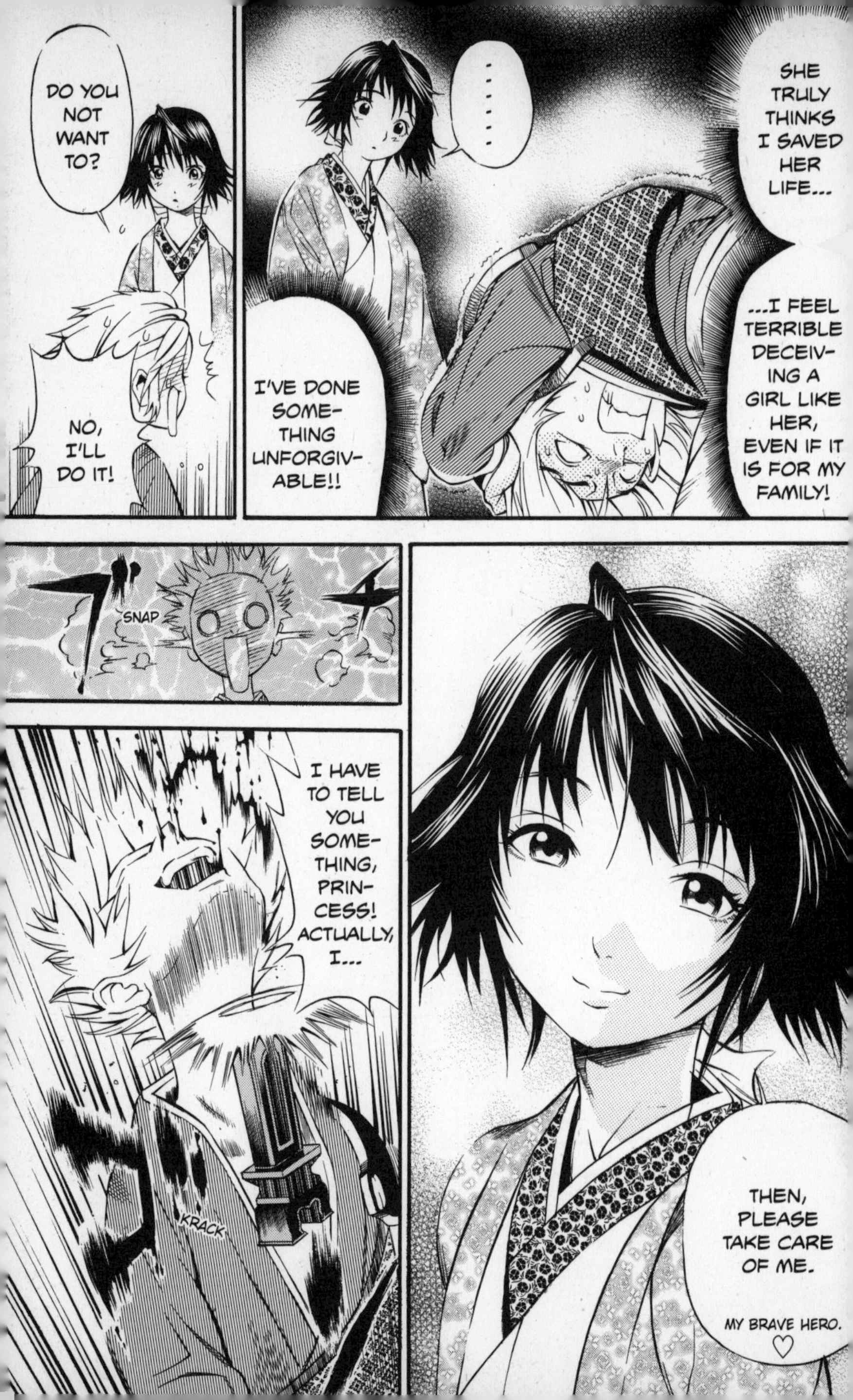
SHE TRULY THINKS I SAVED HER LIFE...
......
...I FEEL TERRIBLE DECEIV-ING A GIRL LIKE HER, EVEN IF IT IS FOR MY FAMILY!
I'VE DONE SOME-THING UNFORGIV-ABLE!!
DO YOU NOT WANT TO?
NO, I'LL DO IT!
THEN, PLEASE TAKE CARE OF ME.
MY BRAVE HERO. ♡
SNAP
I HAVE TO TELL YOU SOME-THING, PRIN-CESS! ACTUALLY, I...
KRACK

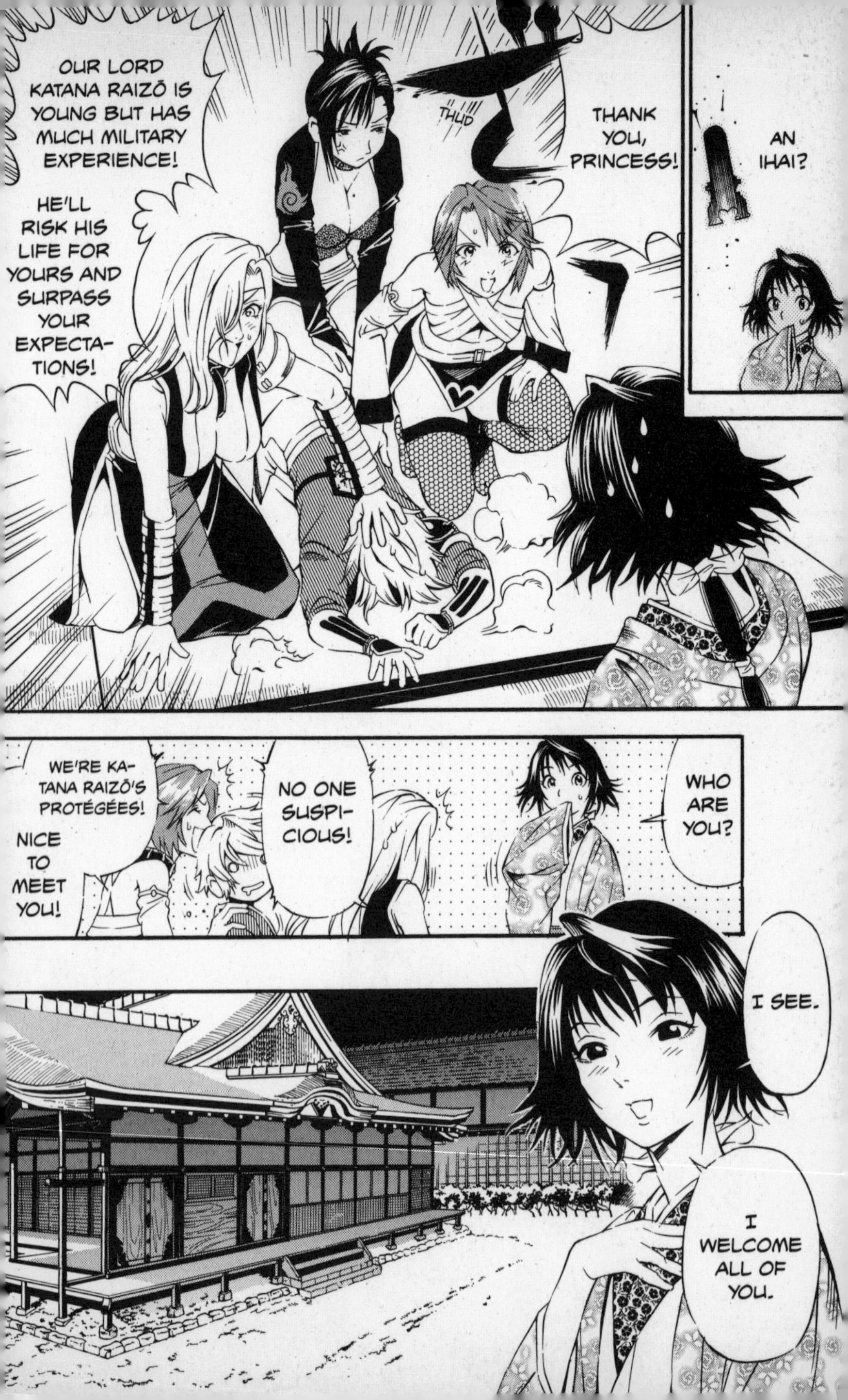
AN IHAI?
THANK YOU, PRINCESS!
THUD
OUR LORD KATANA RAIZŌ IS YOUNG BUT HAS MUCH MILITARY EXPERIENCE!
HE'LL RISK HIS LIFE FOR YOURS AND SURPASS YOUR EXPECTATIONS!
WHO ARE YOU?
NO ONE SUSPICIOUS!
WE'RE KATANA RAIZŌ'S PROTÉGÉES!
NICE TO MEET YOU!
I SEE.
I WELCOME ALL OF YOU.

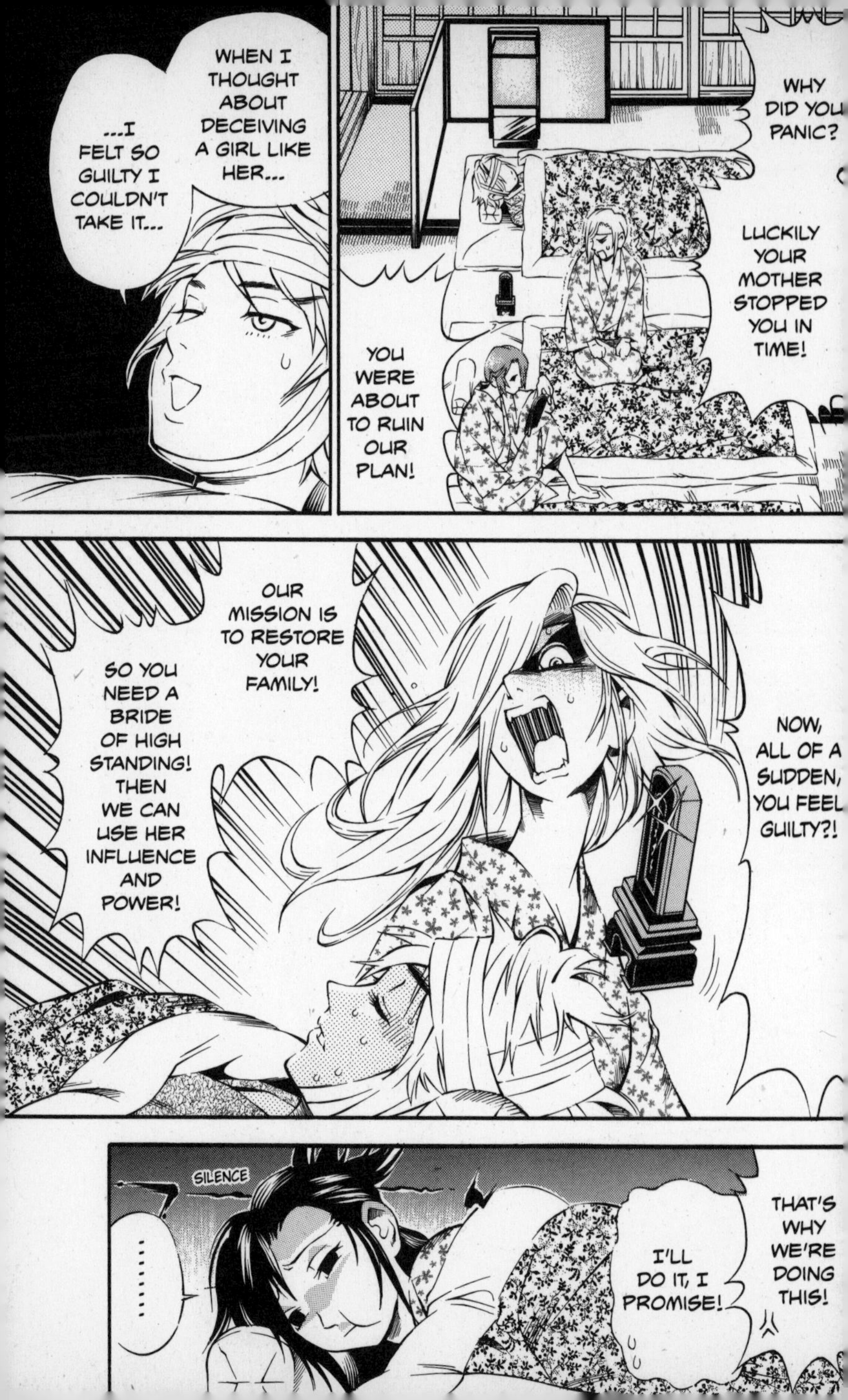
WHY DID YOU PANIC?
LUCKILY YOUR MOTHER STOPPED YOU IN TIME!
YOU WERE ABOUT TO RUIN OUR PLAN!
WHEN I THOUGHT ABOUT DECEIVING A GIRL LIKE HER...
...I FELT SO GUILTY I COULDN'T TAKE IT...
NOW, ALL OF A SUDDEN, YOU FEEL GUILTY?!
OUR MISSION IS TO RESTORE YOUR FAMILY!
SO YOU NEED A BRIDE OF HIGH STANDING! THEN WE CAN USE HER INFLUENCE AND POWER!
THAT'S WHY WE'RE DOING THIS!
I'LL DO IT, I PROMISE!
SILENCE
....

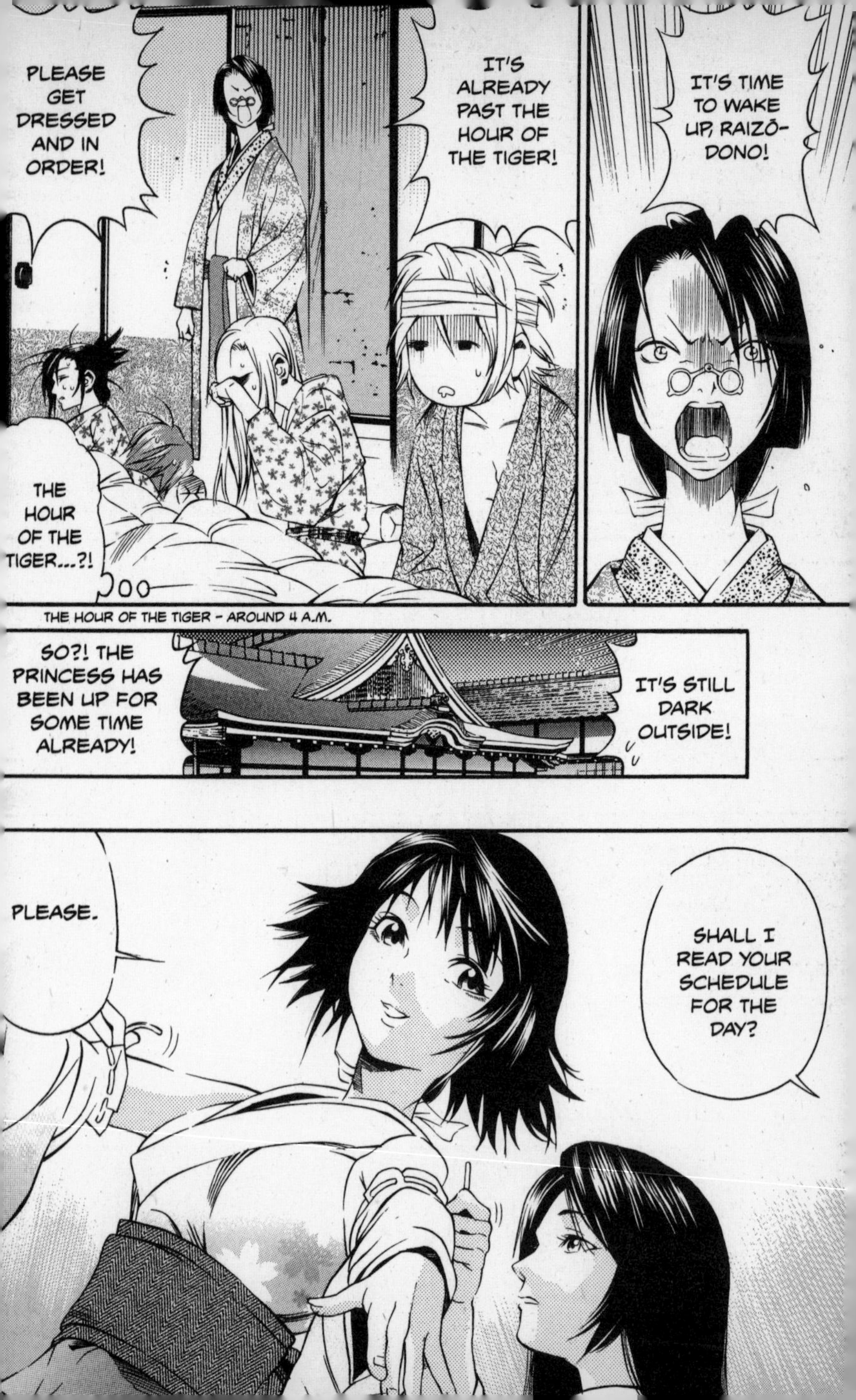
IT'S TIME TO WAKE UP, RAIZŌ-DONO!
IT'S ALREADY PAST THE HOUR OF THE TIGER!
PLEASE GET DRESSED AND IN ORDER!
THE HOUR OF THE TIGER...?!
THE HOUR OF THE TIGER - AROUND 4 A.M.
IT'S STILL DARK OUTSIDE!
SO?! THE PRINCESS HAS BEEN UP FOR SOME TIME ALREADY!
SHALL I READ YOUR SCHEDULE FOR THE DAY?
PLEASE.

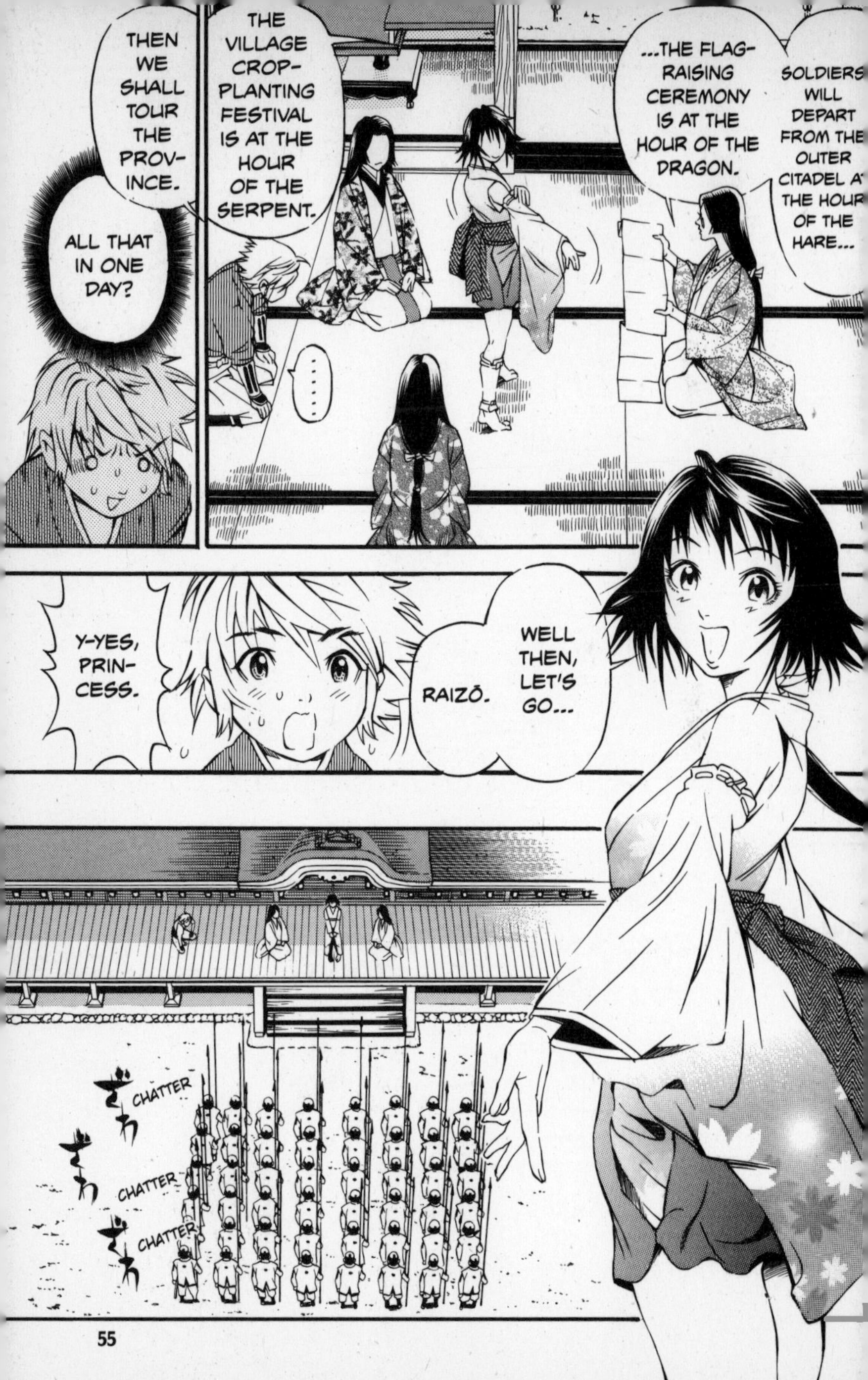
SOLDIERS WILL DEPART FROM THE OUTER CITADEL AT THE HOUR OF THE HARE...
...THE FLAG-RAISING CEREMONY IS AT THE HOUR OF THE DRAGON.
THE VILLAGE CROP-PLANTING FESTIVAL IS AT THE HOUR OF THE SERPENT.
THEN WE SHALL TOUR THE PROVINCE.
......
ALL THAT IN ONE DAY?
WELL THEN, LET'S GO...
RAIZŌ.
Y-YES, PRINCESS.
CHATTER
CHATTER
CHATTER

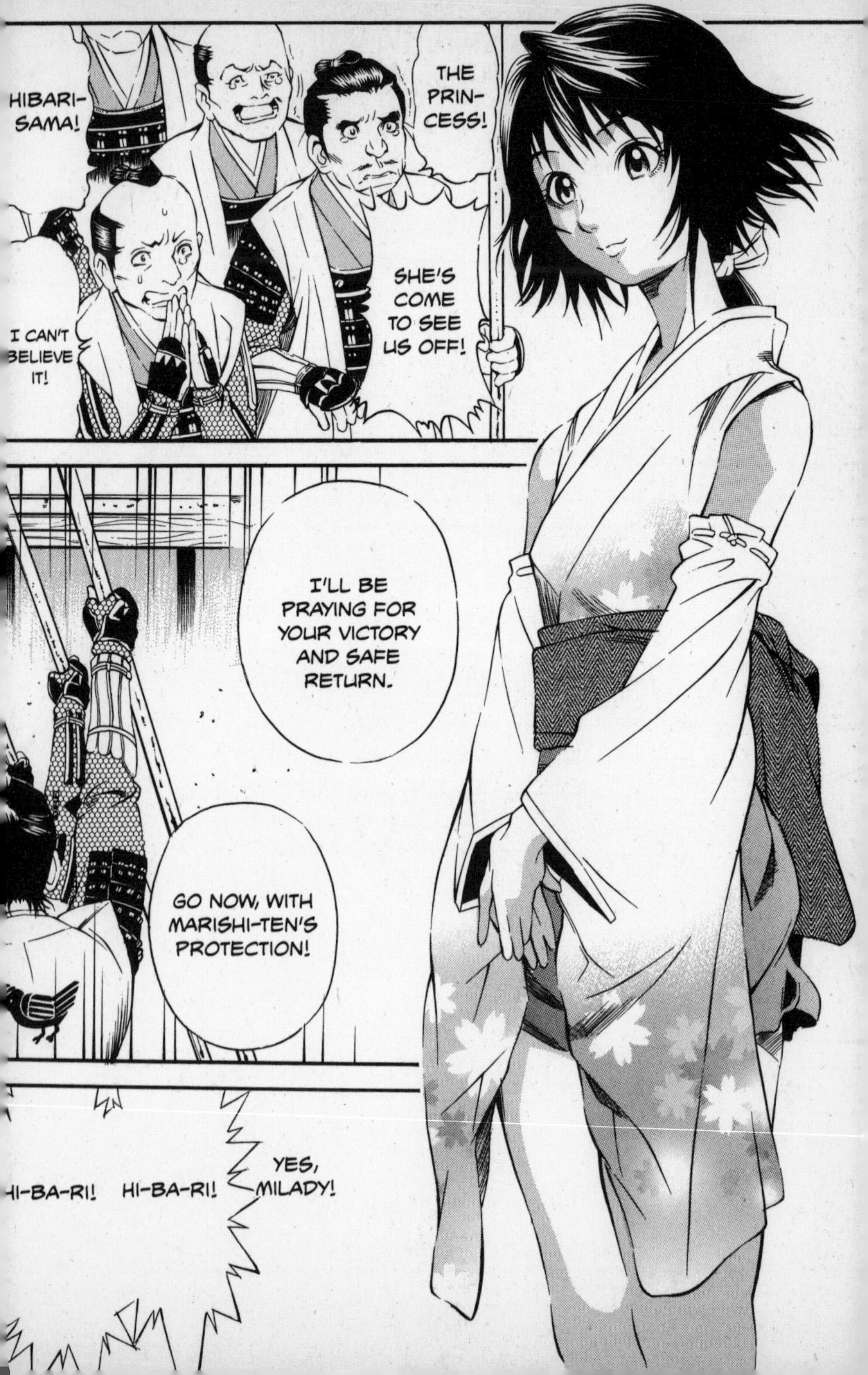
THE PRIN-CESS!
SHE'S COME TO SEE US OFF!
HIBARI-SAMA!
I CAN'T BELIEVE IT!
I'LL BE PRAYING FOR YOUR VICTORY AND SAFE RETURN.
GO NOW, WITH MARISHI-TEN'S PROTECTION!
YES, MILADY!
HI-BA-RI!
HI-BA-RI!

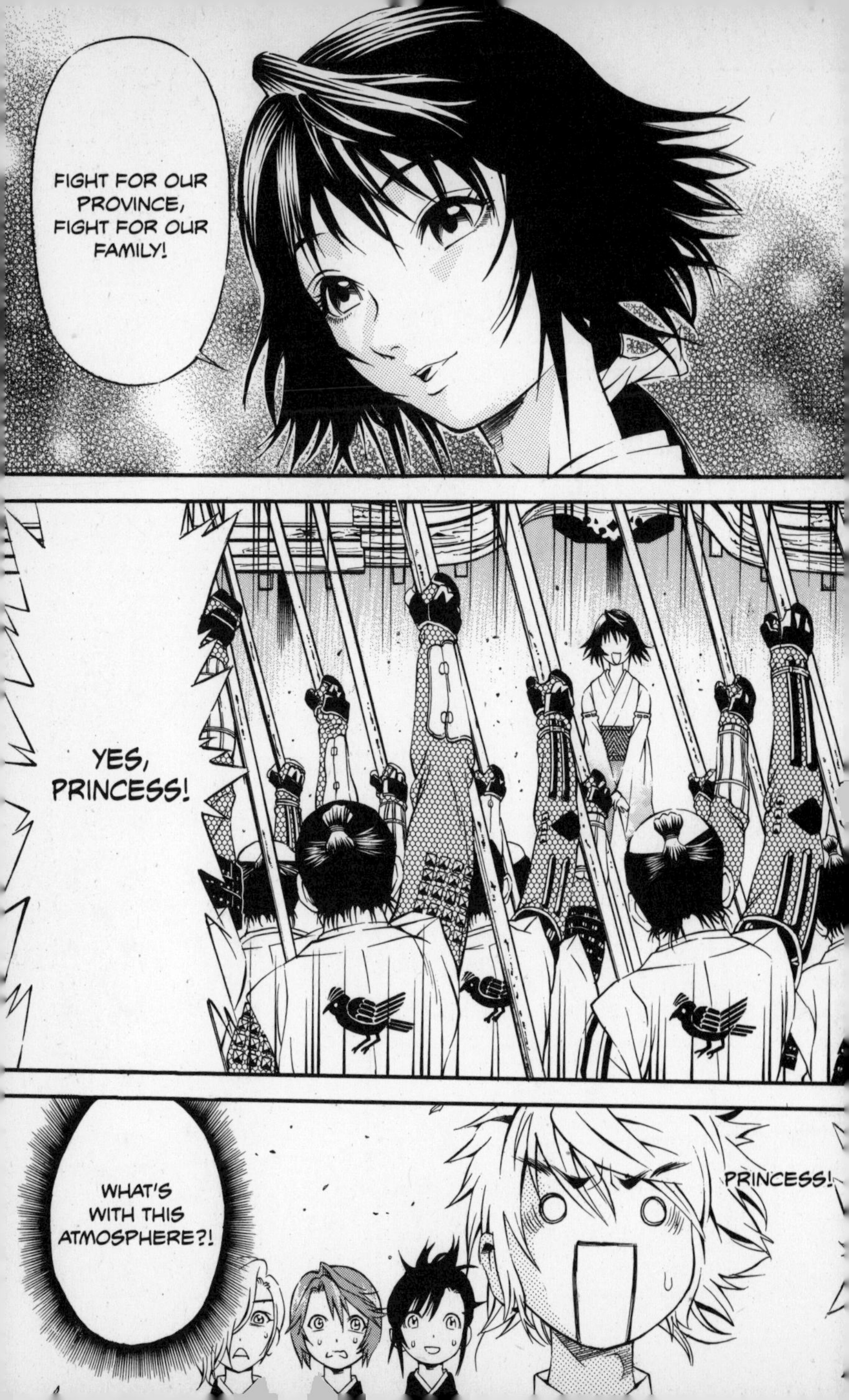
FIGHT FOR OUR PROVINCE, FIGHT FOR OUR FAMILY!
YES, PRINCESS!
PRINCESS!
WHAT'S WITH THIS ATMOSPHERE?!

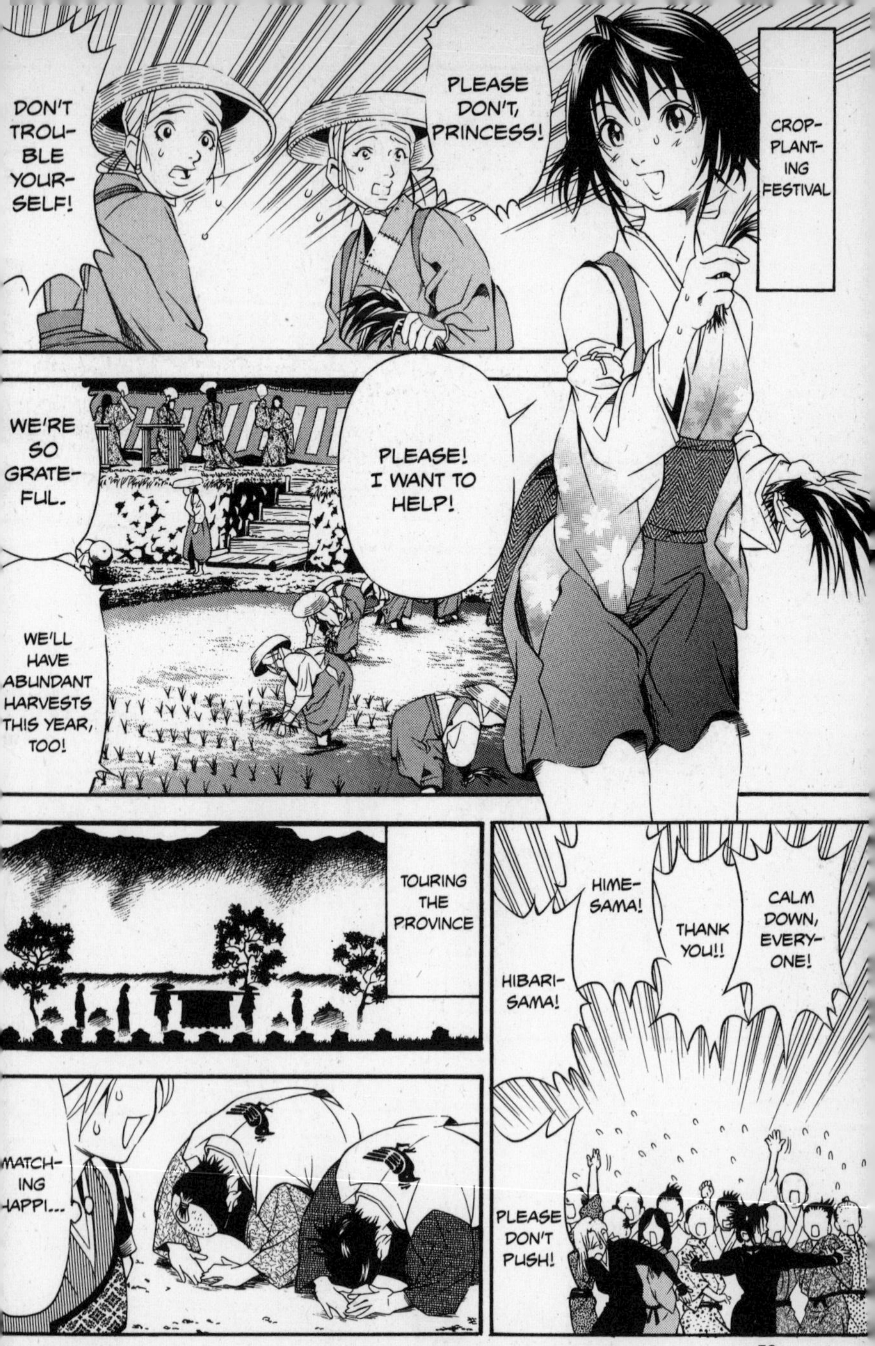
CROP-PLANTING FESTIVAL
PLEASE DON'T, PRINCESS!
DON'T TROUBLE YOURSELF!
PLEASE! I WANT TO HELP!
WE'RE SO GRATEFUL.
WE'LL HAVE ABUNDANT HARVESTS THIS YEAR, TOO!
CALM DOWN, EVERYONE!
THANK YOU!!
HIME-SAMA!
HIBARI-SAMA!
PLEASE DON'T PUSH!
TOURING THE PROVINCE
MATCHING HAPPI...

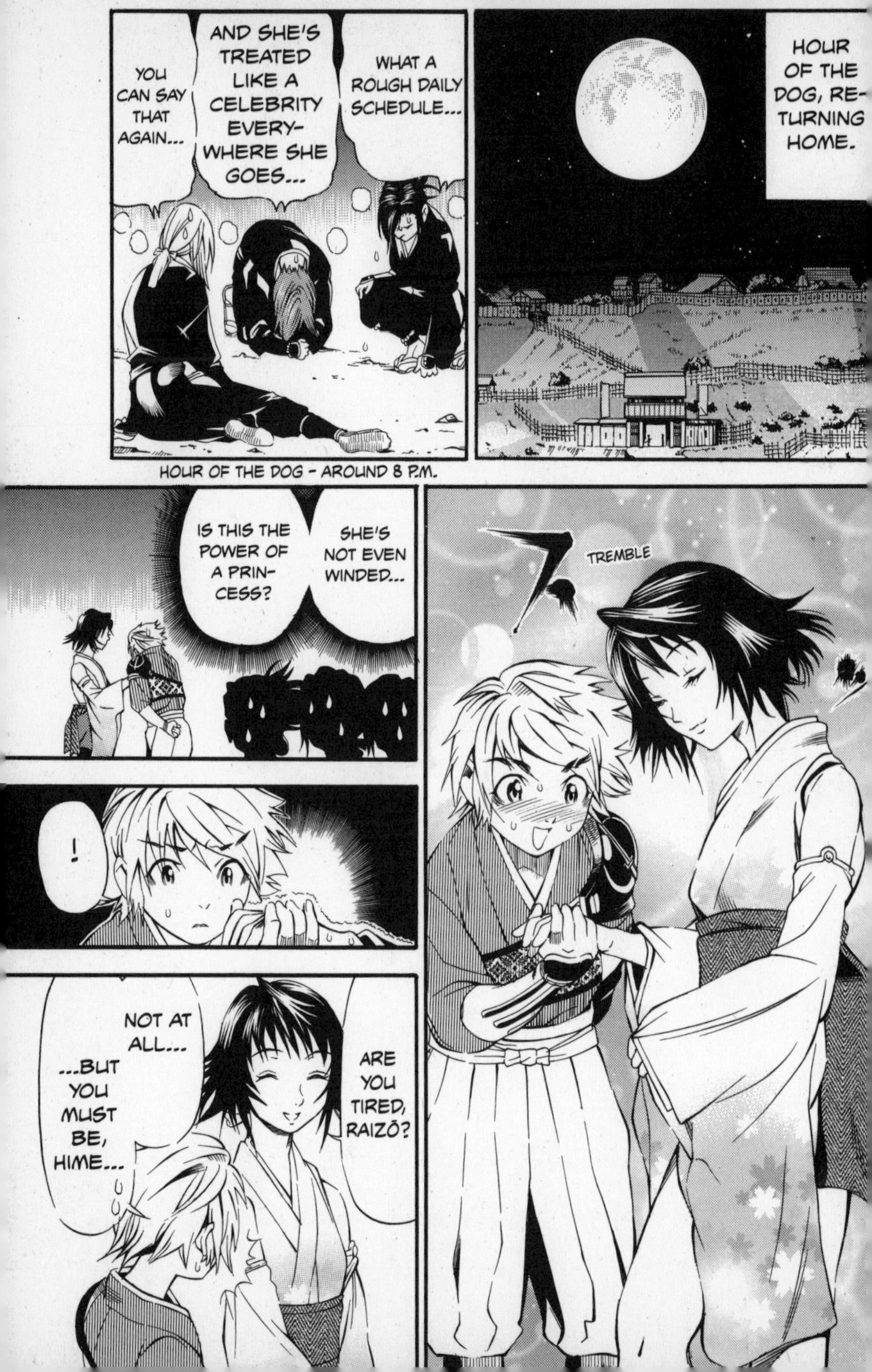
HOUR OF THE DOG, RETURNING HOME.
WHAT A ROUGH DAILY SCHEDULE...
AND SHE'S TREATED LIKE A CELEBRITY EVERYWHERE SHE GOES...
YOU CAN SAY THAT AGAIN...
TREMBLE
SHE'S NOT EVEN WINDED...
IS THIS THE POWER OF A PRINCESS?
!
ARE YOU TIRED, RAIZŌ?
NOT AT ALL...
...BUT YOU MUST BE, HIME...
HOUR OF THE DOG - AROUND 8 P.M.

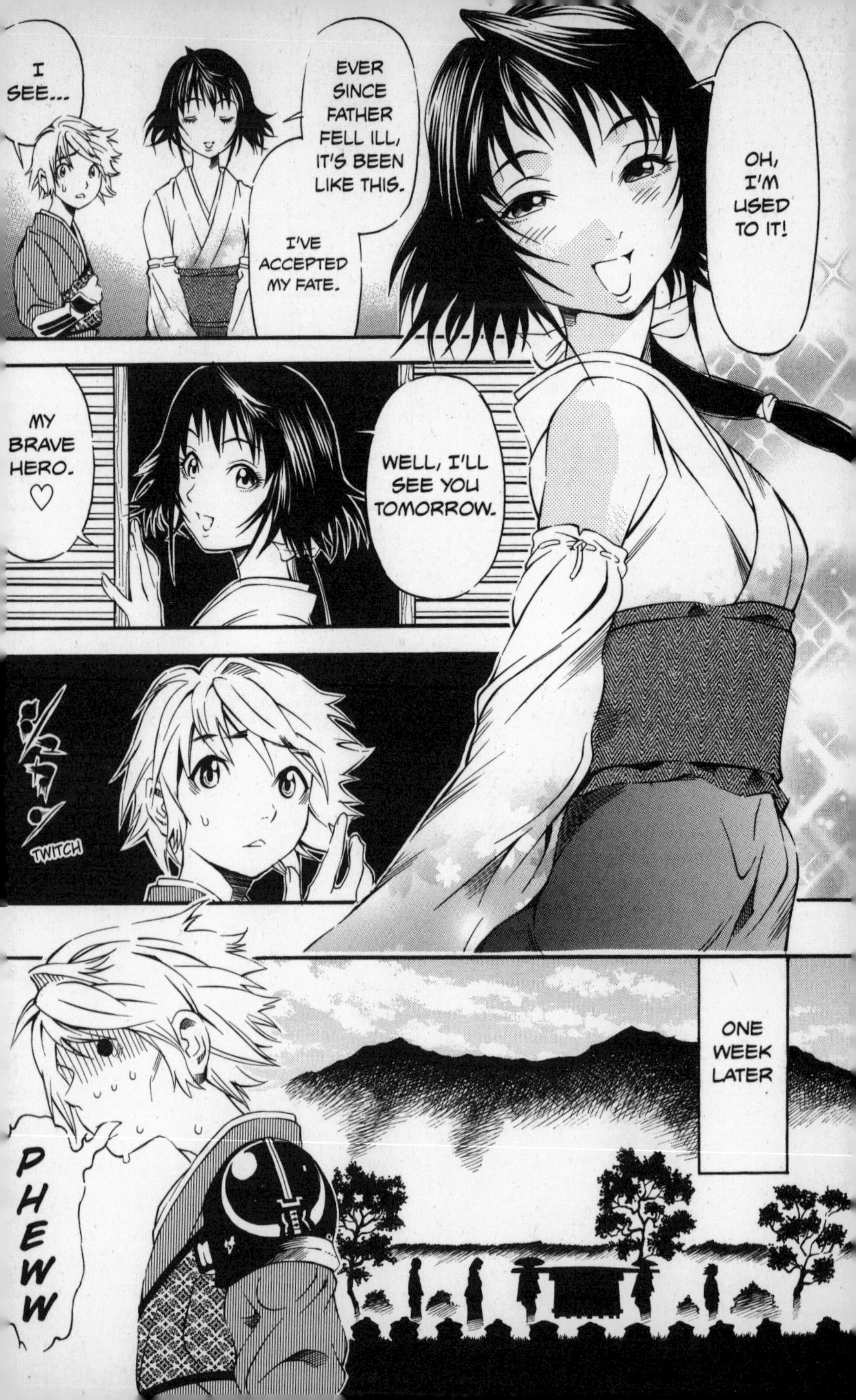
OH, I'M USED TO IT!
EVER SINCE FATHER FELL ILL, IT'S BEEN LIKE THIS.
I'VE ACCEPTED MY FATE.
I SEE...
WELL, I'LL SEE YOU TOMORROW.
MY BRAVE HERO. ♡
TWITCH
ONE WEEK LATER
PHEWW

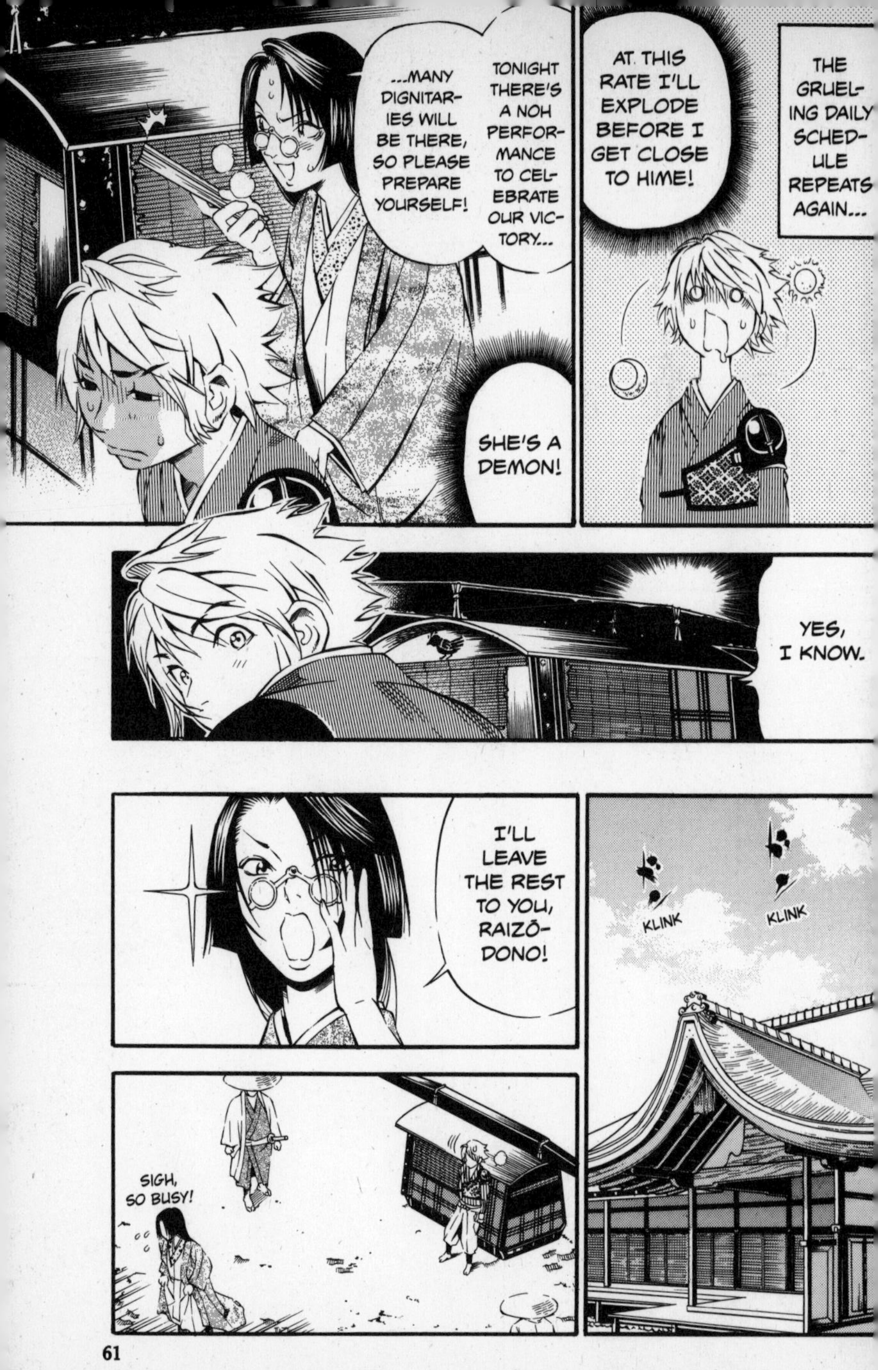
THE GRUELING DAILY SCHEDULE REPEATS AGAIN...
AT THIS RATE I'LL EXPLODE BEFORE I GET CLOSE TO HIME!
TONIGHT THERE'S A NOH PERFORMANCE TO CELEBRATE OUR VICTORY...
...MANY DIGNITARIES WILL BE THERE, SO PLEASE PREPARE YOURSELF!
SHE'S A DEMON!
YES, I KNOW.
KLINK
KLINK
I'LL LEAVE THE REST TO YOU, RAIZŌ-DONO!
SIGH, SO BUSY!

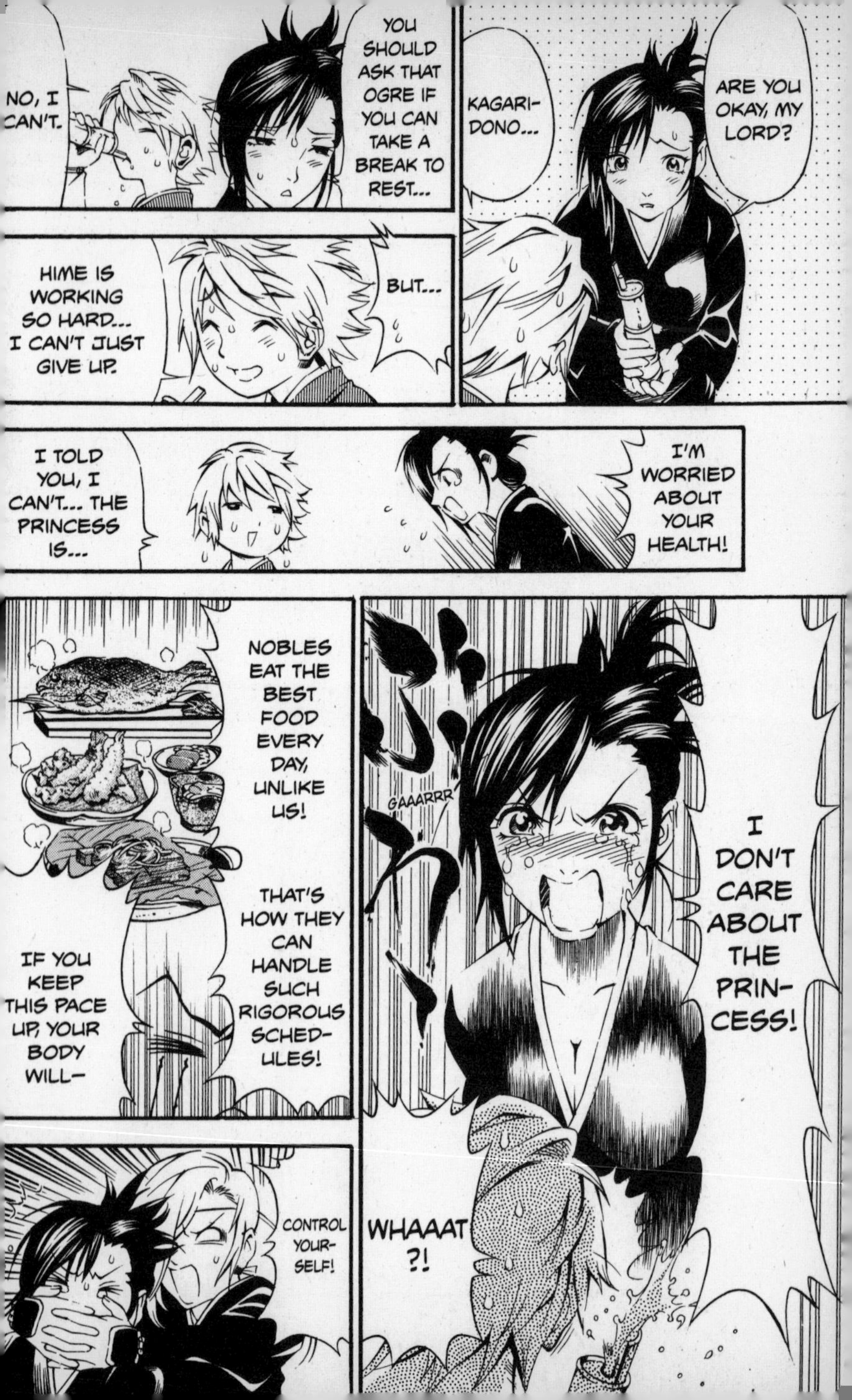
ARE YOU OKAY, MY LORD?
KAGARI-DONO...
YOU SHOULD ASK THAT OGRE IF YOU CAN TAKE A BREAK TO REST...
NO, I CAN'T.
BUT...
HIME IS WORKING SO HARD... I CAN'T JUST GIVE UP.
I'M WORRIED ABOUT YOUR HEALTH!
I TOLD YOU, I CAN'T... THE PRINCESS IS...
GAAARRR
I DON'T CARE ABOUT THE PRIN-CESS!
WHAAAT?!
NOBLES EAT THE BEST FOOD EVERY DAY, UNLIKE US!
THAT'S HOW THEY CAN HANDLE SUCH RIGOROUS SCHED-ULES!
IF YOU KEEP THIS PACE UP, YOUR BODY WILL-
CONTROL YOUR-SELF!

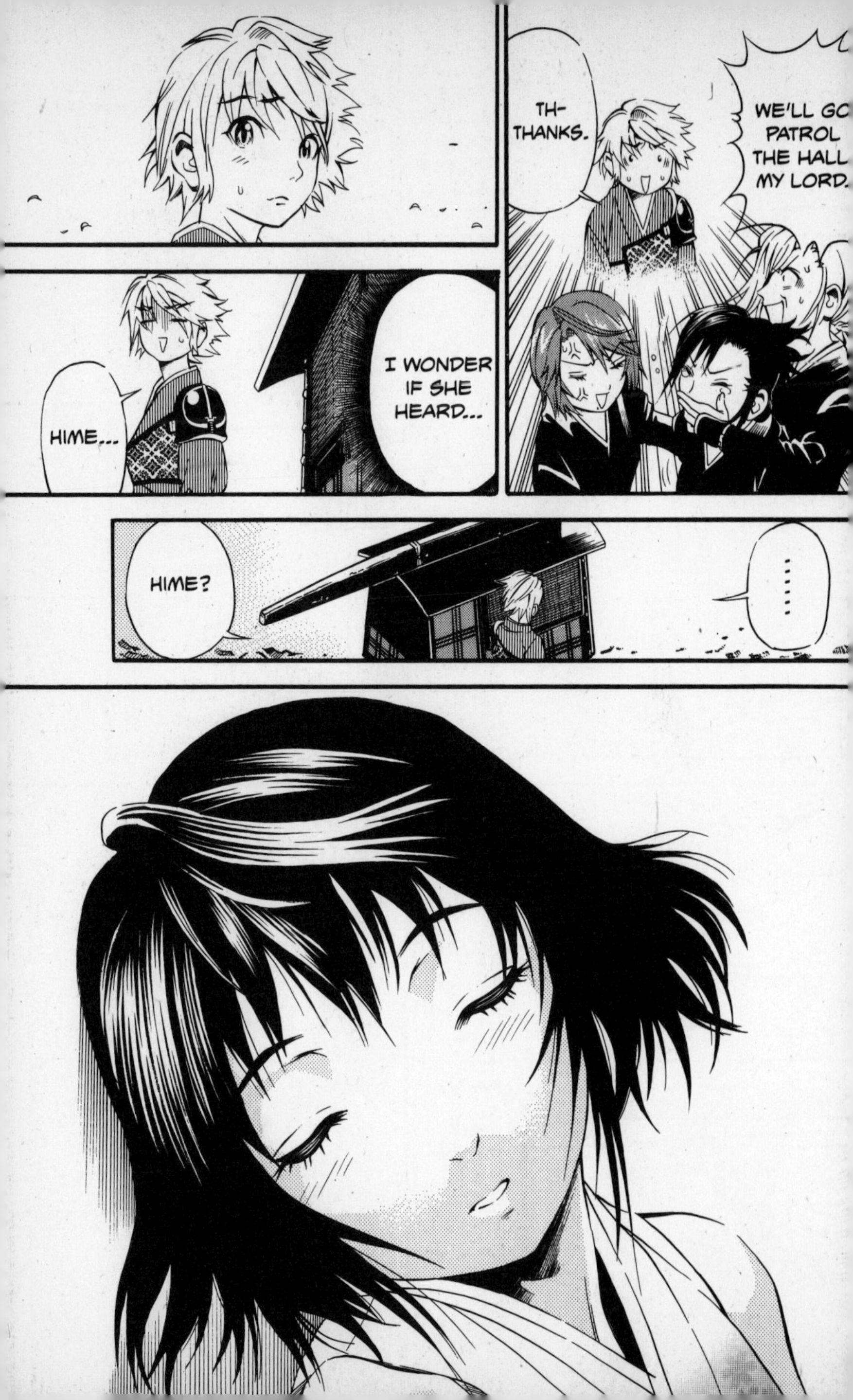
WE'LL GO PATROL THE HALL MY LORD.
TH- THANKS.
I WONDER IF SHE HEARD...
HIME...
......
HIME?

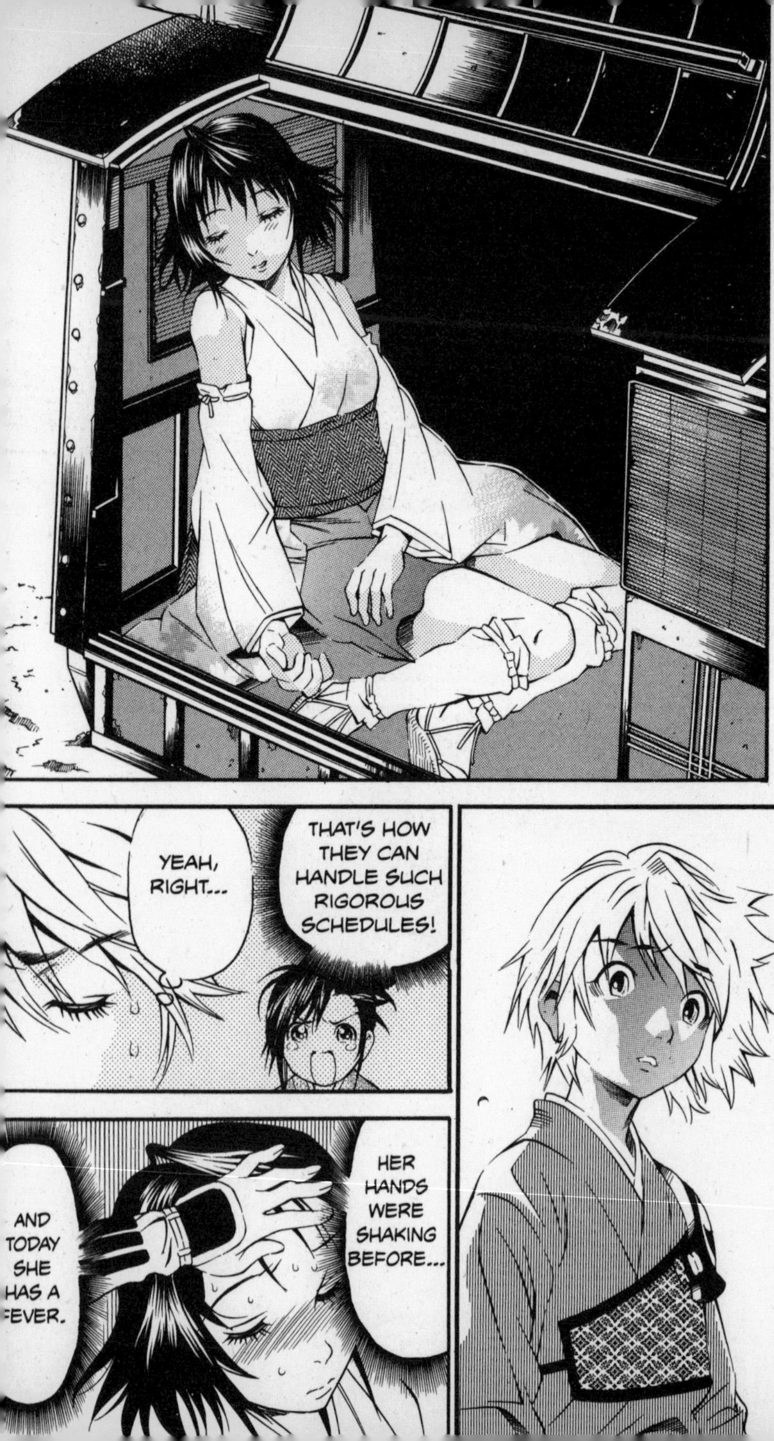
THAT'S HOW THEY CAN HANDLE SUCH RIGOROUS SCHEDULES!
YEAH, RIGHT...
HER HANDS WERE SHAKING BEFORE...
AND TODAY SHE HAS A FEVER.

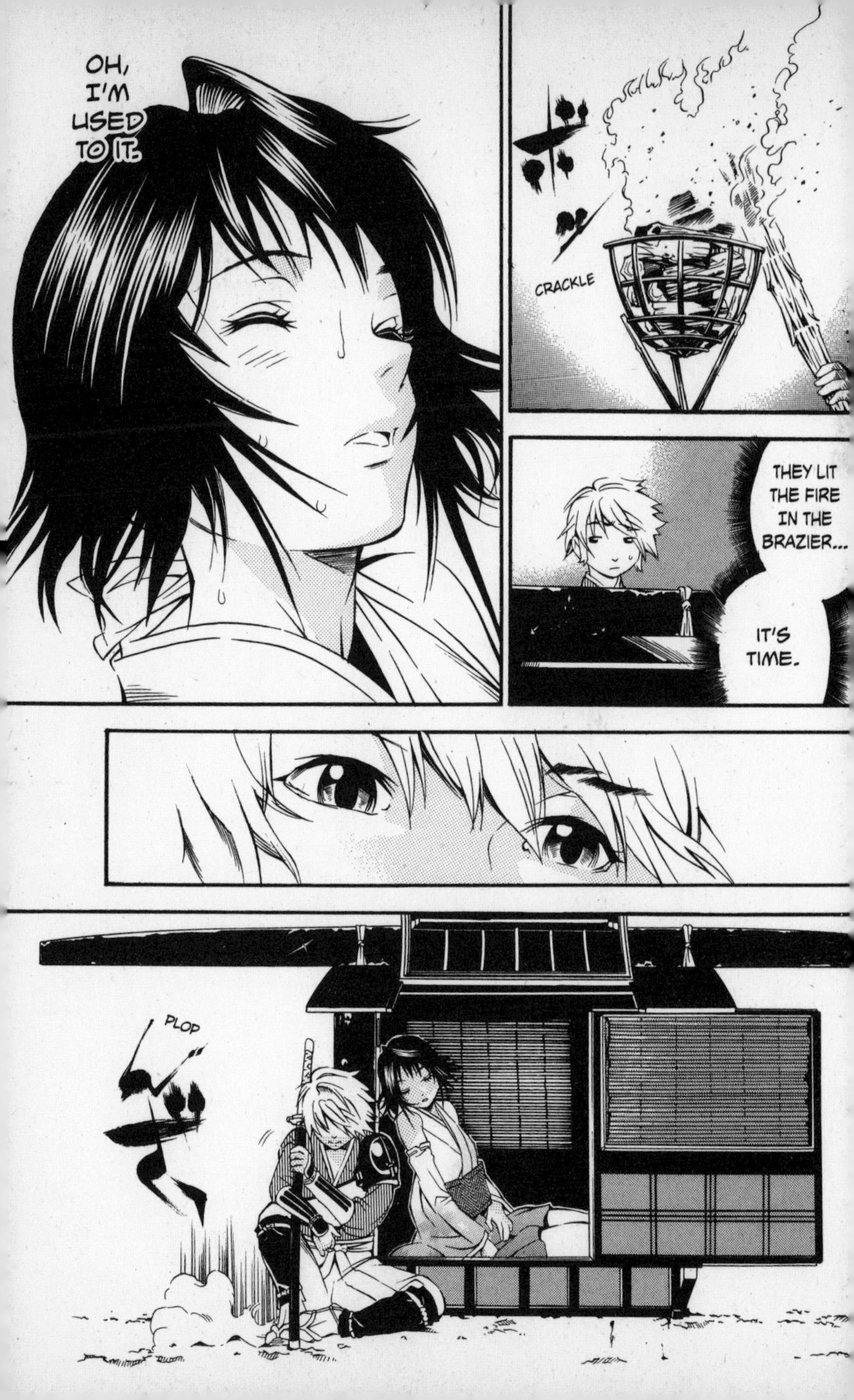
CRACKLE
THEY LIT THE FIRE IN THE BRAZIER...
IT'S TIME.
OH, I'M USED TO IT.
PLOP

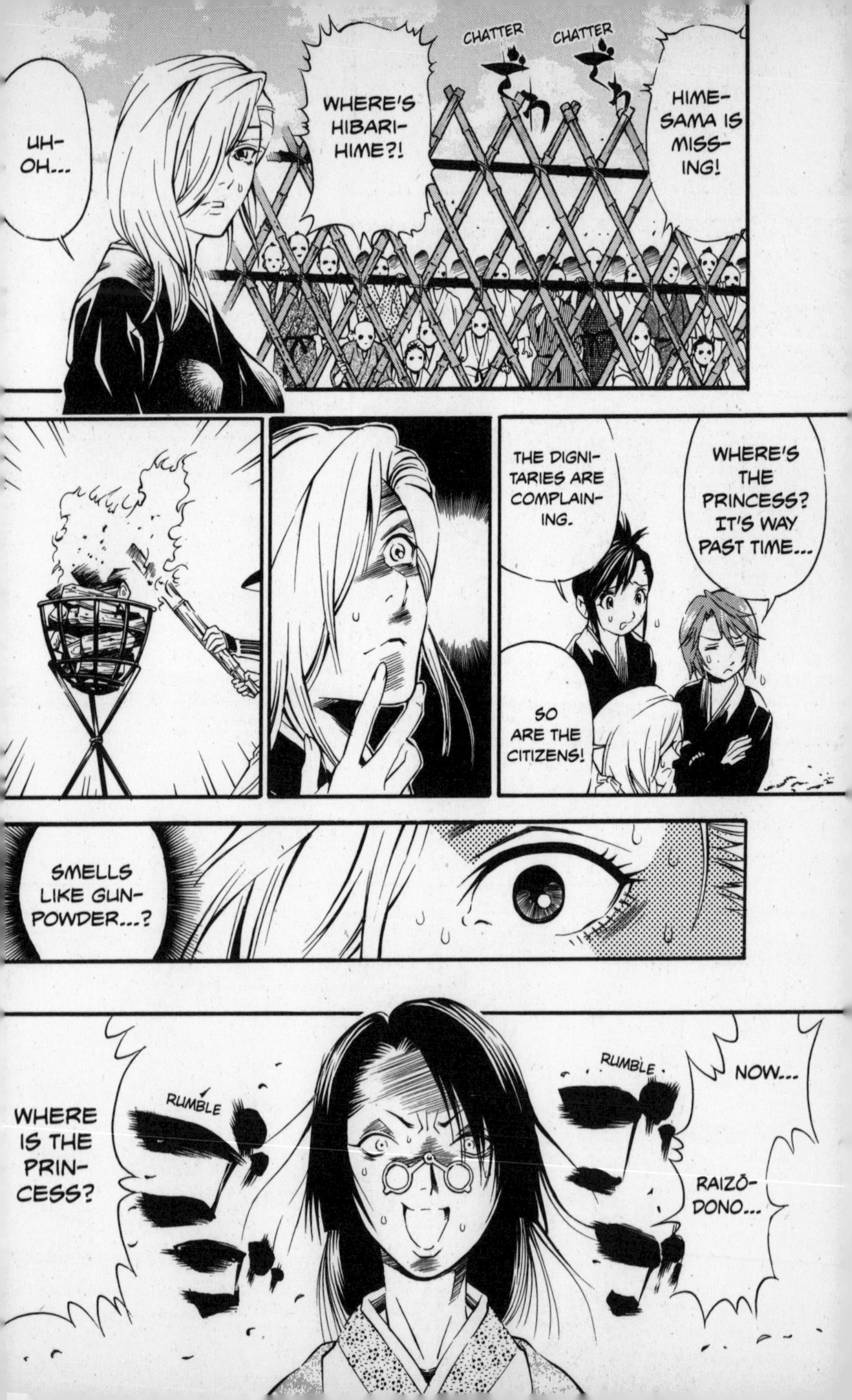
HIME-SAMA IS MISSING!
CHATTER
CHATTER
WHERE'S HIBARI-HIME?!
UH-OH...
WHERE'S THE PRINCESS? IT'S WAY PAST TIME...
THE DIGNITARIES ARE COMPLAINING.
SO ARE THE CITIZENS!
SMELLS LIKE GUNPOWDER...?
NOW...
RUMBLE
RAIZŌ-DONO...
RUMBLE
WHERE IS THE PRINCESS?

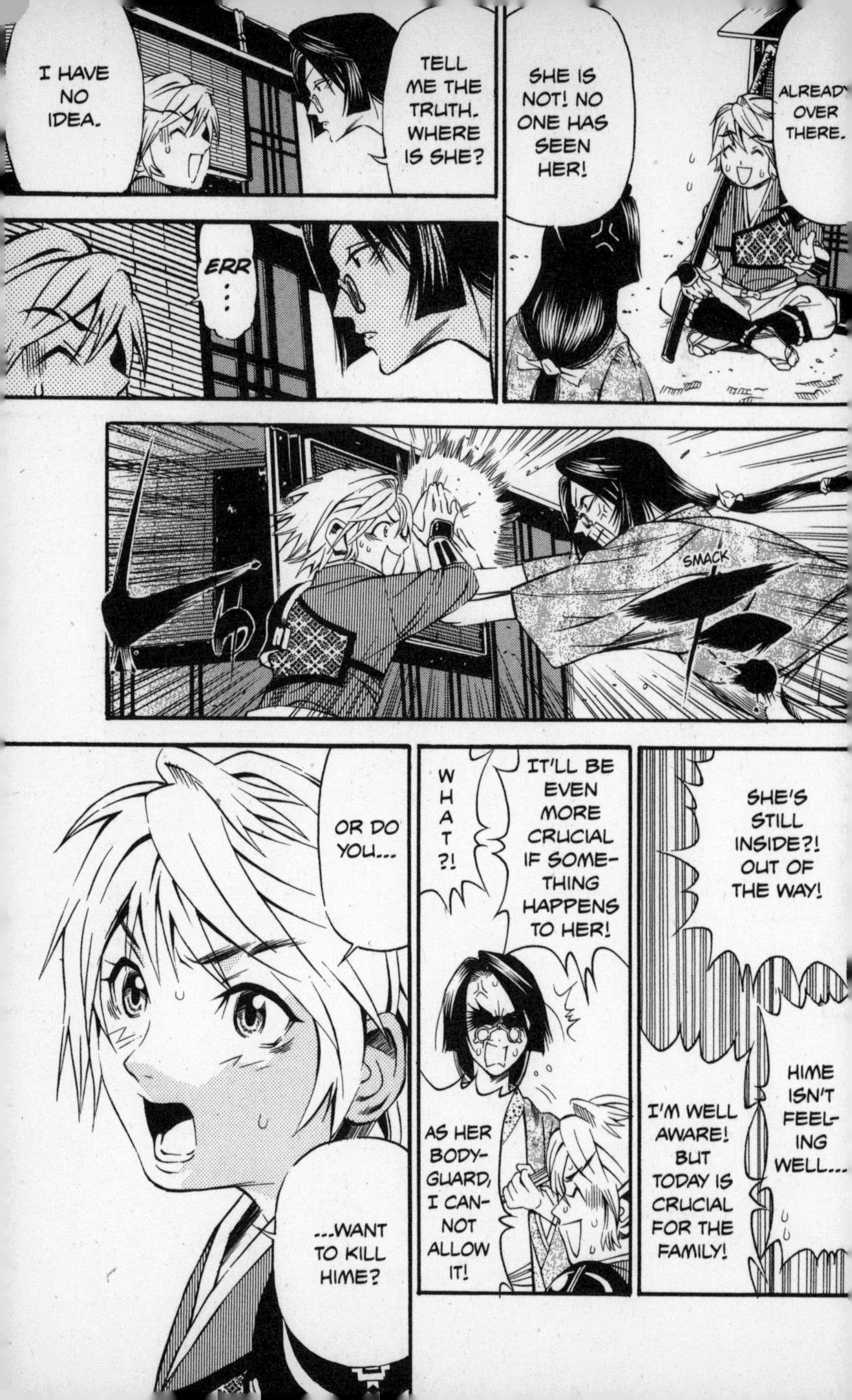
ALREADY OVER THERE.
SHE IS NOT! NO ONE HAS SEEN HER!
TELL ME THE TRUTH. WHERE IS SHE?
I HAVE NO IDEA.
ERR...
SMACK
SHE'S STILL INSIDE?! OUT OF THE WAY!
HIME ISN'T FEEL-ING WELL...
I'M WELL AWARE! BUT TODAY IS CRUCIAL FOR THE FAMILY!
IT'LL BE EVEN MORE CRUCIAL IF SOME-THING HAPPENS TO HER!
WHAT?!
AS HER BODY-GUARD, I CAN-NOT ALLOW IT!
OR DO YOU...
...WANT TO KILL HIME?

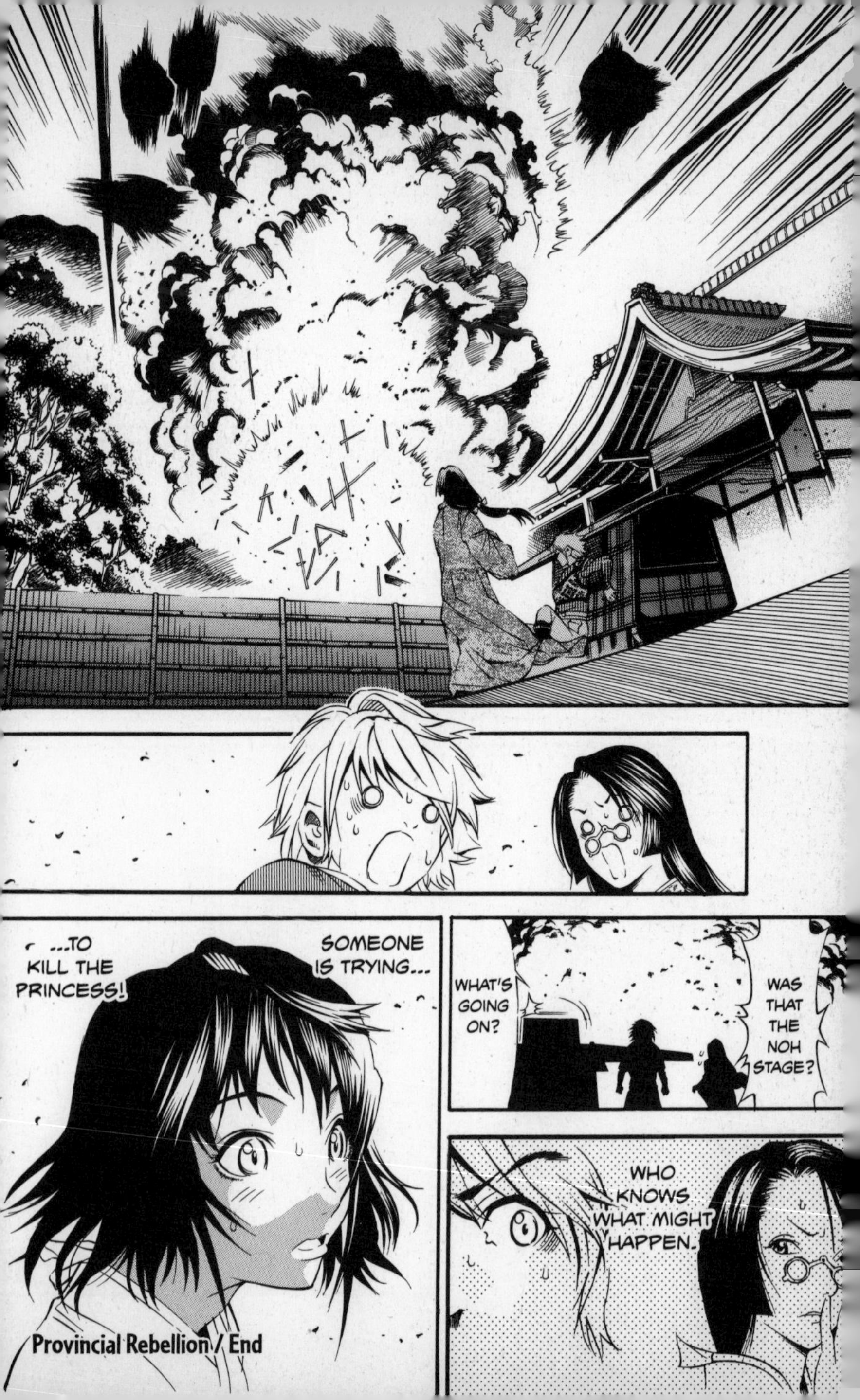
WAS THAT THE NOH STAGE?
WHAT'S GOING ON?
WHO KNOWS WHAT MIGHT HAPPEN.
SOMEONE IS TRYING...
...TO KILL THE PRINCESS!
Provincial Rebellion / End

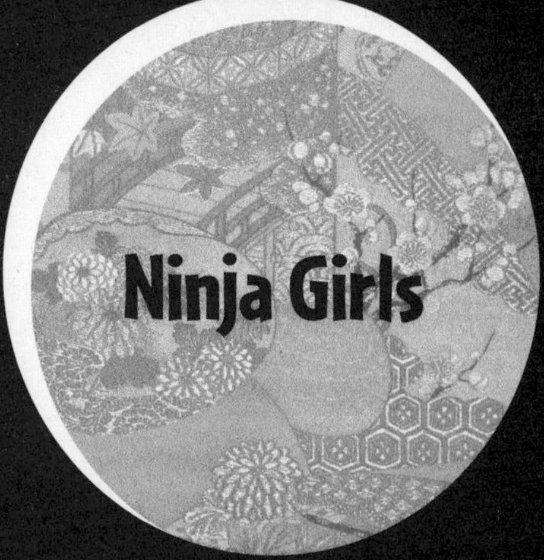
Ninja Girls

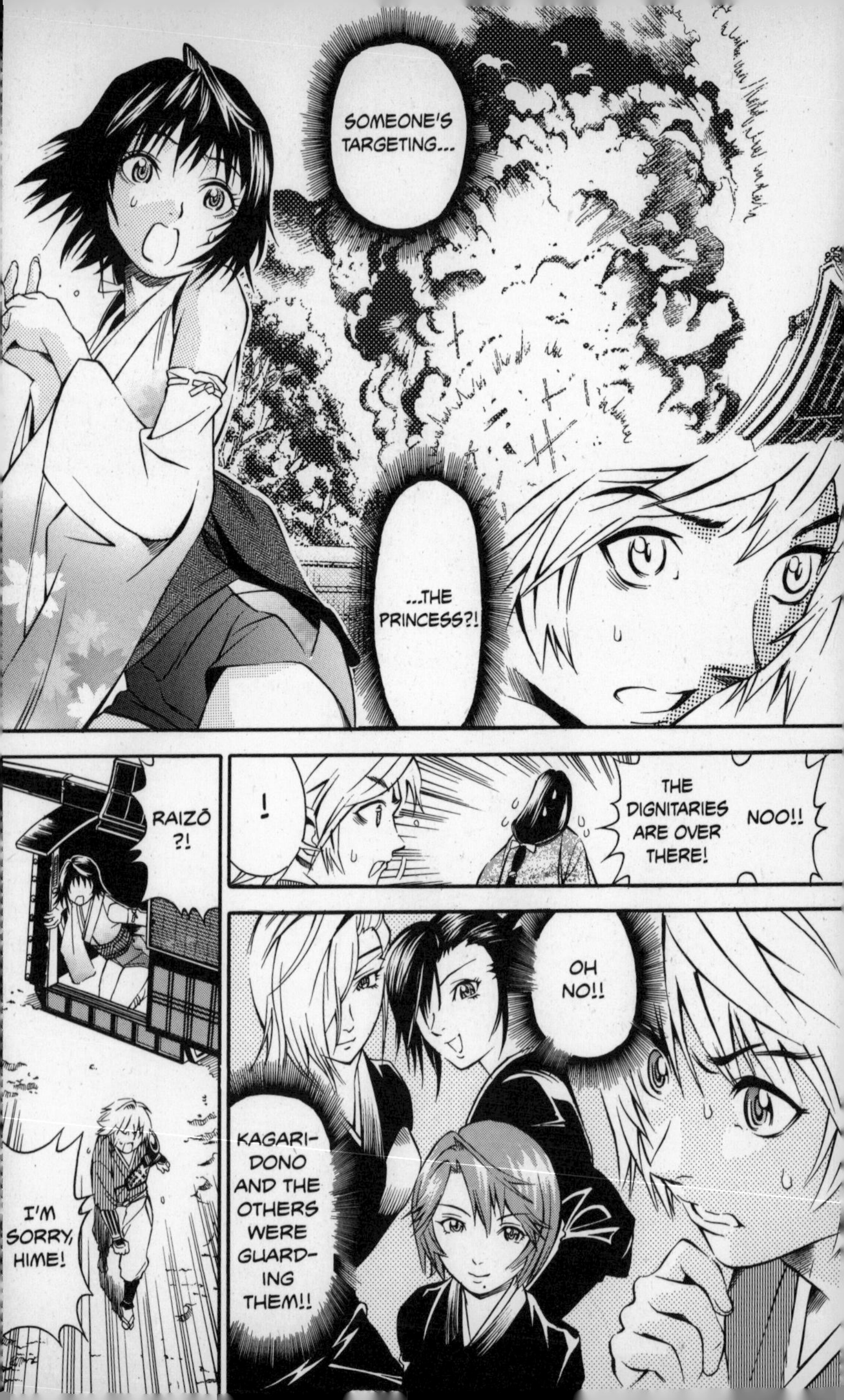
SOMEONE'S TARGETING...
...THE PRINCESS?!
NOO!!
THE DIGNITARIES ARE OVER THERE!
!
OH NO!!
KAGARI-DONO AND THE OTHERS WERE GUARD-ING THEM!!
RAIZŌ ?!
I'M SORRY, HIME!

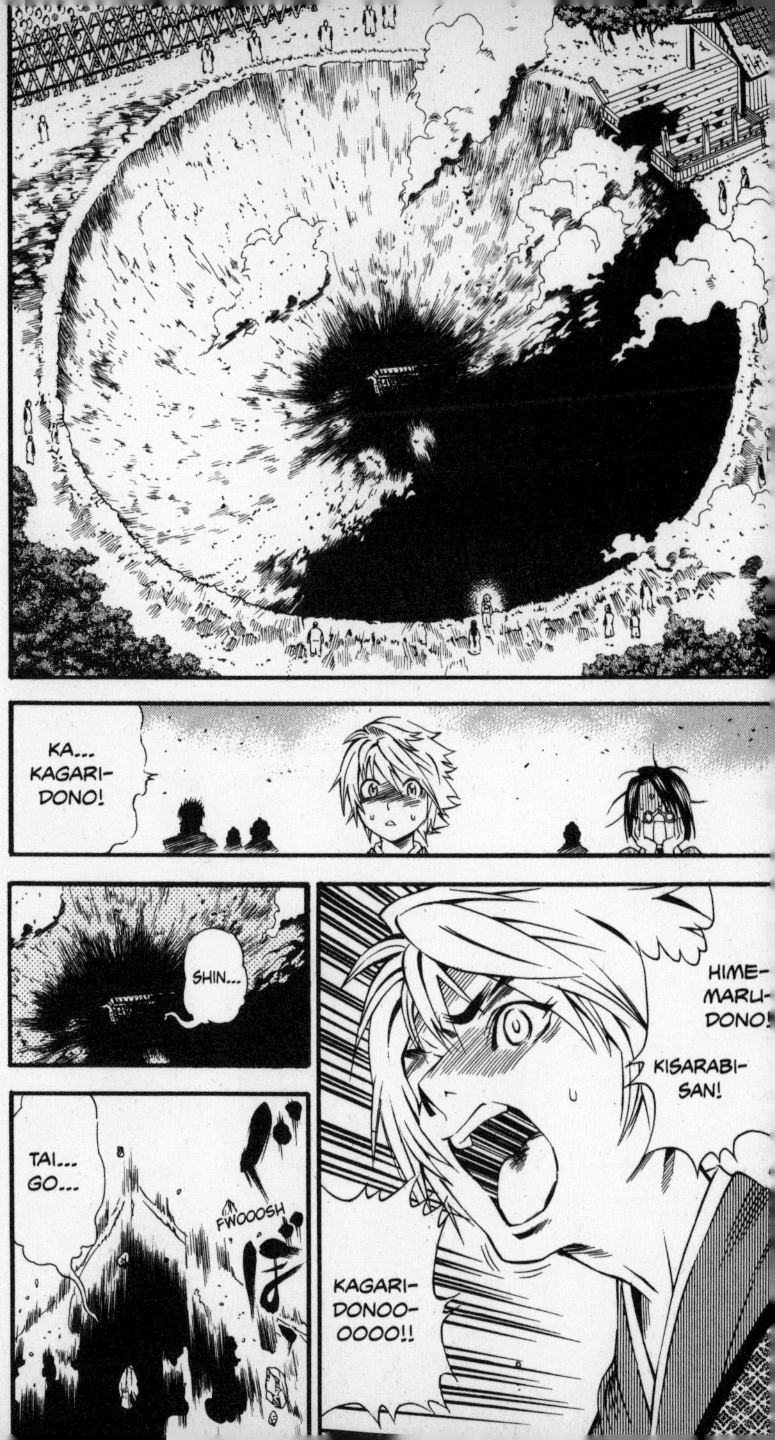
KA... KAGARI-DONO!
HIME-MARU-DONO!
KISARABI-SAN!
KAGARI-DONOO-OOOO!!
SHIN...
TAI... GO...
FWOOOSH

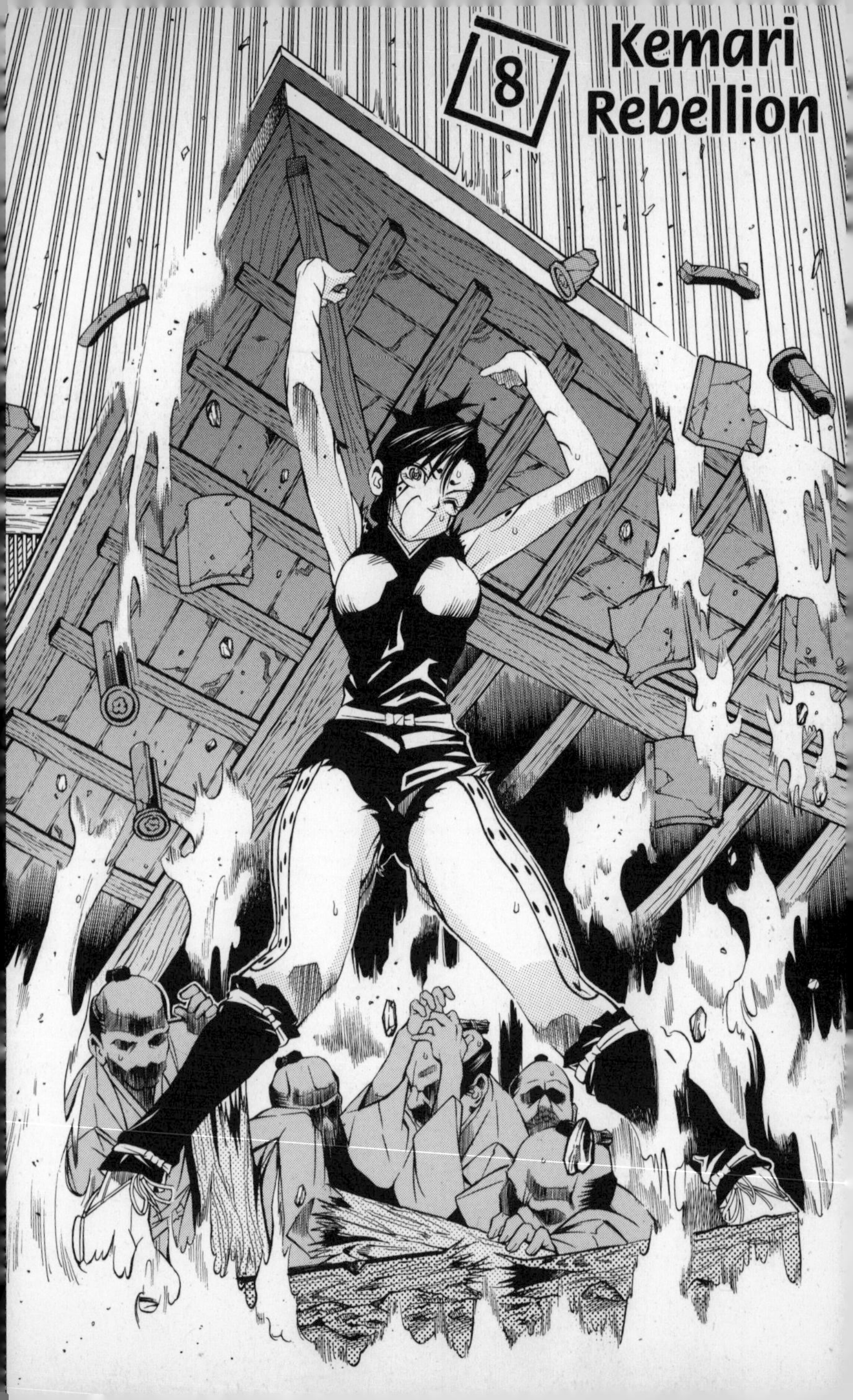
8
Kemari Rebellion

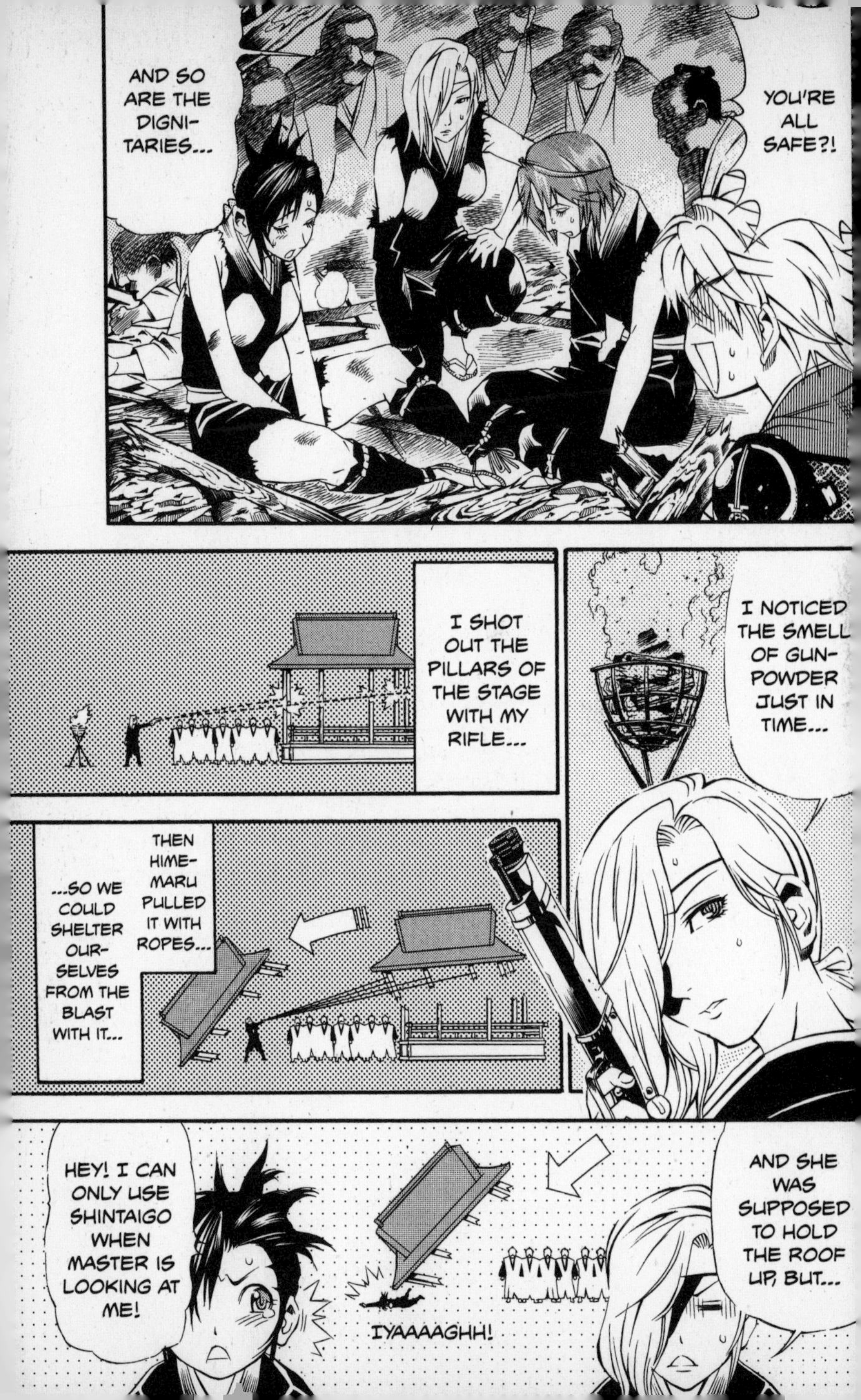
YOU'RE ALL SAFE?!
AND SO ARE THE DIGNITARIES...
I NOTICED THE SMELL OF GUNPOWDER JUST IN TIME...
I SHOT OUT THE PILLARS OF THE STAGE WITH MY RIFLE...
THEN HIMEMARU PULLED IT WITH ROPES...
...SO WE COULD SHELTER OURSELVES FROM THE BLAST WITH IT...
AND SHE WAS SUPPOSED TO HOLD THE ROOF UP, BUT...
IYAAAAGHH!
HEY! I CAN ONLY USE SHINTAIGO WHEN MASTER IS LOOKING AT ME!

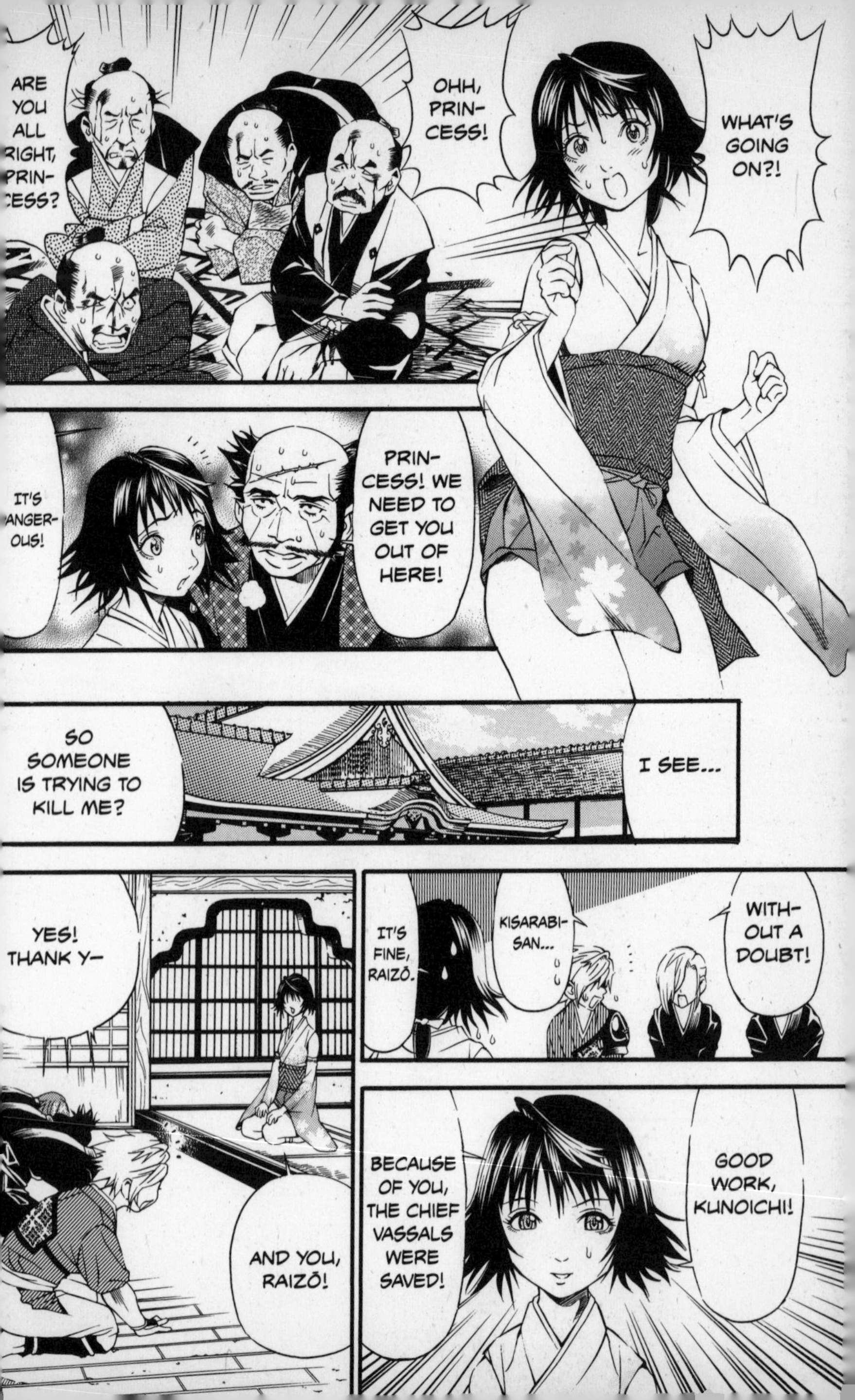

WHAT'S GOING ON?!
OHH, PRINCESS!
ARE YOU ALL RIGHT, PRINCESS?
PRINCESS! WE NEED TO GET YOU OUT OF HERE!
IT'S ANGEROUS!
I SEE...
SO SOMEONE IS TRYING TO KILL ME?
WITHOUT A DOUBT!
KISARABI-SAN...
IT'S FINE, RAIZŌ.
GOOD WORK, KUNOICHI!
BECAUSE OF YOU, THE CHIEF VASSALS WERE SAVED!
AND YOU, RAIZŌ!
YES! THANK Y—

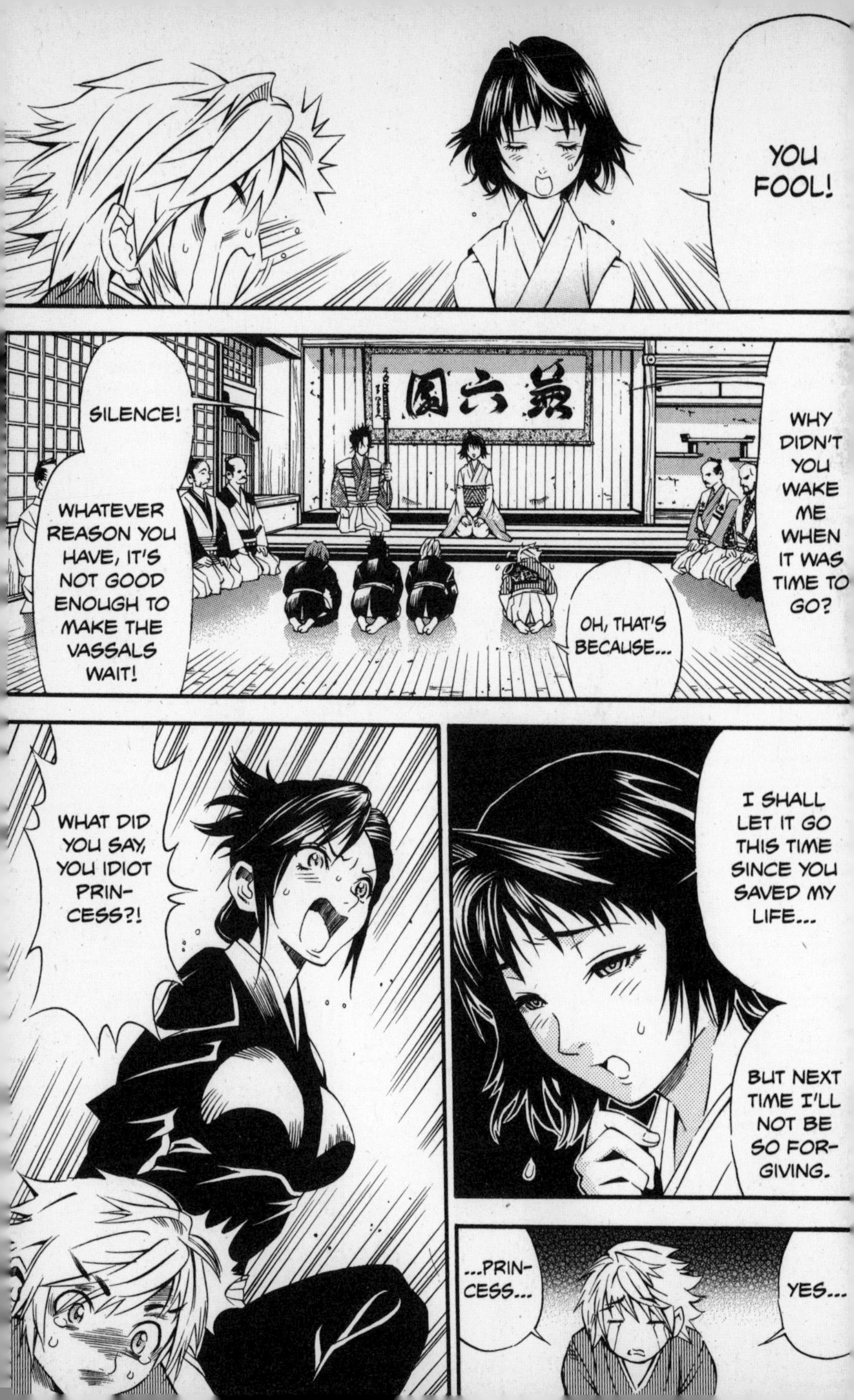
YOU FOOL!
WHY DIDN'T YOU WAKE ME WHEN IT WAS TIME TO GO?
OH, THAT'S BECAUSE...
SILENCE!
WHATEVER REASON YOU HAVE, IT'S NOT GOOD ENOUGH TO MAKE THE VASSALS WAIT!
I SHALL LET IT GO THIS TIME SINCE YOU SAVED MY LIFE...
BUT NEXT TIME I'LL NOT BE SO FOR-GIVING.
YES...
...PRIN-CESS...
WHAT DID YOU SAY, YOU IDIOT PRIN-CESS?!

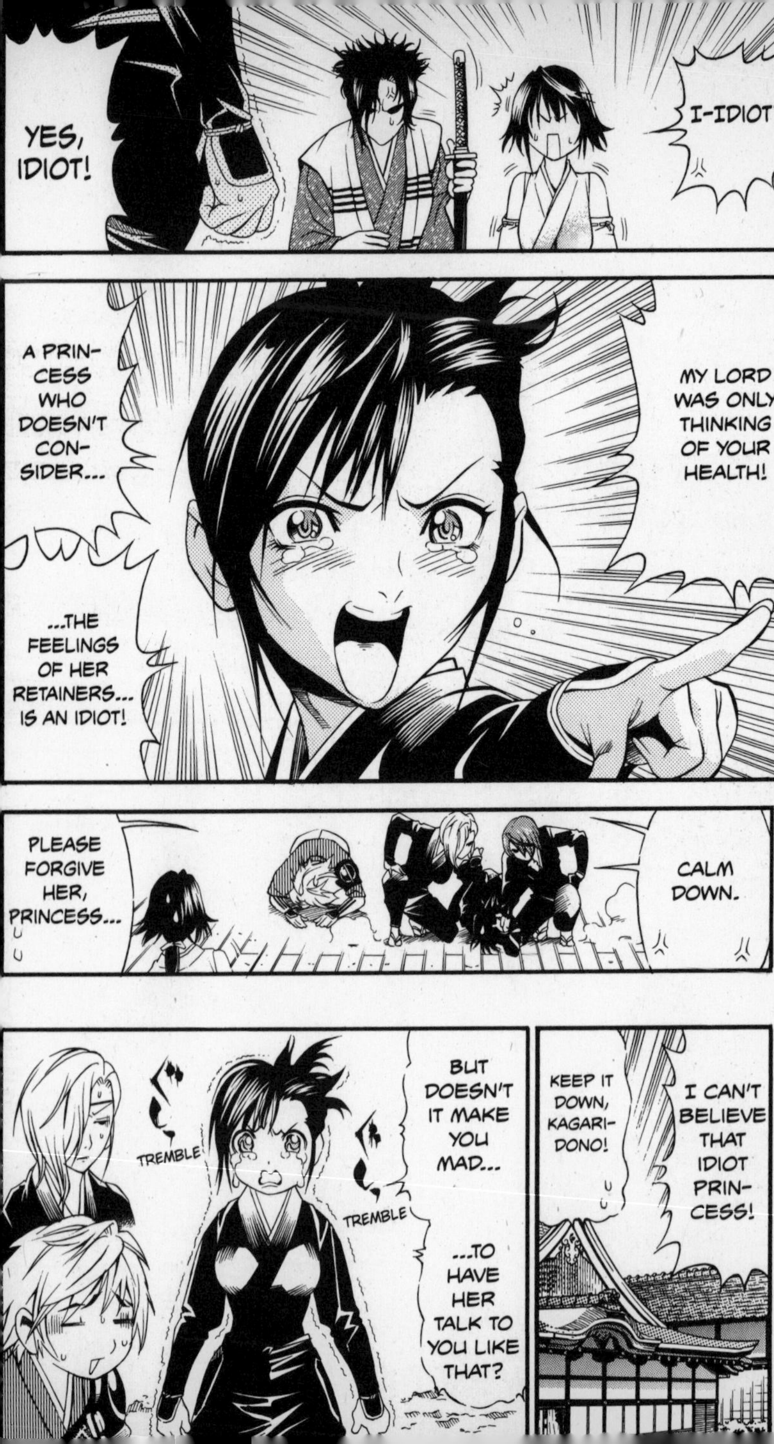

I-IDIOT?!
YES, IDIOT!
MY LORD WAS ONLY THINKING OF YOUR HEALTH!
A PRINCESS WHO DOESN'T CONSIDER...
...THE FEELINGS OF HER RETAINERS... IS AN IDIOT!
CALM DOWN.
PLEASE FORGIVE HER, PRINCESS...
I CAN'T BELIEVE THAT IDIOT PRINCESS!
KEEP IT DOWN, KAGARI-DONO!
BUT DOESN'T IT MAKE YOU MAD...
...TO HAVE HER TALK TO YOU LIKE THAT?
TREMBLE
TREMBLE

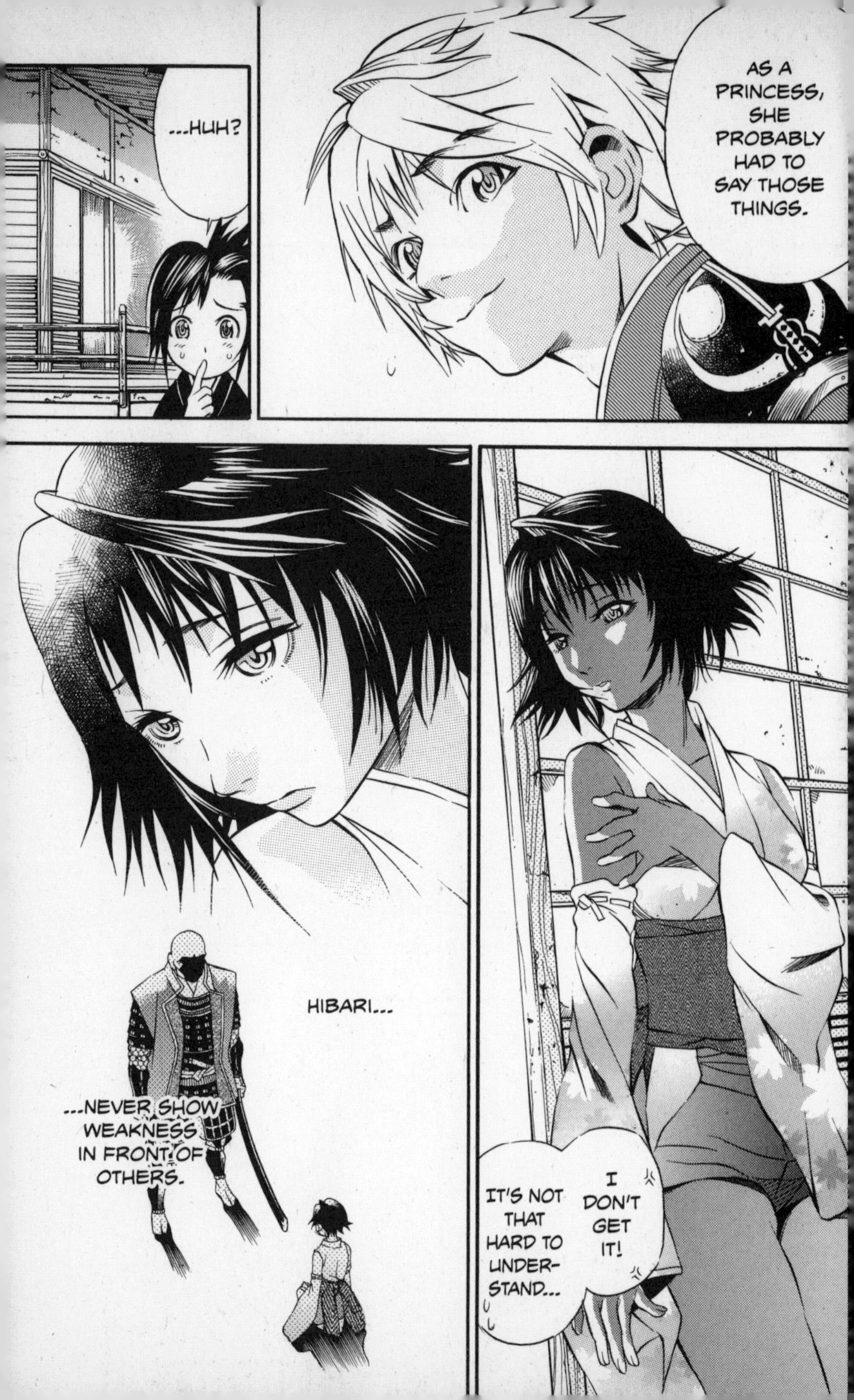
AS A PRINCESS, SHE PROBABLY HAD TO SAY THOSE THINGS.
...HUH?
I DON'T GET IT!
IT'S NOT THAT HARD TO UNDER-STAND...
HIBARI...
...NEVER SHOW WEAKNESS IN FRONT OF OTHERS.

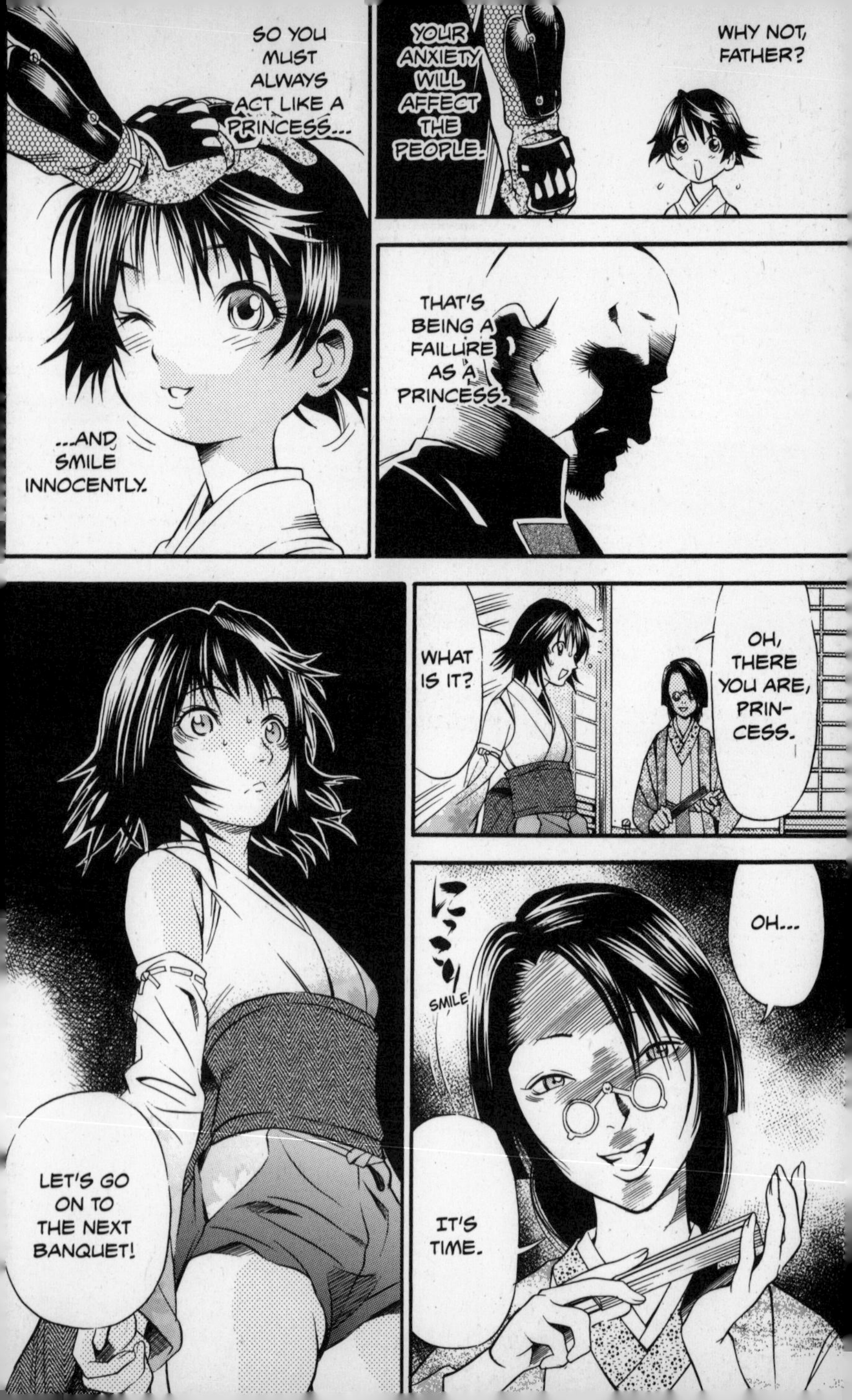
WHY NOT, FATHER?
YOUR ANXIETY WILL AFFECT THE PEOPLE.
THAT'S BEING A FAILURE AS A PRINCESS.
SO YOU MUST ALWAYS ACT LIKE A PRINCESS...
...AND SMILE INNOCENTLY.
OH, THERE YOU ARE, PRIN-CESS.
WHAT IS IT?
OH...
にっこり
SMILE
IT'S TIME.
LET'S GO ON TO THE NEXT BANQUET!

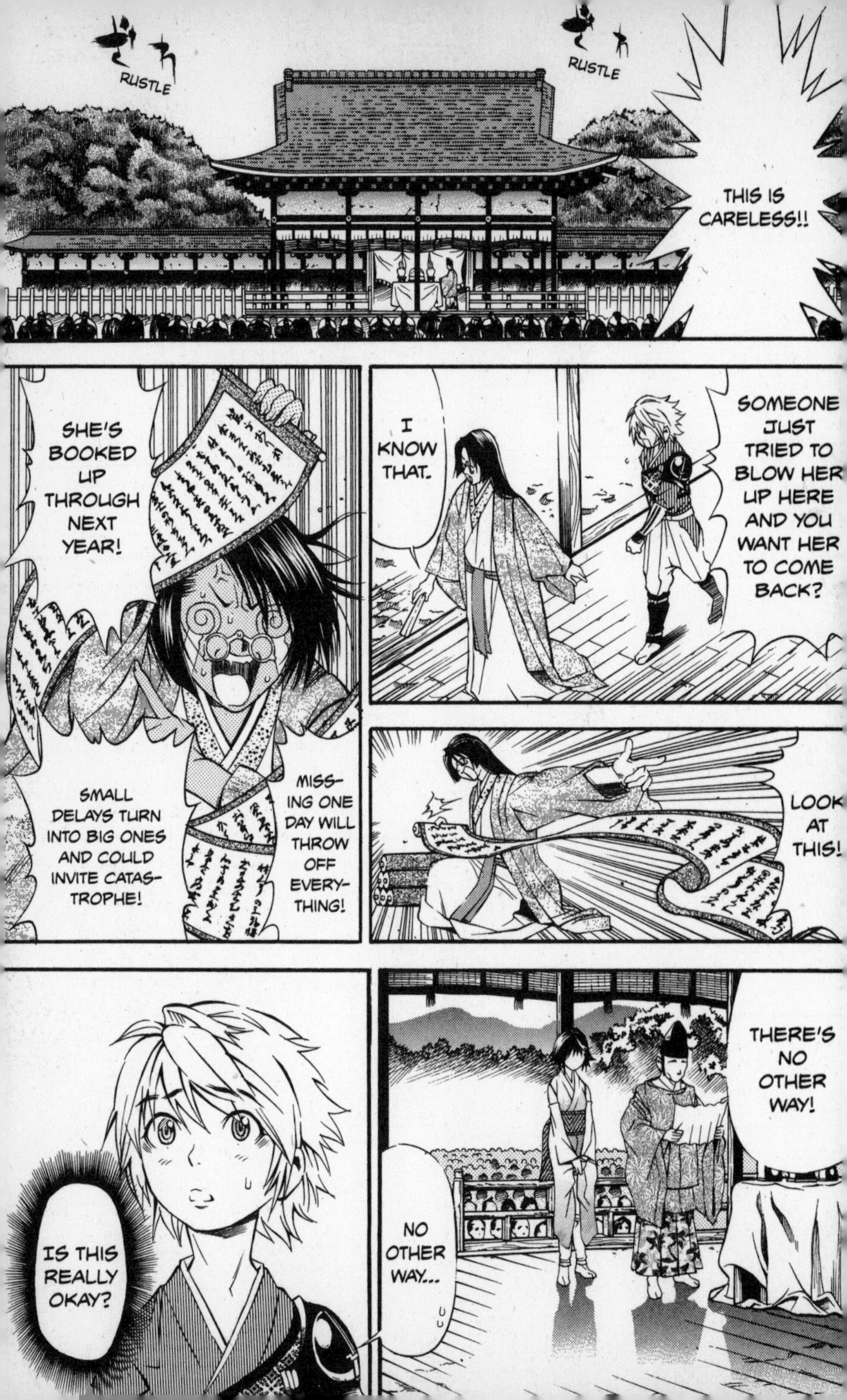
RUSTLE
THIS IS CARELESS!!
RUSTLE
SOMEONE JUST TRIED TO BLOW HER UP HERE AND YOU WANT HER TO COME BACK?
I KNOW THAT.
LOOK AT THIS!
SHE'S BOOKED UP THROUGH NEXT YEAR!
MISS-ING ONE DAY WILL THROW OFF EVERY-THING!
SMALL DELAYS TURN INTO BIG ONES AND COULD INVITE CATAS-TROPHE!
THERE'S NO OTHER WAY!
NO OTHER WAY...
IS THIS REALLY OKAY?

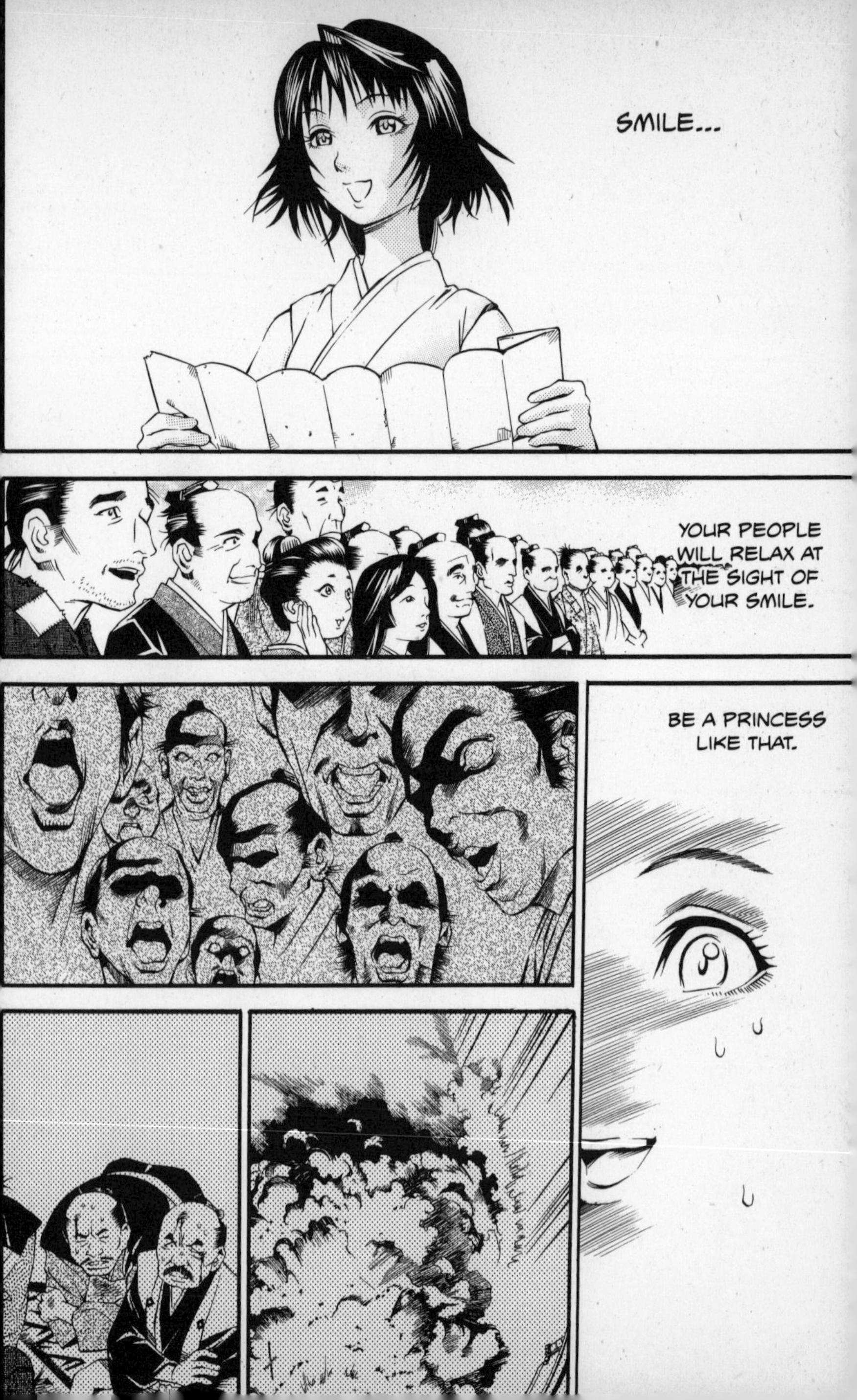
SMILE...
YOUR PEOPLE WILL RELAX AT THE SIGHT OF YOUR SMILE.
BE A PRINCESS LIKE THAT.

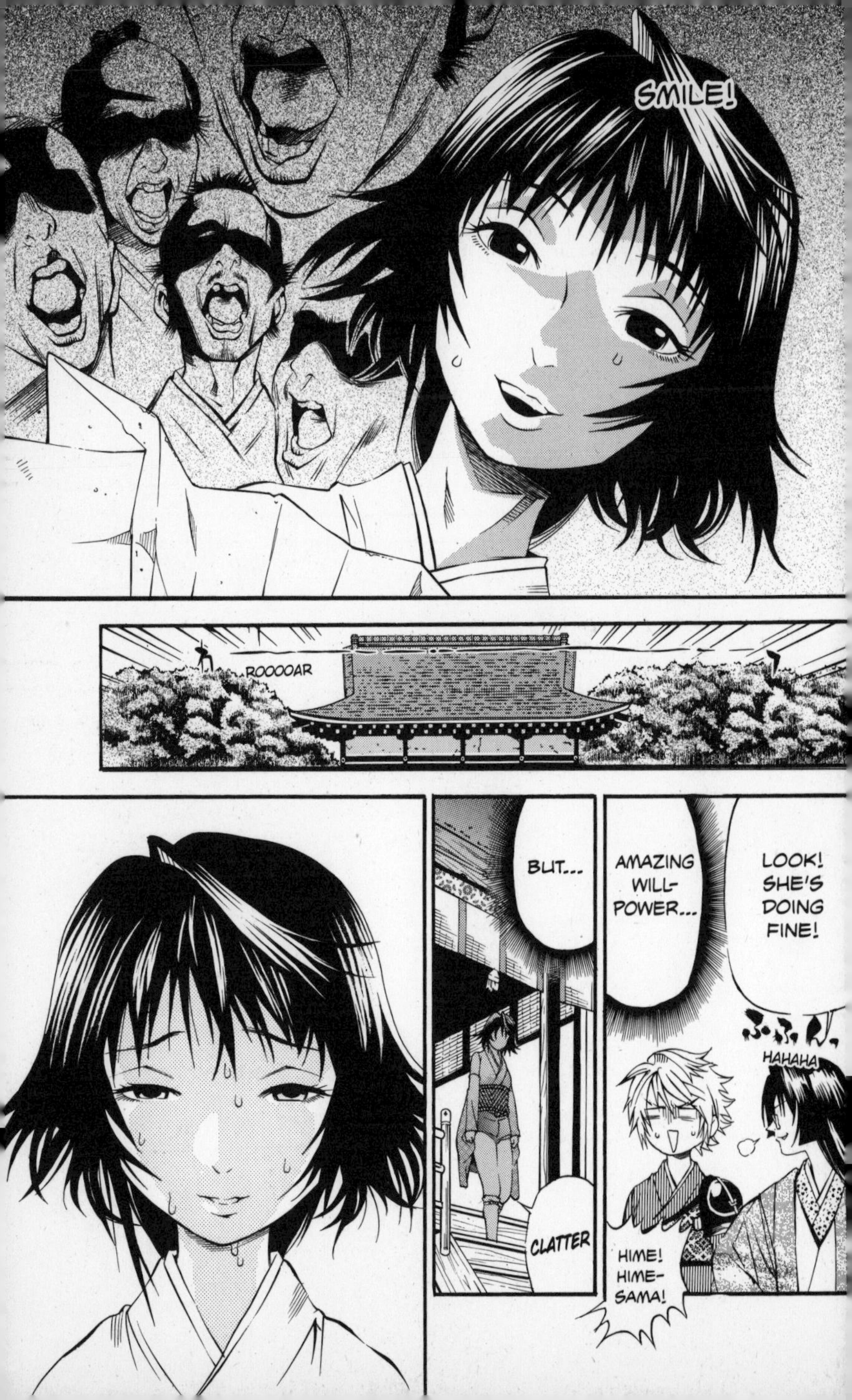
SMILE!
ROOOOAR
LOOK! SHE'S DOING FINE!
AMAZING WILL-POWER...
ふふん
HAHAHA
BUT...
CLATTER
HIME! HIME-SAMA!

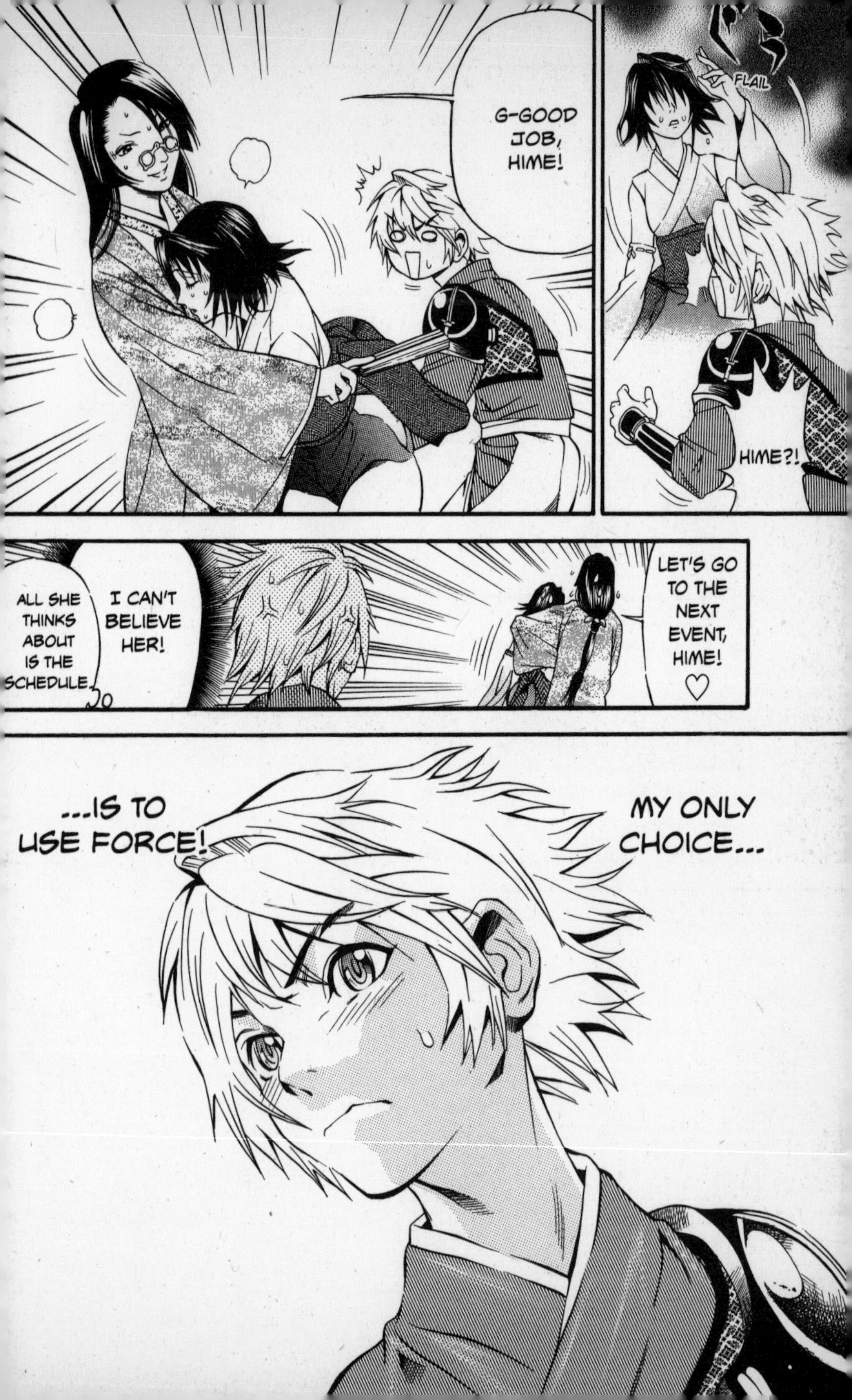
FLAIL
HIME?!
G-GOOD JOB, HIME!
LET'S GO TO THE NEXT EVENT, HIME! ♡
I CAN'T BELIEVE HER!
ALL SHE THINKS ABOUT IS THE SCHEDULE.
MY ONLY CHOICE...
...IS TO USE FORCE!

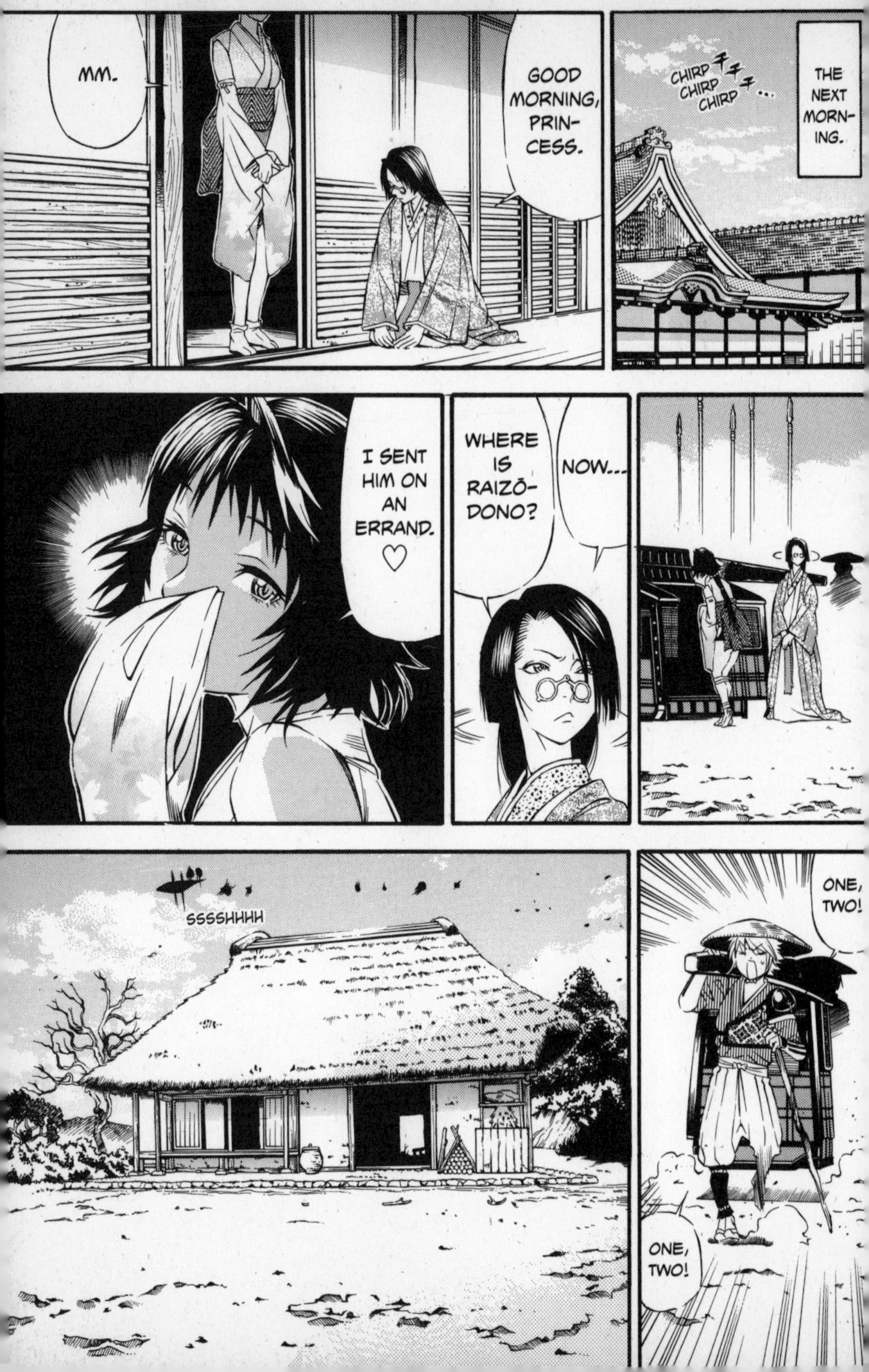

THE NEXT MORNING.
CHIRP CHIRP CHIRP
チチチ...
GOOD MORNING, PRINCESS.
MM.
NOW...
WHERE IS RAIZŌ-DONO?
I SENT HIM ON AN ERRAND. ♡
ONE, TWO!
ONE, TWO!
SSSSHHHH

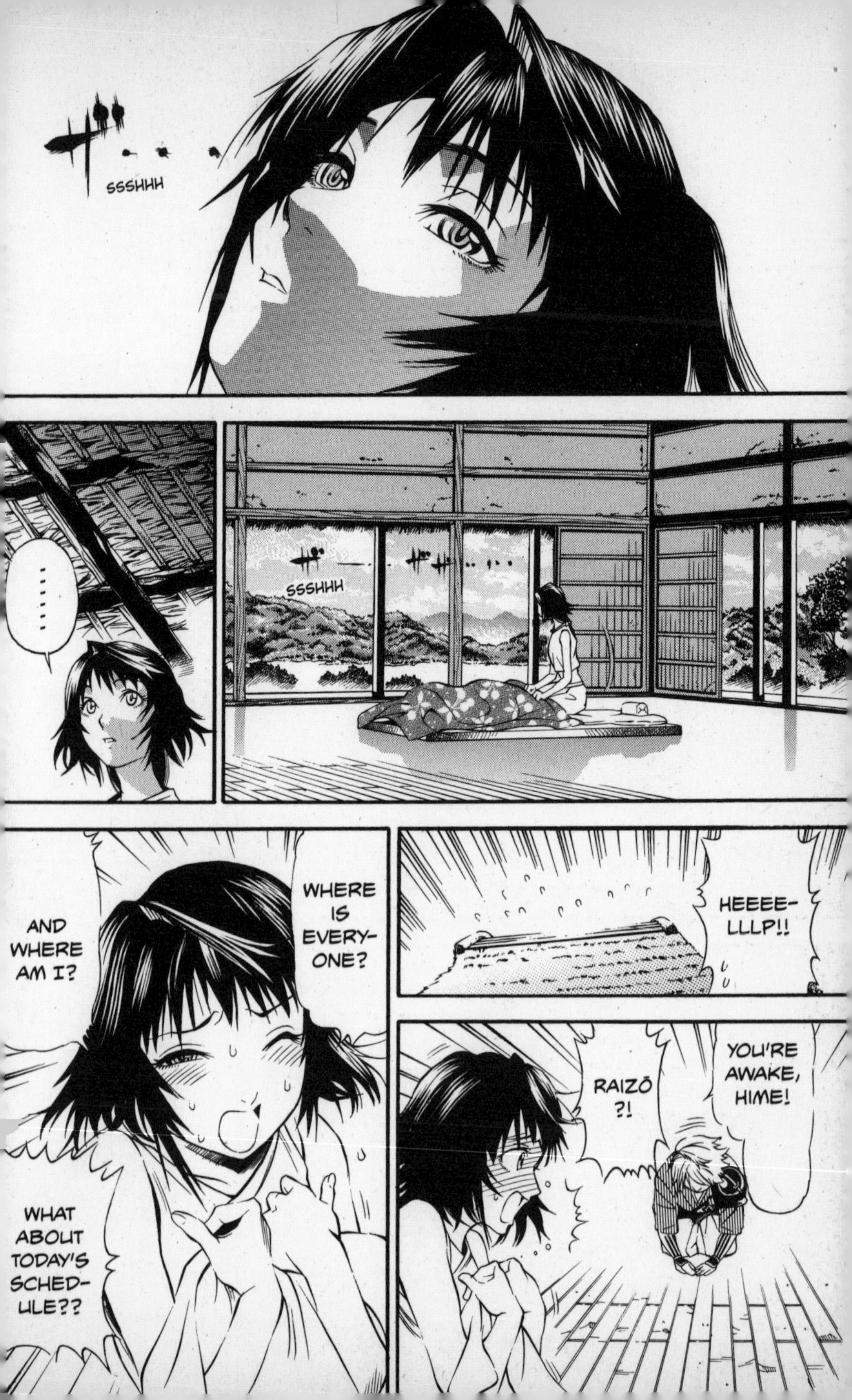
SSSHHH
SSSHHH
......
HEEEE-LLLP!!
YOU'RE AWAKE, HIME!
RAIZŌ ?!
WHERE IS EVERY-ONE?
AND WHERE AM I?
WHAT ABOUT TODAY'S SCHED-ULE??

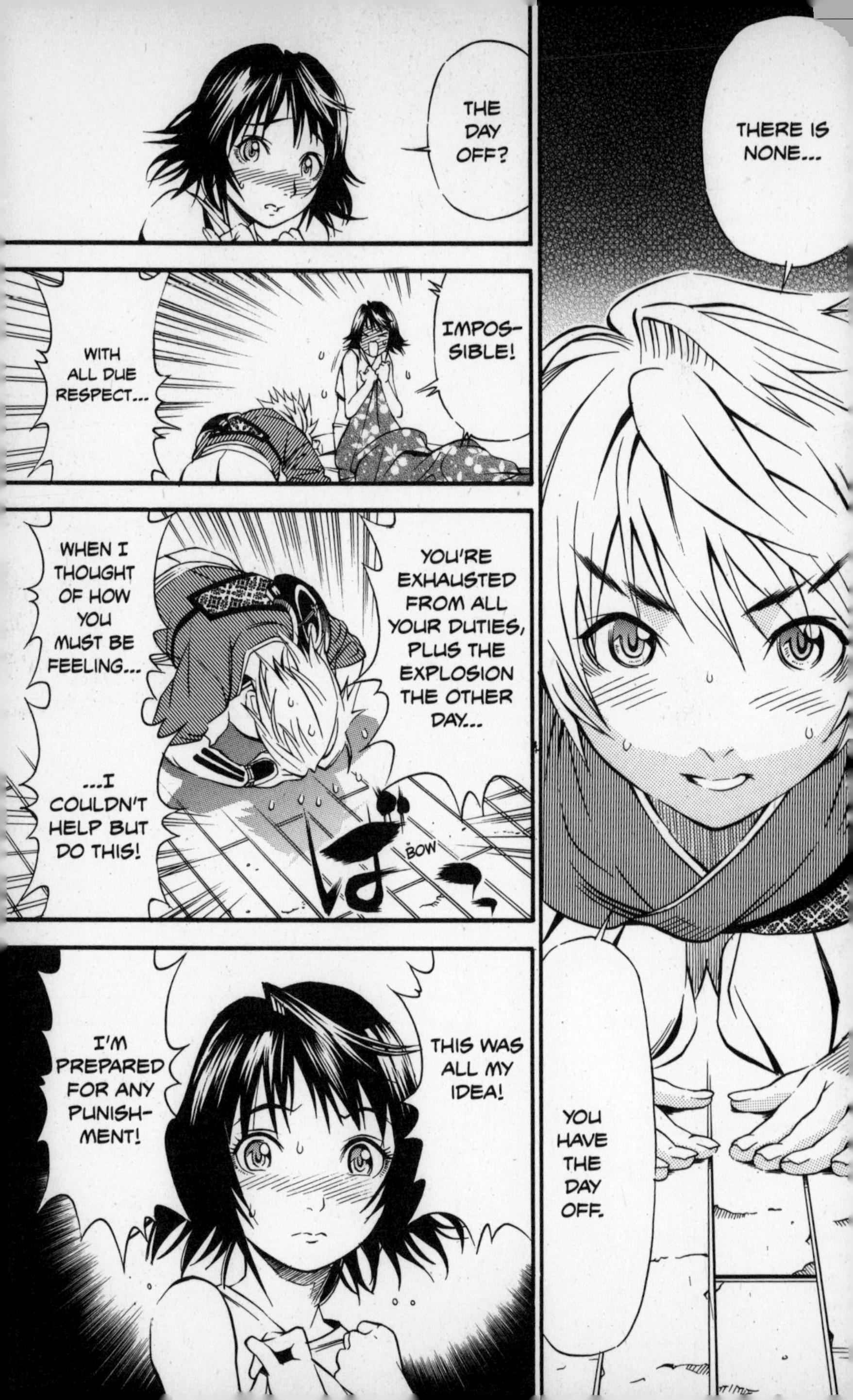
THERE IS NONE...
YOU HAVE THE DAY OFF.
THE DAY OFF?
IMPOS-SIBLE!
WITH ALL DUE RESPECT...
YOU'RE EXHAUSTED FROM ALL YOUR DUTIES, PLUS THE EXPLOSION THE OTHER DAY...
WHEN I THOUGHT OF HOW YOU MUST BE FEELING...
...I COULDN'T HELP BUT DO THIS!
BOW
THIS WAS ALL MY IDEA!
I'M PREPARED FOR ANY PUNISH-MENT!

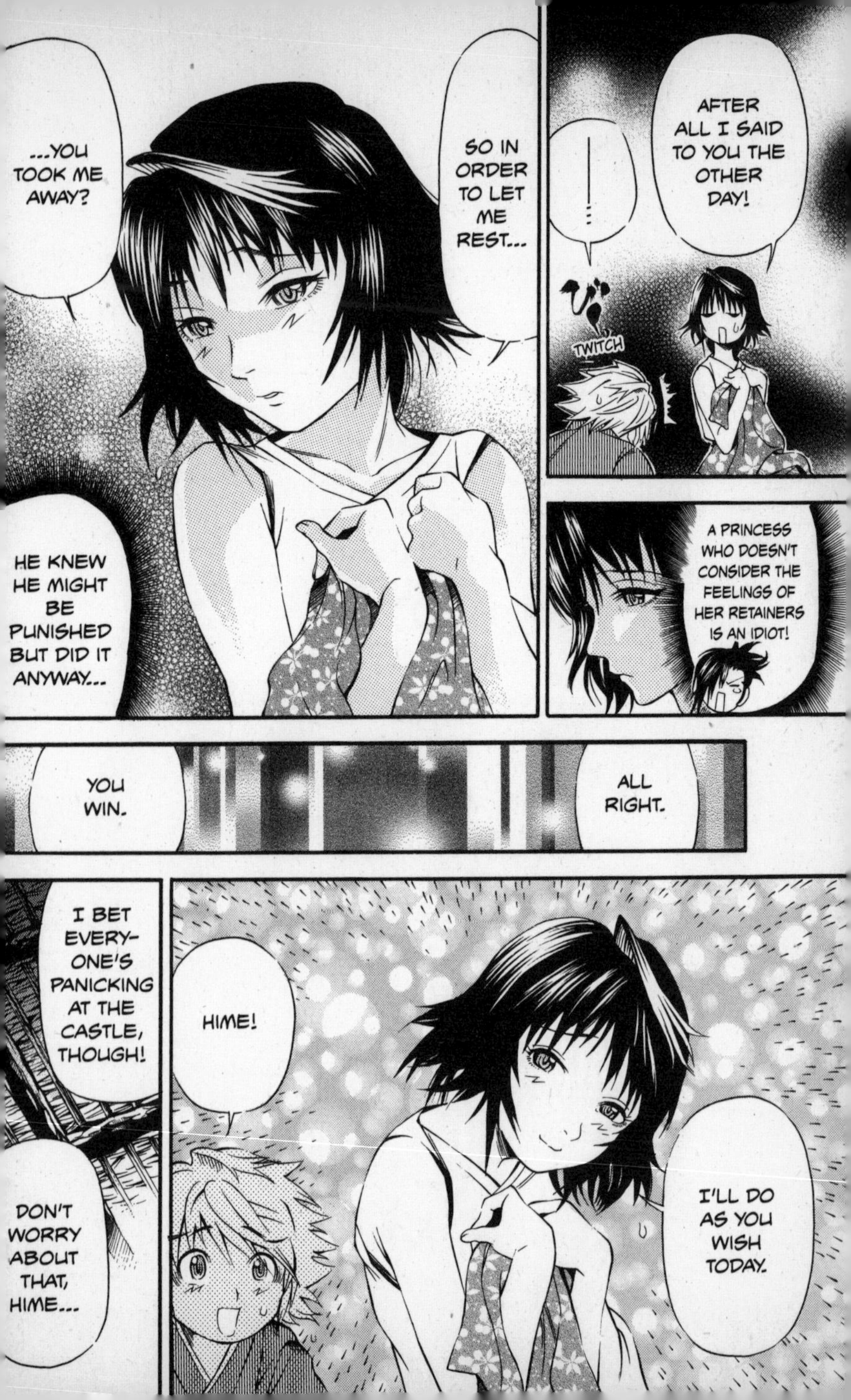
AFTER ALL I SAID TO YOU THE OTHER DAY!
—...
TWITCH
A PRINCESS WHO DOESN'T CONSIDER THE FEELINGS OF HER RETAINERS IS AN IDIOT!
SO IN ORDER TO LET ME REST...
...YOU TOOK ME AWAY?
HE KNEW HE MIGHT BE PUNISHED BUT DID IT ANYWAY...
ALL RIGHT.
YOU WIN.
I'LL DO AS YOU WISH TODAY.
HIME!
I BET EVERYONE'S PANICKING AT THE CASTLE, THOUGH!
DON'T WORRY ABOUT THAT, HIME...

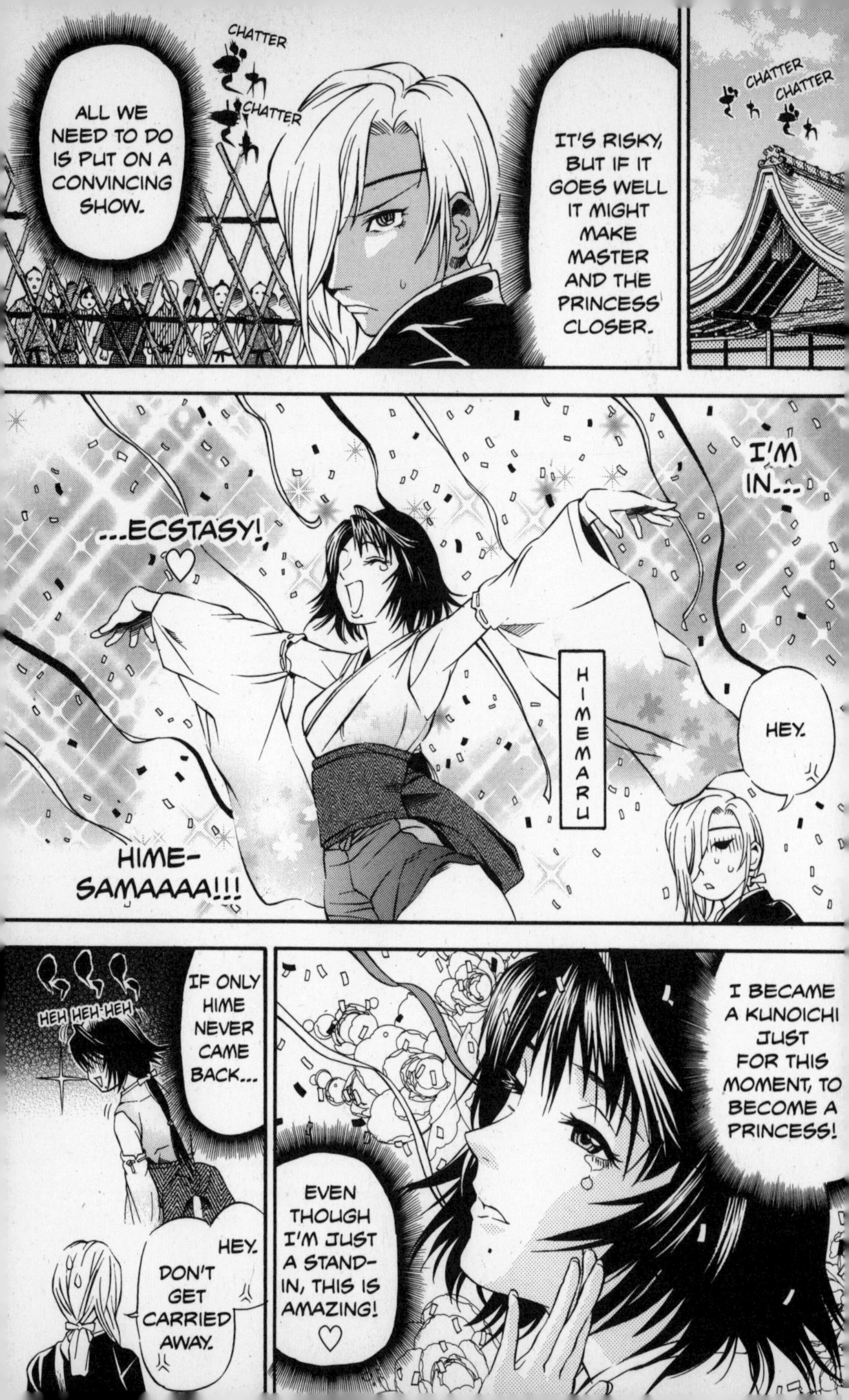
CHATTER
CHATTER
IT'S RISKY, BUT IF IT GOES WELL IT MIGHT MAKE MASTER AND THE PRINCESS CLOSER.
CHATTER
CHATTER
ALL WE NEED TO DO IS PUT ON A CONVINCING SHOW.
I'M IN...
HEY.
HIMEMARU
...ECSTASY! ♥
HIME-SAMAAAAA!!!
I BECAME A KUNOICHI JUST FOR THIS MOMENT, TO BECOME A PRINCESS!
EVEN THOUGH I'M JUST A STAND-IN, THIS IS AMAZING! ♡
IF ONLY HIME NEVER CAME BACK...
HEH HEH HEH
HEY. DON'T GET CARRIED AWAY.

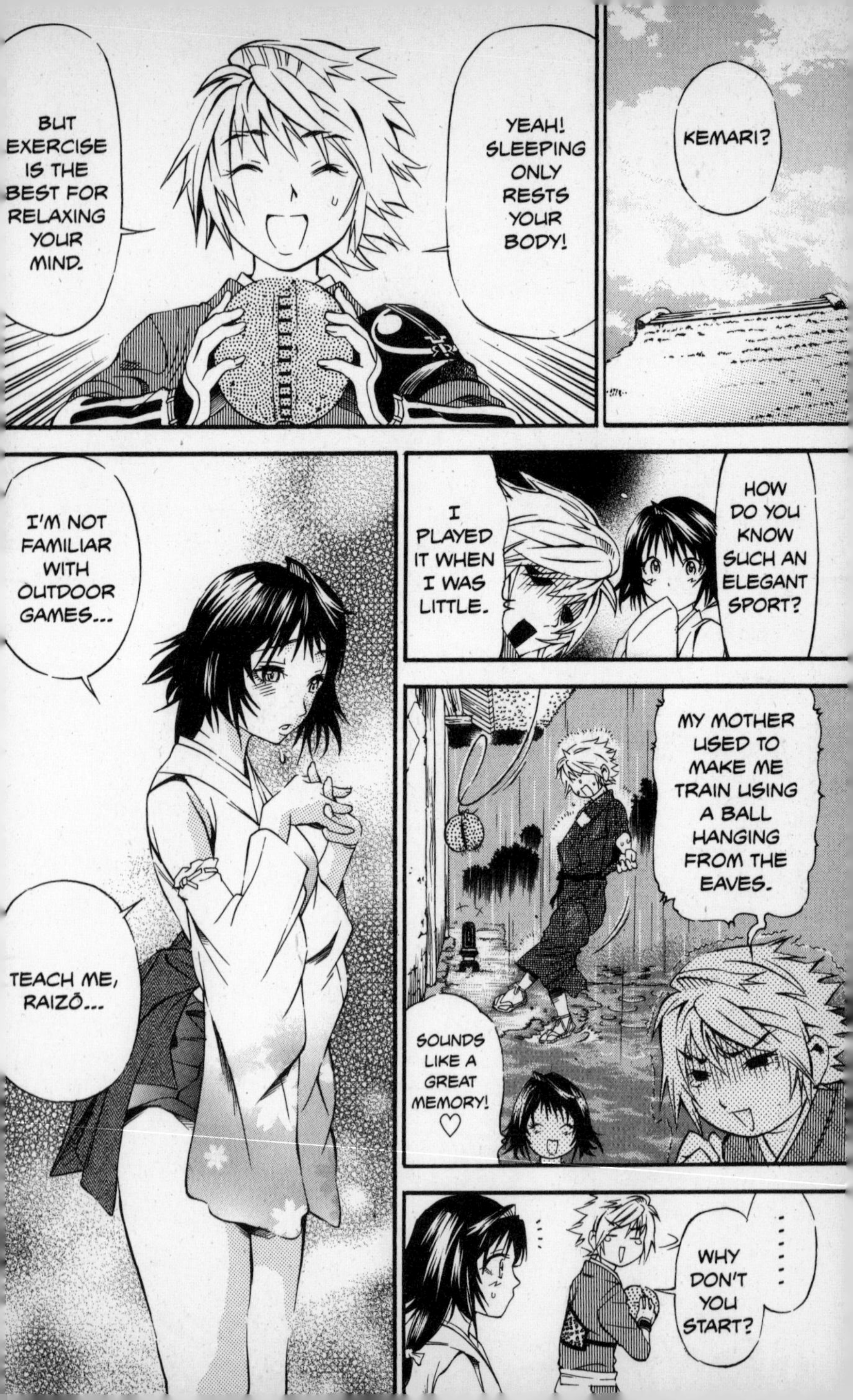
KEMARI?
YEAH! SLEEPING ONLY RESTS YOUR BODY!
BUT EXERCISE IS THE BEST FOR RELAXING YOUR MIND.
HOW DO YOU KNOW SUCH AN ELEGANT SPORT?
I PLAYED IT WHEN I WAS LITTLE.
MY MOTHER USED TO MAKE ME TRAIN USING A BALL HANGING FROM THE EAVES.
SOUNDS LIKE A GREAT MEMORY! ♡
......
WHY DON'T YOU START?
...
I'M NOT FAMILIAR WITH OUTDOOR GAMES...
TEACH ME, RAIZŌ...

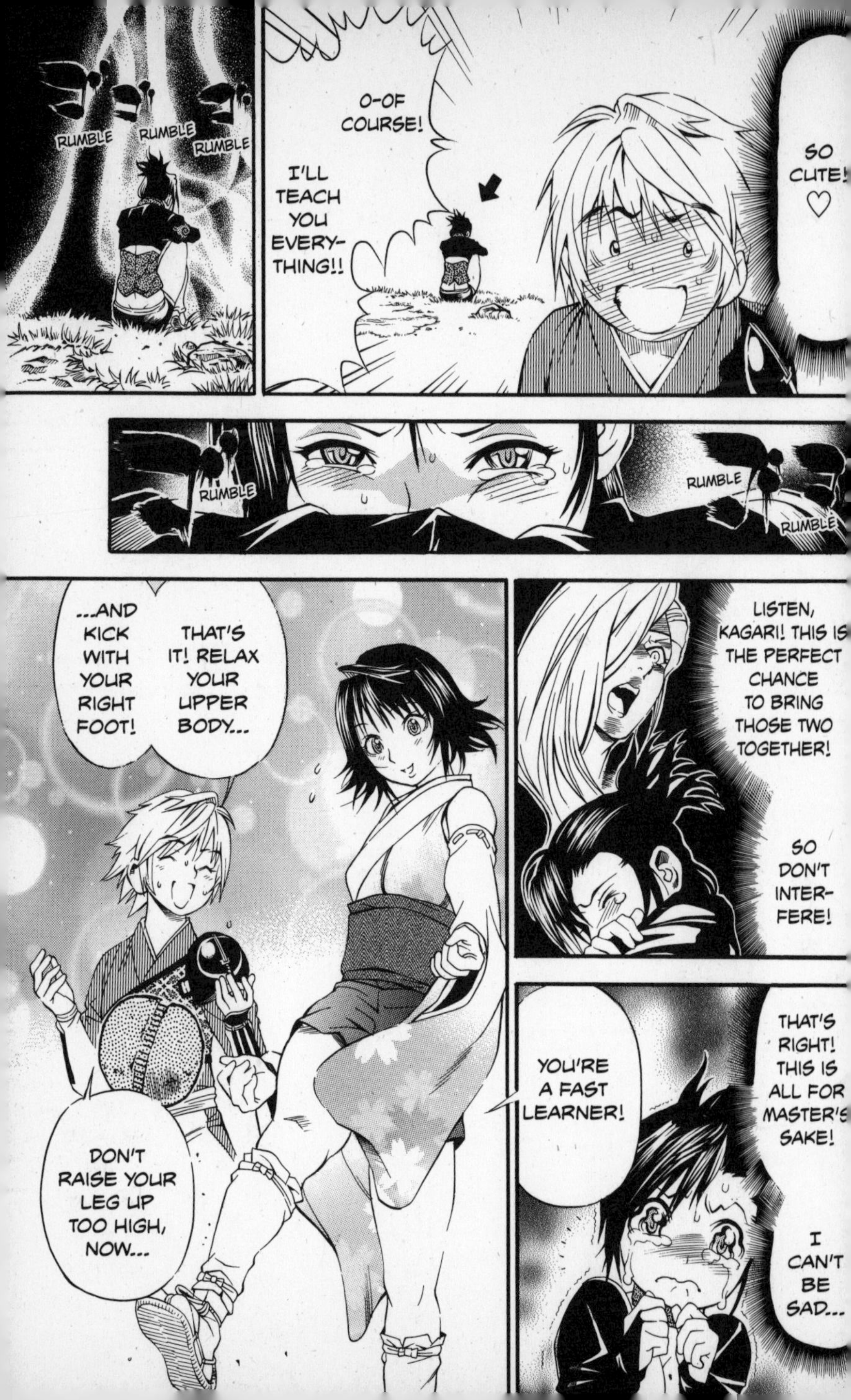
SO CUTE! ♡
O-OF COURSE!
I'LL TEACH YOU EVERYTHING!!
RUMBLE
RUMBLE
RUMBLE
RUMBLE
RUMBLE
RUMBLE
LISTEN, KAGARI! THIS IS THE PERFECT CHANCE TO BRING THOSE TWO TOGETHER!
SO DON'T INTERFERE!
THAT'S RIGHT! THIS IS ALL FOR MASTER'S SAKE!
I CAN'T BE SAD...
YOU'RE A FAST LEARNER!
THAT'S IT! RELAX YOUR UPPER BODY...
...AND KICK WITH YOUR RIGHT FOOT!
DON'T RAISE YOUR LEG UP TOO HIGH, NOW...

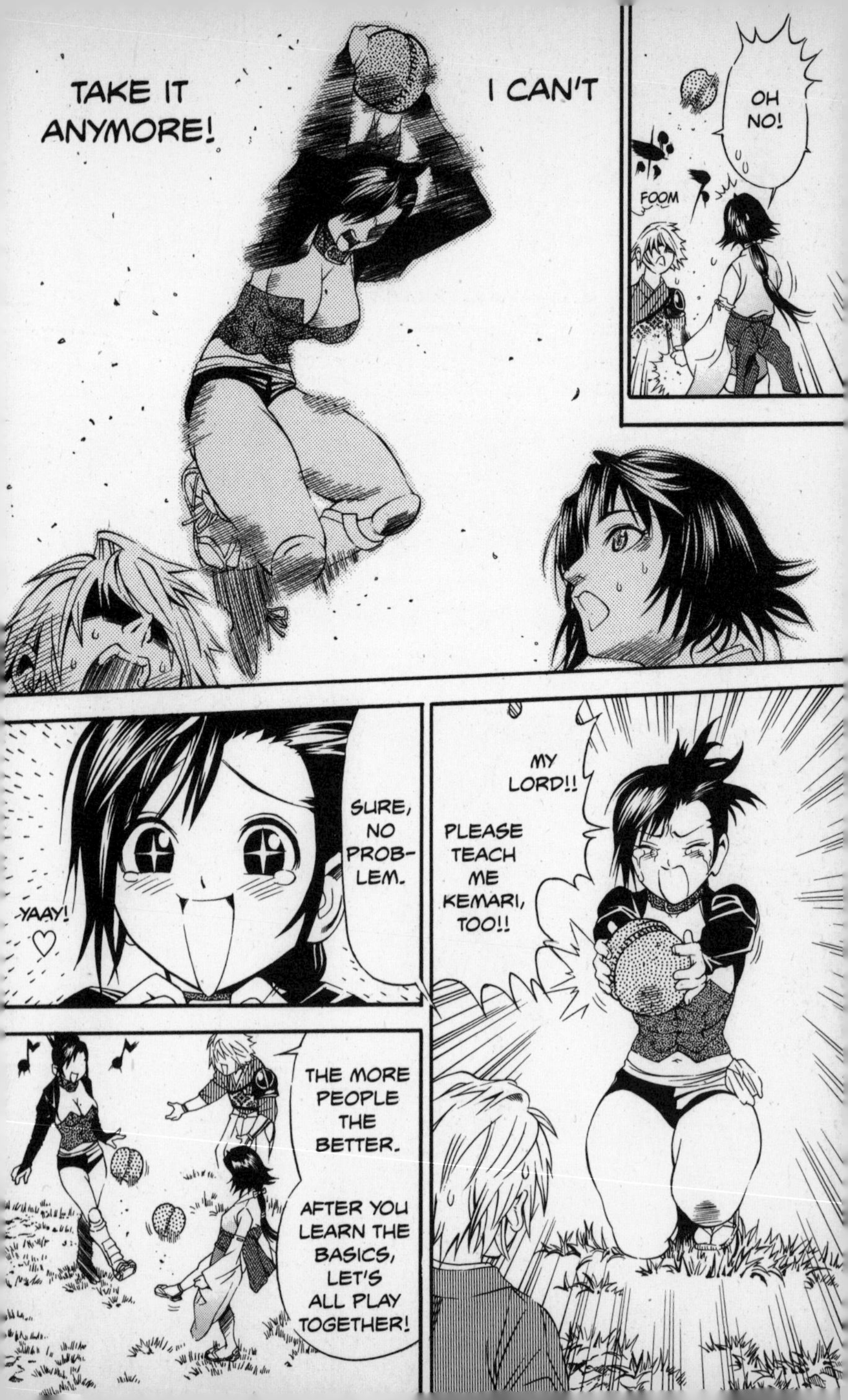
OH NO!
FOOM
I CAN'T
TAKE IT ANYMORE!
MY LORD!!
PLEASE TEACH ME KEMARI, TOO!!
SURE, NO PROB-LEM.
YAAY! ♡
THE MORE PEOPLE THE BETTER.
AFTER YOU LEARN THE BASICS, LET'S ALL PLAY TOGETHER!

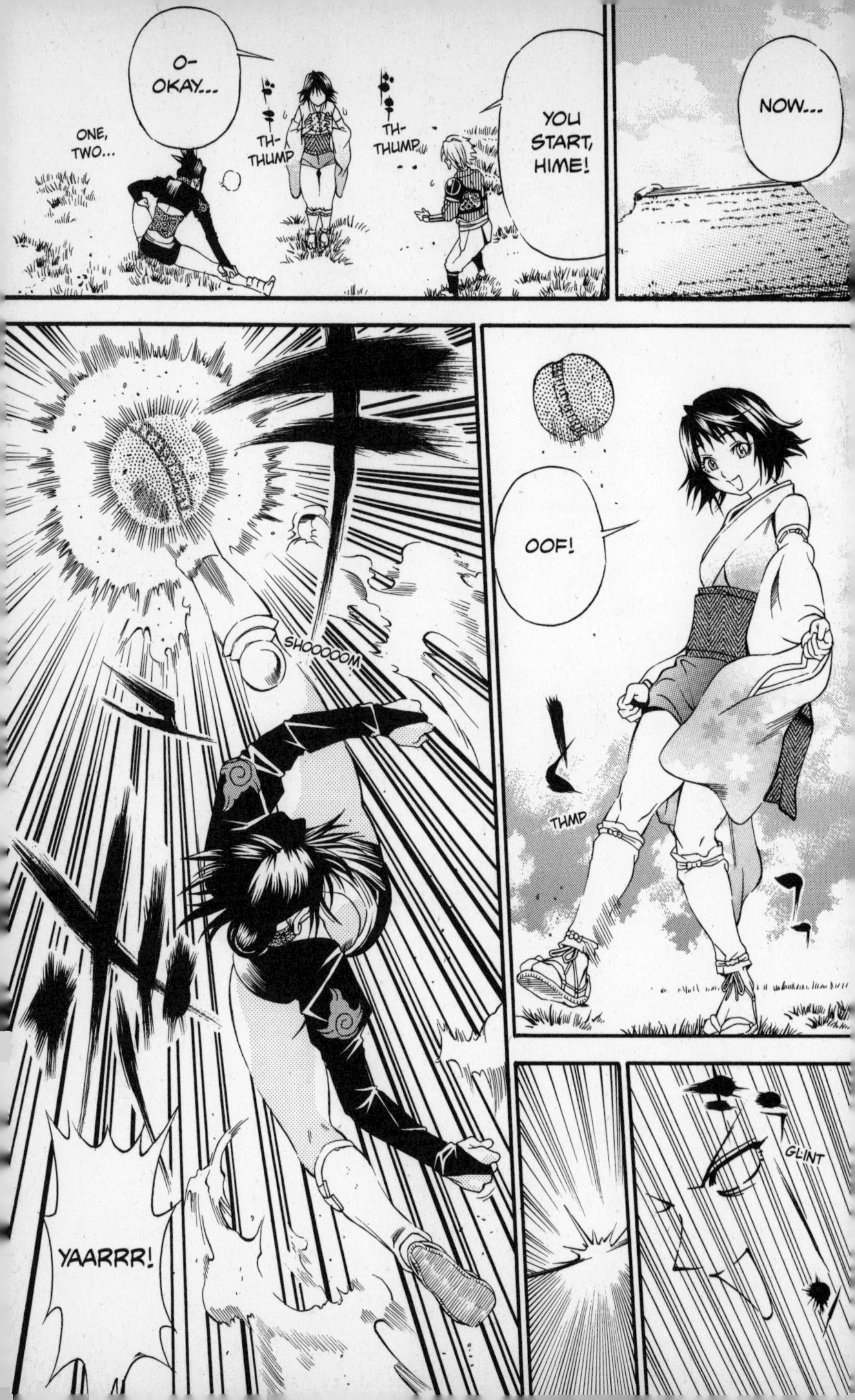
NOW...
YOU START, HIME!
TH-THUMP
TH-THUMP
O-OKAY...
ONE, TWO...
OOF!
THMP
GLINT
SHOOOOOM
YAARRR!

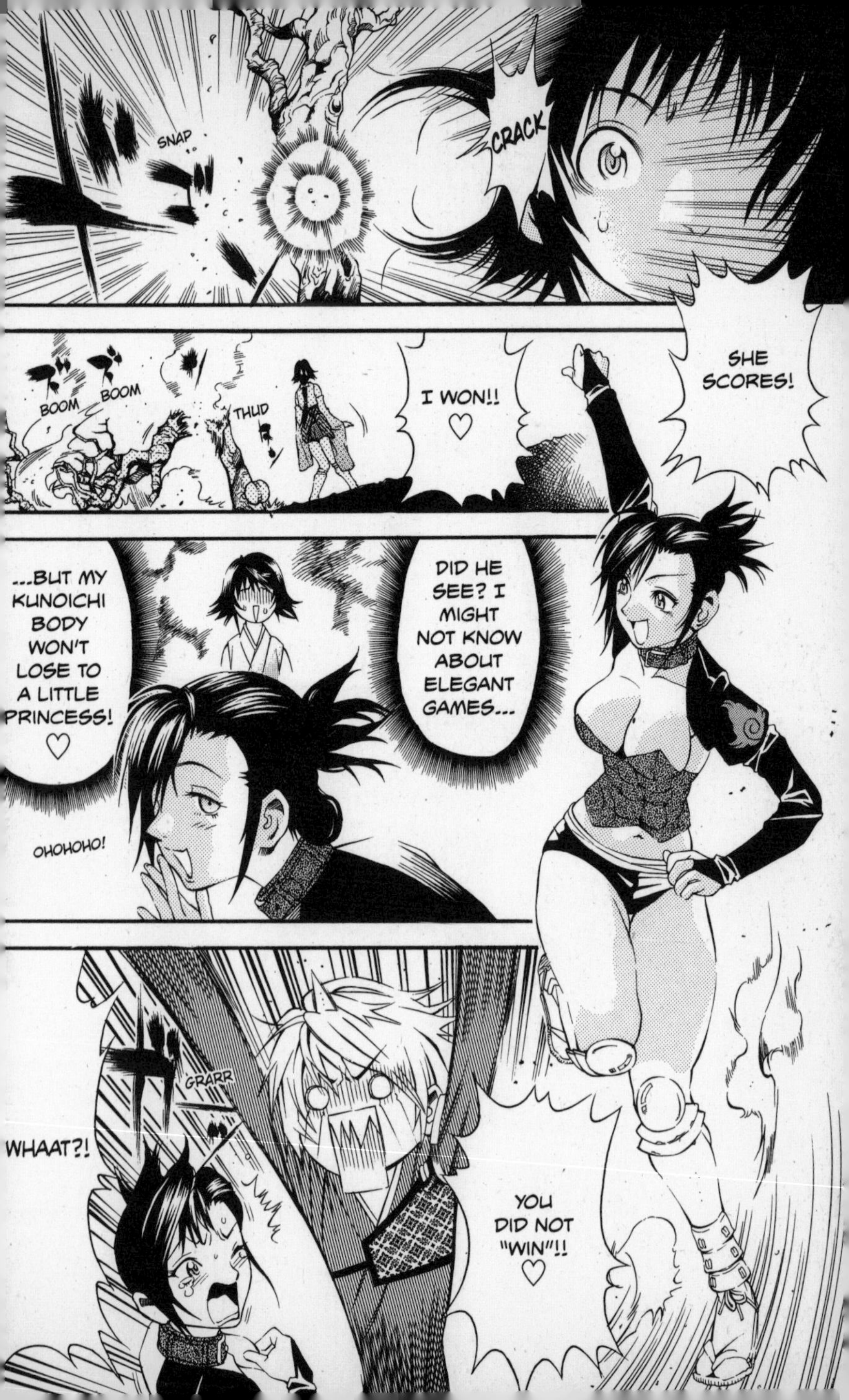
CRACK
SNAP
SHE SCORES!
I WON!! ♡
THUD
BOOM
BOOM
DID HE SEE? I MIGHT NOT KNOW ABOUT ELEGANT GAMES...
...BUT MY KUNOICHI BODY WON'T LOSE TO A LITTLE PRINCESS! ♡
OHOHOHO!
YOU DID NOT "WIN"!! ♡
GRARR
WHAAT?!

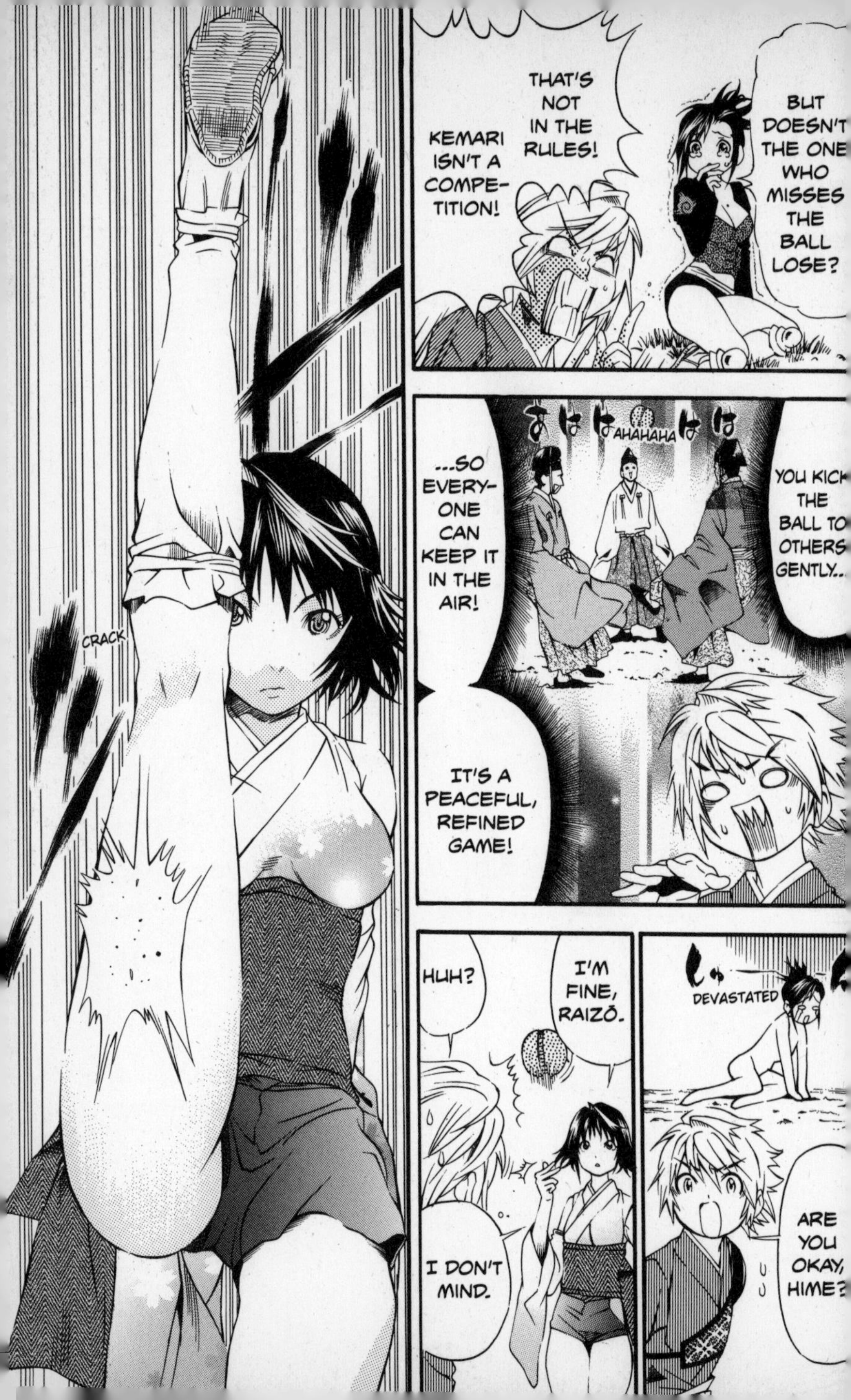
BUT DOESN'T THE ONE WHO MISSES THE BALL LOSE?
THAT'S NOT IN THE RULES!
KEMARI ISN'T A COMPETITION!
YOU KICK THE BALL TO OTHERS GENTLY...
AHAHAHA
...SO EVERYONE CAN KEEP IT IN THE AIR!
IT'S A PEACEFUL, REFINED GAME!
DEVASTATED
ARE YOU OKAY, HIME?
I'M FINE, RAIZŌ.
HUH?
I DON'T MIND.
CRACK

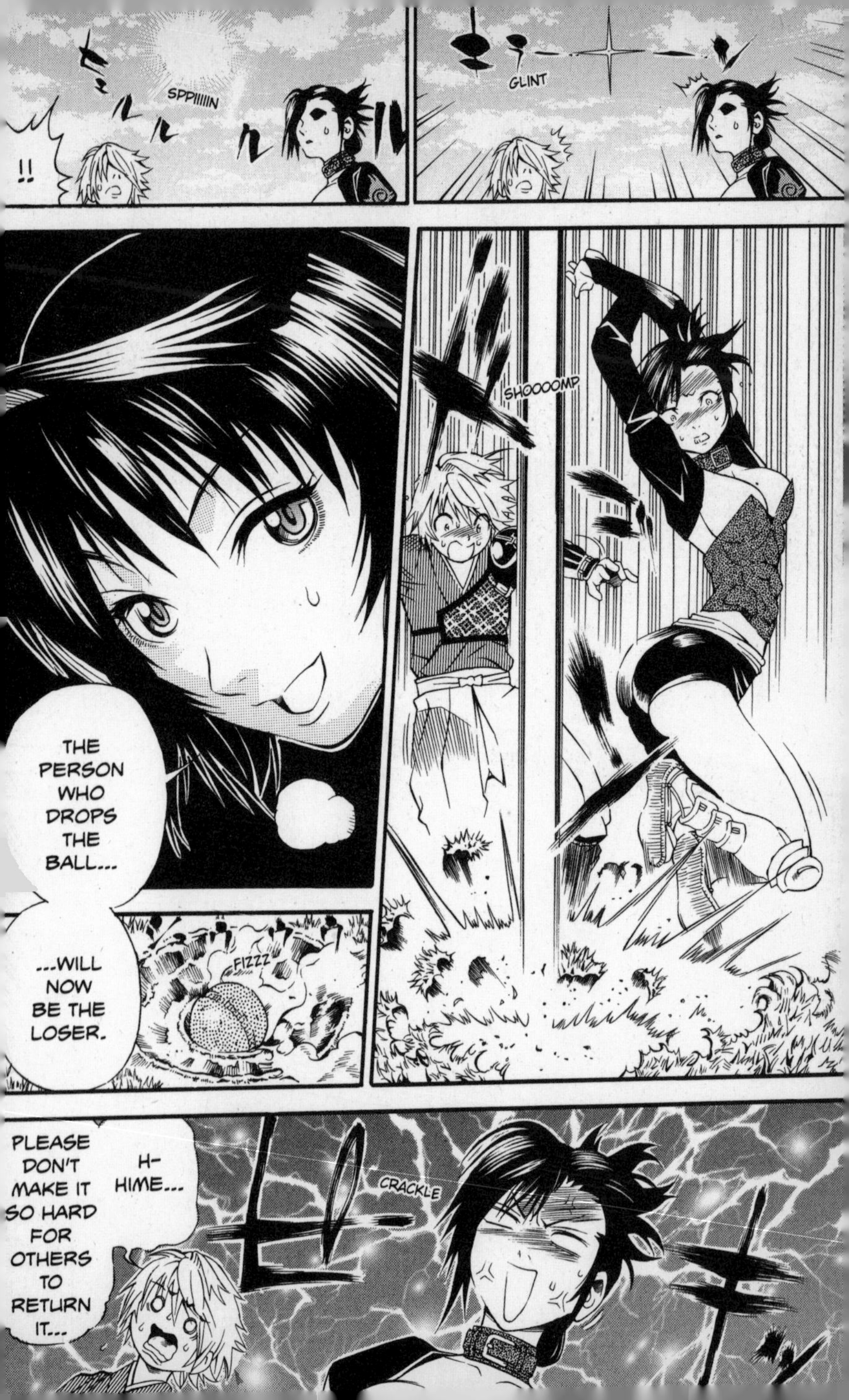
GLINT
SPPIIIIN
!!
SHOOOOMP
THE PERSON WHO DROPS THE BALL...
FIZZZ
...WILL NOW BE THE LOSER.
CRACKLE
H- HIME...
PLEASE DON'T MAKE IT SO HARD FOR OTHERS TO RETURN IT...

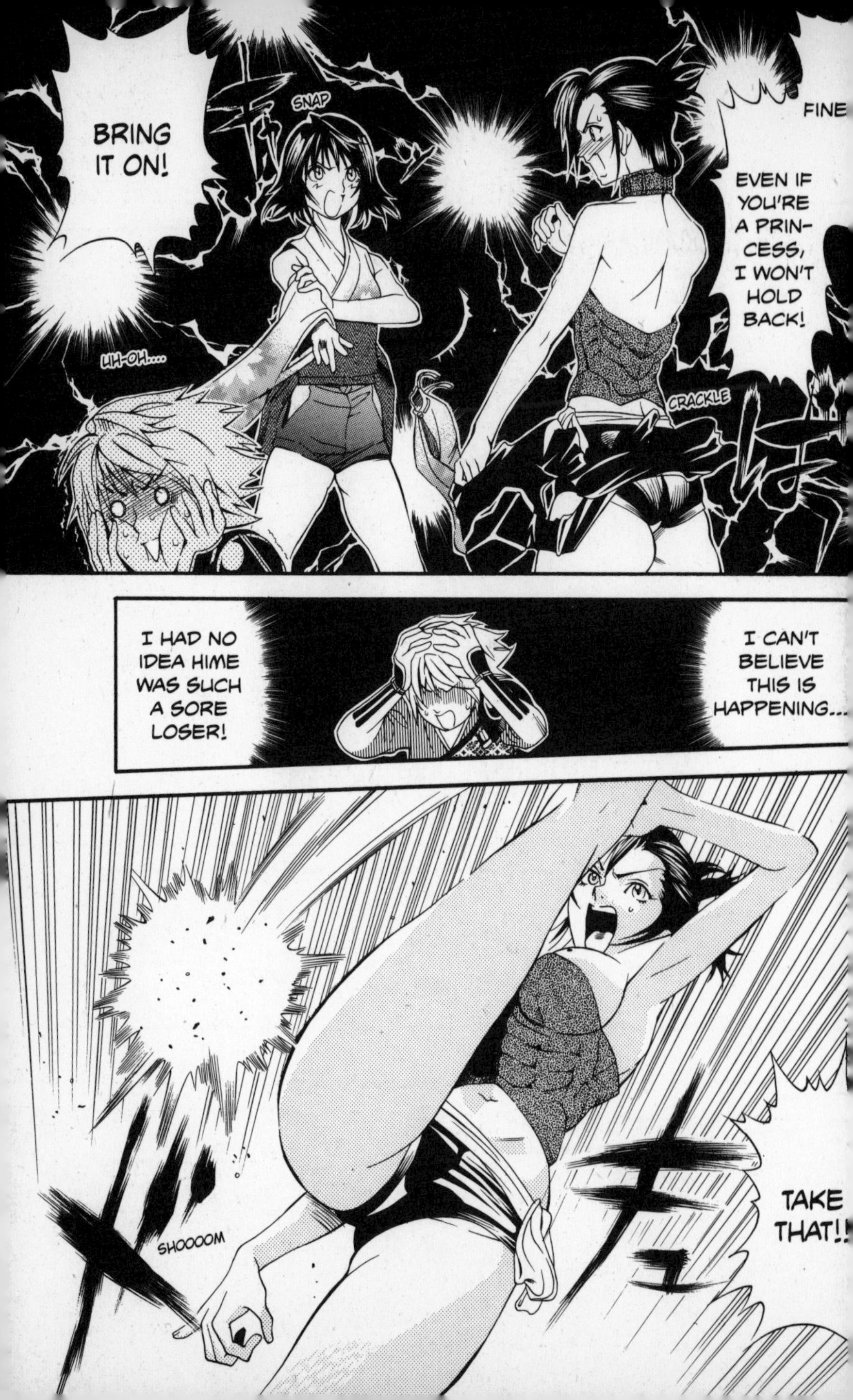
FINE
EVEN IF YOU'RE A PRIN-CESS, I WON'T HOLD BACK!
CRACKLE
SNAP
BRING IT ON!
UH-OH....
I CAN'T BELIEVE THIS IS HAPPENING...
I HAD NO IDEA HIME WAS SUCH A SORE LOSER!
TAKE THAT!!
SHOOOOM

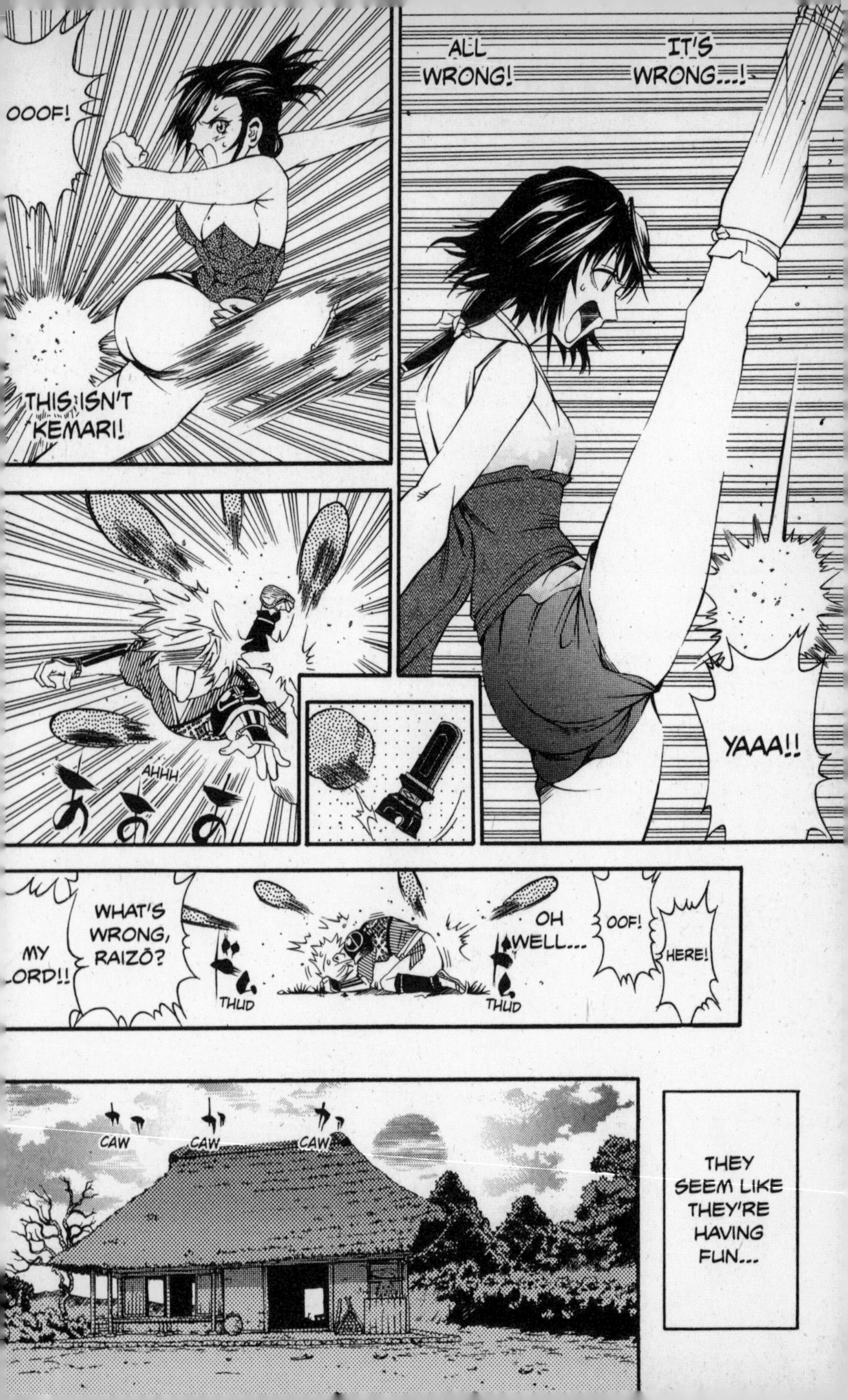
IT'S WRONG...!
ALL WRONG!
YAAA!!
OOOF!
THIS ISN'T KEMARI!
AHHH
HERE!
OOF!
OH WELL...
THUD
WHAT'S WRONG, RAIZŌ?
THUD
MY LORD!!
THEY SEEM LIKE THEY'RE HAVING FUN...
CAW
CAW
CAW

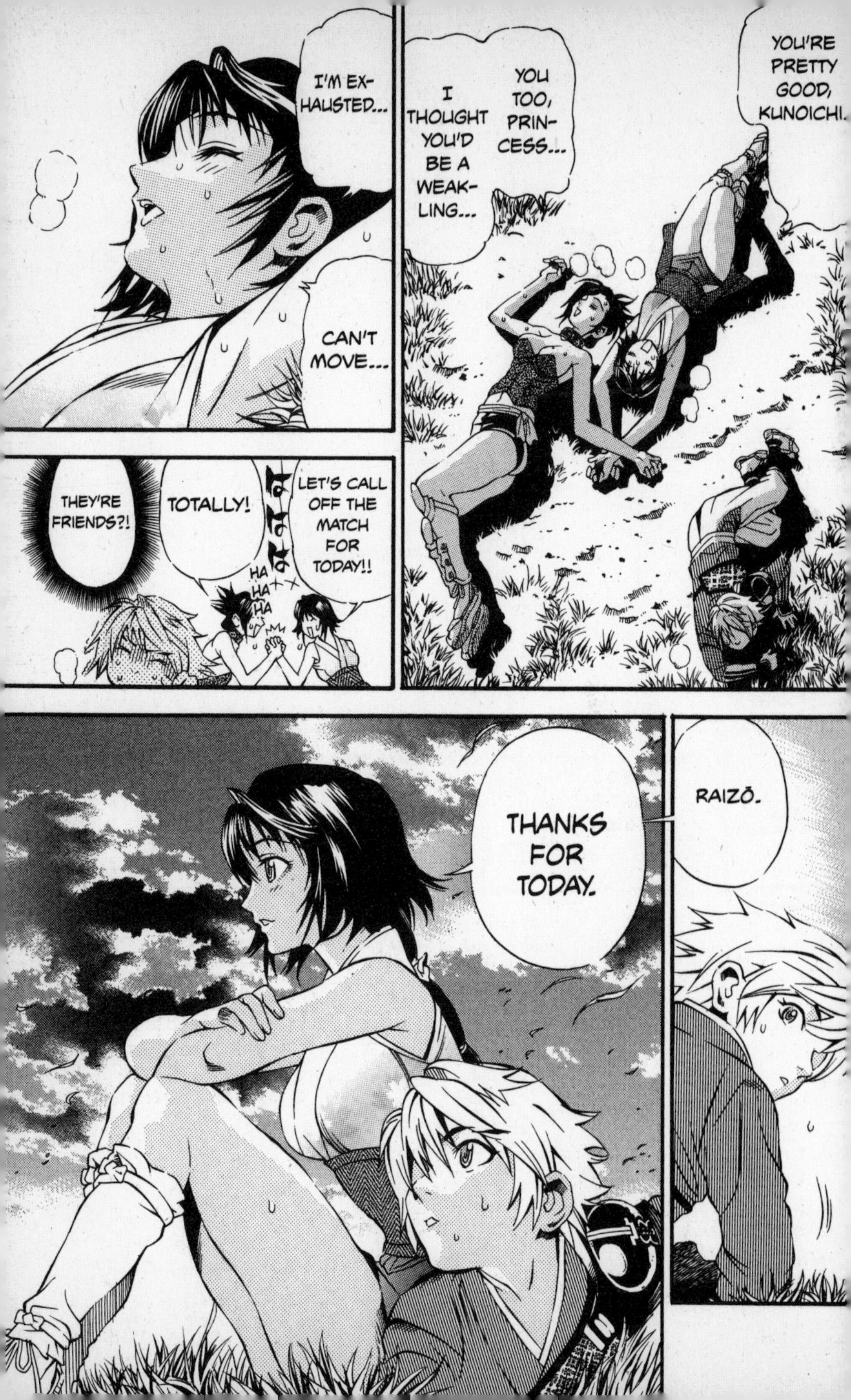
YOU'RE PRETTY GOOD, KUNOICHI.
YOU TOO, PRIN- CESS...
I THOUGHT YOU'D BE A WEAK- LING...
I'M EX- HAUSTED...
CAN'T MOVE...
LET'S CALL OFF THE MATCH FOR TODAY!!
HA HA HA
TOTALLY!
THEY'RE FRIENDS?!
RAIZŌ.
THANKS FOR TODAY.

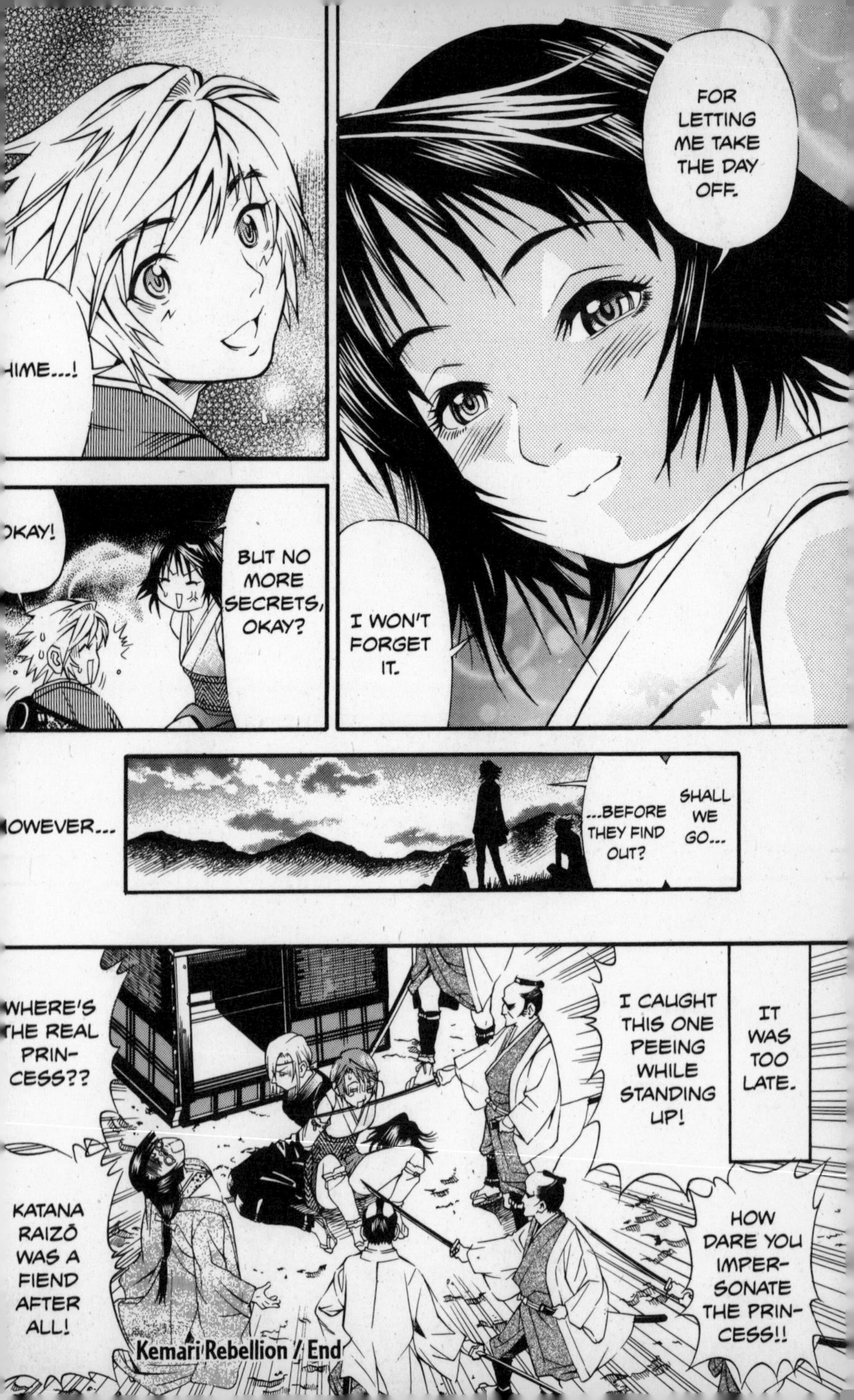
FOR LETTING ME TAKE THE DAY OFF.
I WON'T FORGET IT.
HIME...!
BUT NO MORE SECRETS, OKAY?
OKAY!
SHALL WE GO...
...BEFORE THEY FIND OUT?
HOWEVER...
IT WAS TOO LATE.
I CAUGHT THIS ONE PEEING WHILE STANDING UP!
WHERE'S THE REAL PRINCESS??
HOW DARE YOU IMPERSONATE THE PRINCESS!!
KATANA RAIZŌ WAS A FIEND AFTER ALL!
Kemari Rebellion / End

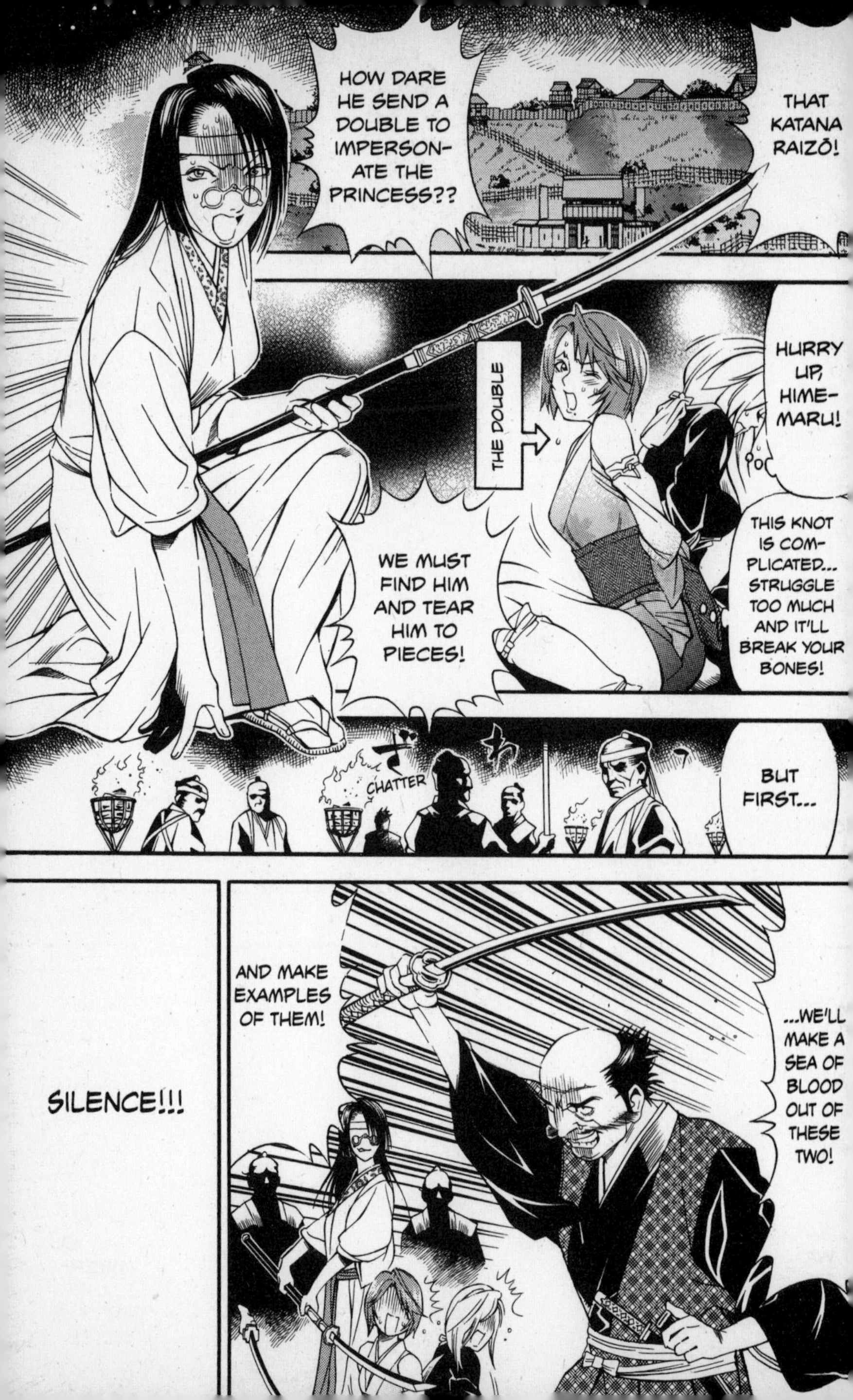
THAT KATANA RAIZŌ!
HOW DARE HE SEND A DOUBLE TO IMPERSON-ATE THE PRINCESS??
HURRY UP, HIME-MARU!
THIS KNOT IS COM-PLICATED... STRUGGLE TOO MUCH AND IT'LL BREAK YOUR BONES!
THE DOUBLE
WE MUST FIND HIM AND TEAR HIM TO PIECES!
BUT FIRST...
CHATTER
...WE'LL MAKE A SEA OF BLOOD OUT OF THESE TWO!
AND MAKE EXAMPLES OF THEM!
SILENCE!!!

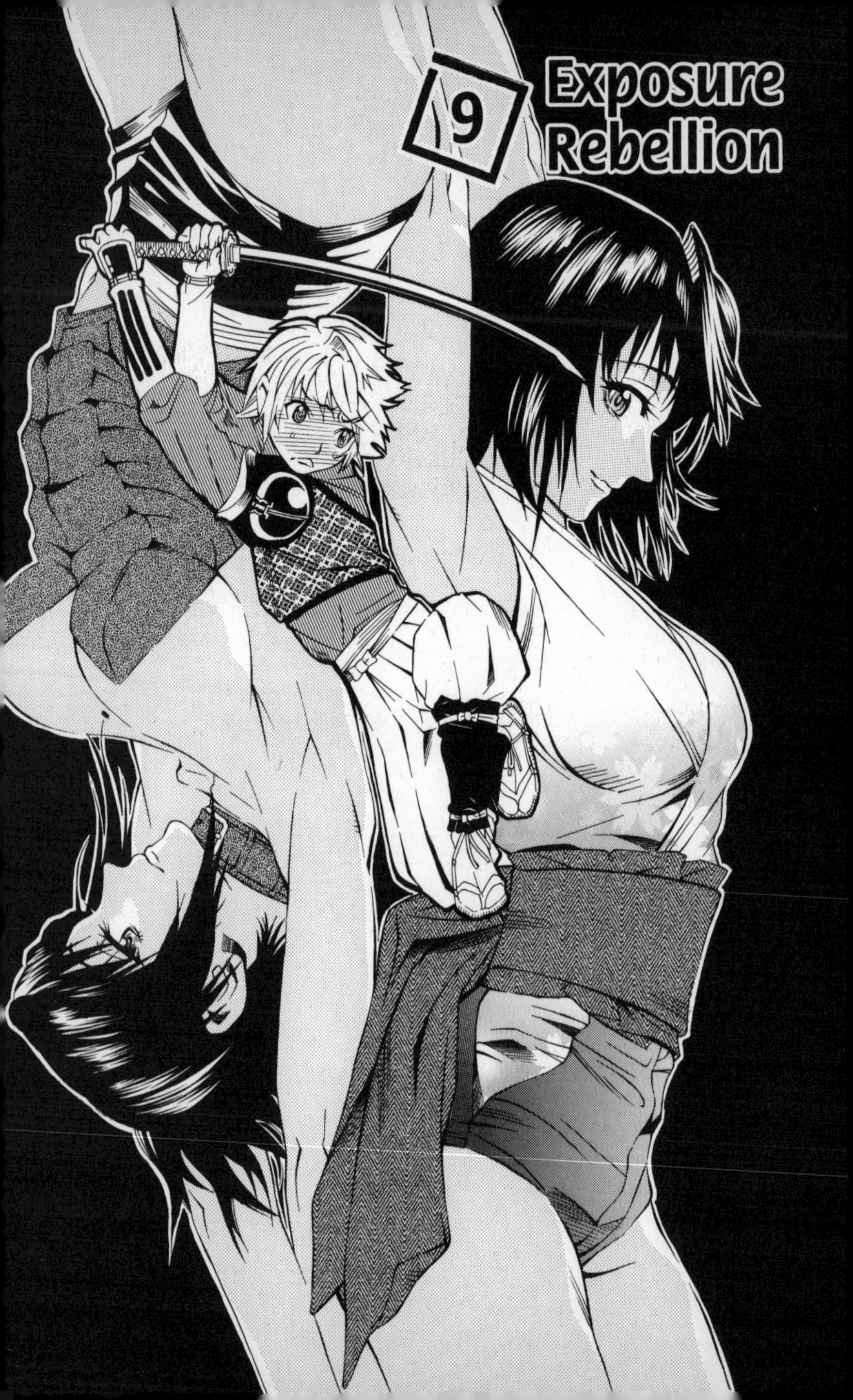
9
Exposure
Rebellion

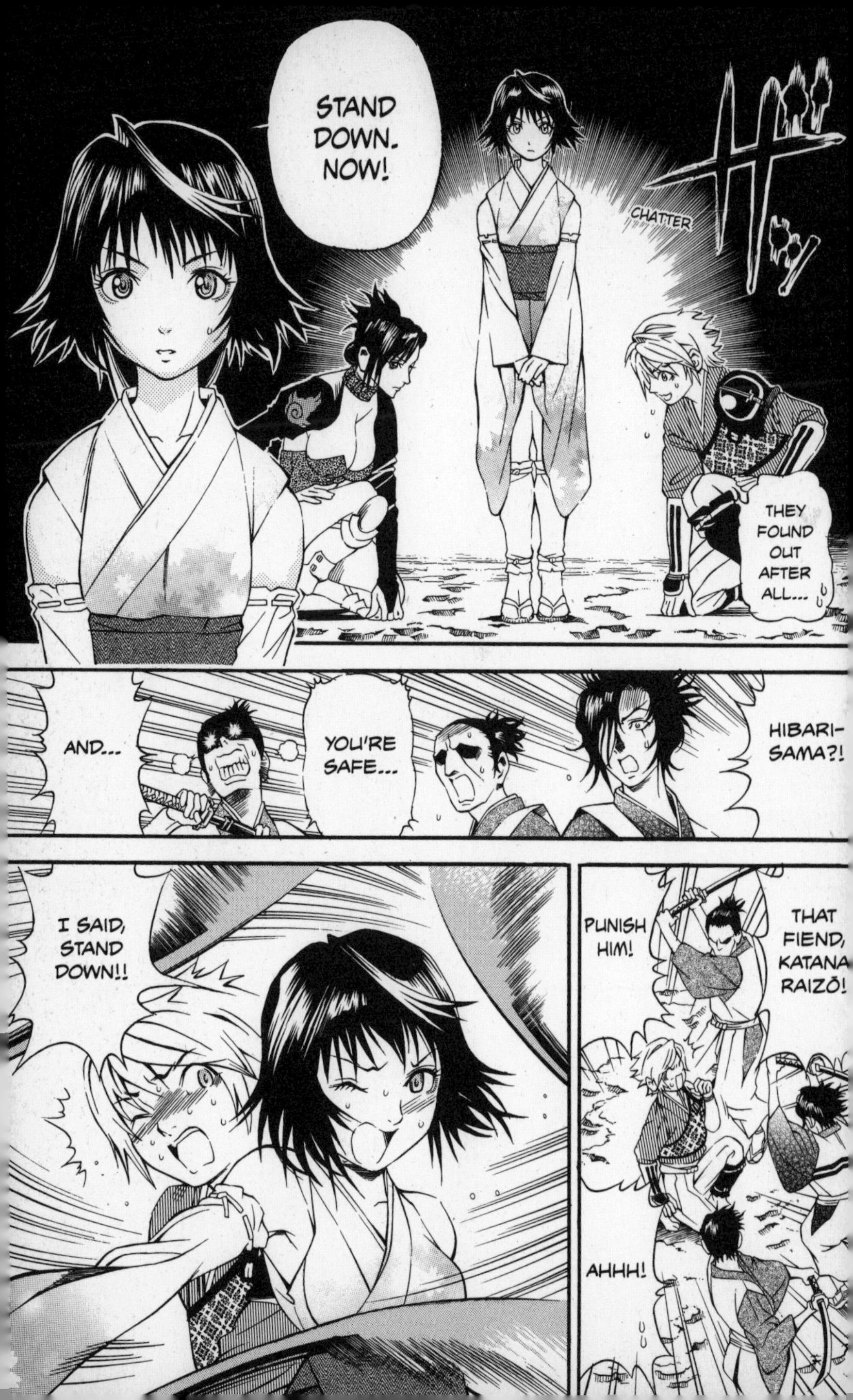
CHATTER
STAND DOWN. NOW!
THEY FOUND OUT AFTER ALL...
HIBARI-SAMA?!
YOU'RE SAFE...
AND...
THAT FIEND, KATANA RAIZŌ!
PUNISH HIM!
AHHH!
I SAID, STAND DOWN!!

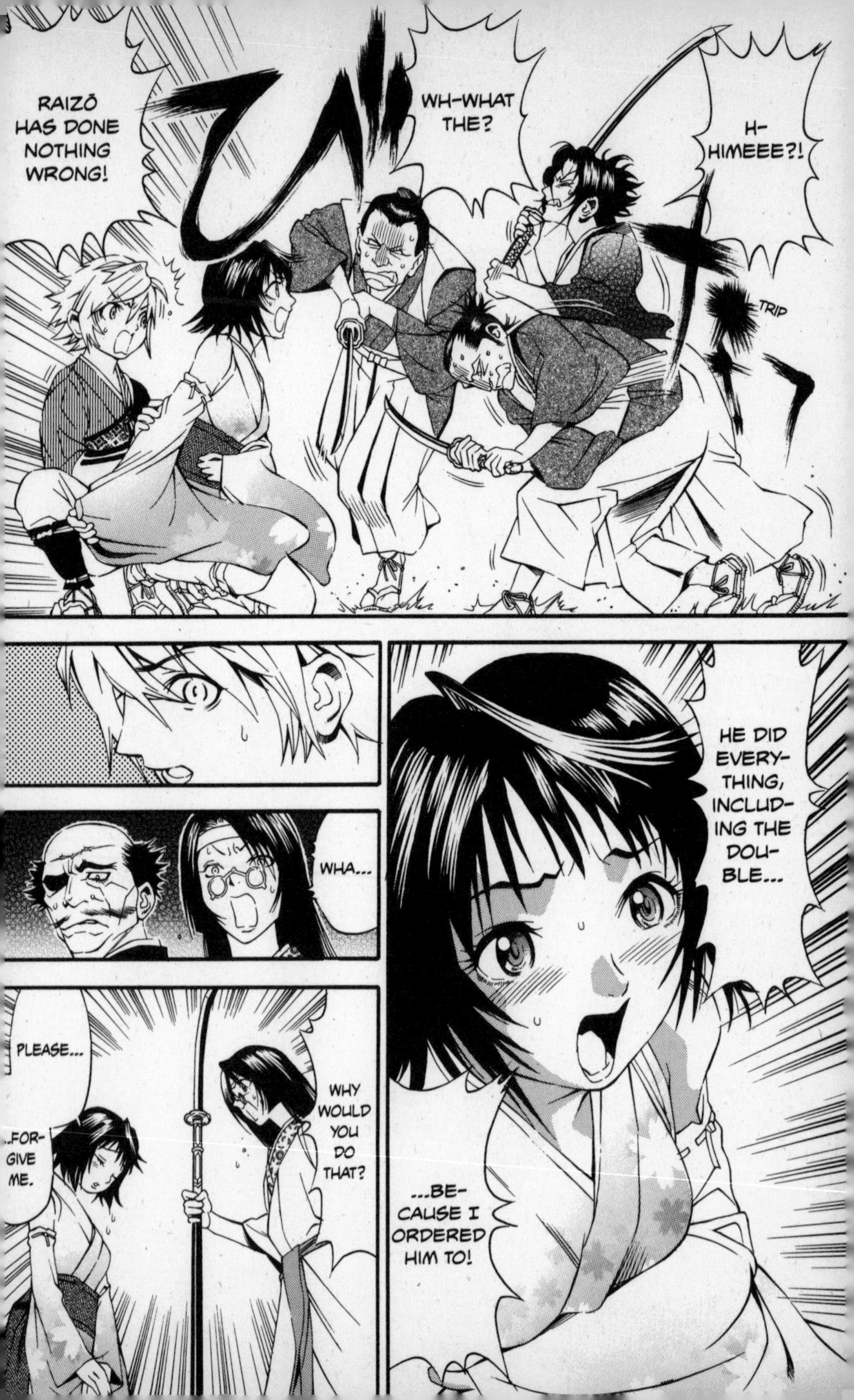
H-HIMEEE?!
WH-WHAT THE?
TRIP
RAIZŌ HAS DONE NOTHING WRONG!
HE DID EVERY-THING, INCLUD-ING THE DOU-BLE...
...BE-CAUSE I ORDERED HIM TO!
WHA...
WHY WOULD YOU DO THAT?
PLEASE...
...FOR-GIVE ME.

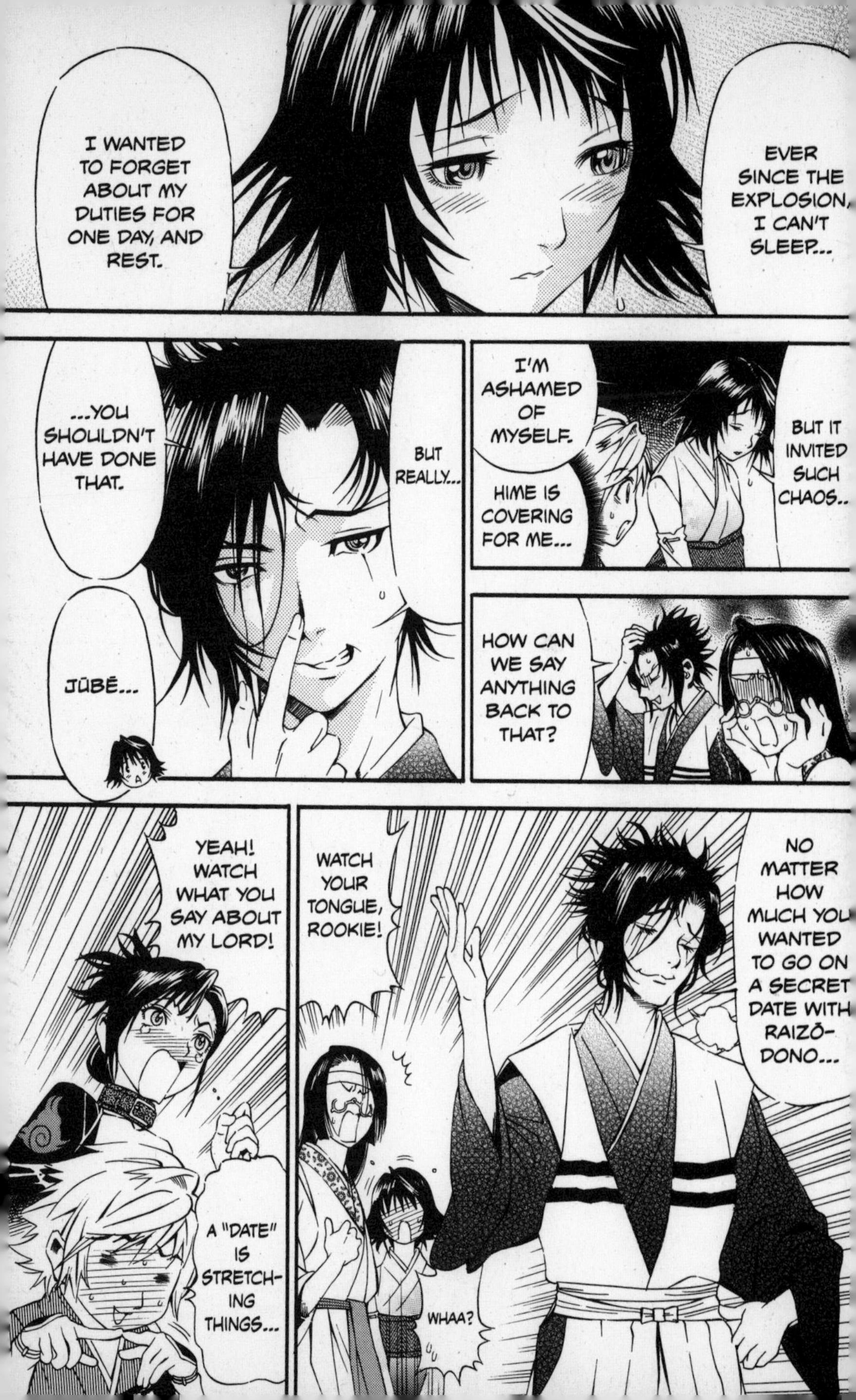
EVER SINCE THE EXPLOSION, I CAN'T SLEEP...
I WANTED TO FORGET ABOUT MY DUTIES FOR ONE DAY, AND REST.
BUT IT INVITED SUCH CHAOS..
I'M ASHAMED OF MYSELF.
HIME IS COVERING FOR ME...
HOW CAN WE SAY ANYTHING BACK TO THAT?
BUT REALLY...
...YOU SHOULDN'T HAVE DONE THAT.
JŪBĒ...
NO MATTER HOW MUCH YOU WANTED TO GO ON A SECRET DATE WITH RAIZŌ-DONO...
WATCH YOUR TONGUE, ROOKIE!
WHAA?
YEAH! WATCH WHAT YOU SAY ABOUT MY LORD!
A "DATE" IS STRETCHING THINGS...

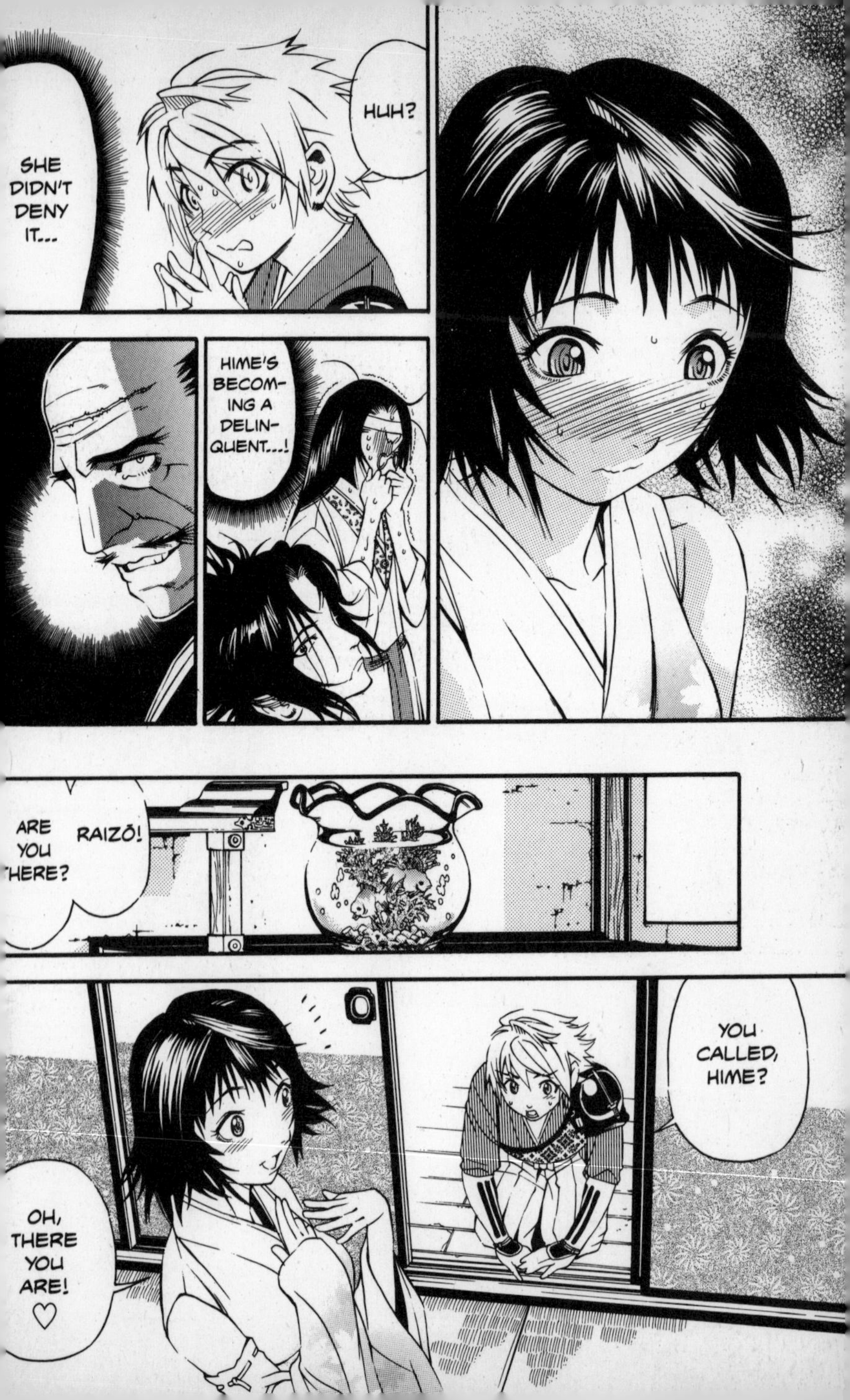
HUH?
SHE DIDN'T DENY IT...
HIME'S BECOMING A DELINQUENT...!
RAIZŌ!
ARE YOU THERE?
YOU CALLED, HIME?
OH, THERE YOU ARE! ♡

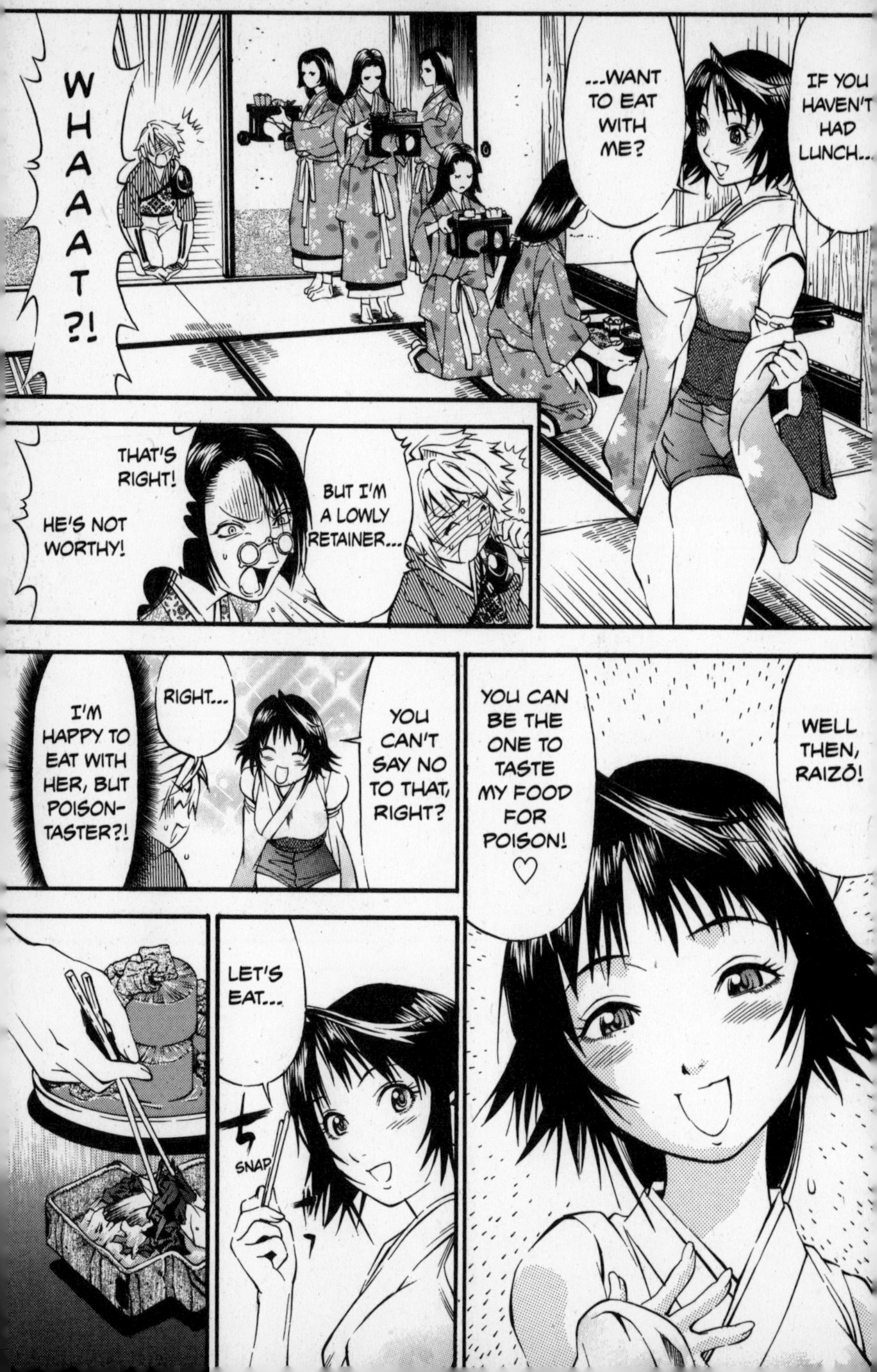
IF YOU HAVEN'T HAD LUNCH...
...WANT TO EAT WITH ME?
WHAAAAT?!
BUT I'M A LOWLY RETAINER...
THAT'S RIGHT!
HE'S NOT WORTHY!
WELL THEN, RAIZŌ!
YOU CAN BE THE ONE TO TASTE MY FOOD FOR POISON! ♡
YOU CAN'T SAY NO TO THAT, RIGHT?
RIGHT...
I'M HAPPY TO EAT WITH HER, BUT POISON-TASTER?!
LET'S EAT...
SNAP

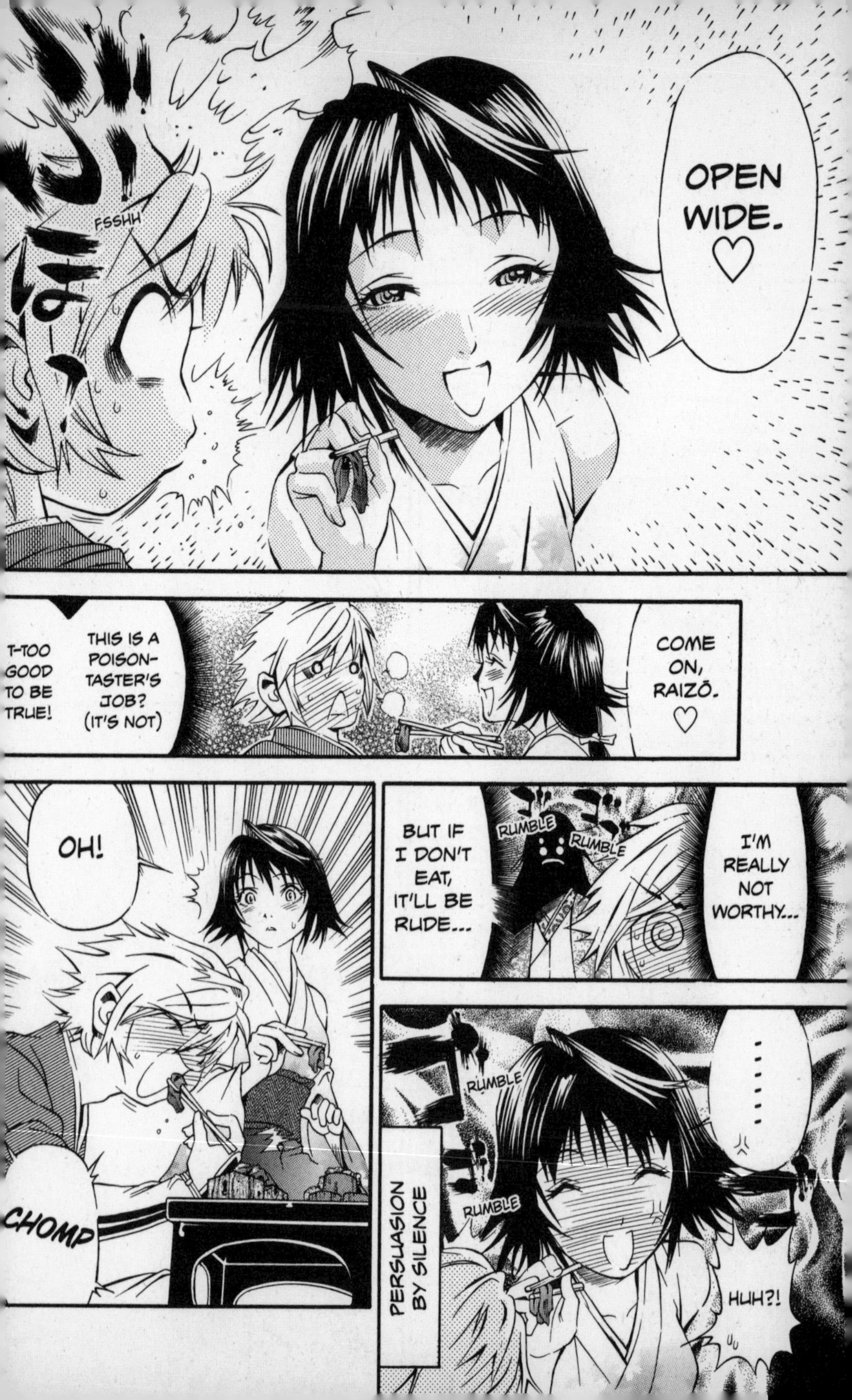
OPEN WIDE. ♡
FSSHH
COME ON, RAIZŌ. ♡
THIS IS A POISON-TASTER'S JOB? (IT'S NOT)
T-TOO GOOD TO BE TRUE!
I'M REALLY NOT WORTHY...
RUMBLE
RUMBLE
BUT IF I DON'T EAT, IT'LL BE RUDE...
......
RUMBLE
HUH?!
RUMBLE
PERSUASION BY SILENCE
OH!
CHOMP

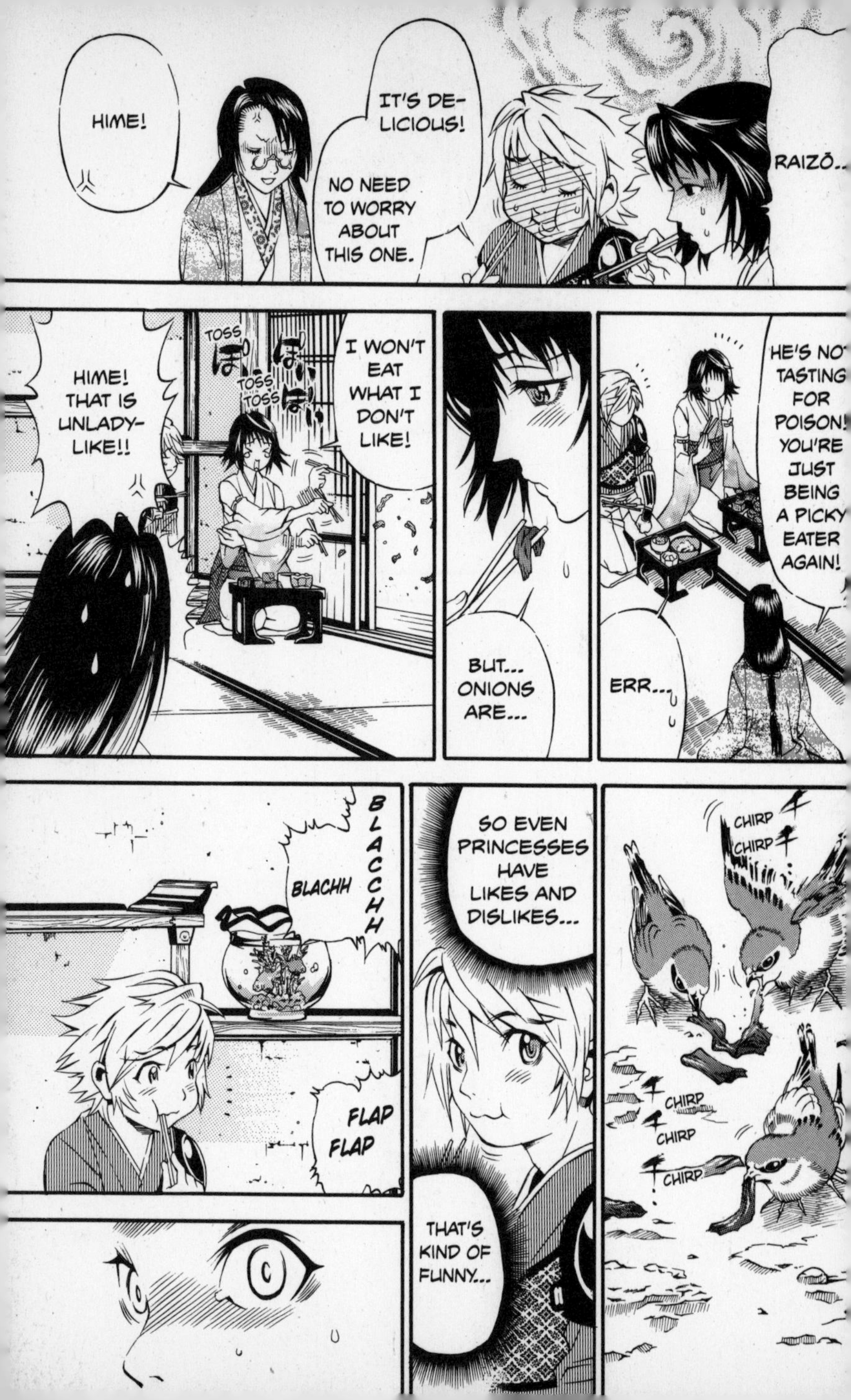
RAIZŌ...
IT'S DE-LICIOUS!
NO NEED TO WORRY ABOUT THIS ONE.
HIME!
HE'S NOT TASTING FOR POISON! YOU'RE JUST BEING A PICKY EATER AGAIN!
ERR...
BUT... ONIONS ARE...
I WON'T EAT WHAT I DON'T LIKE!
TOSS
TOSS
TOSS
HIME! THAT IS UNLADY-LIKE!!
CHIRP
CHIRP
CHIRP
CHIRP
CHIRP
SO EVEN PRINCESSES HAVE LIKES AND DISLIKES...
THAT'S KIND OF FUNNY...
BLACCHH
BLACHH
FLAP FLAP

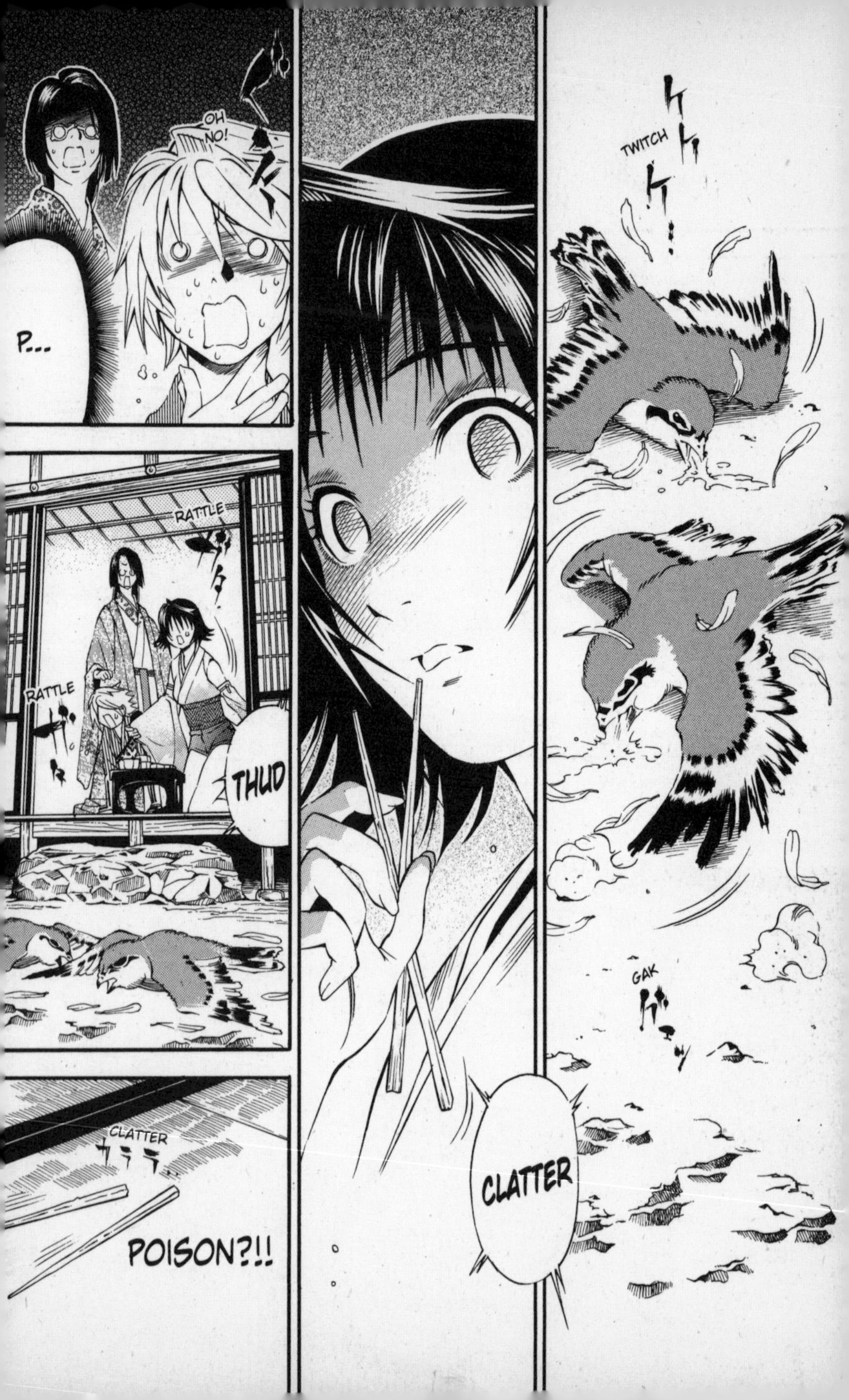
TWITCH
GAK
CLATTER
OH NO!
P...
RATTLE
RATTLE
THUD
CLATTER
POISON?!!

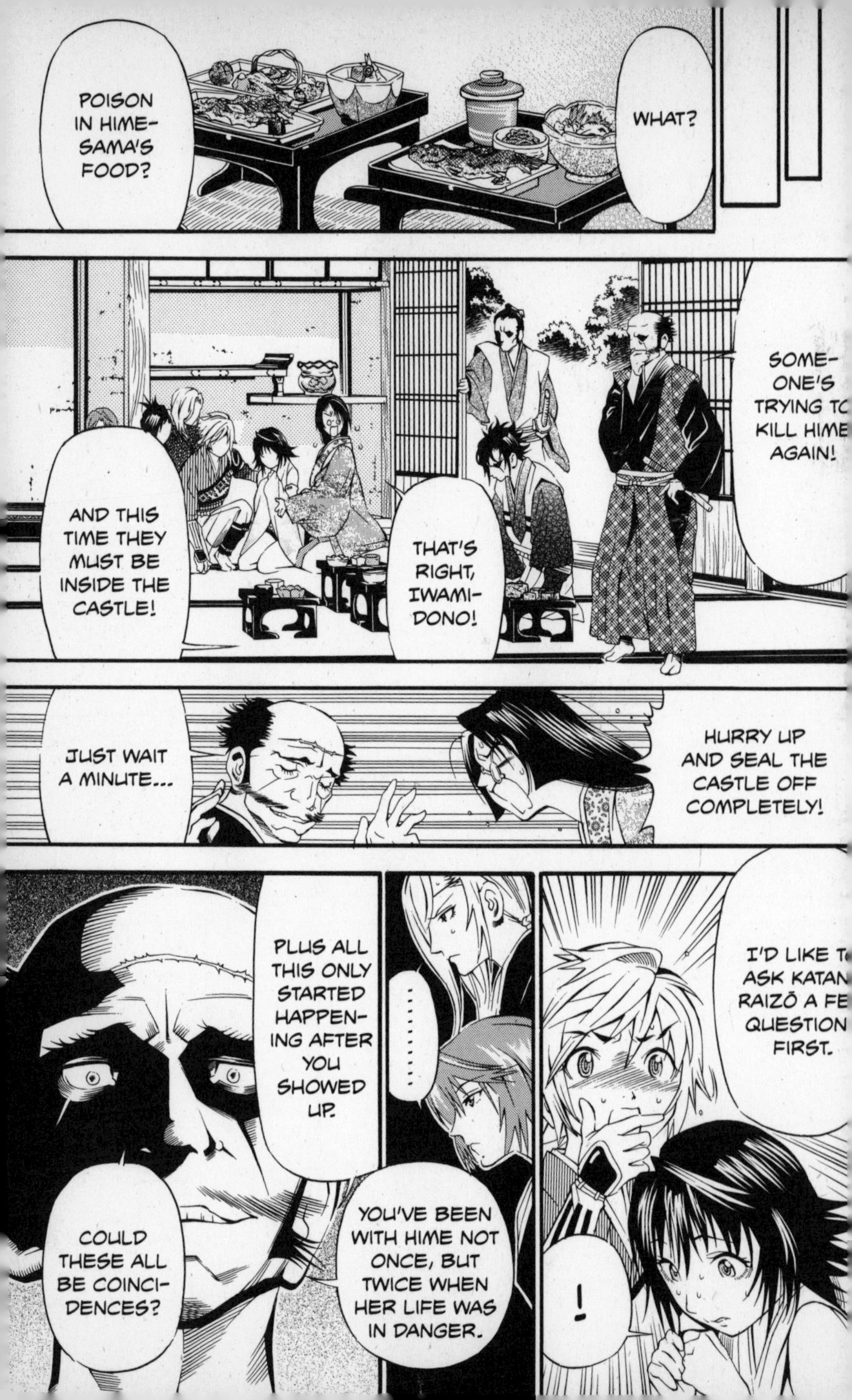

WHAT?
POISON IN HIME-SAMA'S FOOD?
SOME-ONE'S TRYING TO KILL HIME AGAIN!
THAT'S RIGHT, IWAMI-DONO!
AND THIS TIME THEY MUST BE INSIDE THE CASTLE!
HURRY UP AND SEAL THE CASTLE OFF COMPLETELY!
JUST WAIT A MINUTE...
I'D LIKE T ASK KATAN RAIZŌ A FE QUESTION FIRST.
!
......
PLUS ALL THIS ONLY STARTED HAPPEN-ING AFTER YOU SHOWED UP.
YOU'VE BEEN WITH HIME NOT ONCE, BUT TWICE WHEN HER LIFE WAS IN DANGER.
COULD THESE ALL BE COINCI-DENCES?

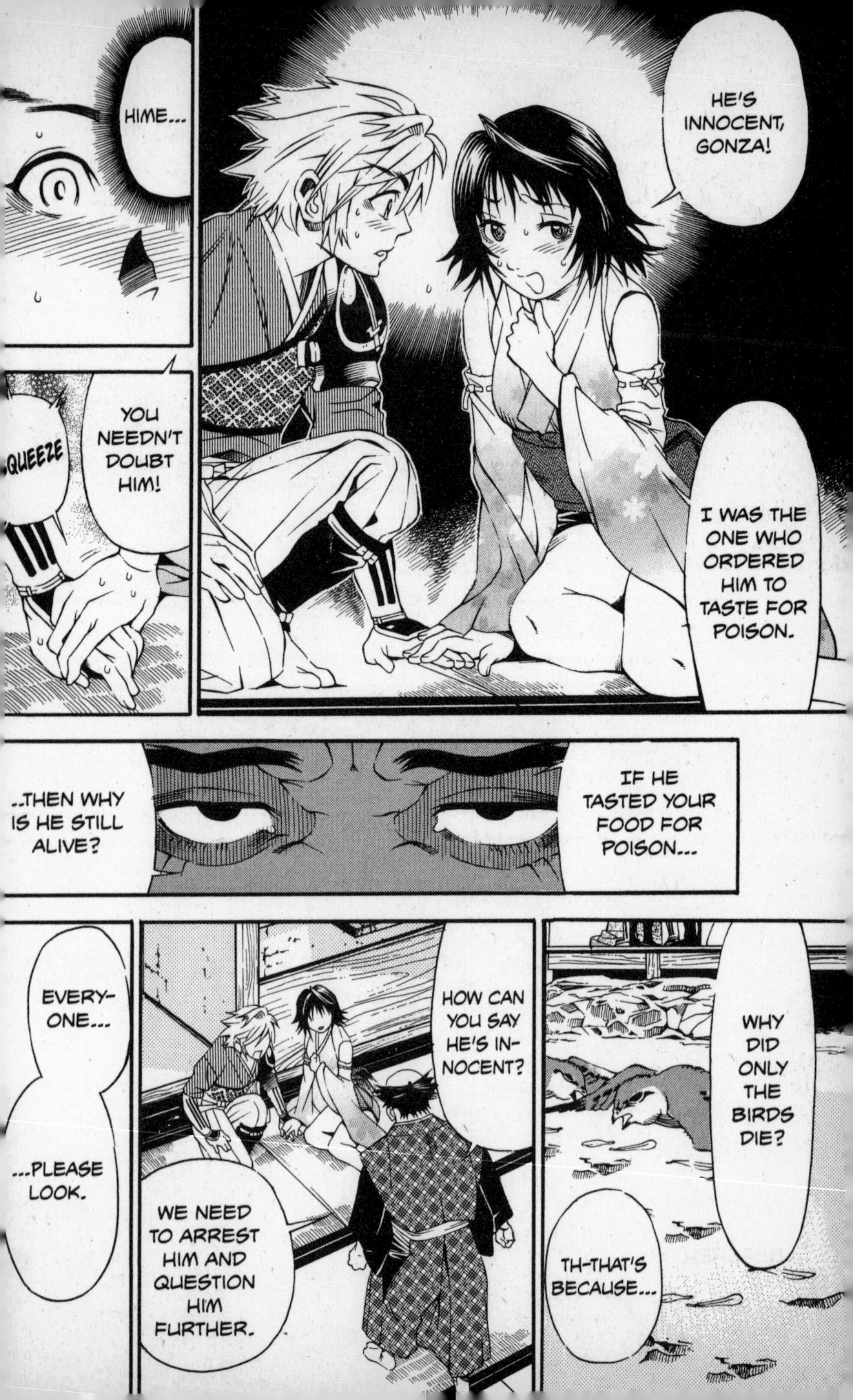
HE'S INNOCENT, GONZA!
I WAS THE ONE WHO ORDERED HIM TO TASTE FOR POISON.
HIME...
YOU NEEDN'T DOUBT HIM!
QUEEZE
IF HE TASTED YOUR FOOD FOR POISON...
..THEN WHY IS HE STILL ALIVE?
WHY DID ONLY THE BIRDS DIE?
TH-THAT'S BECAUSE...
HOW CAN YOU SAY HE'S IN-NOCENT?
WE NEED TO ARREST HIM AND QUESTION HIM FURTHER.
EVERY-ONE...
...PLEASE LOOK.

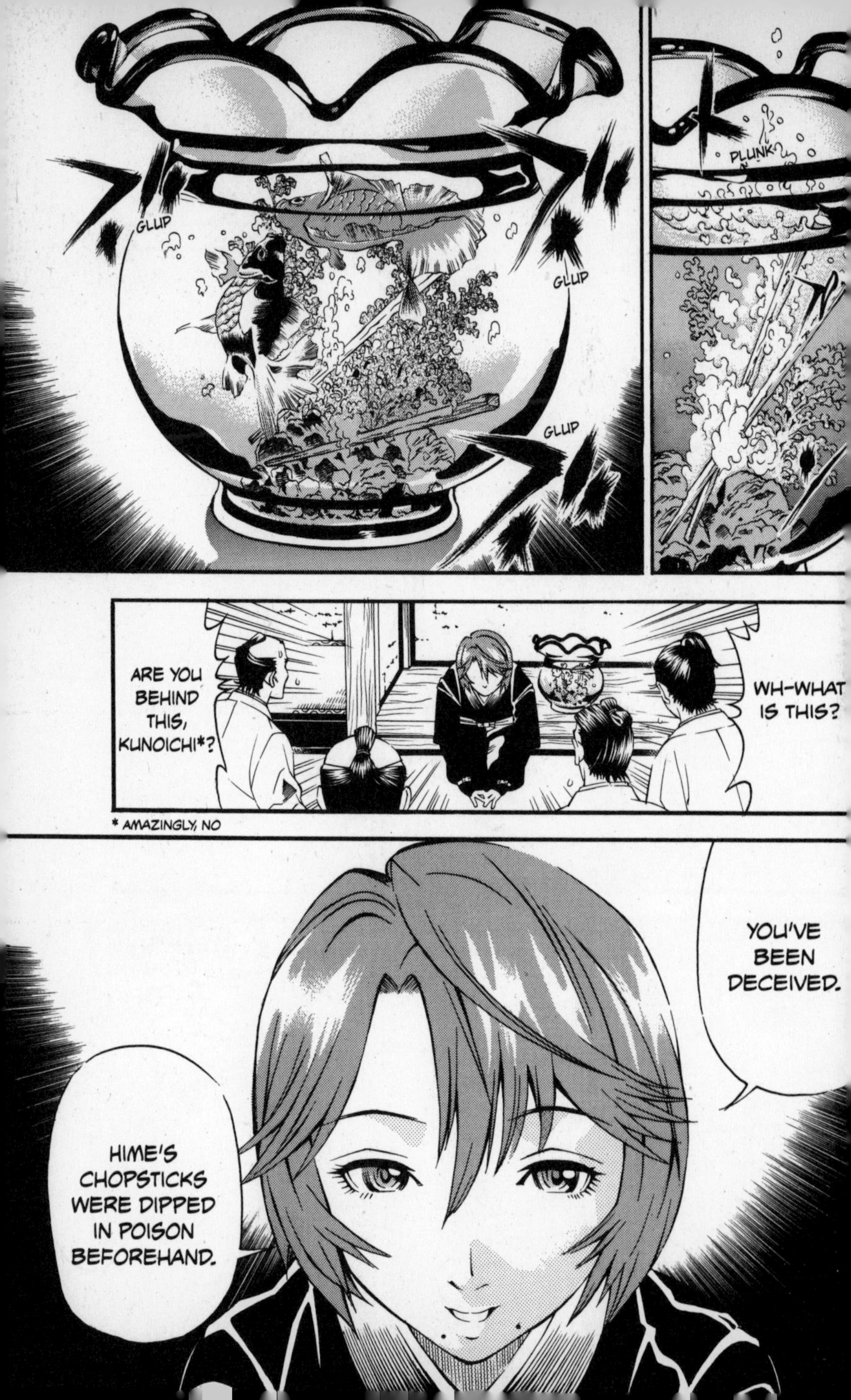
PLUNK
GLUP
GLUP
GLUP
WH-WHAT IS THIS?
ARE YOU BEHIND THIS, KUNOICHI*?
* AMAZINGLY, NO
YOU'VE BEEN DECEIVED.
HIME'S CHOPSTICKS WERE DIPPED IN POISON BEFOREHAND.

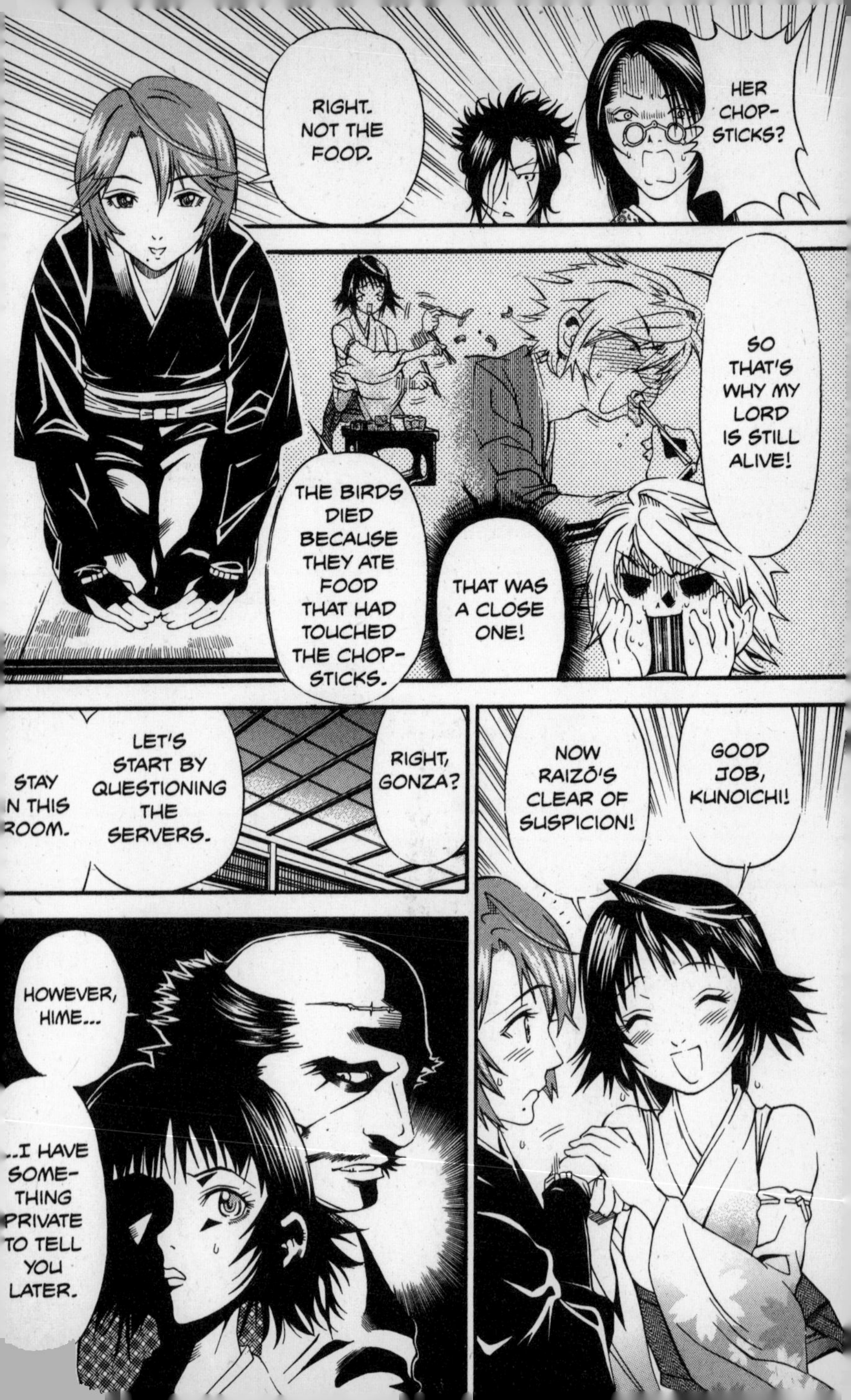
HER CHOP-STICKS?
RIGHT. NOT THE FOOD.
SO THAT'S WHY MY LORD IS STILL ALIVE!
THAT WAS A CLOSE ONE!
THE BIRDS DIED BECAUSE THEY ATE FOOD THAT HAD TOUCHED THE CHOP-STICKS.
GOOD JOB, KUNOICHI!
NOW RAIZŌ'S CLEAR OF SUSPICION!
RIGHT, GONZA?
LET'S START BY QUESTIONING THE SERVERS.
STAY N THIS ROOM.
HOWEVER, HIME...
..I HAVE SOME-THING PRIVATE TO TELL YOU LATER.

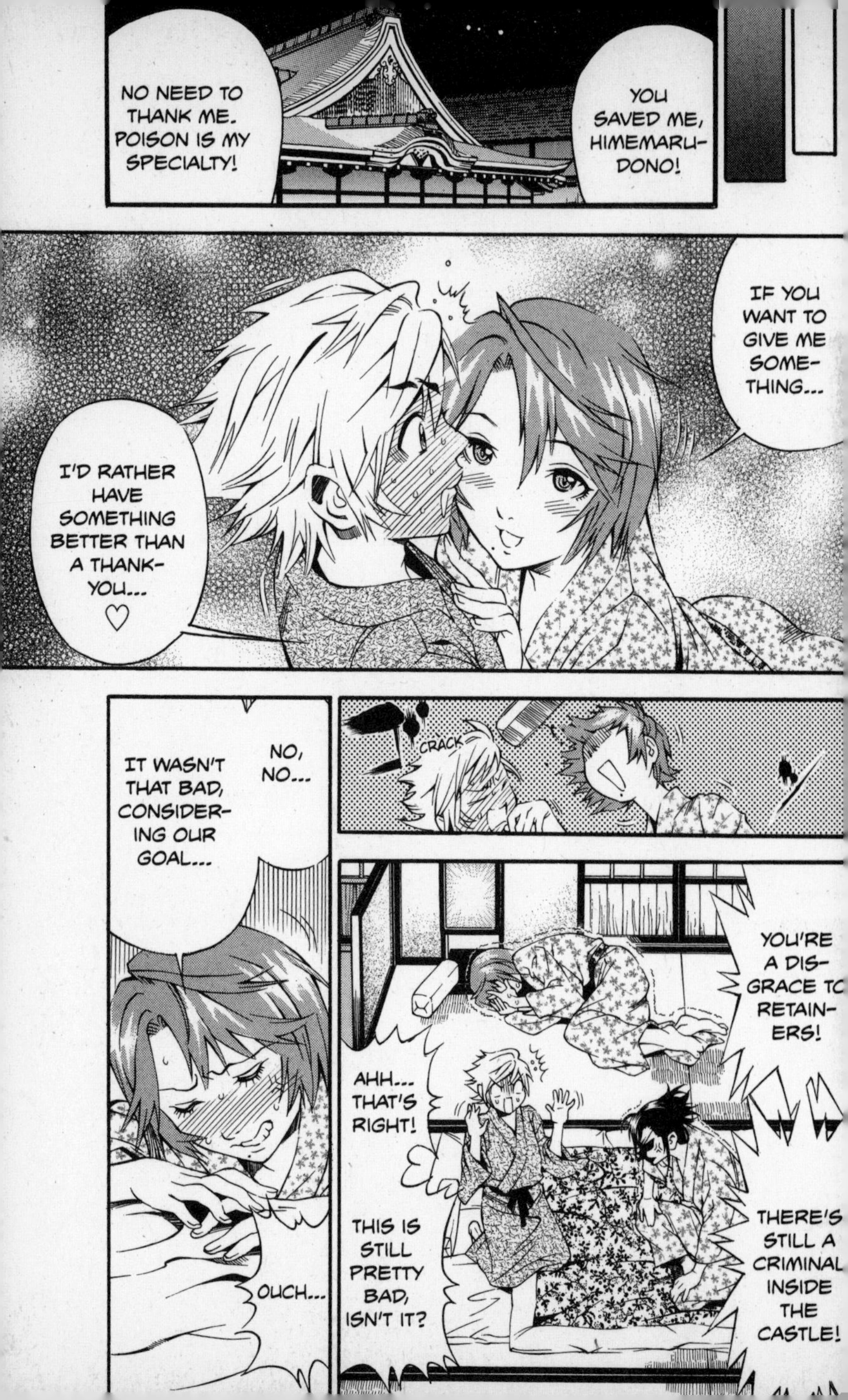
YOU SAVED ME, HIMEMARU-DONO!
NO NEED TO THANK ME. POISON IS MY SPECIALTY!
IF YOU WANT TO GIVE ME SOME-THING...
I'D RATHER HAVE SOMETHING BETTER THAN A THANK-YOU... ♡
CRACK
YOU'RE A DIS-GRACE TO RETAIN-ERS!
THERE'S STILL A CRIMINAL INSIDE THE CASTLE!
AHH... THAT'S RIGHT!
THIS IS STILL PRETTY BAD, ISN'T IT?
NO, NO...
IT WASN'T THAT BAD, CONSIDER-ING OUR GOAL...
OUCH...

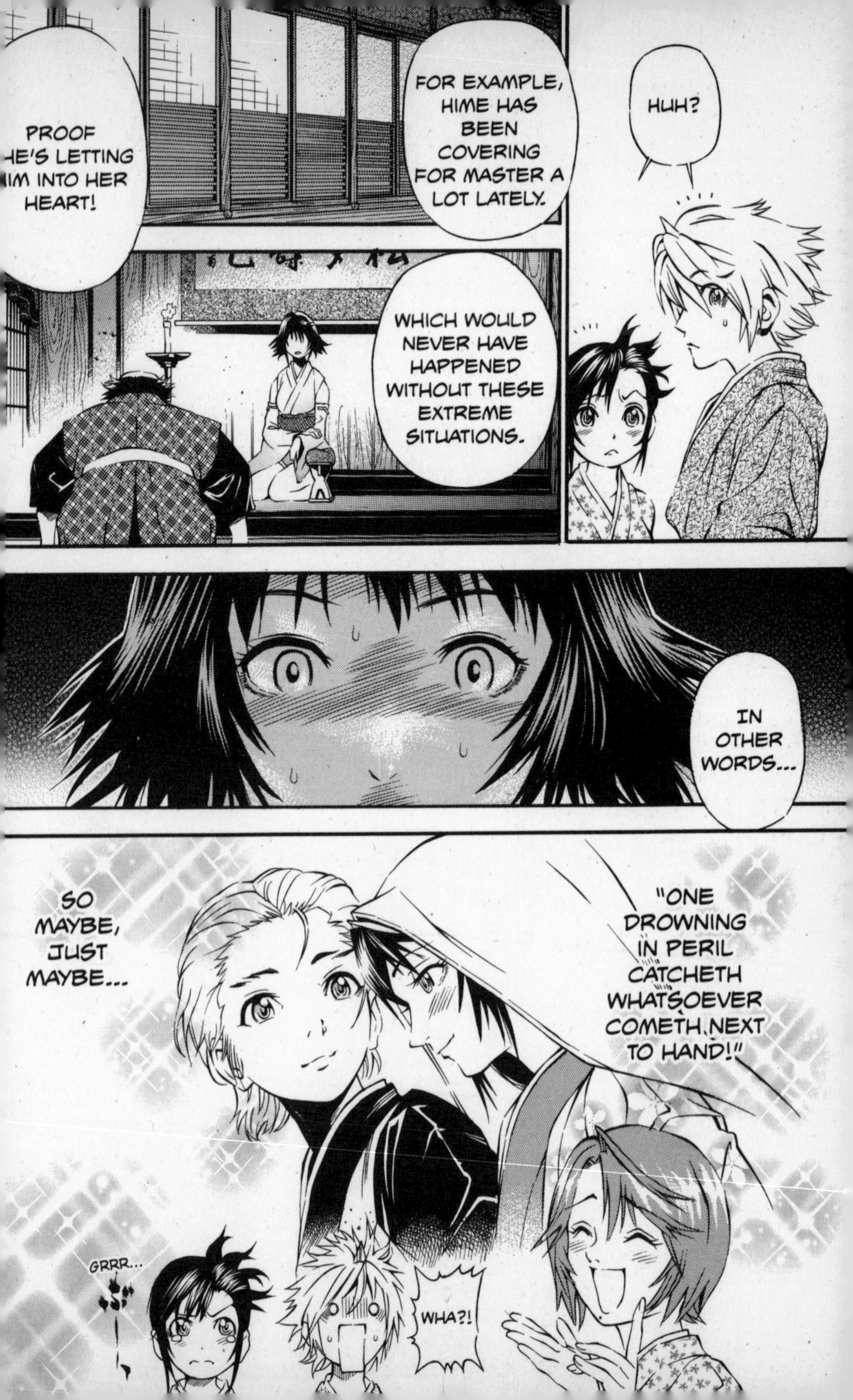
HUH?
FOR EXAMPLE, HIME HAS BEEN COVERING FOR MASTER A LOT LATELY.
WHICH WOULD NEVER HAVE HAPPENED WITHOUT THESE EXTREME SITUATIONS.
PROOF HE'S LETTING IM INTO HER HEART!
IN OTHER WORDS...
"ONE DROWNING IN PERIL CATCHETH WHATSOEVER COMETH NEXT TO HAND!"
SO MAYBE, JUST MAYBE...
WHA?!
GRRR...

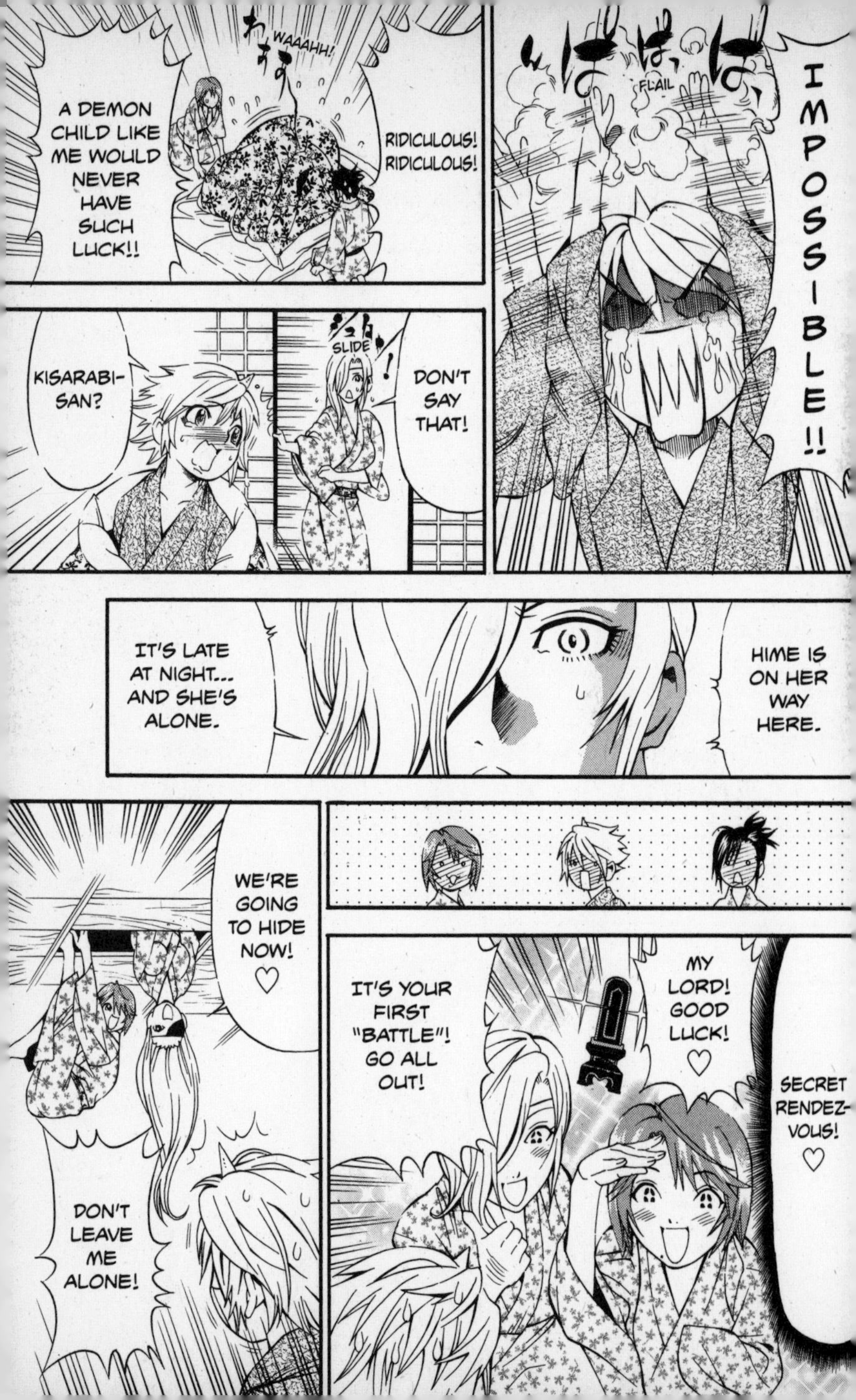
IMPOSSIBLE!!
FLAIL
WAAAHH!
RIDICULOUS! RIDICULOUS!
A DEMON CHILD LIKE ME WOULD NEVER HAVE SUCH LUCK!!
SLIDE
DON'T SAY THAT!
KISARABI-SAN?
HIME IS ON HER WAY HERE.
IT'S LATE AT NIGHT... AND SHE'S ALONE.
SECRET RENDEZ-VOUS! ♡
MY LORD! GOOD LUCK! ♡
IT'S YOUR FIRST "BATTLE"! GO ALL OUT!
WE'RE GOING TO HIDE NOW! ♡
DON'T LEAVE ME ALONE!

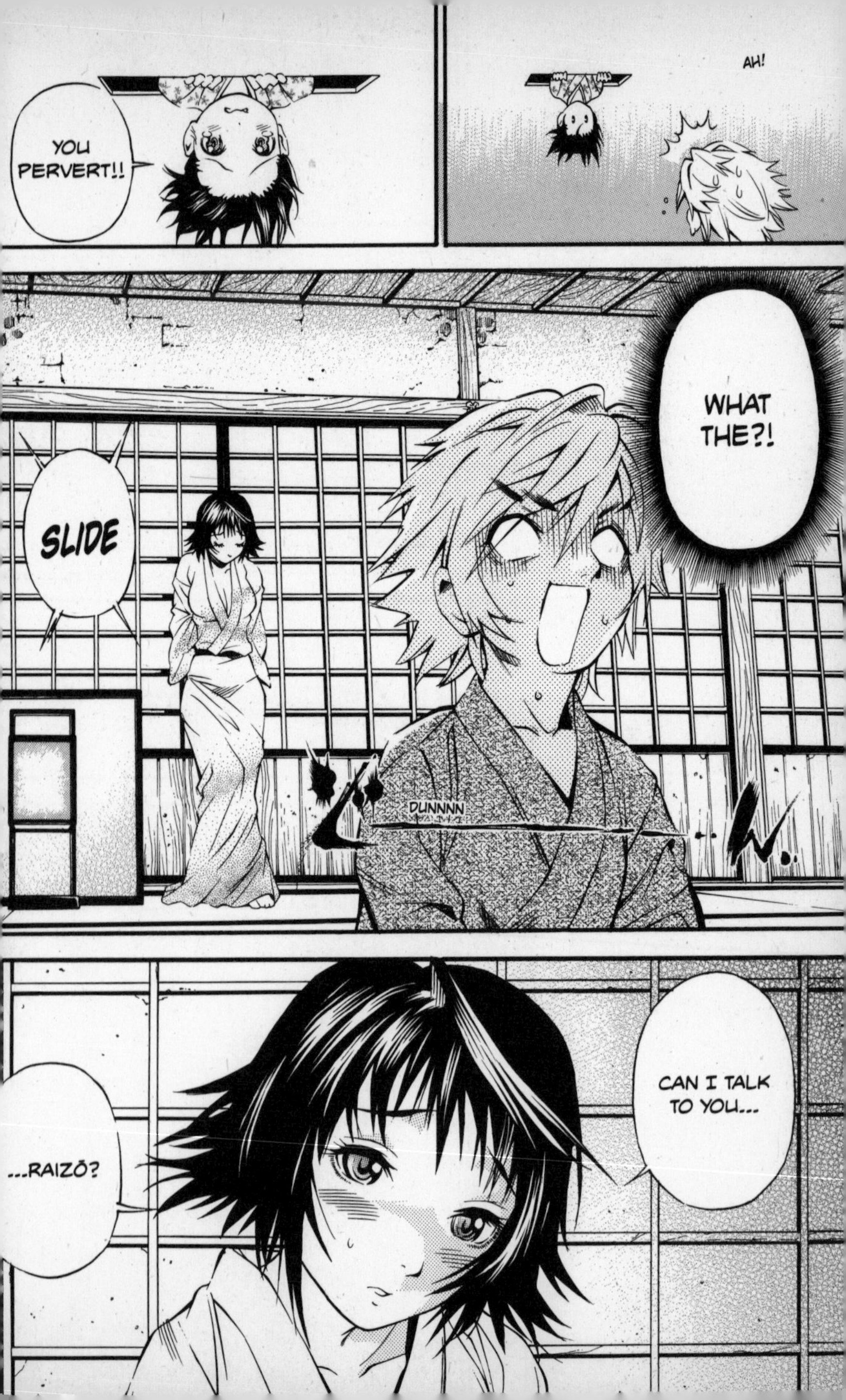
AH!
YOU PERVERT!!
WHAT THE?!
SLIDE
DUNNNN
CAN I TALK TO YOU...
...RAIZŌ?

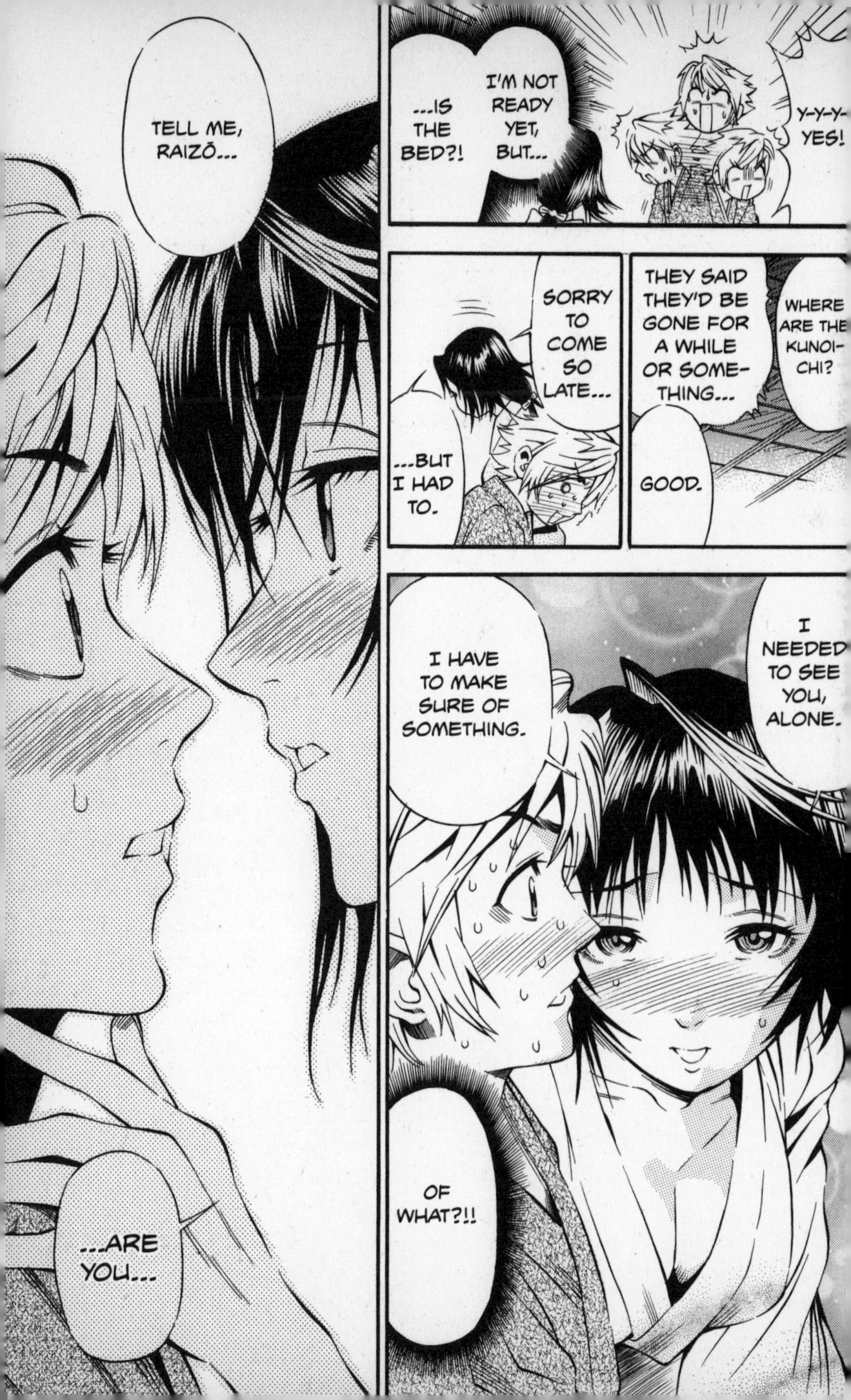
Y-Y-Y-YES!
I'M NOT READY YET, BUT...
...IS THE BED?!
WHERE ARE THE KUNOICHI?
THEY SAID THEY'D BE GONE FOR A WHILE OR SOMETHING...
GOOD.
SORRY TO COME SO LATE...
...BUT I HAD TO.
I NEEDED TO SEE YOU, ALONE.
I HAVE TO MAKE SURE OF SOMETHING.
OF WHAT?!!
TELL ME, RAIZŌ...
...ARE YOU...

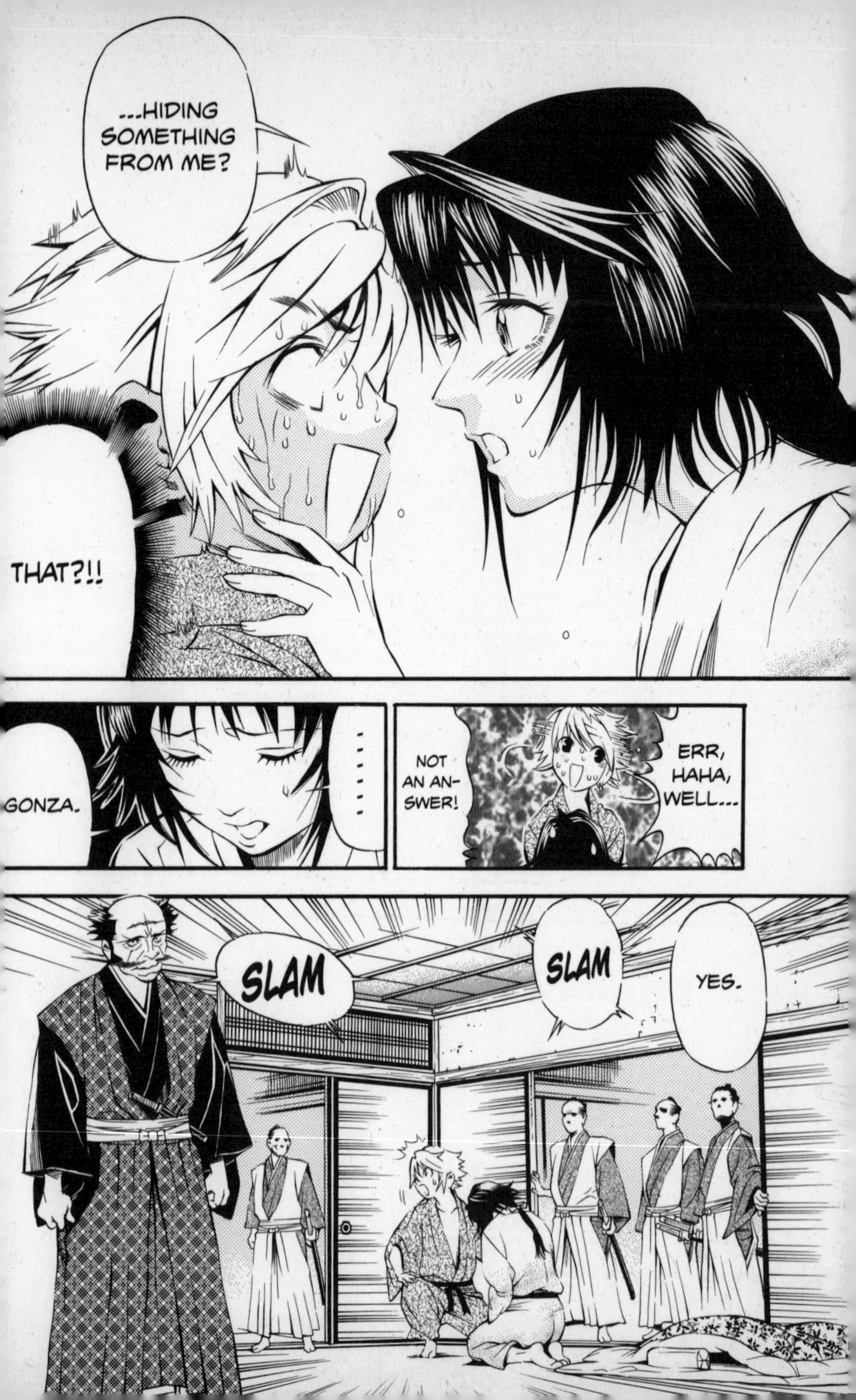
...HIDING SOMETHING FROM ME?
THAT?!!
ERR, HAHA, WELL...
NOT AN AN-SWER!
......
GONZA.
YES.
SLAM
SLAM

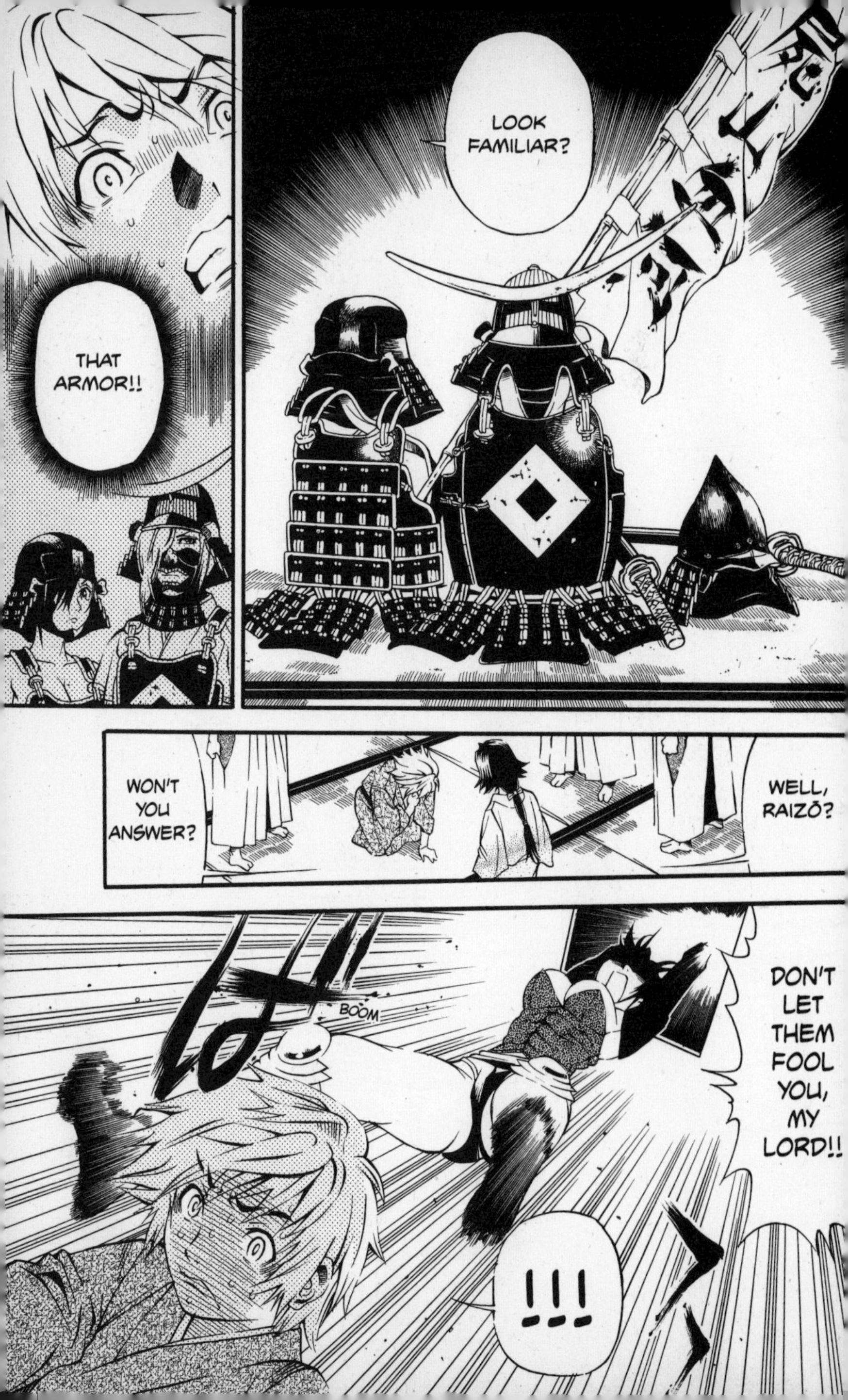
LOOK FAMILIAR?
THAT ARMOR!!
WELL, RAIZŌ?
WON'T YOU ANSWER?
DON'T LET THEM FOOL YOU, MY LORD!!
BOOM
!!!

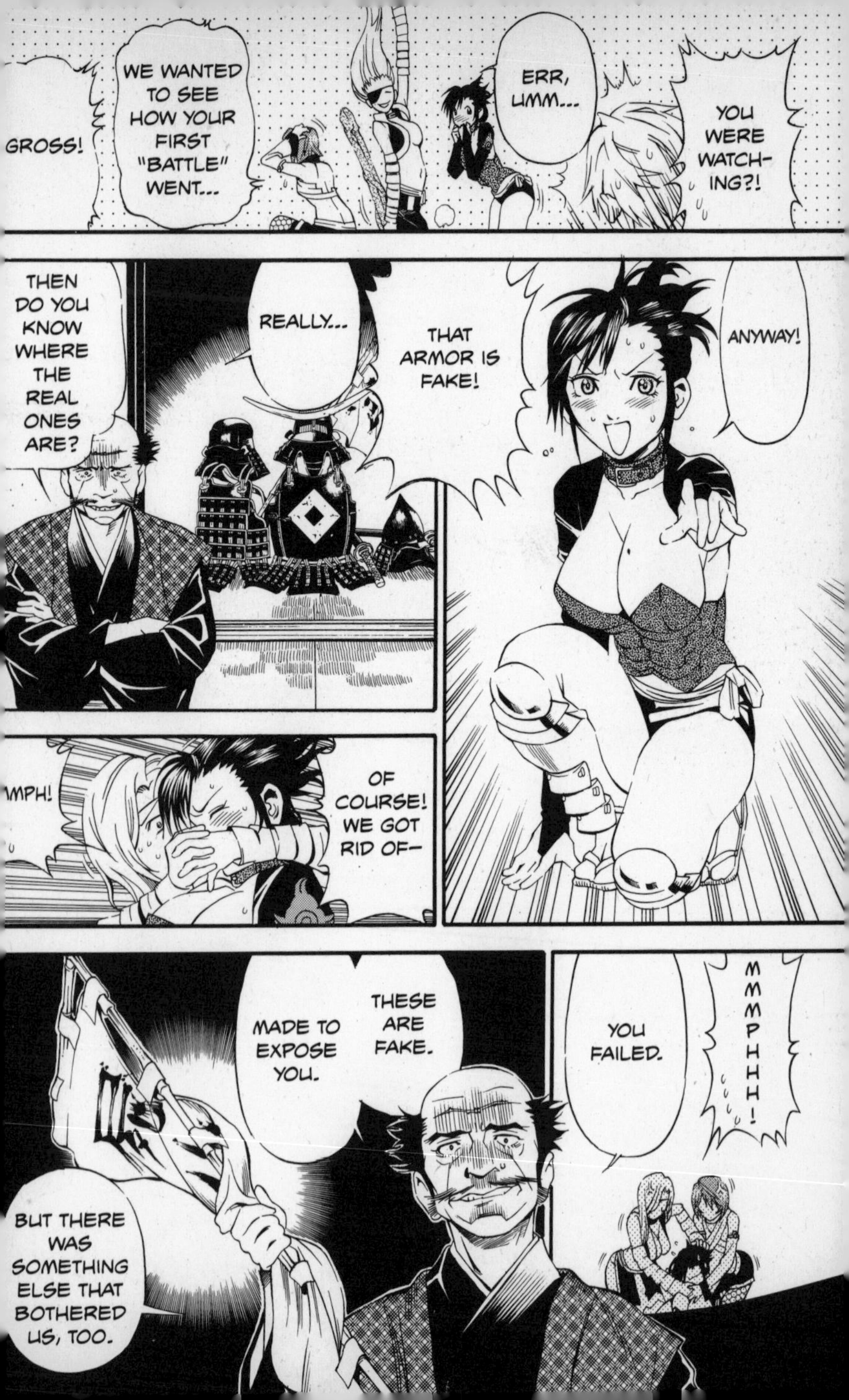
YOU WERE WATCHING?!
ERR, UMM...
WE WANTED TO SEE HOW YOUR FIRST "BATTLE" WENT...
GROSS!
ANYWAY!
THAT ARMOR IS FAKE!
REALLY...
THEN DO YOU KNOW WHERE THE REAL ONES ARE?
OF COURSE! WE GOT RID OF—
MPH!
MMMPHHH!
YOU FAILED.
THESE ARE FAKE.
MADE TO EXPOSE YOU.
BUT THERE WAS SOMETHING ELSE THAT BOTHERED US, TOO.

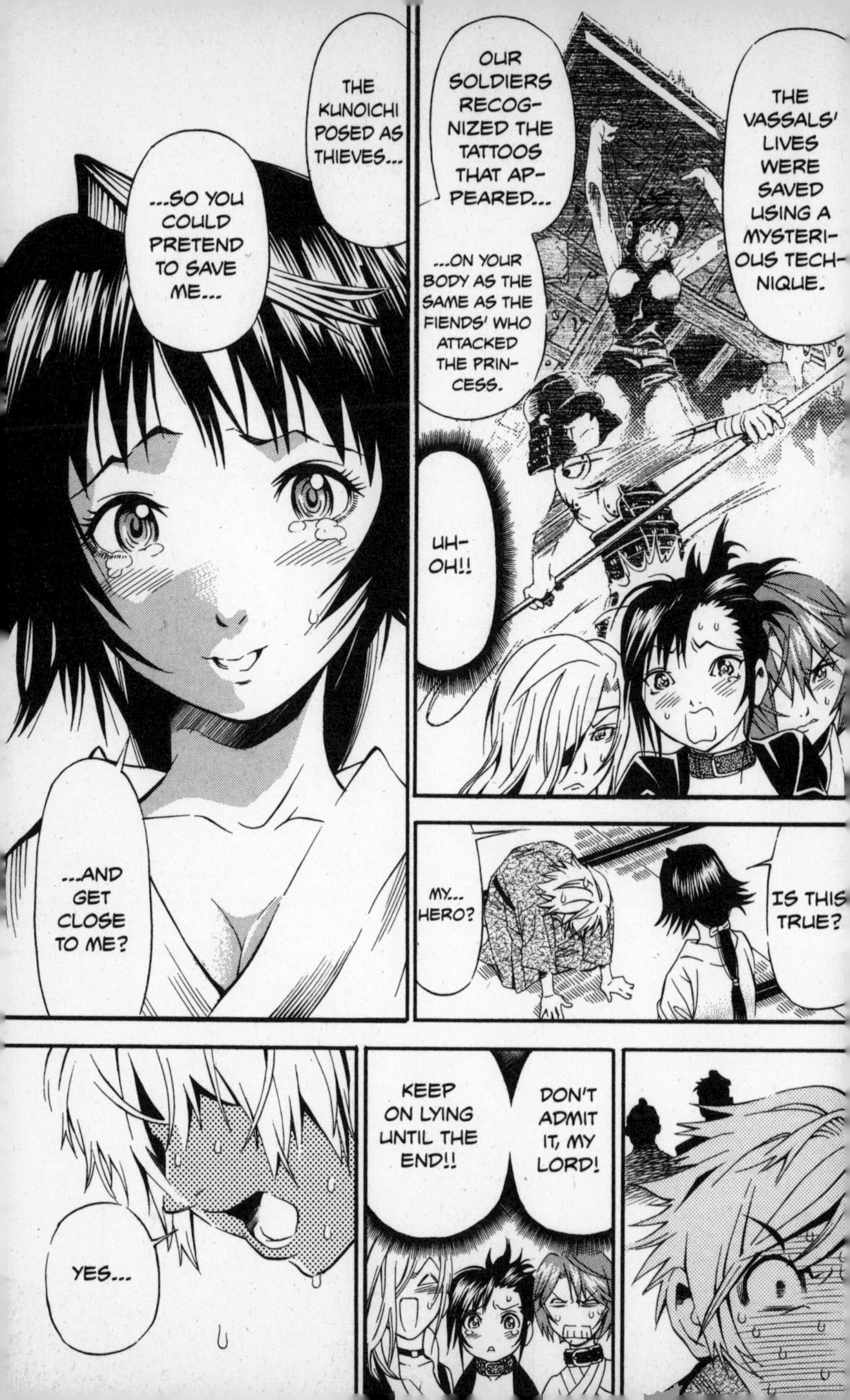
THE VASSALS' LIVES WERE SAVED USING A MYSTERIOUS TECHNIQUE.
OUR SOLDIERS RECOGNIZED THE TATTOOS THAT APPEARED...
...ON YOUR BODY AS THE SAME AS THE FIENDS' WHO ATTACKED THE PRINCESS.
UH-OH!!
IS THIS TRUE?
MY... HERO?
THE KUNOICHI POSED AS THIEVES...
...SO YOU COULD PRETEND TO SAVE ME...
...AND GET CLOSE TO ME?
DON'T ADMIT IT, MY LORD!
KEEP ON LYING UNTIL THE END!!
YES...

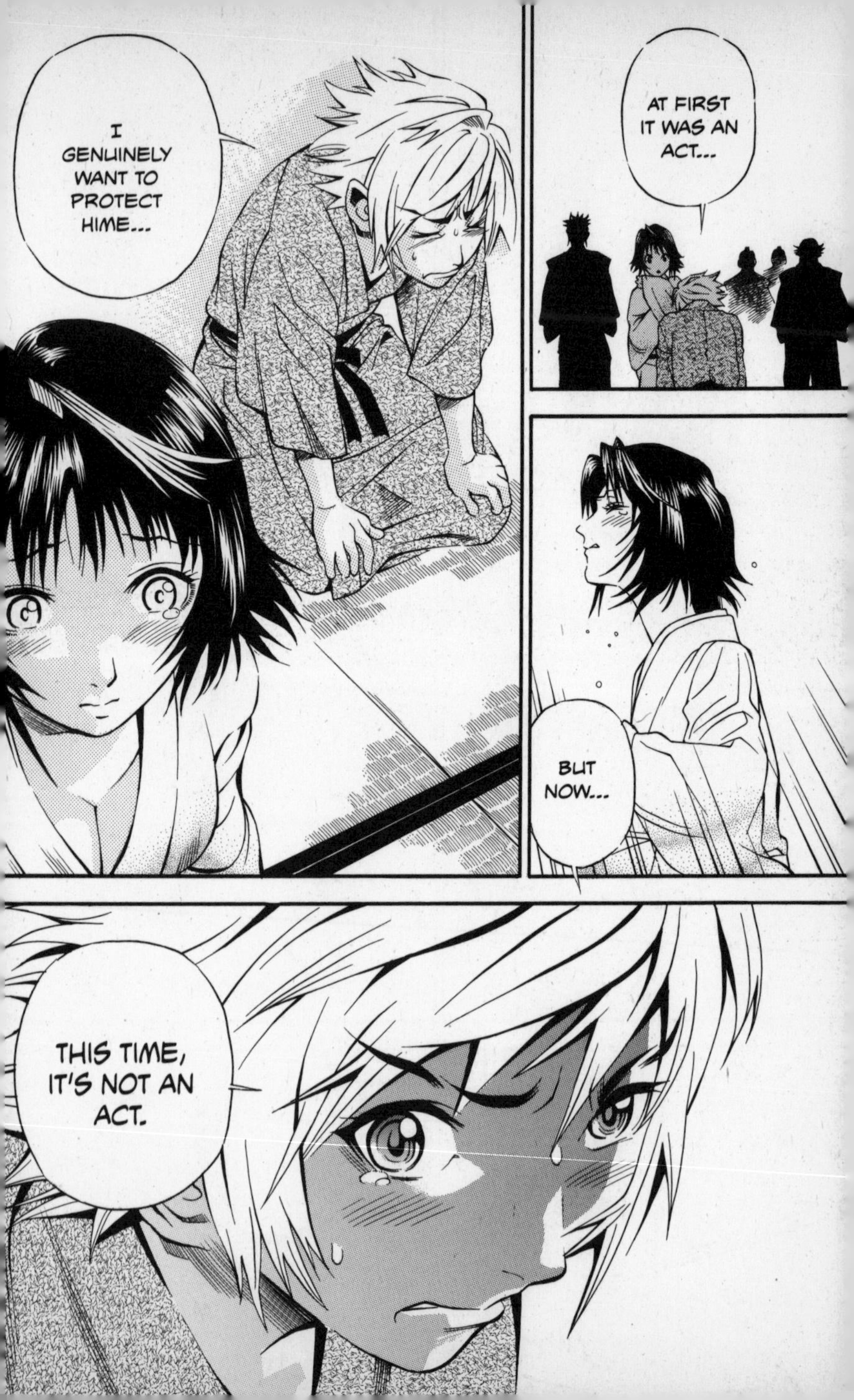
AT FIRST IT WAS AN ACT...
BUT NOW...
I GENUINELY WANT TO PROTECT HIME...
THIS TIME, IT'S NOT AN ACT.

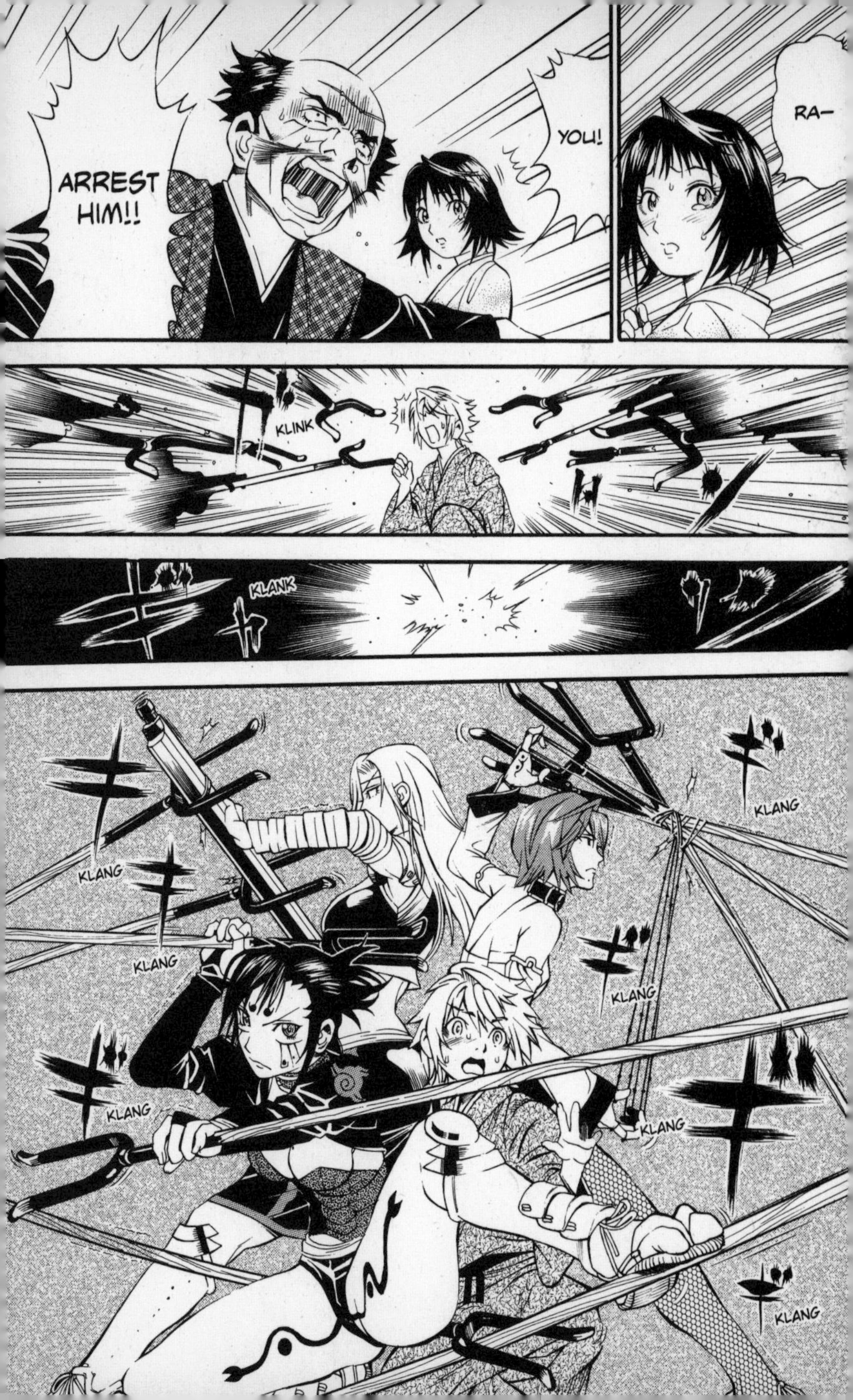
RA–
YOU!
ARREST HIM!!
KLINK
KLANK
KLANG
KLANG
KLANG
KLANG
KLANG
KLANG
KLANG

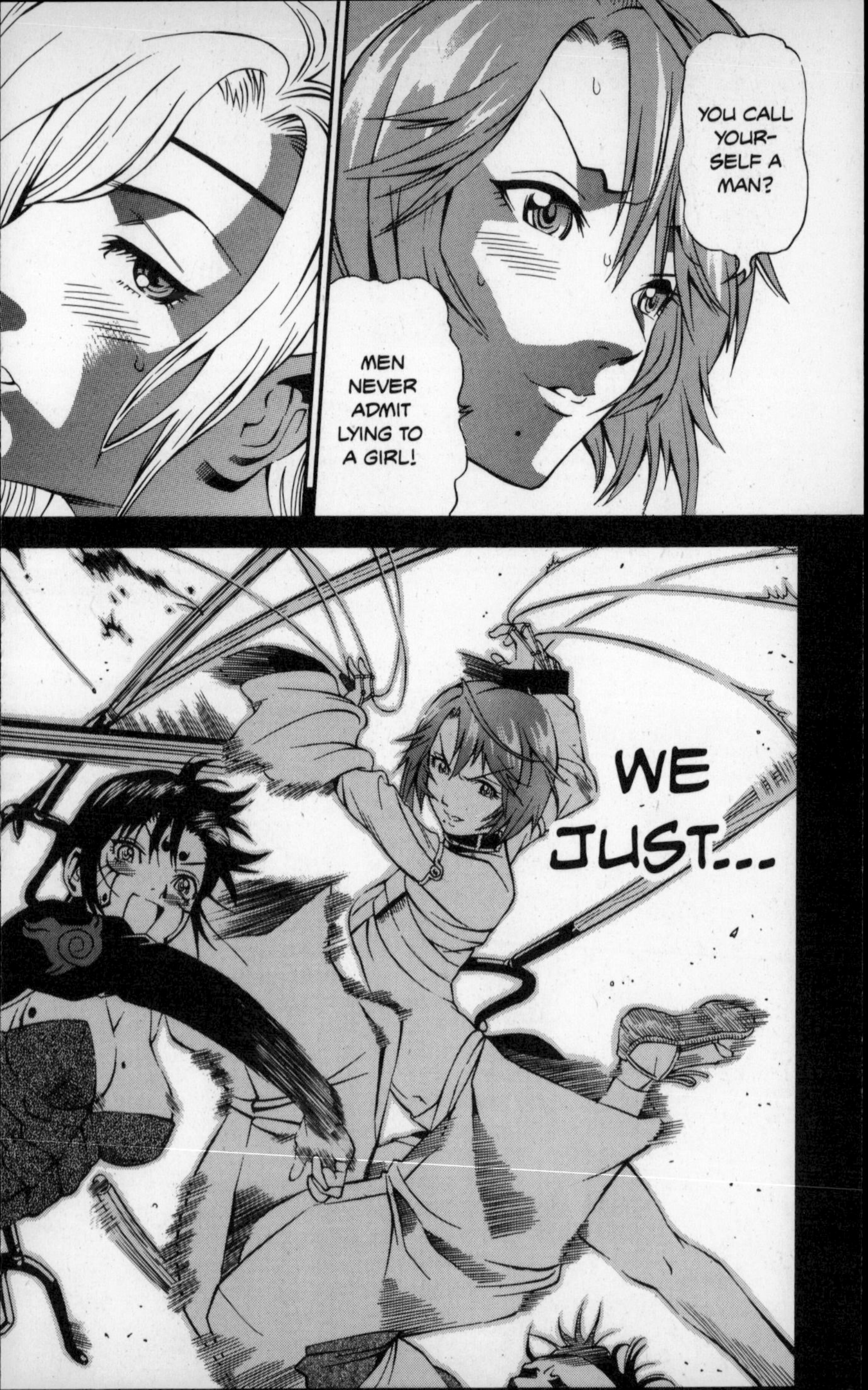
YOU CALL YOUR-SELF A MAN?
MEN NEVER ADMIT LYING TO A GIRL!
WE JUST...

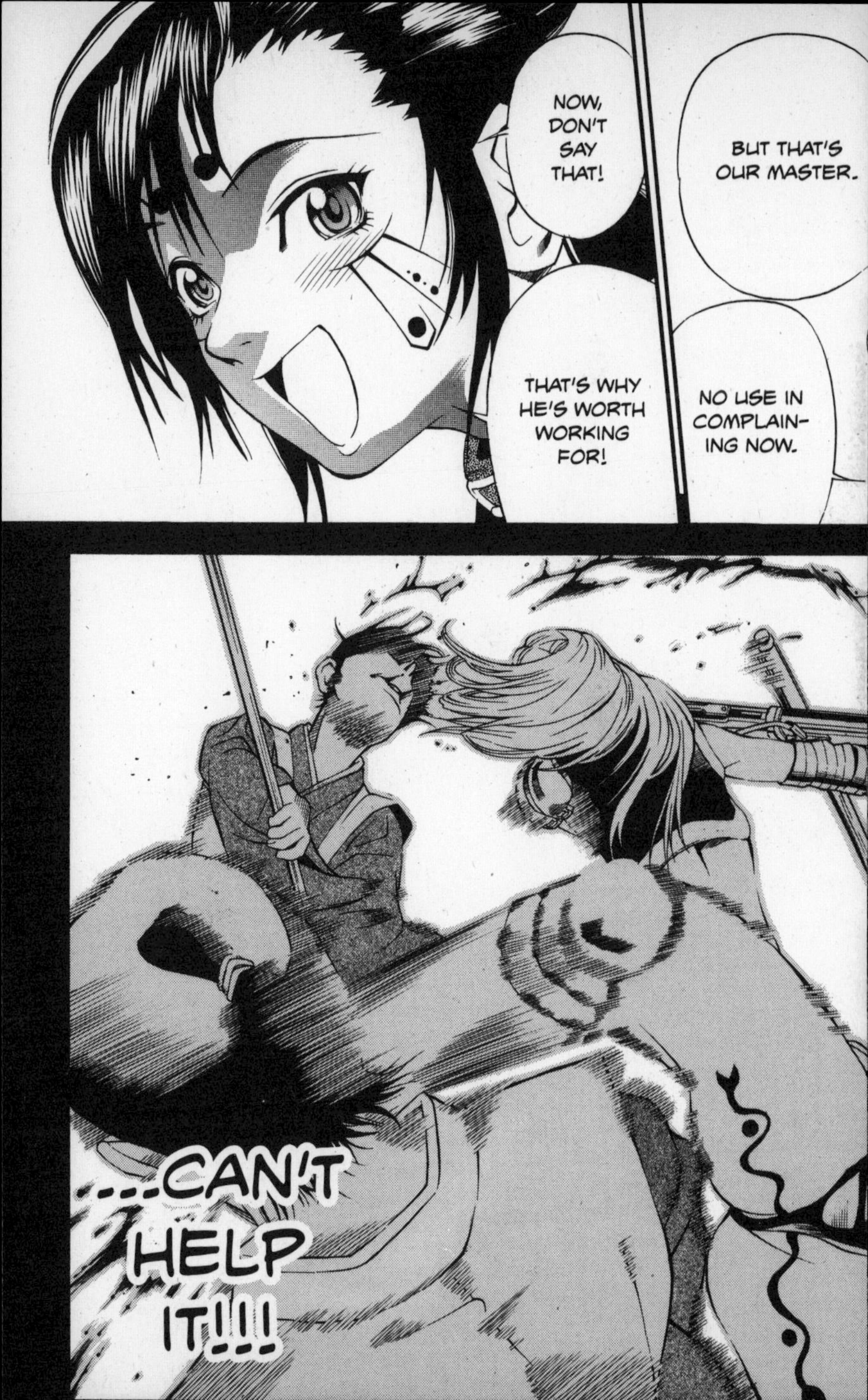
BUT THAT'S OUR MASTER.
NO USE IN COMPLAIN-ING NOW.
NOW, DON'T SAY THAT!
THAT'S WHY HE'S WORTH WORKING FOR!
...CAN'T HELP IT!!!

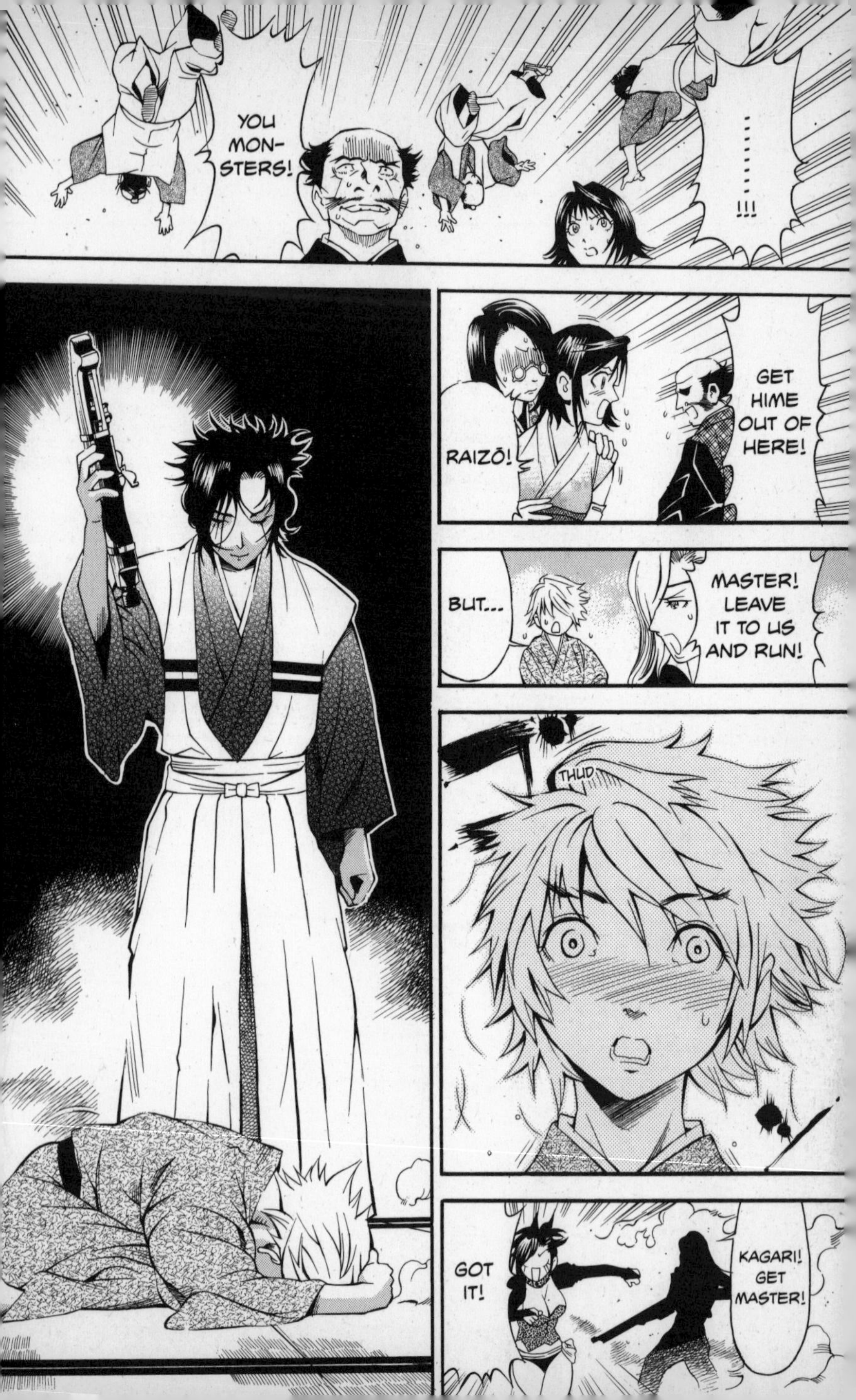
....
!!!
YOU MON-STERS!
GET HIME OUT OF HERE!
RAIZŌ!
MASTER! LEAVE IT TO US AND RUN!
BUT...
THUD
KAGARI! GET MASTER!
GOT IT!

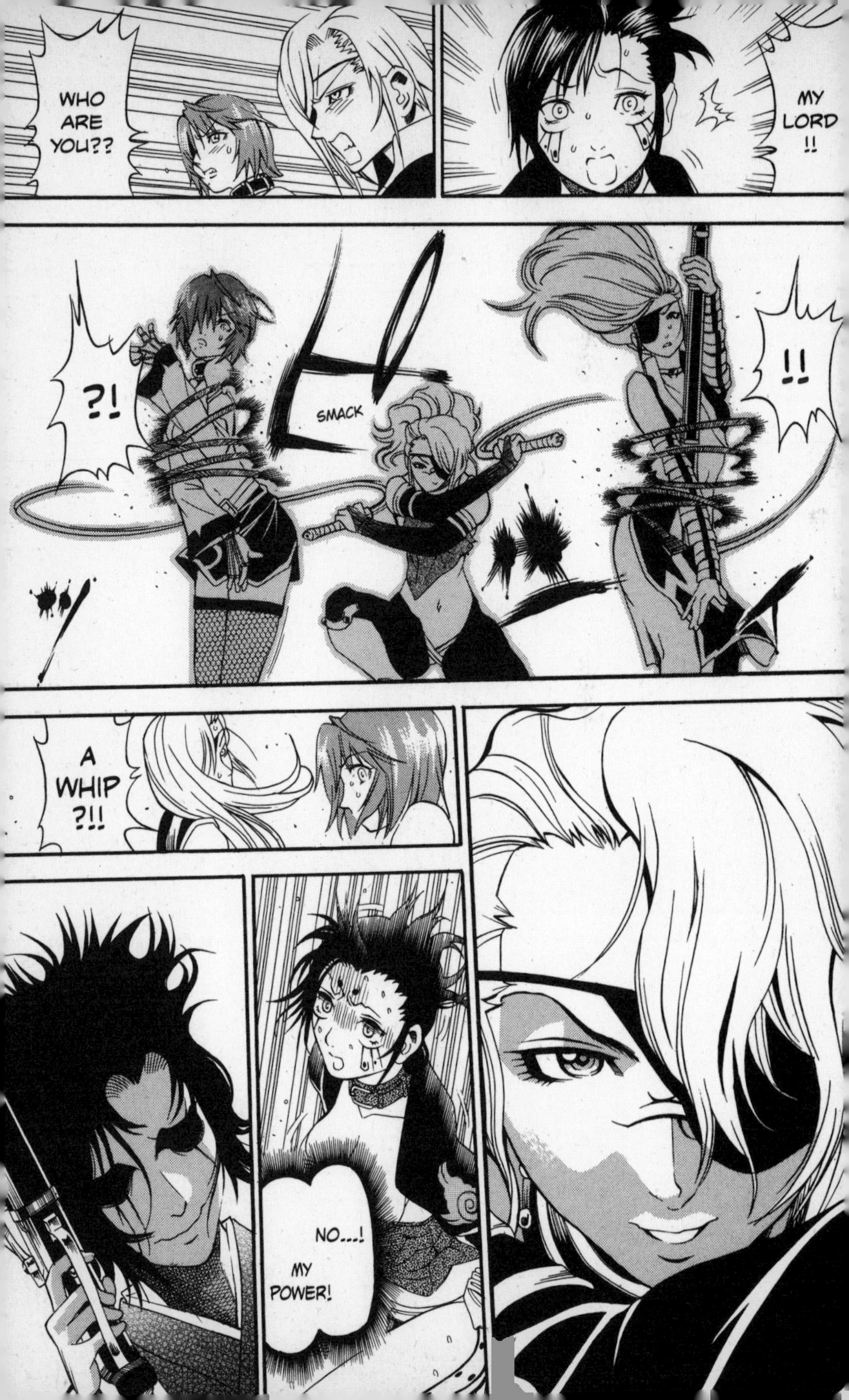
MY LORD !!
WHO ARE YOU??
!!
SMACK
?!
A WHIP ?!!
NO...!
MY POWER!

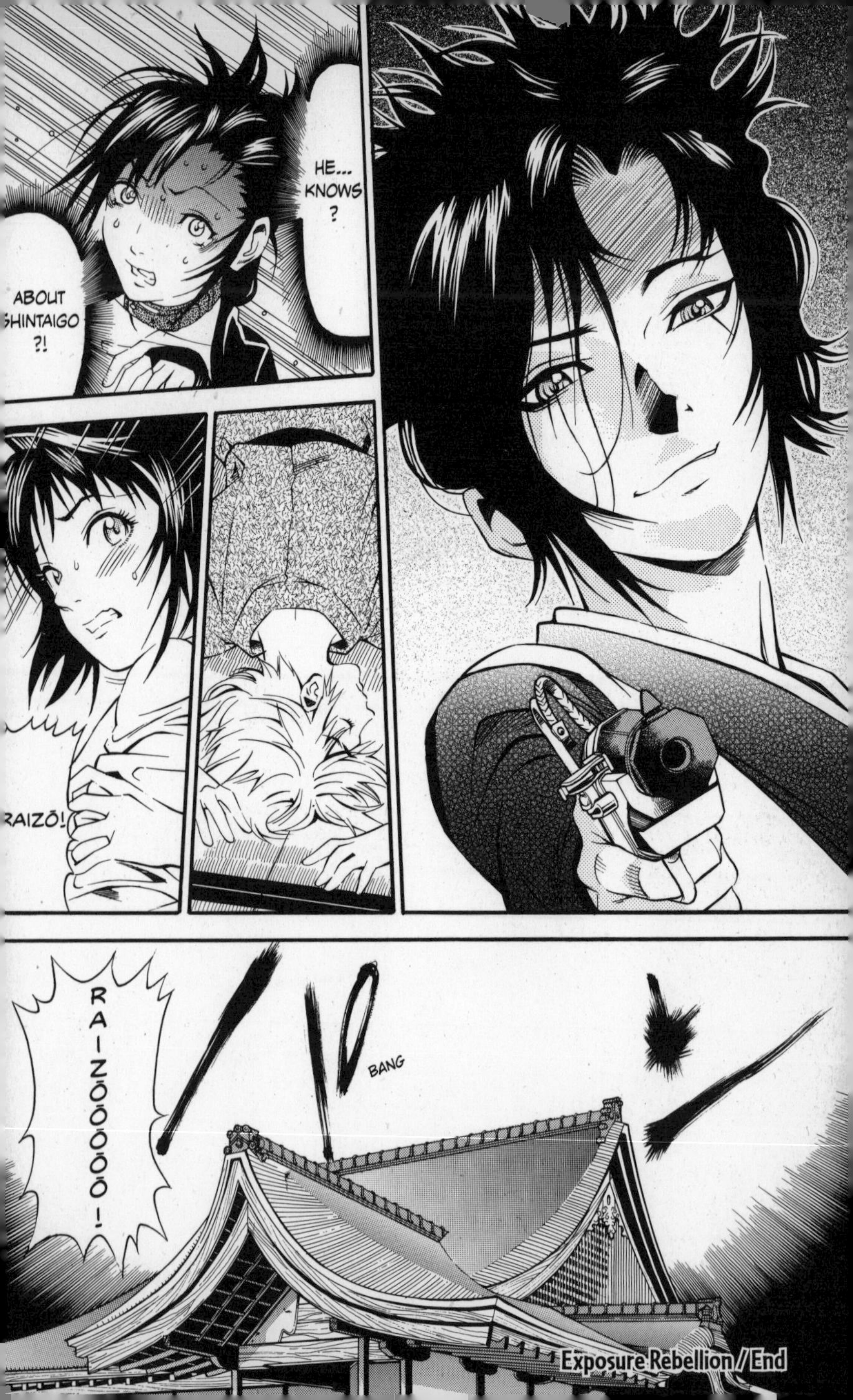
HE... KNOWS?
ABOUT SHINTAIGO?!
RAIZŌ!
BANG
RAIZŌŌŌŌŌ!
Exposure Rebellion / End

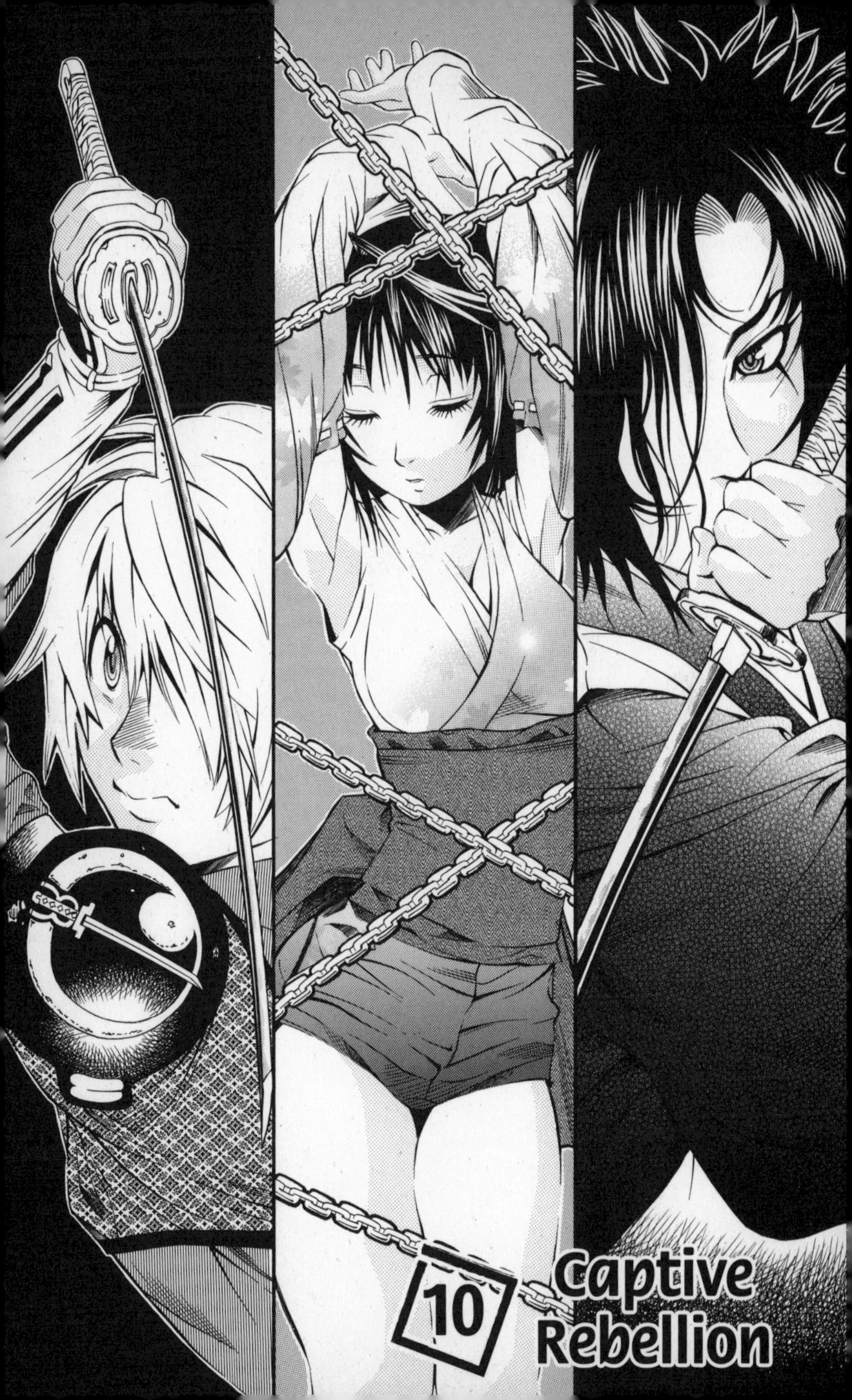
10
Captive
Rebellion

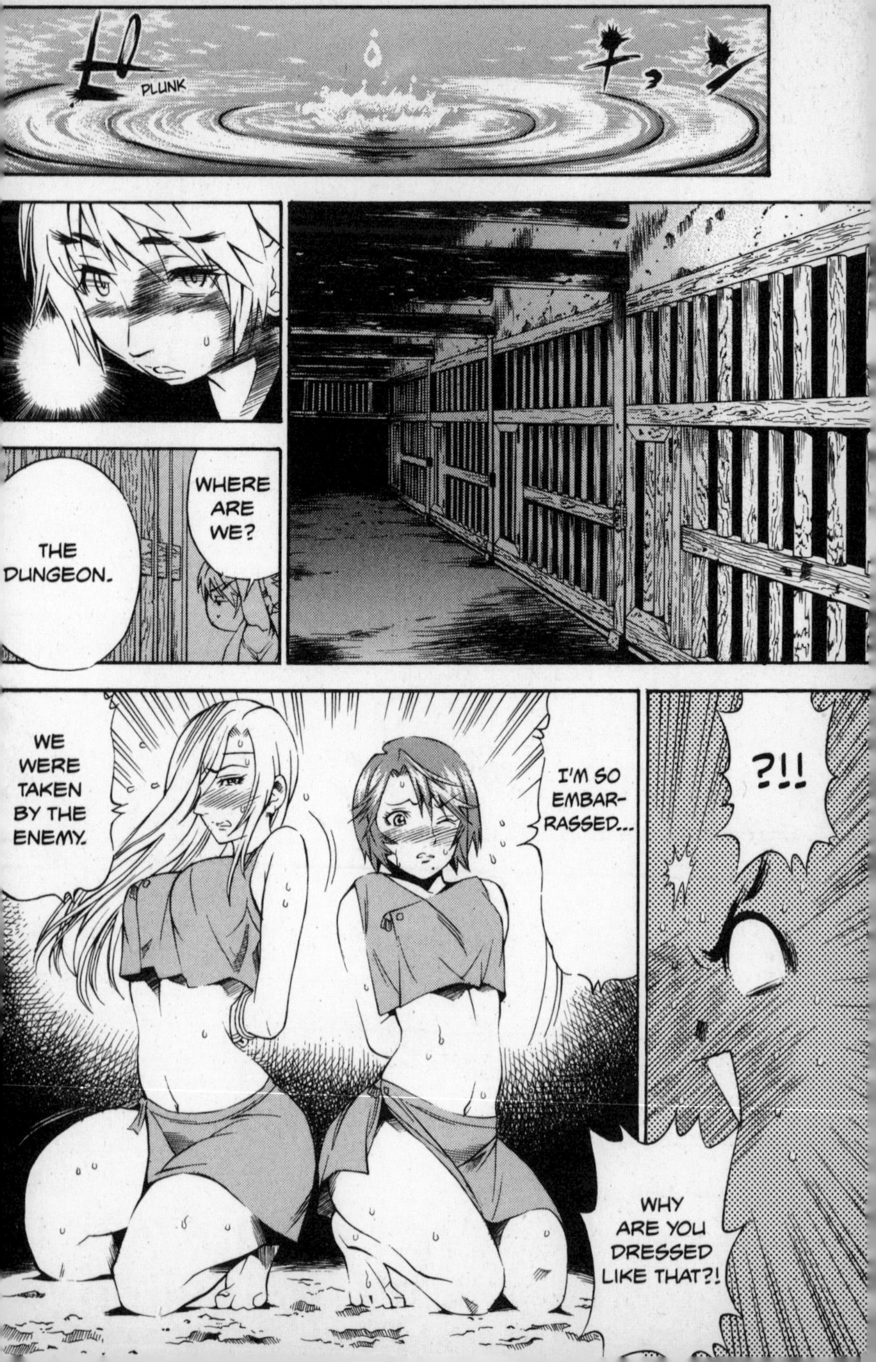
PLUNK
WHERE ARE WE?
THE DUNGEON.
?!!
WHY ARE YOU DRESSED LIKE THAT?!
I'M SO EMBARRASSED...
WE WERE TAKEN BY THE ENEMY.

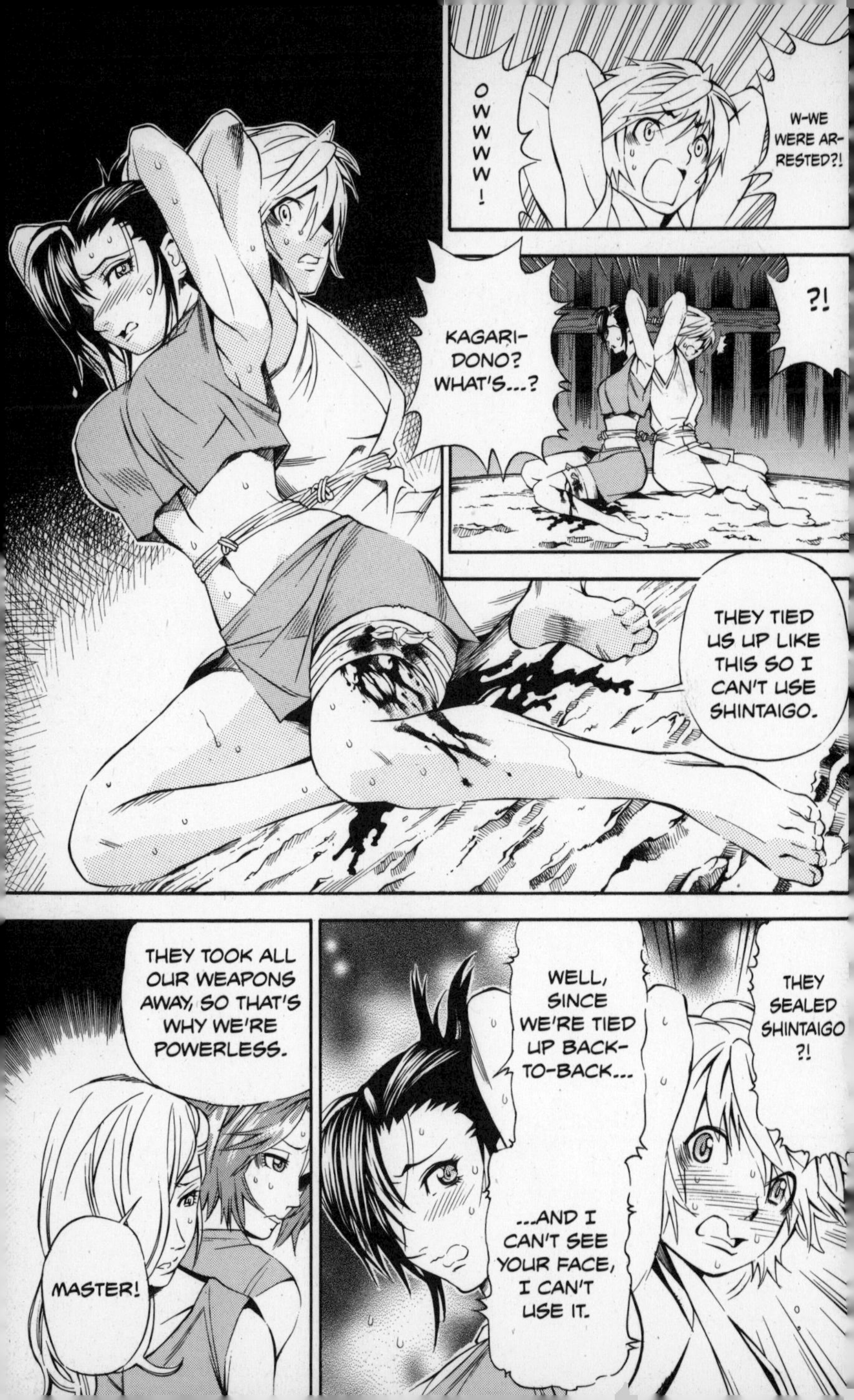
W-WE WERE ARRESTED?!
OWWWW!
?!
KAGARI-DONO? WHAT'S...?
THEY TIED US UP LIKE THIS SO I CAN'T USE SHINTAIGO.
THEY SEALED SHINTAIGO?!
WELL, SINCE WE'RE TIED UP BACK-TO-BACK...
...AND I CAN'T SEE YOUR FACE, I CAN'T USE IT.
THEY TOOK ALL OUR WEAPONS AWAY, SO THAT'S WHY WE'RE POWERLESS.
MASTER!

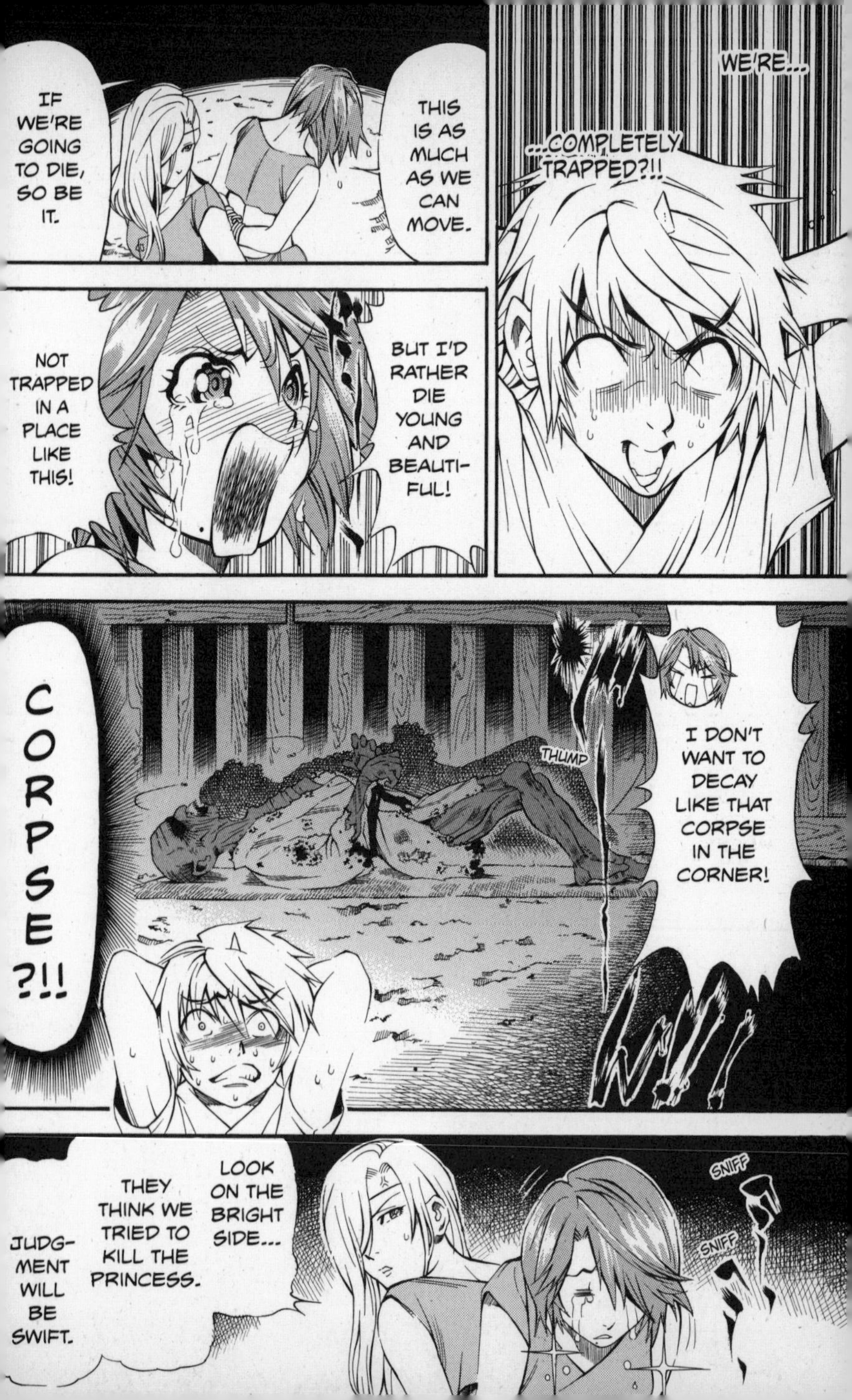
WE'RE...
...COMPLETELY TRAPPED?!!
THIS IS AS MUCH AS WE CAN MOVE.
IF WE'RE GOING TO DIE, SO BE IT.
BUT I'D RATHER DIE YOUNG AND BEAUTIFUL!
NOT TRAPPED IN A PLACE LIKE THIS!
I DON'T WANT TO DECAY LIKE THAT CORPSE IN THE CORNER!
THUMP
CORPSE?!!
SNIFF
SNIFF
LOOK ON THE BRIGHT SIDE...
THEY THINK WE TRIED TO KILL THE PRINCESS.
JUDGMENT WILL BE SWIFT.

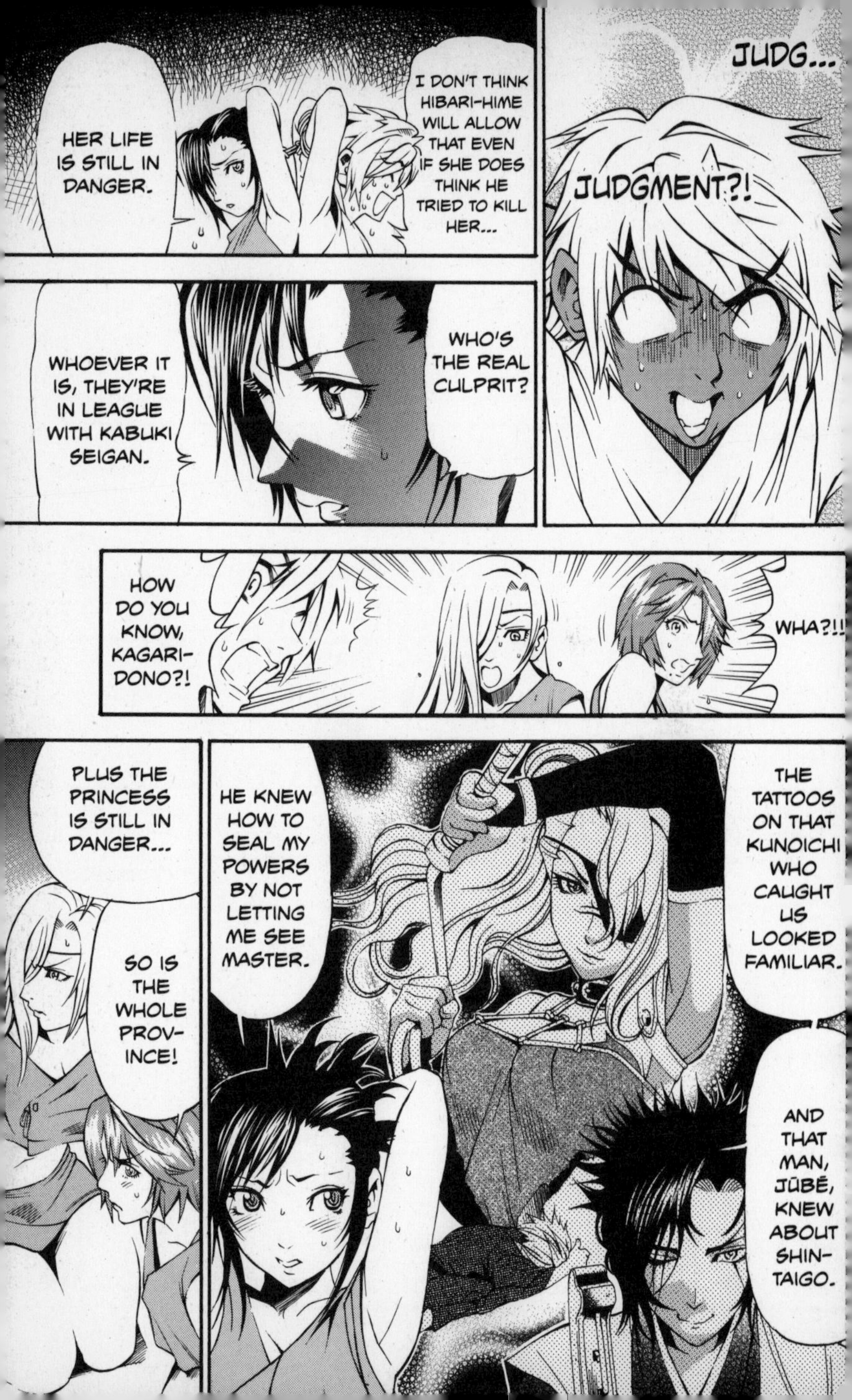

JUDG...
JUDGMENT?!
I DON'T THINK HIBARI-HIME WILL ALLOW THAT EVEN IF SHE DOES THINK HE TRIED TO KILL HER...
HER LIFE IS STILL IN DANGER.
WHO'S THE REAL CULPRIT?
WHOEVER IT IS, THEY'RE IN LEAGUE WITH KABUKI SEIGAN.
WHA?!!
HOW DO YOU KNOW, KAGARI-DONO?!
THE TATTOOS ON THAT KUNOICHI WHO CAUGHT US LOOKED FAMILIAR.
AND THAT MAN, JŪBĒ, KNEW ABOUT SHIN-TAIGO.
HE KNEW HOW TO SEAL MY POWERS BY NOT LETTING ME SEE MASTER.
PLUS THE PRINCESS IS STILL IN DANGER...
SO IS THE WHOLE PROVINCE!

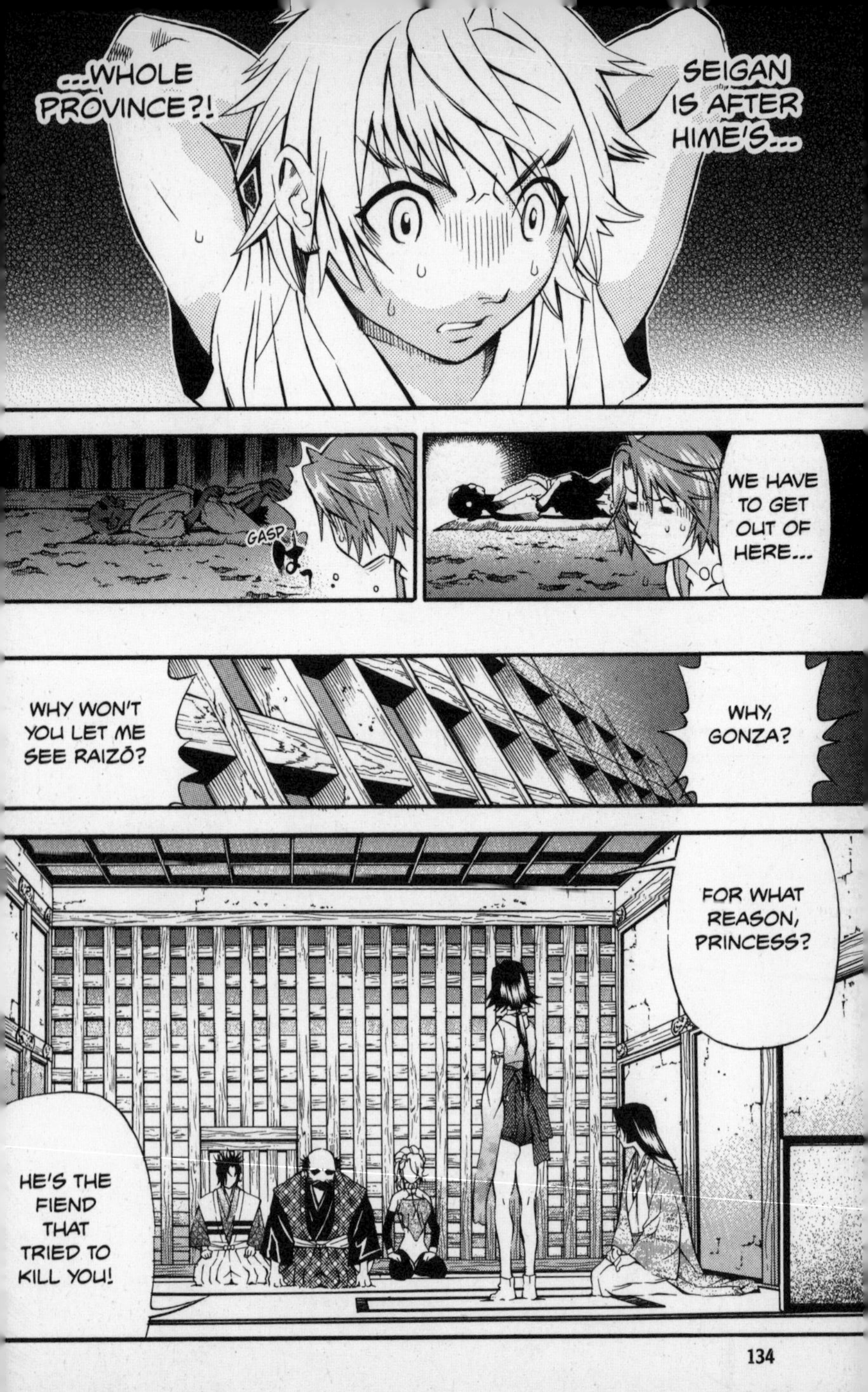
SEIGAN IS AFTER HIME'S...
...WHOLE PROVINCE?!
WE HAVE TO GET OUT OF HERE...
GASP
WHY, GONZA?
WHY WON'T YOU LET ME SEE RAIZŌ?
FOR WHAT REASON, PRINCESS?
HE'S THE FIEND THAT TRIED TO KILL YOU!

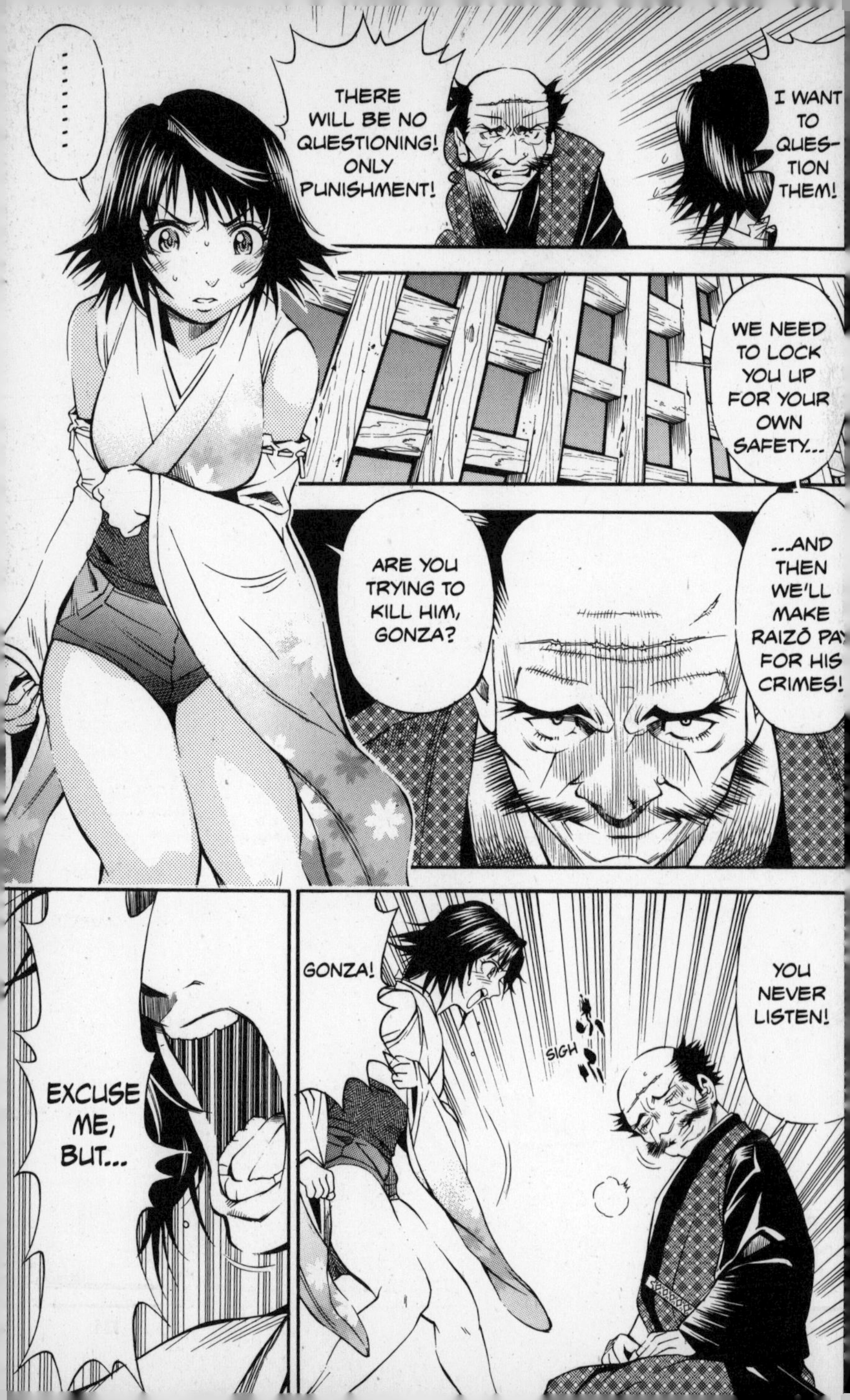
I WANT TO QUESTION THEM!
THERE WILL BE NO QUESTIONING! ONLY PUNISHMENT!
WE NEED TO LOCK YOU UP FOR YOUR OWN SAFETY...
...AND THEN WE'LL MAKE RAIZŌ PAY FOR HIS CRIMES!
ARE YOU TRYING TO KILL HIM, GONZA?
......
YOU NEVER LISTEN!
SIGH
GONZA!
EXCUSE ME, BUT...

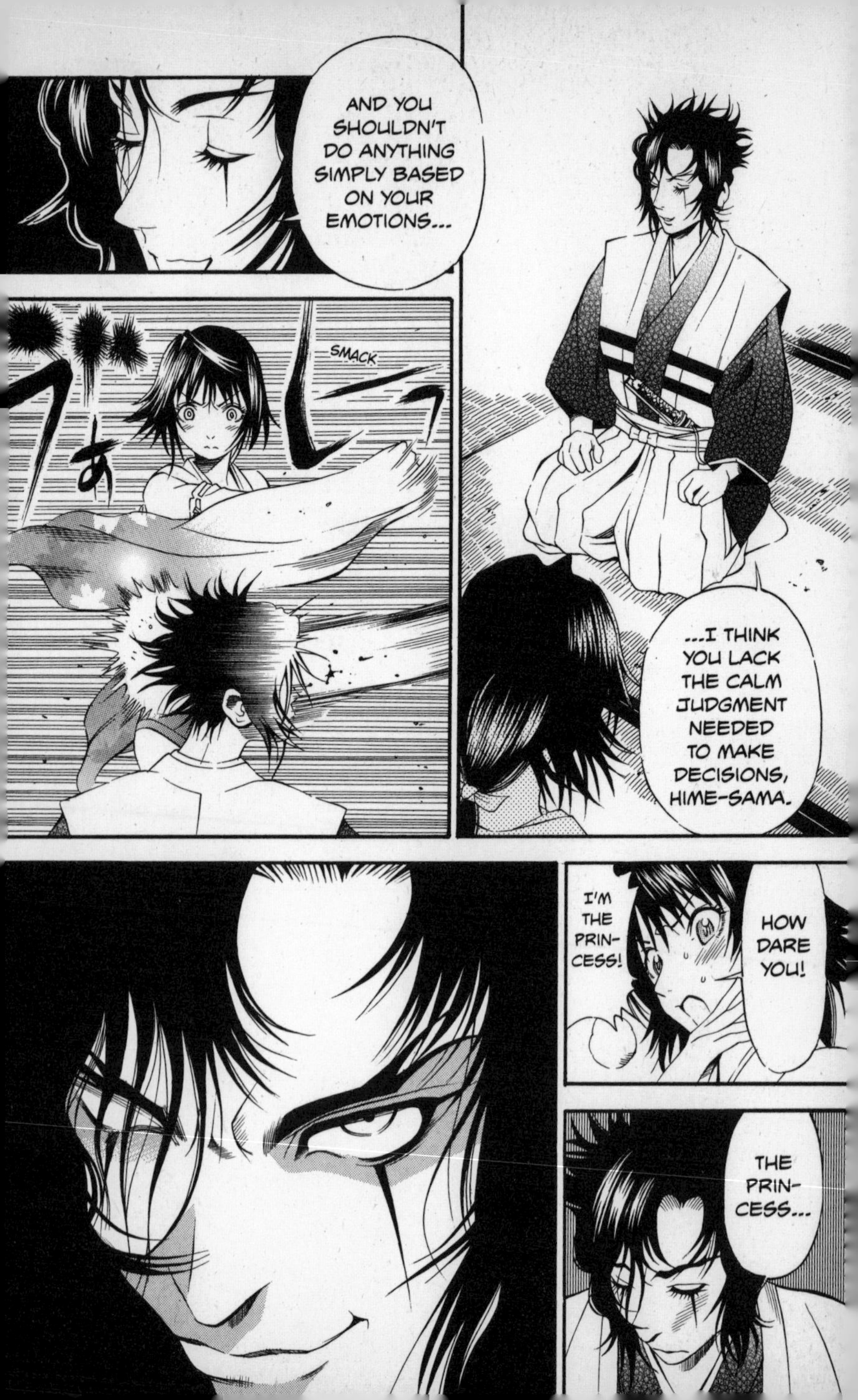
...I THINK YOU LACK THE CALM JUDGMENT NEEDED TO MAKE DECISIONS, HIME-SAMA.
AND YOU SHOULDN'T DO ANYTHING SIMPLY BASED ON YOUR EMOTIONS...
SMACK
HOW DARE YOU!
I'M THE PRIN-CESS!
THE PRIN-CESS...

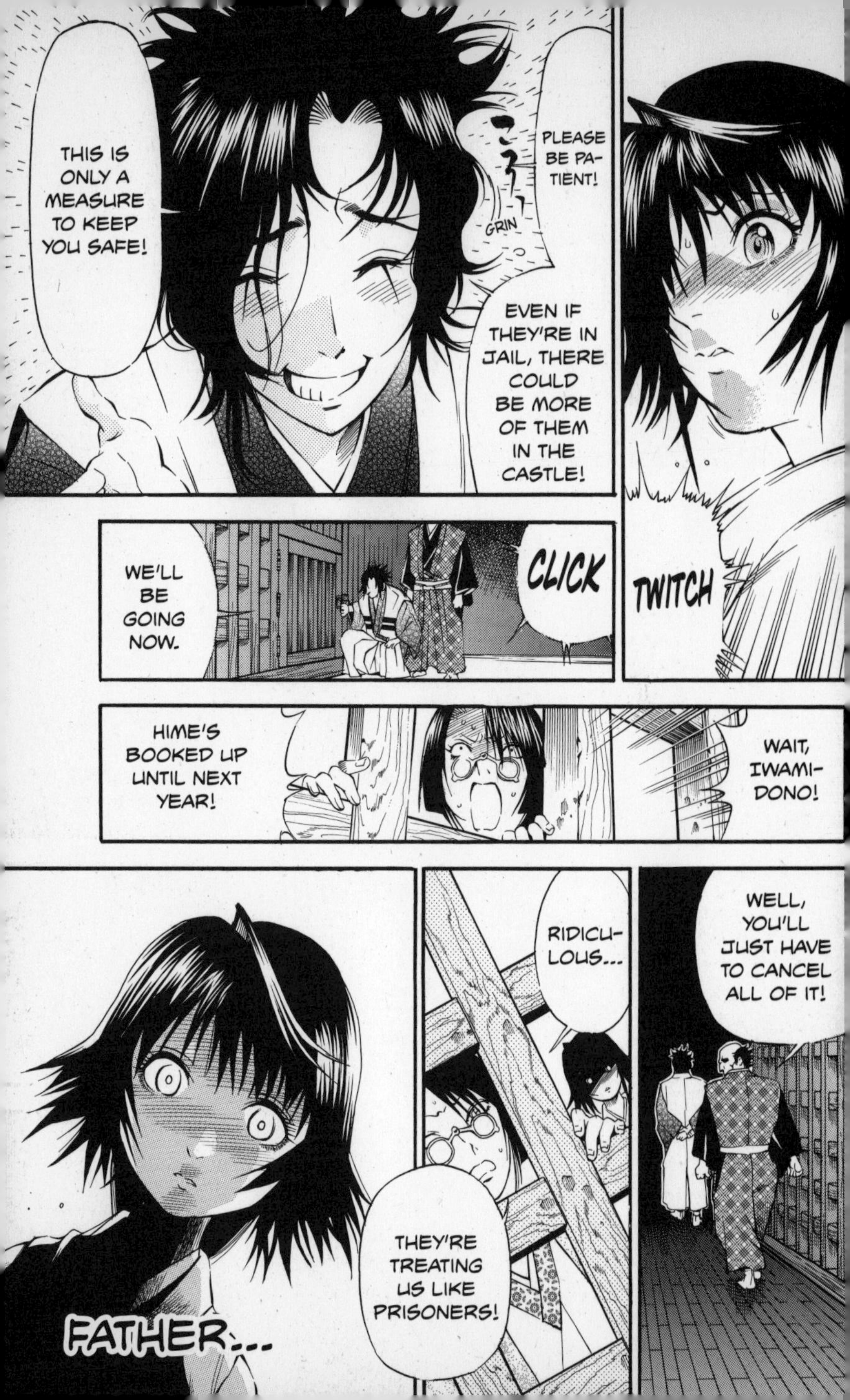
TWITCH
PLEASE BE PATIENT!
GRIN
EVEN IF THEY'RE IN JAIL, THERE COULD BE MORE OF THEM IN THE CASTLE!
THIS IS ONLY A MEASURE TO KEEP YOU SAFE!
CLICK
WE'LL BE GOING NOW.
WAIT, IWAMI-DONO!
HIME'S BOOKED UP UNTIL NEXT YEAR!
WELL, YOU'LL JUST HAVE TO CANCEL ALL OF IT!
RIDICULOUS...
THEY'RE TREATING US LIKE PRISONERS!
FATHER...

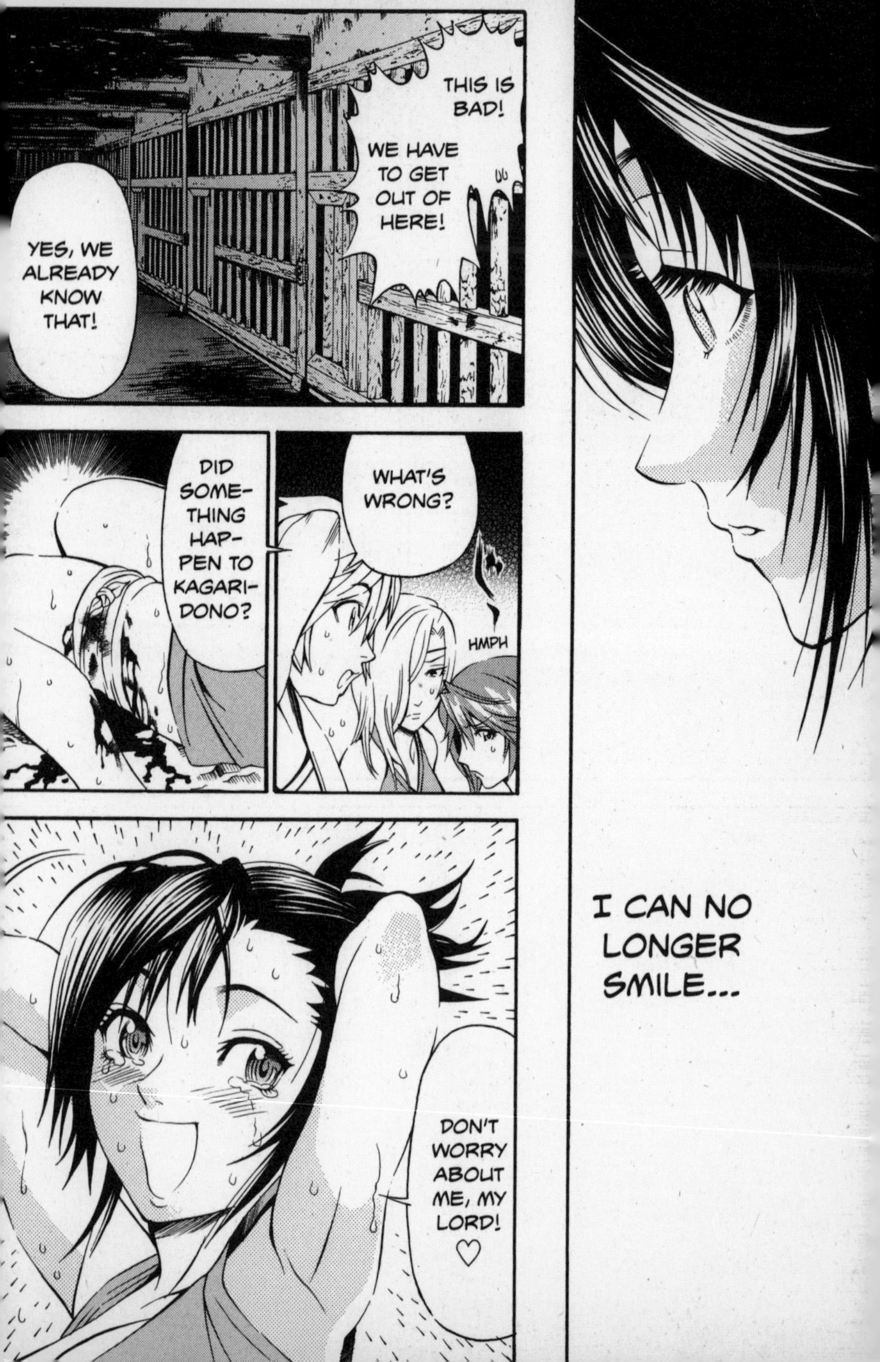
I CAN NO LONGER SMILE...
THIS IS BAD!
WE HAVE TO GET OUT OF HERE!
YES, WE ALREADY KNOW THAT!
WHAT'S WRONG?
HMPH
DID SOMETHING HAPPEN TO KAGARI-DONO?
DON'T WORRY ABOUT ME, MY LORD! ♡

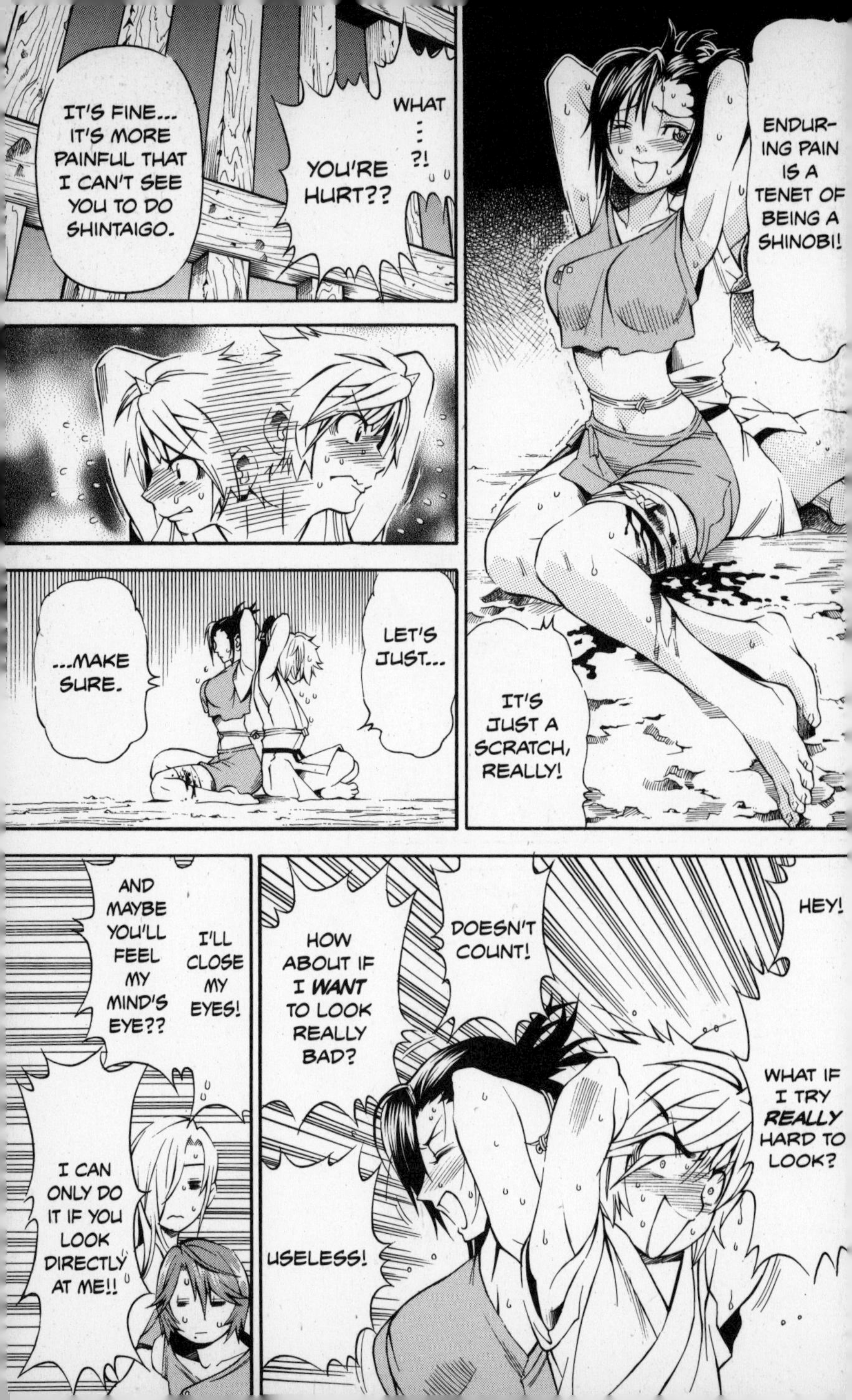
ENDURING PAIN IS A TENET OF BEING A SHINOBI!
IT'S JUST A SCRATCH, REALLY!
WHAT...?!
YOU'RE HURT??
IT'S FINE... IT'S MORE PAINFUL THAT I CAN'T SEE YOU TO DO SHINTAIGO.
LET'S JUST...
...MAKE SURE.
HEY!
DOESN'T COUNT!
HOW ABOUT IF I *WANT* TO LOOK REALLY BAD?
WHAT IF I TRY *REALLY* HARD TO LOOK?
USELESS!
I'LL CLOSE MY EYES!
AND MAYBE YOU'LL FEEL MY MIND'S EYE??
I CAN ONLY DO IT IF YOU LOOK DIRECTLY AT ME!!

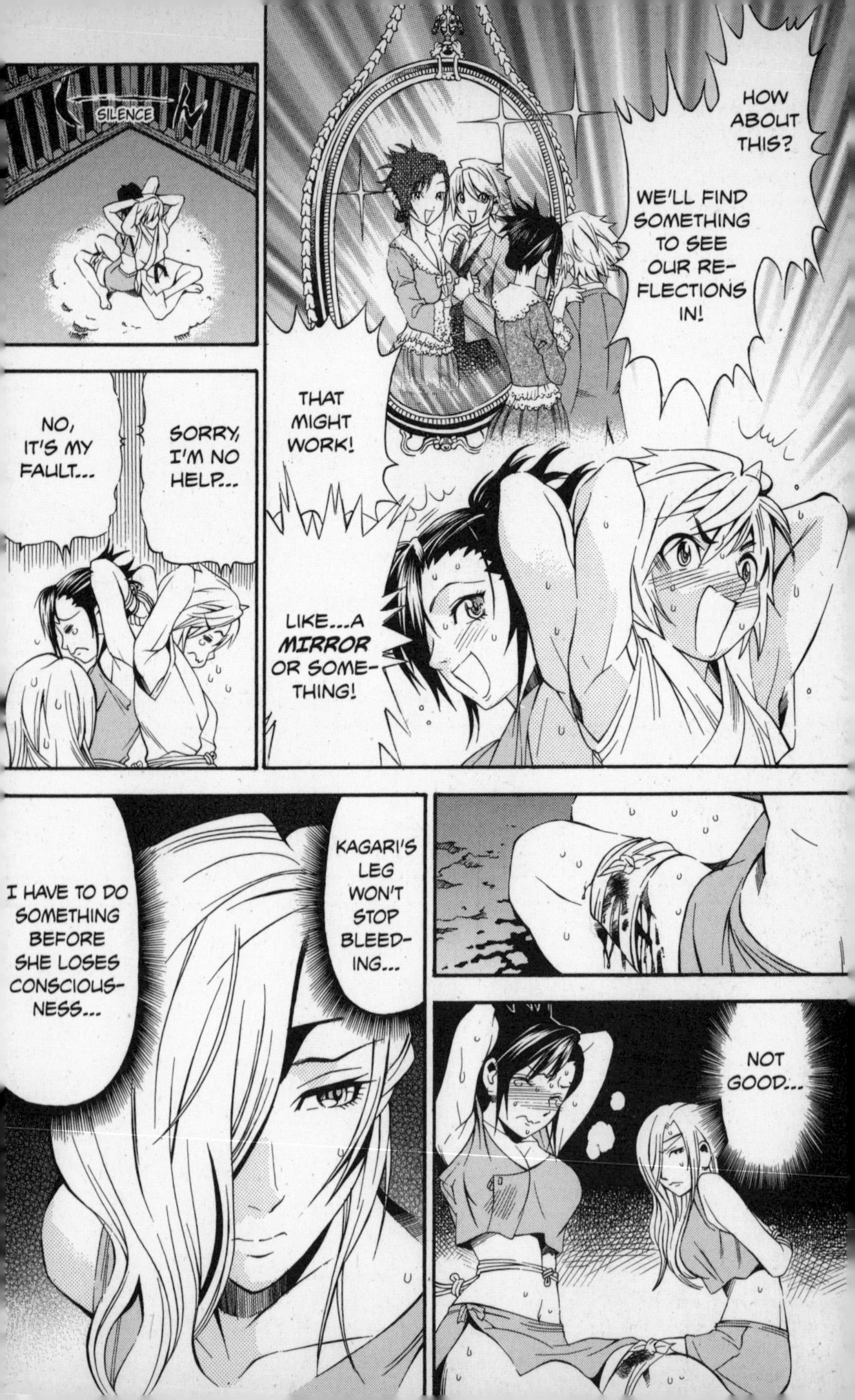
HOW ABOUT THIS?
WE'LL FIND SOMETHING TO SEE OUR RE-FLECTIONS IN!
THAT MIGHT WORK!
LIKE...A *MIRROR* OR SOME-THING!
SILENCE
SORRY, I'M NO HELP...
NO, IT'S MY FAULT...
NOT GOOD...
KAGARI'S LEG WON'T STOP BLEED-ING...
I HAVE TO DO SOMETHING BEFORE SHE LOSES CONSCIOUS-NESS...

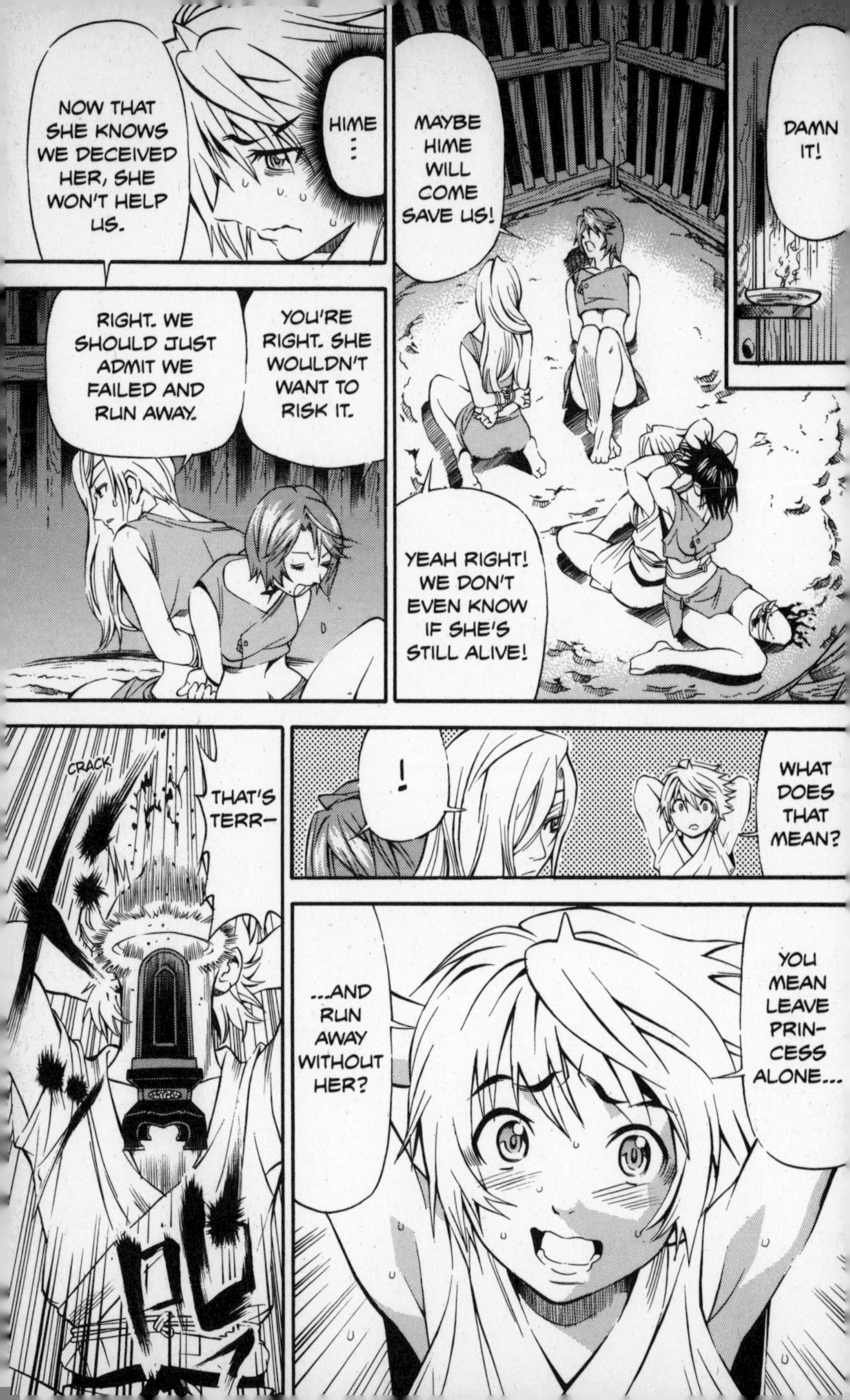
DAMN IT!
MAYBE HIME WILL COME SAVE US!
YEAH RIGHT! WE DON'T EVEN KNOW IF SHE'S STILL ALIVE!
HIME...
NOW THAT SHE KNOWS WE DECEIVED HER, SHE WON'T HELP US.
YOU'RE RIGHT. SHE WOULDN'T WANT TO RISK IT.
RIGHT. WE SHOULD JUST ADMIT WE FAILED AND RUN AWAY.
WHAT DOES THAT MEAN?
!
YOU MEAN LEAVE PRIN-CESS ALONE...
...AND RUN AWAY WITHOUT HER?
CRACK
THAT'S TERR—

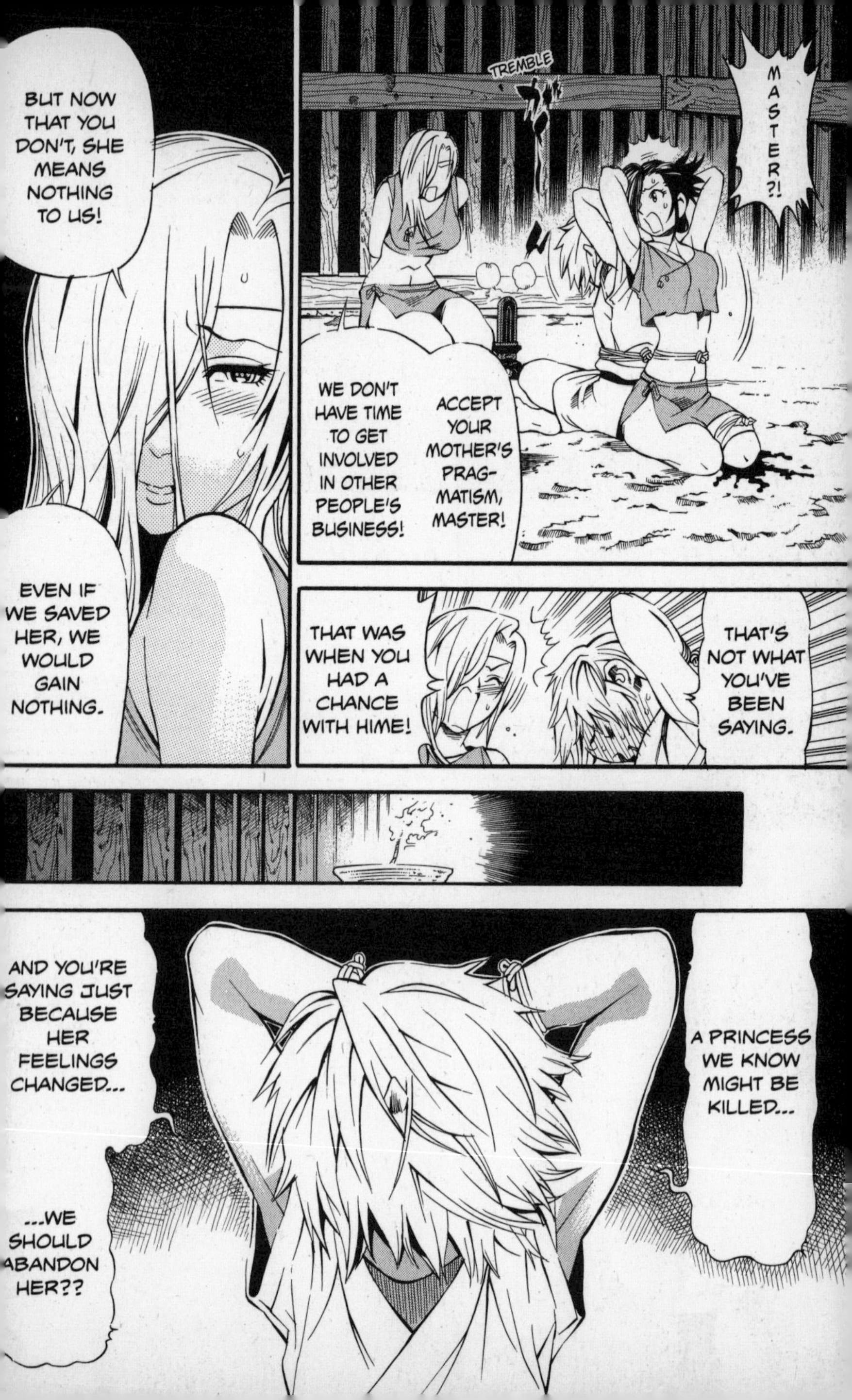
MASTER?!
TREMBLE
ACCEPT YOUR MOTHER'S PRAG-MATISM, MASTER!
WE DON'T HAVE TIME TO GET INVOLVED IN OTHER PEOPLE'S BUSINESS!
THAT'S NOT WHAT YOU'VE BEEN SAYING.
THAT WAS WHEN YOU HAD A CHANCE WITH HIME!
BUT NOW THAT YOU DON'T, SHE MEANS NOTHING TO US!
EVEN IF WE SAVED HER, WE WOULD GAIN NOTHING.
A PRINCESS WE KNOW MIGHT BE KILLED...
AND YOU'RE SAYING JUST BECAUSE HER FEELINGS CHANGED...
...WE SHOULD ABANDON HER??

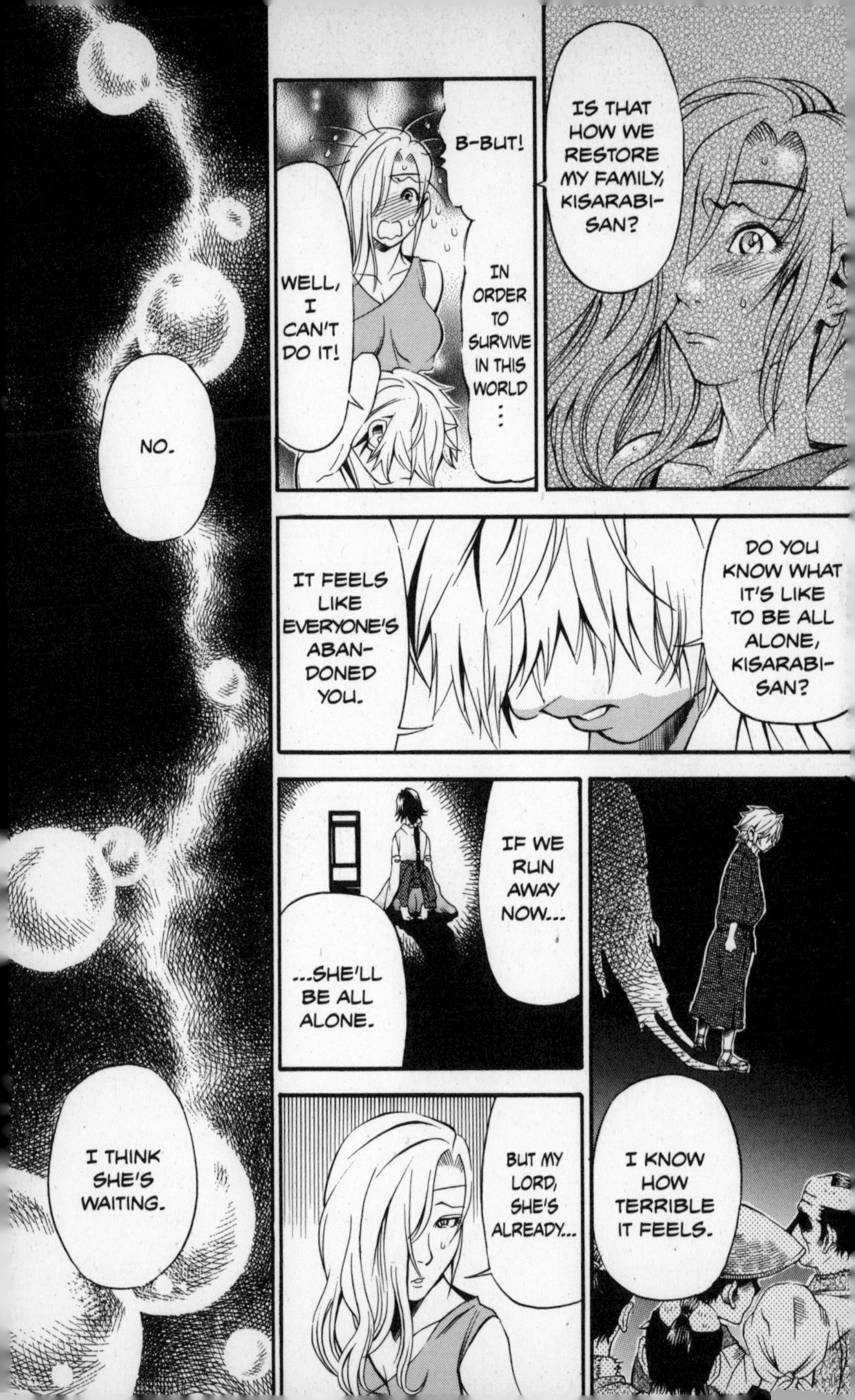
IS THAT HOW WE RESTORE MY FAMILY, KISARABI-SAN?
B-BUT!
IN ORDER TO SURVIVE IN THIS WORLD...
WELL, I CAN'T DO IT!
DO YOU KNOW WHAT IT'S LIKE TO BE ALL ALONE, KISARABI-SAN?
IT FEELS LIKE EVERYONE'S ABAN-DONED YOU.
I KNOW HOW TERRIBLE IT FEELS.
IF WE RUN AWAY NOW...
...SHE'LL BE ALL ALONE.
BUT MY LORD, SHE'S ALREADY...
NO.
I THINK SHE'S WAITING.

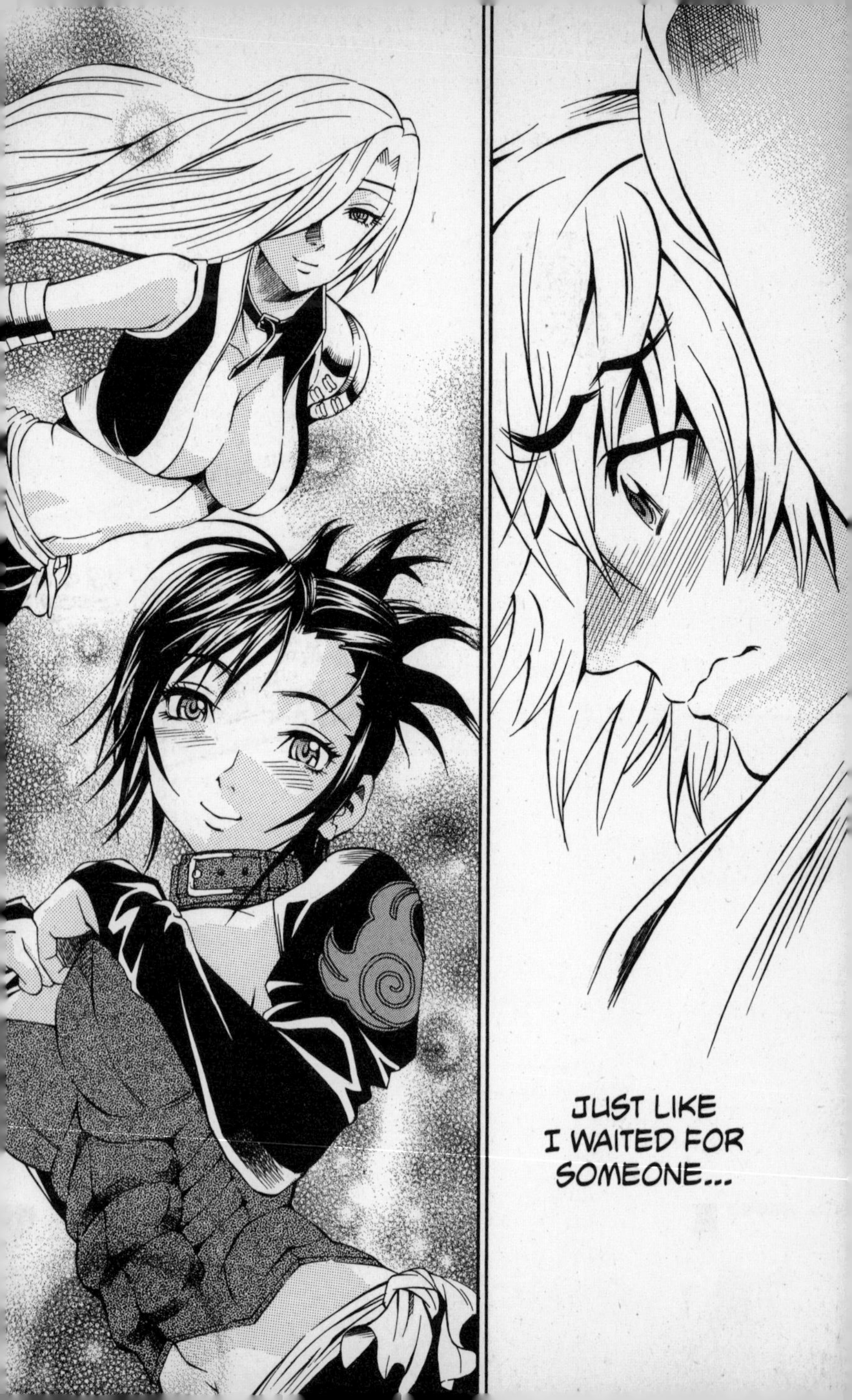
JUST LIKE
I WAITED FOR
SOMEONE...

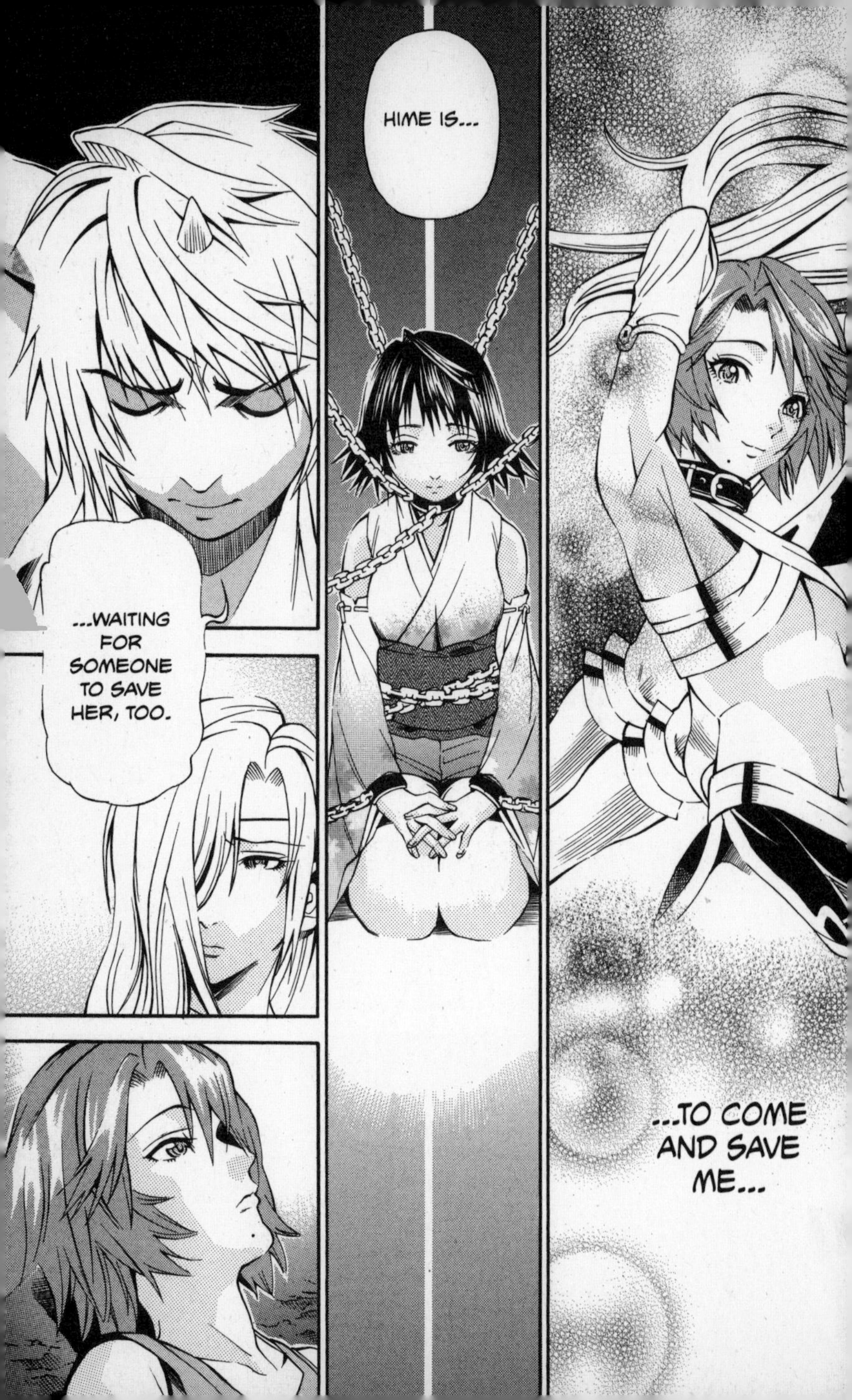
...TO COME AND SAVE ME...
HIME IS...
...WAITING FOR SOMEONE TO SAVE HER, TOO.

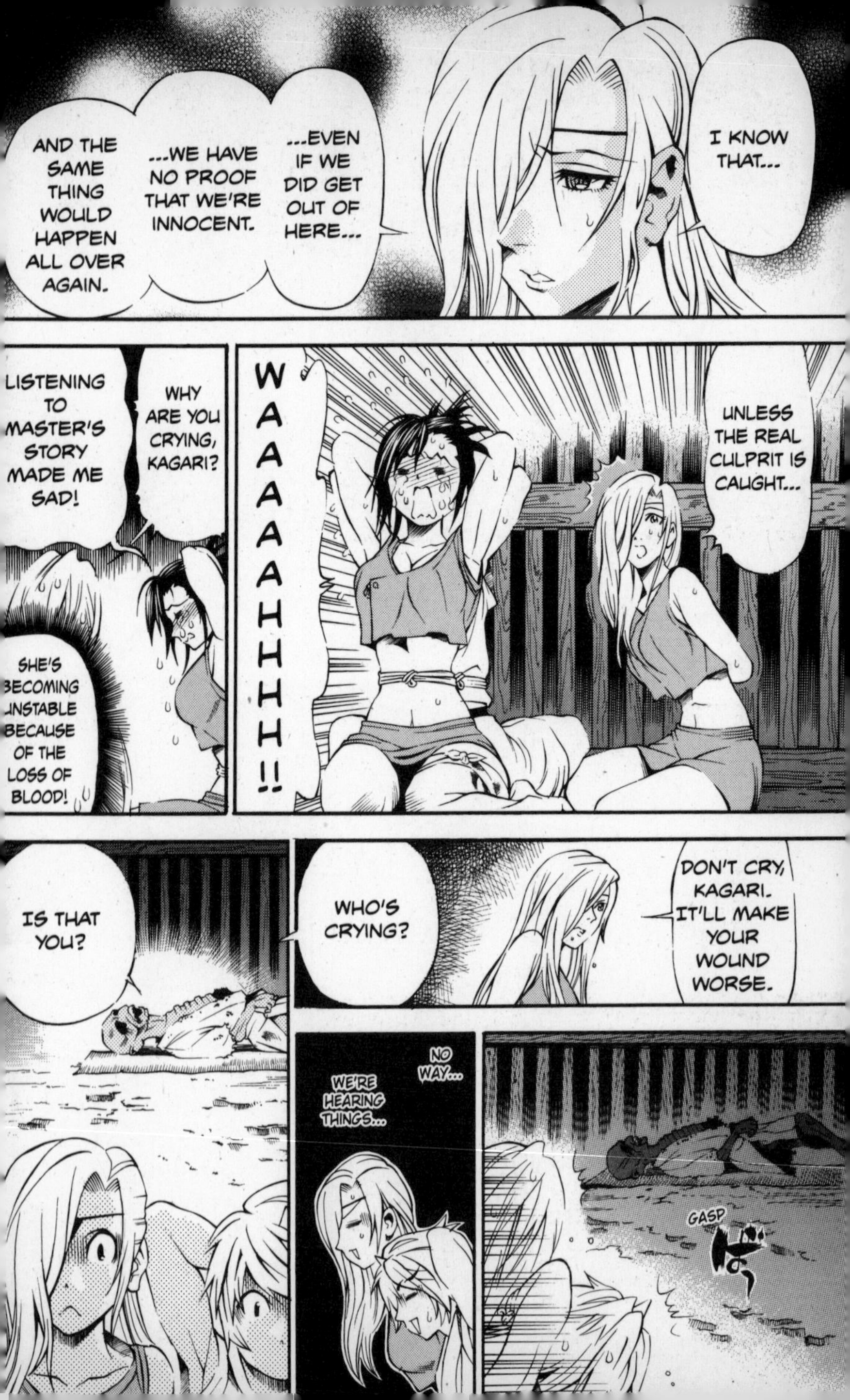
I KNOW THAT...
...EVEN IF WE DID GET OUT OF HERE...
...WE HAVE NO PROOF THAT WE'RE INNOCENT.
AND THE SAME THING WOULD HAPPEN ALL OVER AGAIN.
UNLESS THE REAL CULPRIT IS CAUGHT...
WAAAAAHHHH!!
WHY ARE YOU CRYING, KAGARI?
LISTENING TO MASTER'S STORY MADE ME SAD!
SHE'S BECOMING UNSTABLE BECAUSE OF THE LOSS OF BLOOD!
DON'T CRY, KAGARI. IT'LL MAKE YOUR WOUND WORSE.
WHO'S CRYING?
GASP
NO WAY...
WE'RE HEARING THINGS...
IS THAT YOU?

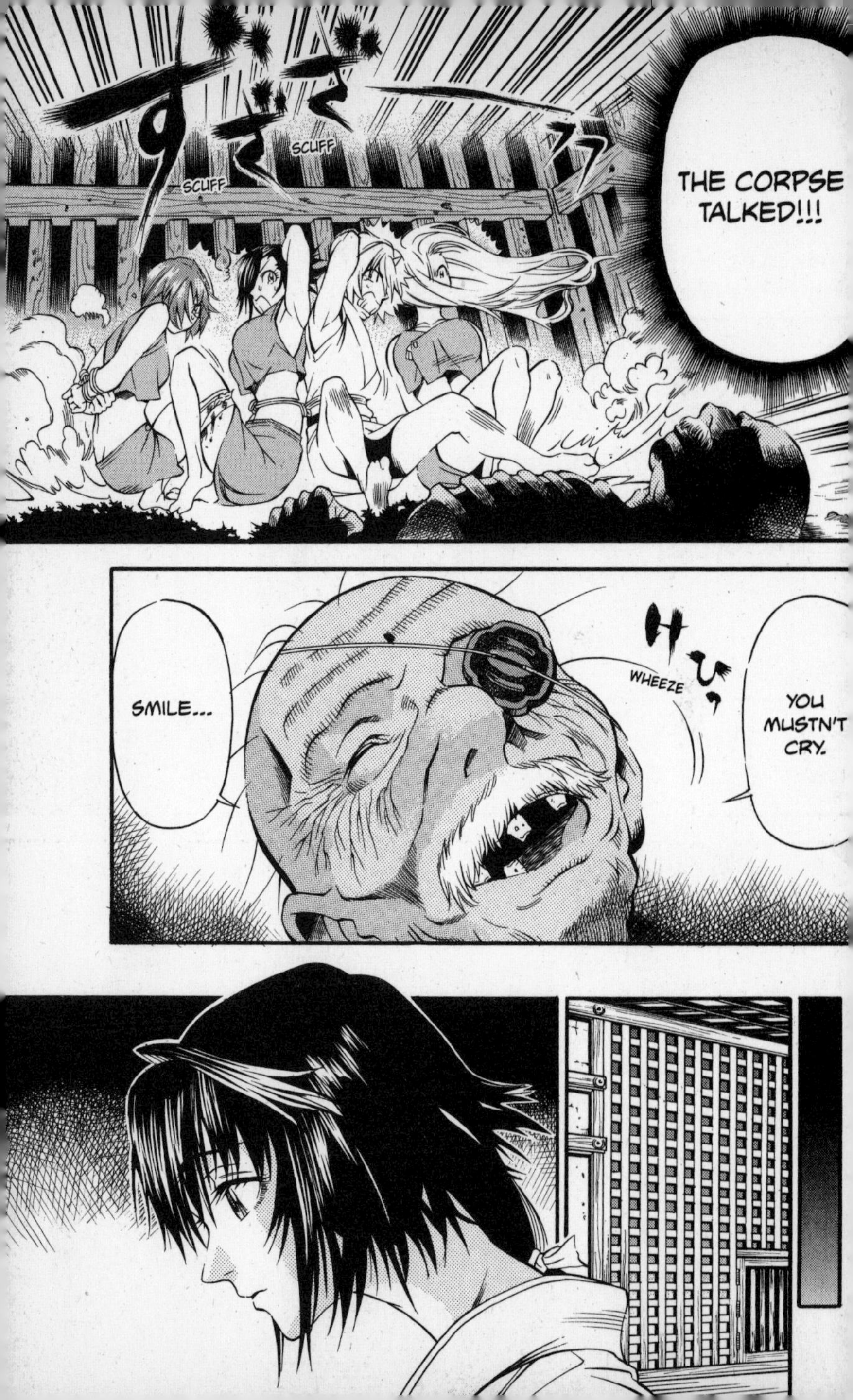
THE CORPSE TALKED!!!
SCUFF
SCUFF
YOU MUSTN'T CRY.
WHEEZE
SMILE...

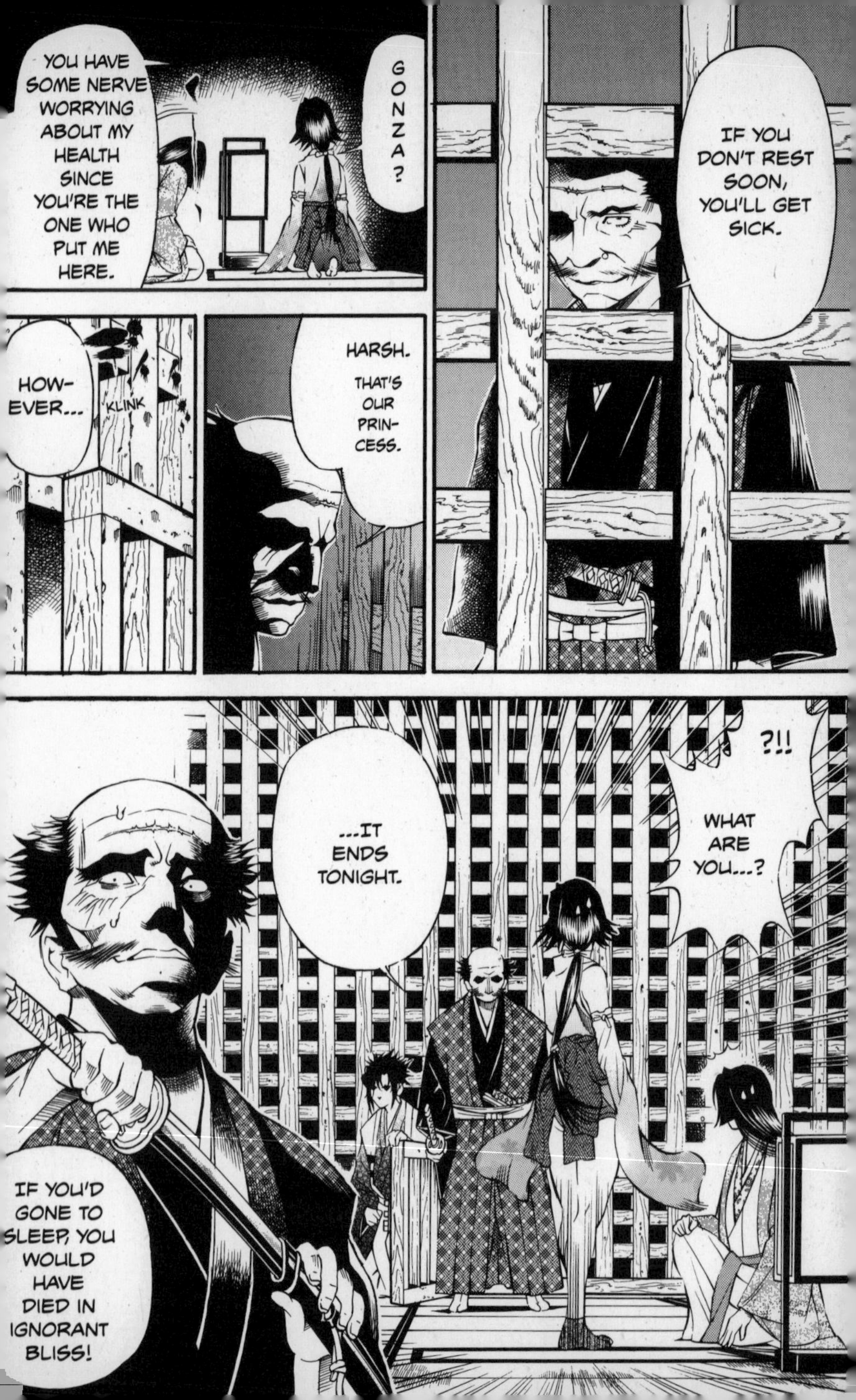
IF YOU DON'T REST SOON, YOU'LL GET SICK.
GONZA?
YOU HAVE SOME NERVE WORRYING ABOUT MY HEALTH SINCE YOU'RE THE ONE WHO PUT ME HERE.
HARSH. THAT'S OUR PRINCESS.
HOW-EVER...
KLINK
?!!
WHAT ARE YOU...?
...IT ENDS TONIGHT.
IF YOU'D GONE TO SLEEP, YOU WOULD HAVE DIED IN IGNORANT BLISS!

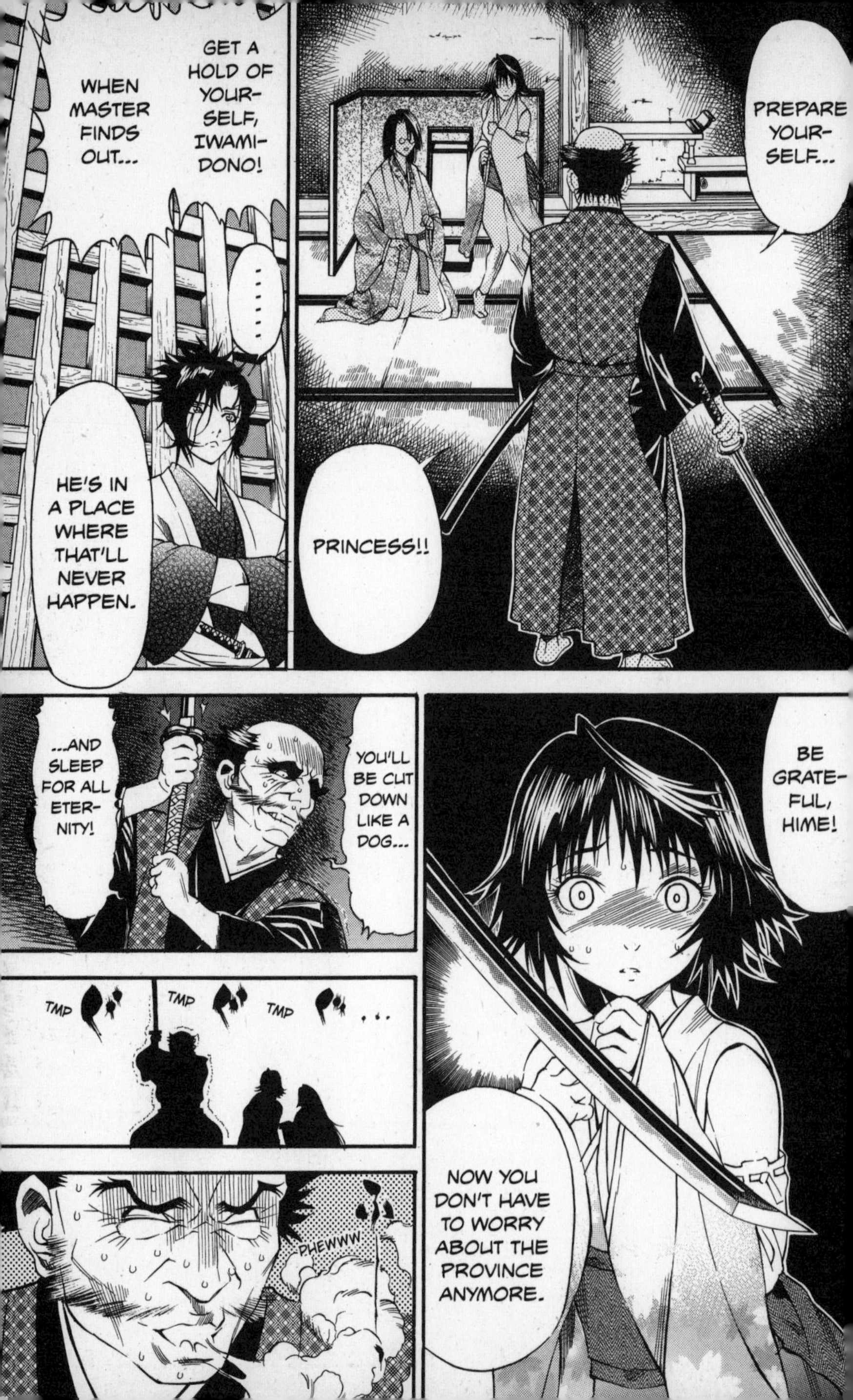
PREPARE YOURSELF...
PRINCESS!!
GET A HOLD OF YOURSELF, IWAMI-DONO!
WHEN MASTER FINDS OUT...
......
HE'S IN A PLACE WHERE THAT'LL NEVER HAPPEN.
BE GRATEFUL, HIME!
NOW YOU DON'T HAVE TO WORRY ABOUT THE PROVINCE ANYMORE.
YOU'LL BE CUT DOWN LIKE A DOG...
...AND SLEEP FOR ALL ETERNITY!
TMP
TMP
TMP
...
PHEWWW

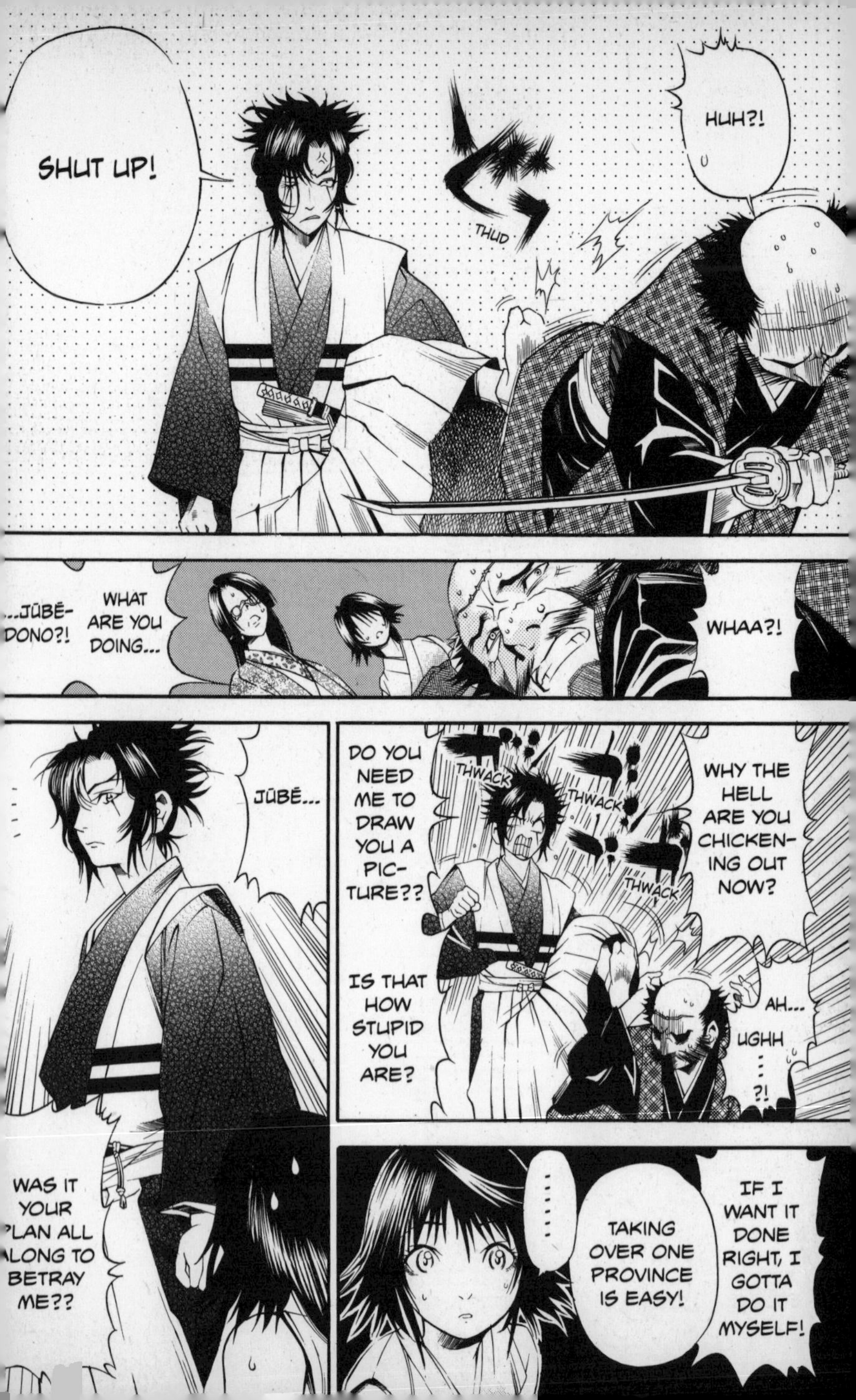
HUH?!
THUD
SHUT UP!
WHAA?!
WHAT ARE YOU DOING...
...JŪBĒ-DONO?!
WHY THE HELL ARE YOU CHICKEN-ING OUT NOW?
THWACK
THWACK
THWACK
DO YOU NEED ME TO DRAW YOU A PIC-TURE??
AH... UGHH ...?!
IS THAT HOW STUPID YOU ARE?
IF I WANT IT DONE RIGHT, I GOTTA DO IT MYSELF!
TAKING OVER ONE PROVINCE IS EASY!
......
JŪBĒ...
...
WAS IT YOUR PLAN ALL ALONG TO BETRAY ME??

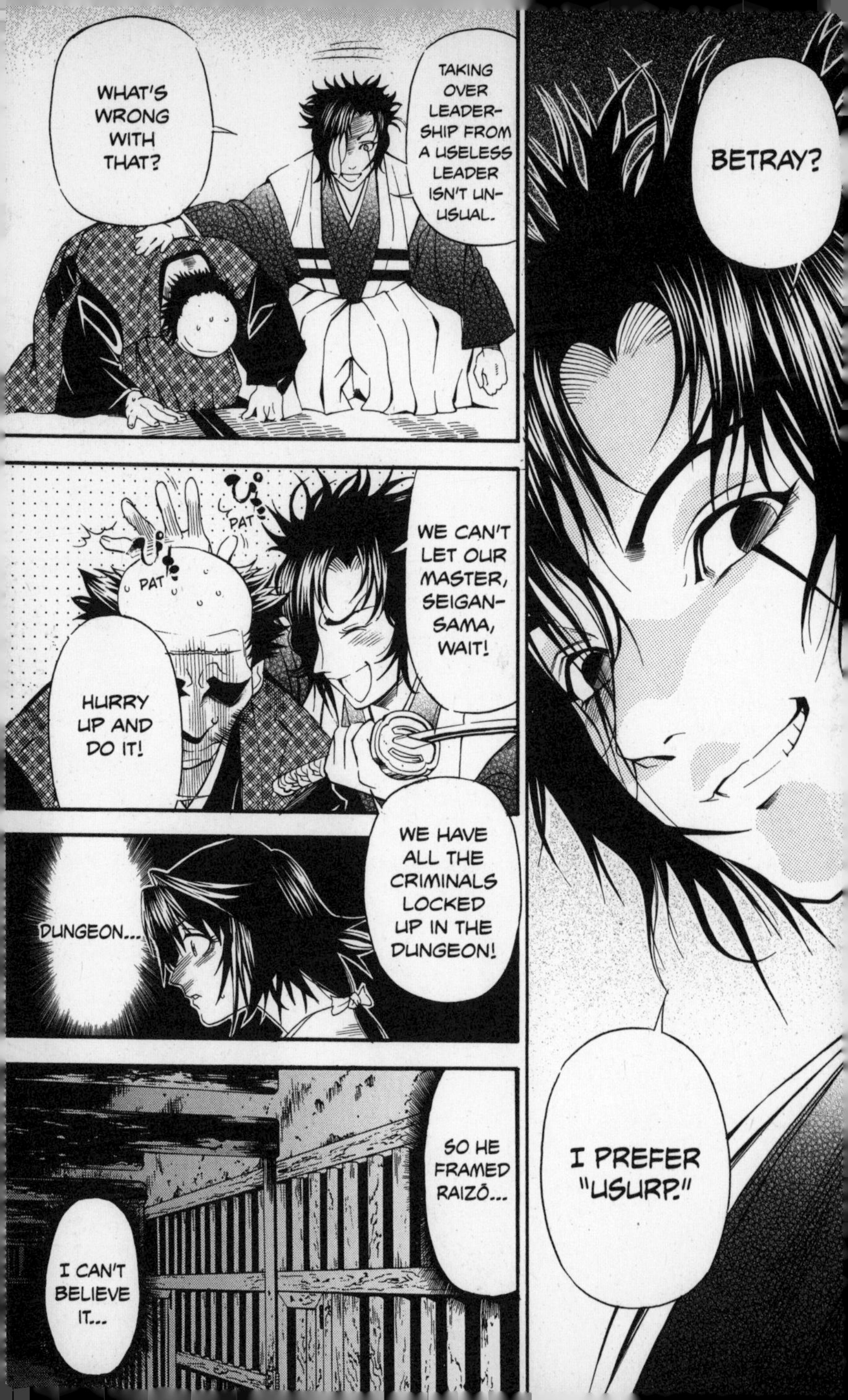
BETRAY?
I PREFER "USURP."
TAKING OVER LEADER-SHIP FROM A USELESS LEADER ISN'T UN-USUAL.
WHAT'S WRONG WITH THAT?
WE CAN'T LET OUR MASTER, SEIGAN-SAMA, WAIT!
PAT
PAT
HURRY UP AND DO IT!
WE HAVE ALL THE CRIMINALS LOCKED UP IN THE DUNGEON!
DUNGEON...
SO HE FRAMED RAIZŌ...
I CAN'T BELIEVE IT...

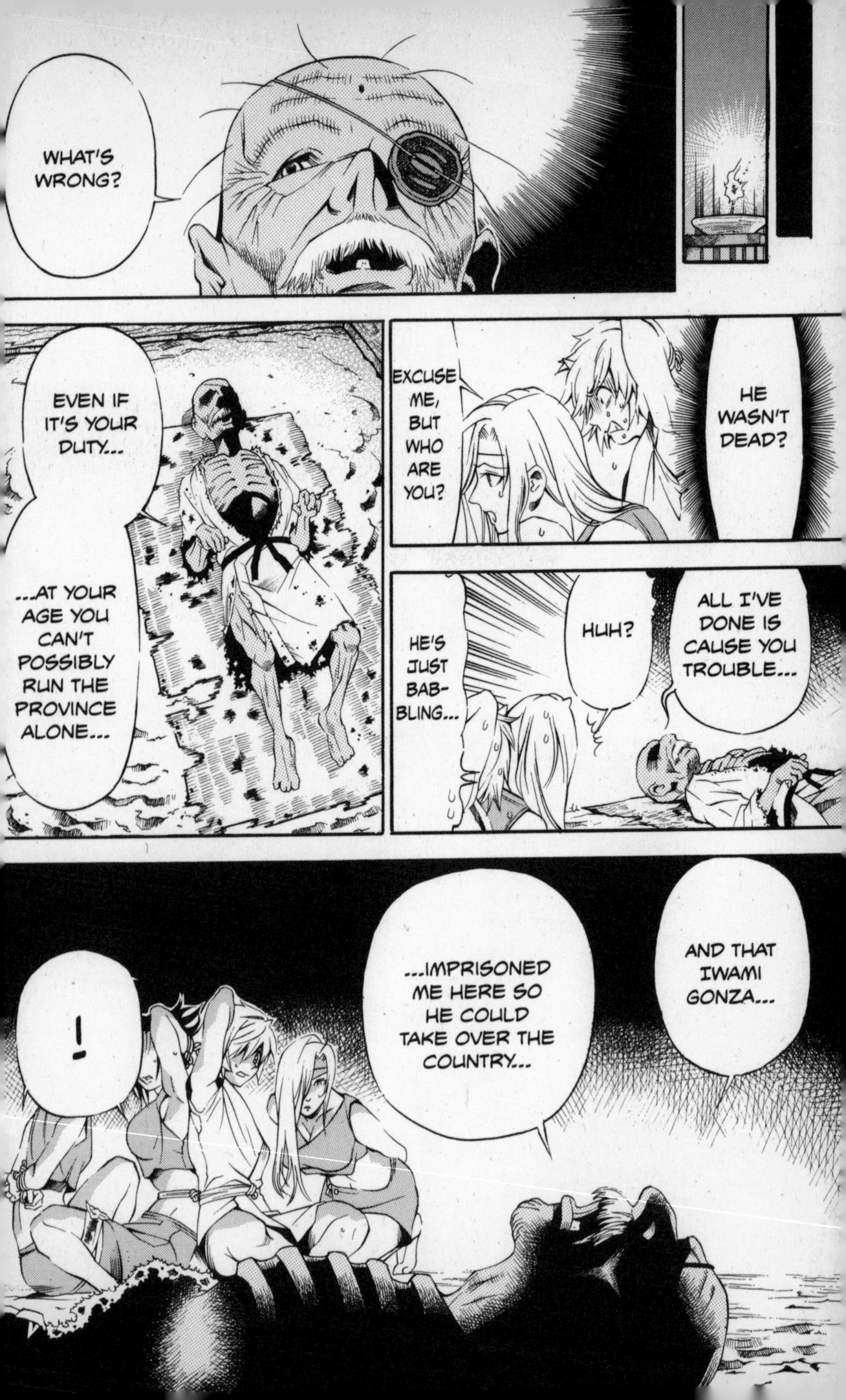
WHAT'S WRONG?
HE WASN'T DEAD?
EXCUSE ME, BUT WHO ARE YOU?
ALL I'VE DONE IS CAUSE YOU TROUBLE...
HUH?
HE'S JUST BAB-BLING...
EVEN IF IT'S YOUR DUTY...
...AT YOUR AGE YOU CAN'T POSSIBLY RUN THE PROVINCE ALONE...
AND THAT IWAMI GONZA...
...IMPRISONED ME HERE SO HE COULD TAKE OVER THE COUNTRY...
!

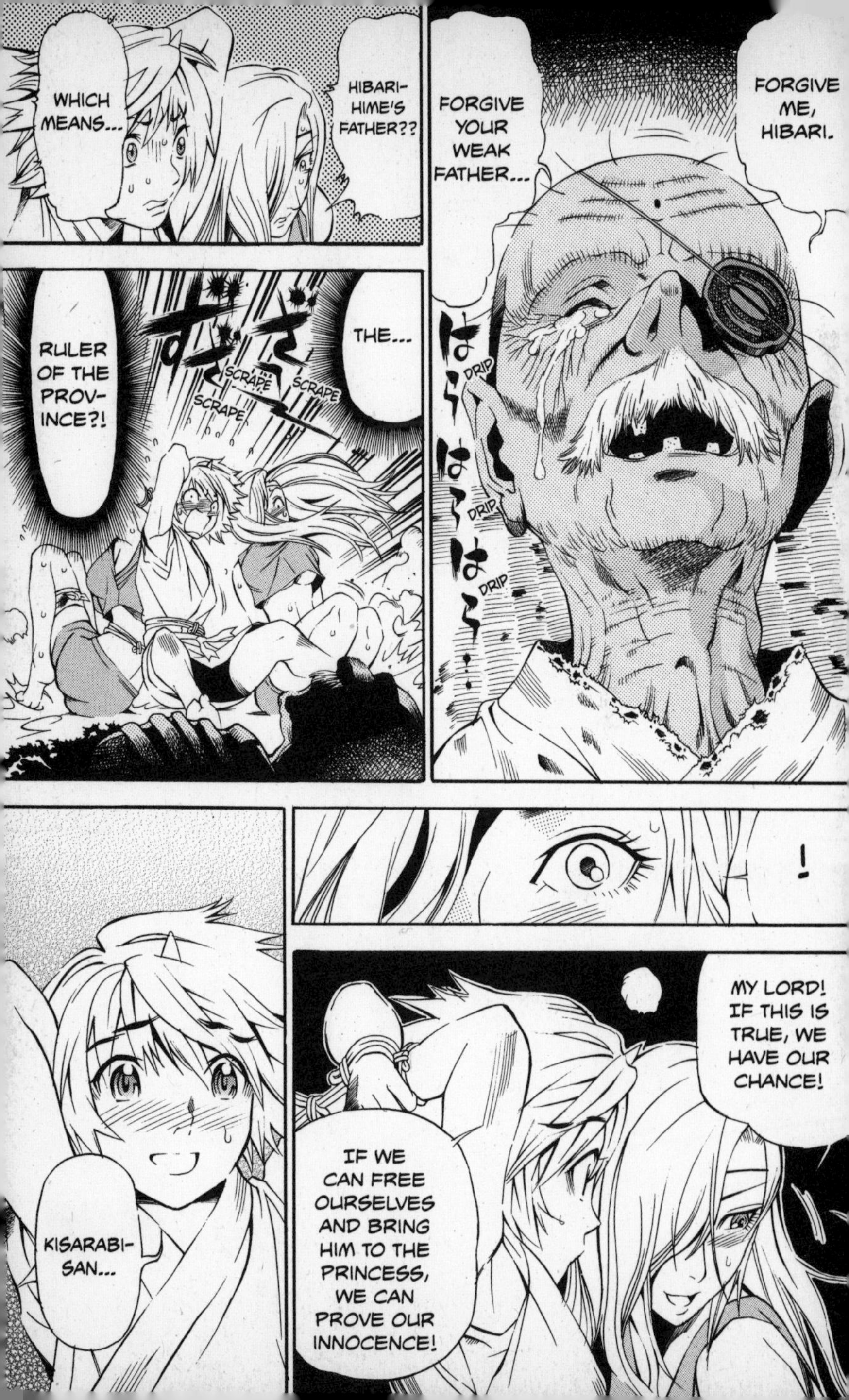
FORGIVE ME, HIBARI.
FORGIVE YOUR WEAK FATHER...
DRIP
DRIP
DRIP
HIBARI-HIME'S FATHER??
WHICH MEANS...
THE...
RULER OF THE PROVINCE?!
SCRAPE
SCRAPE
SCRAPE
!
MY LORD! IF THIS IS TRUE, WE HAVE OUR CHANCE!
IF WE CAN FREE OURSELVES AND BRING HIM TO THE PRINCESS, WE CAN PROVE OUR INNOCENCE!
KISARABI-SAN...

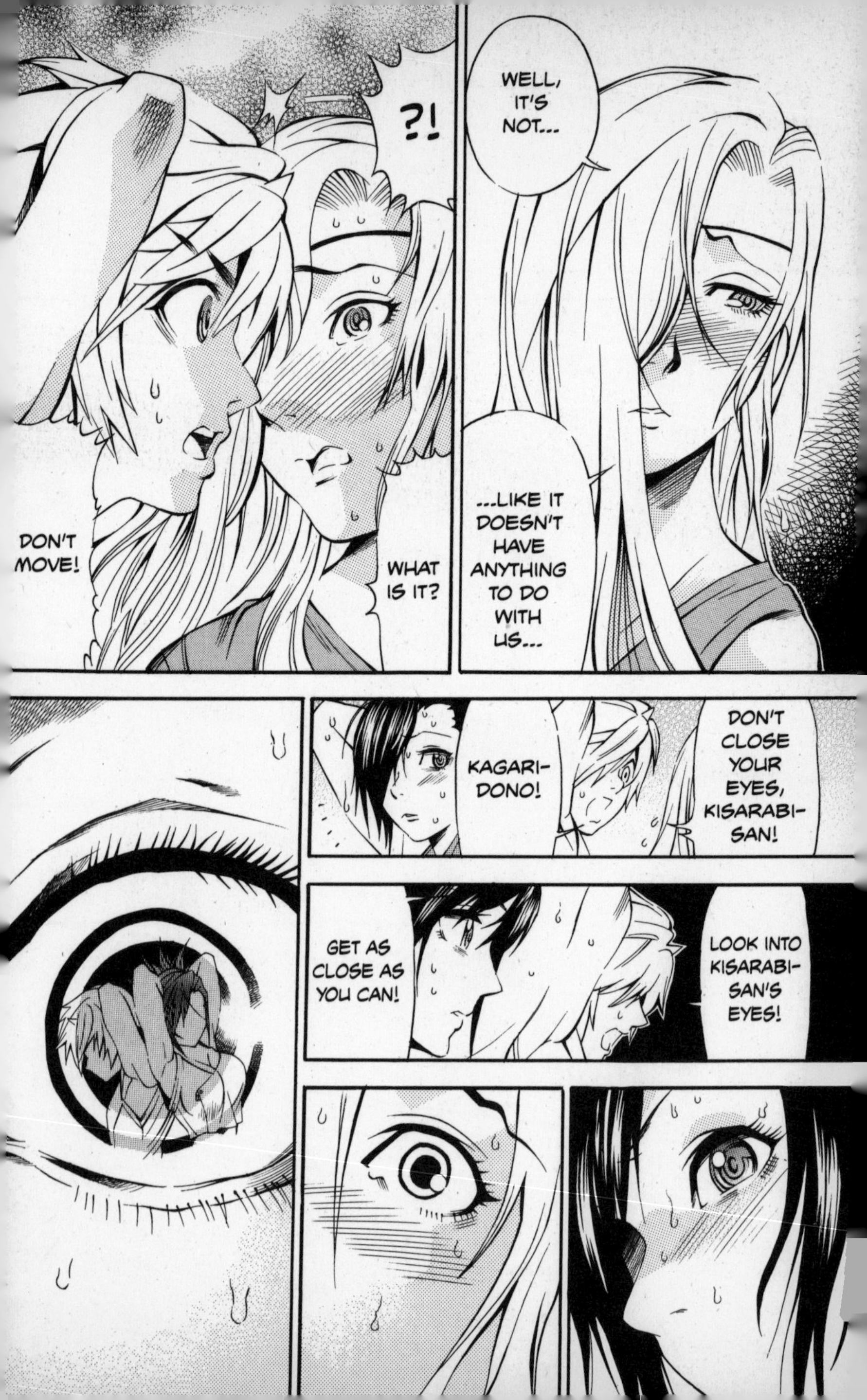
WELL, IT'S NOT...
...LIKE IT DOESN'T HAVE ANYTHING TO DO WITH US...
?!
WHAT IS IT?
DON'T MOVE!
DON'T CLOSE YOUR EYES, KISARABI-SAN!
KAGARI-DONO!
LOOK INTO KISARABI-SAN'S EYES!
GET AS CLOSE AS YOU CAN!

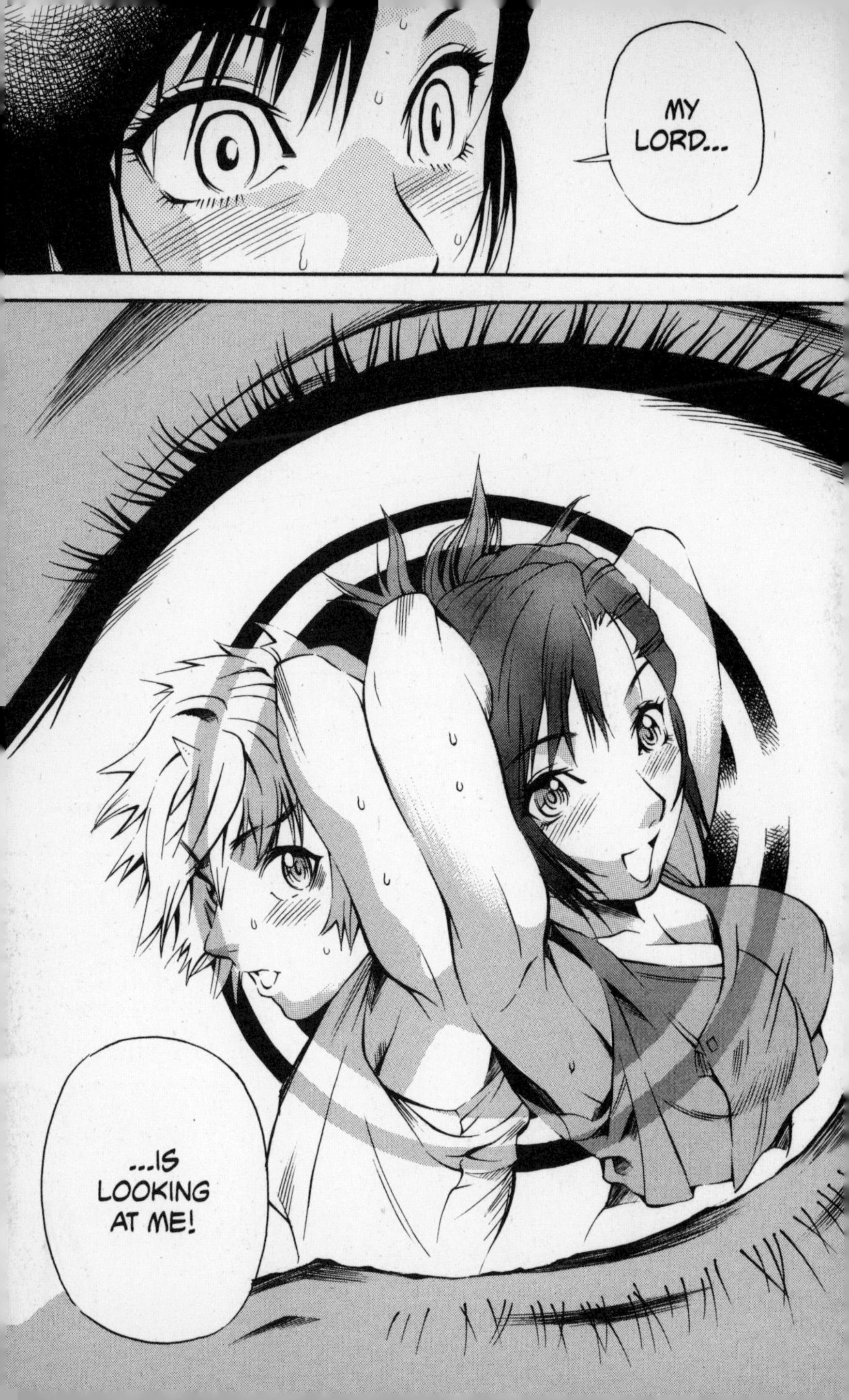
MY LORD...
...IS LOOKING AT ME!

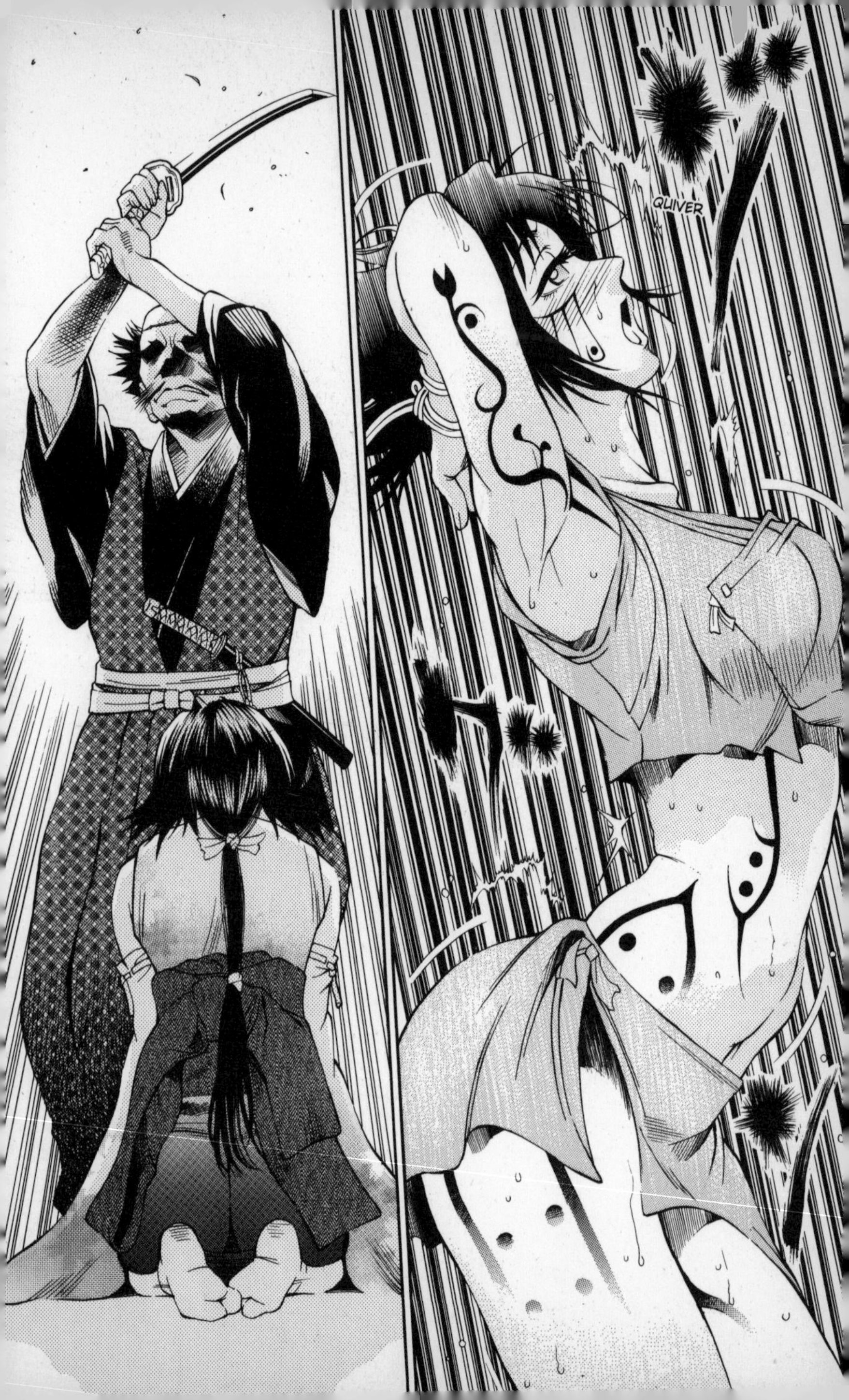
QUIVER

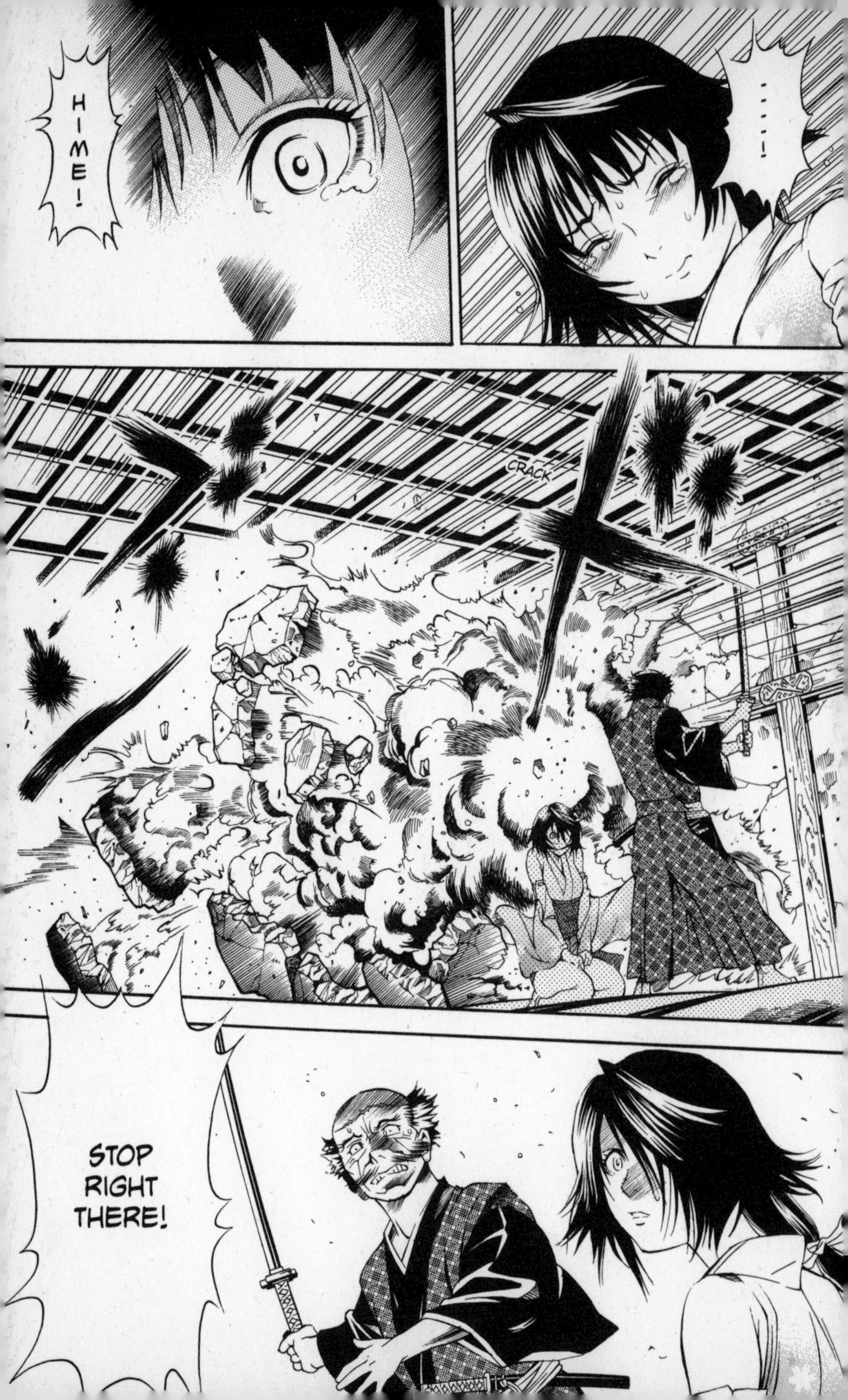
....!
HIME!
CRACK
STOP RIGHT THERE!

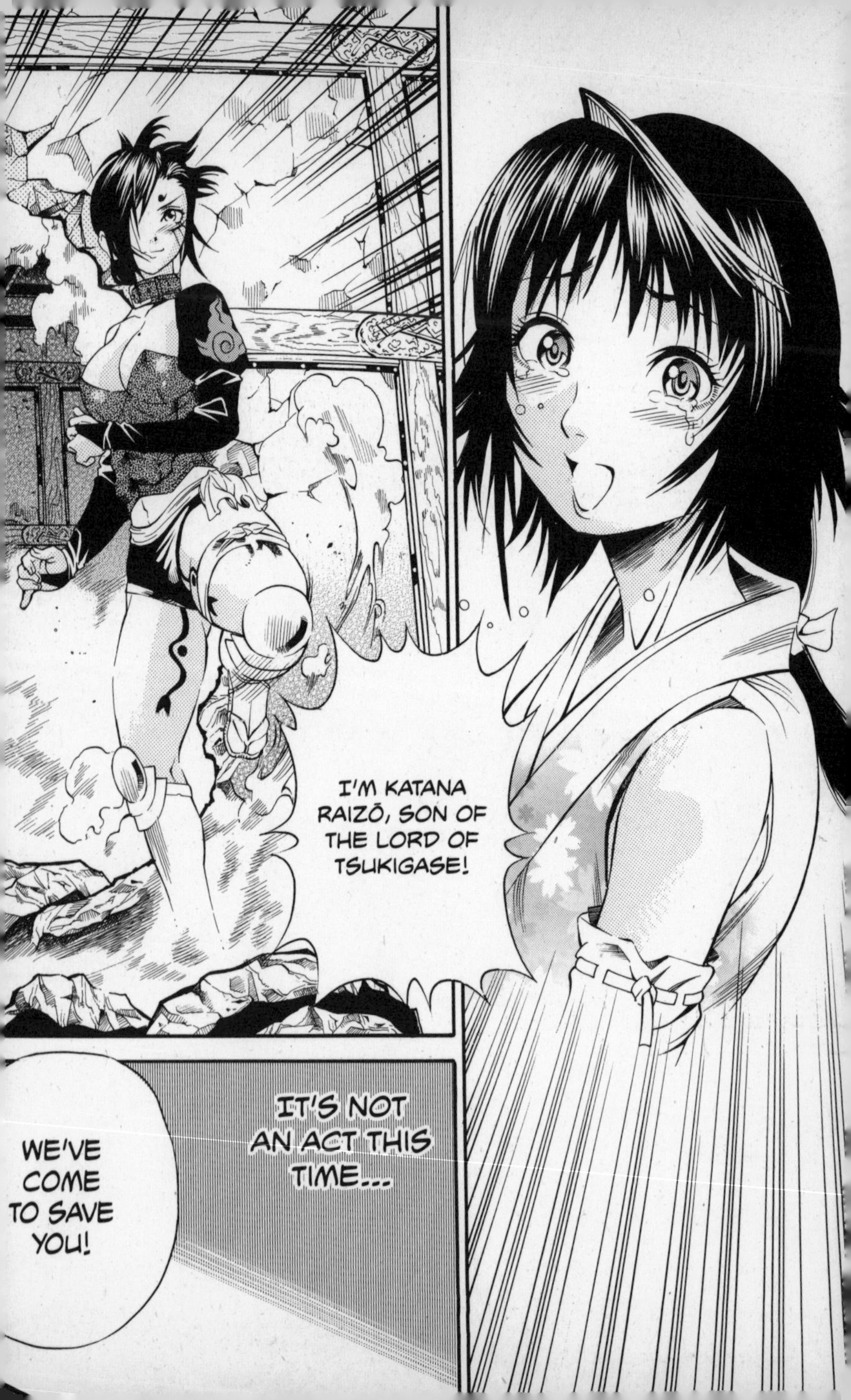

I'M KATANA RAIZŌ, SON OF THE LORD OF TSUKIGASE!
IT'S NOT AN ACT THIS TIME...
WE'VE COME TO SAVE YOU!

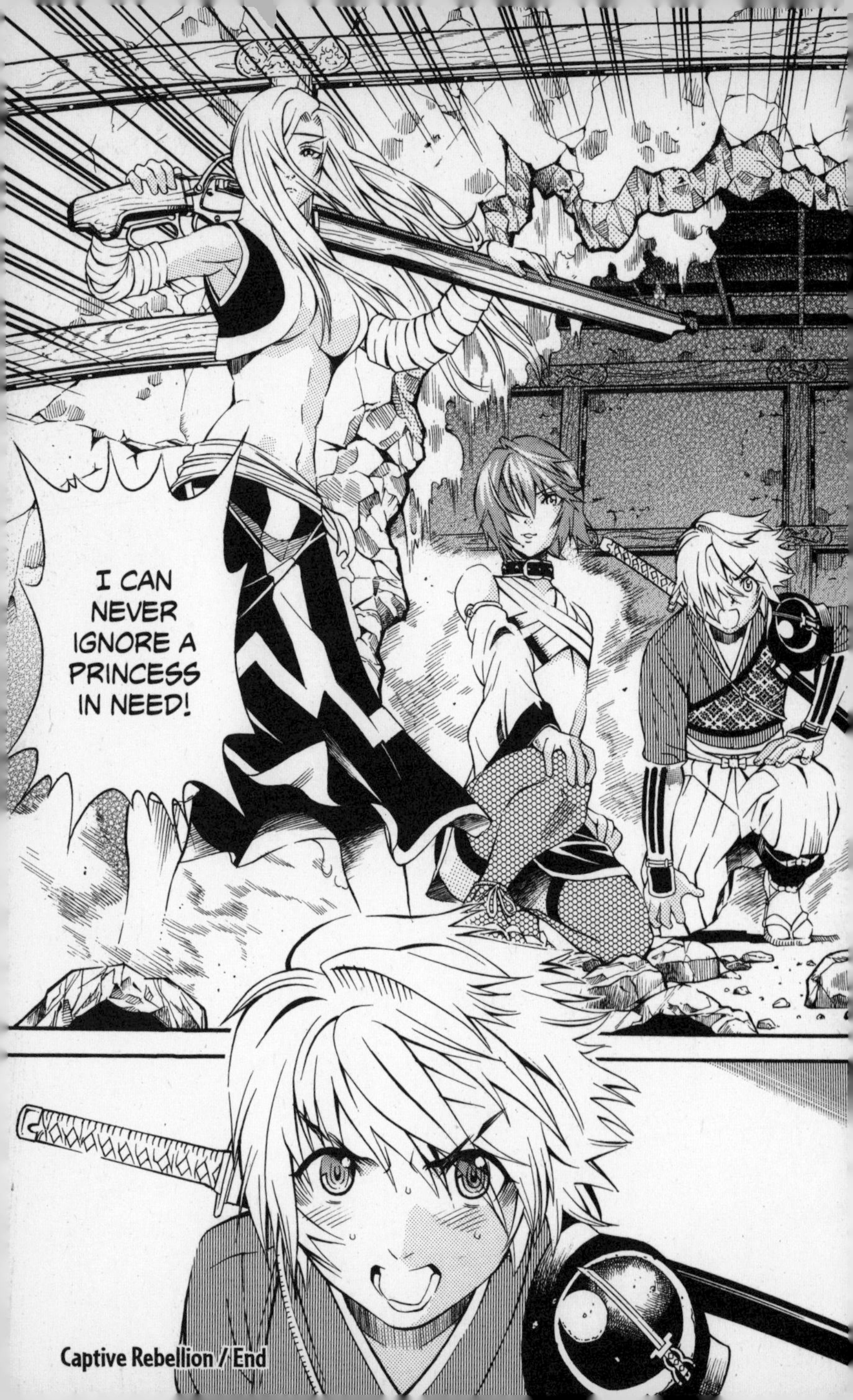
I CAN NEVER IGNORE A PRINCESS IN NEED!
Captive Rebellion / End

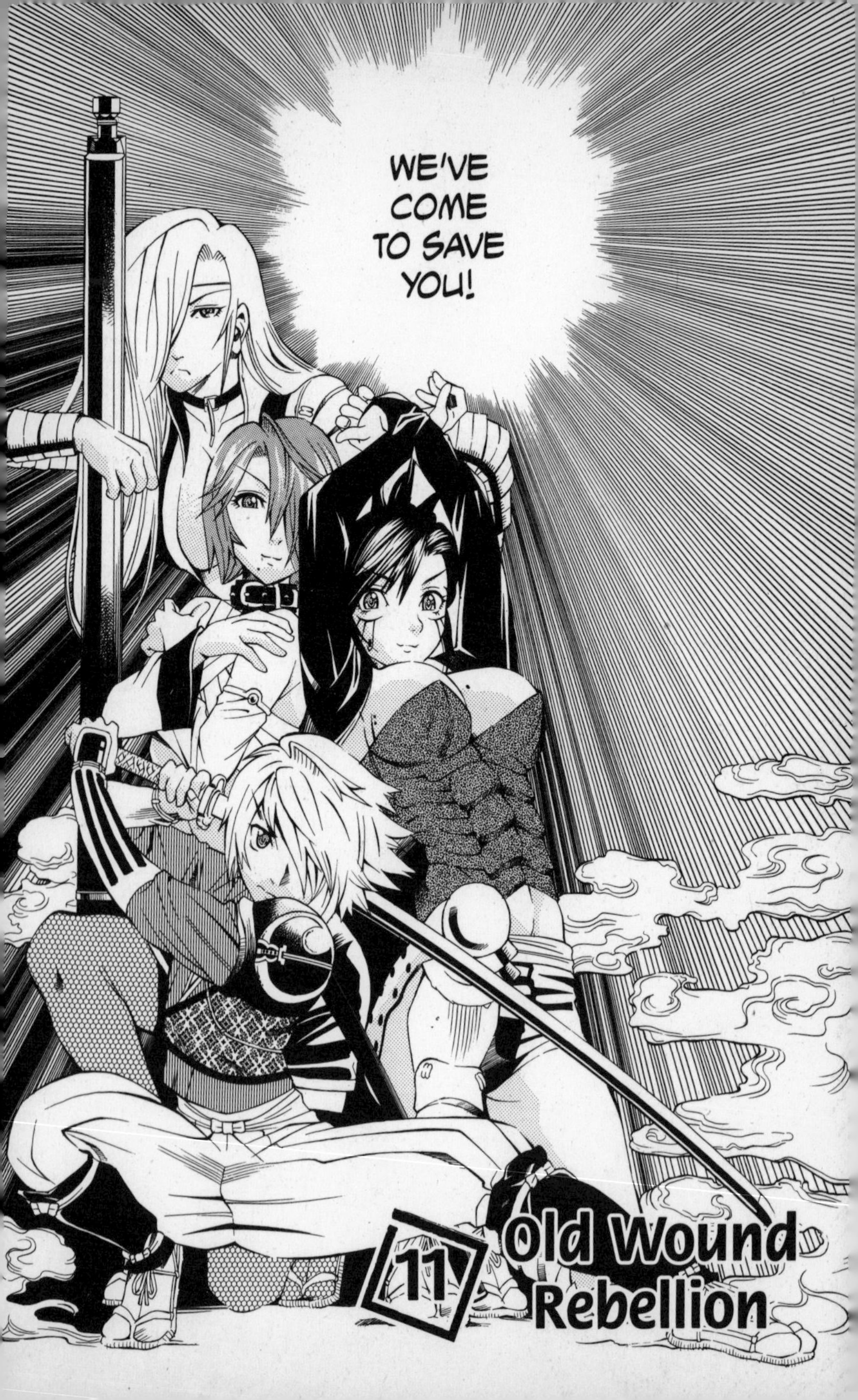
WE'VE COME TO SAVE YOU!
11
Old Wound Rebellion

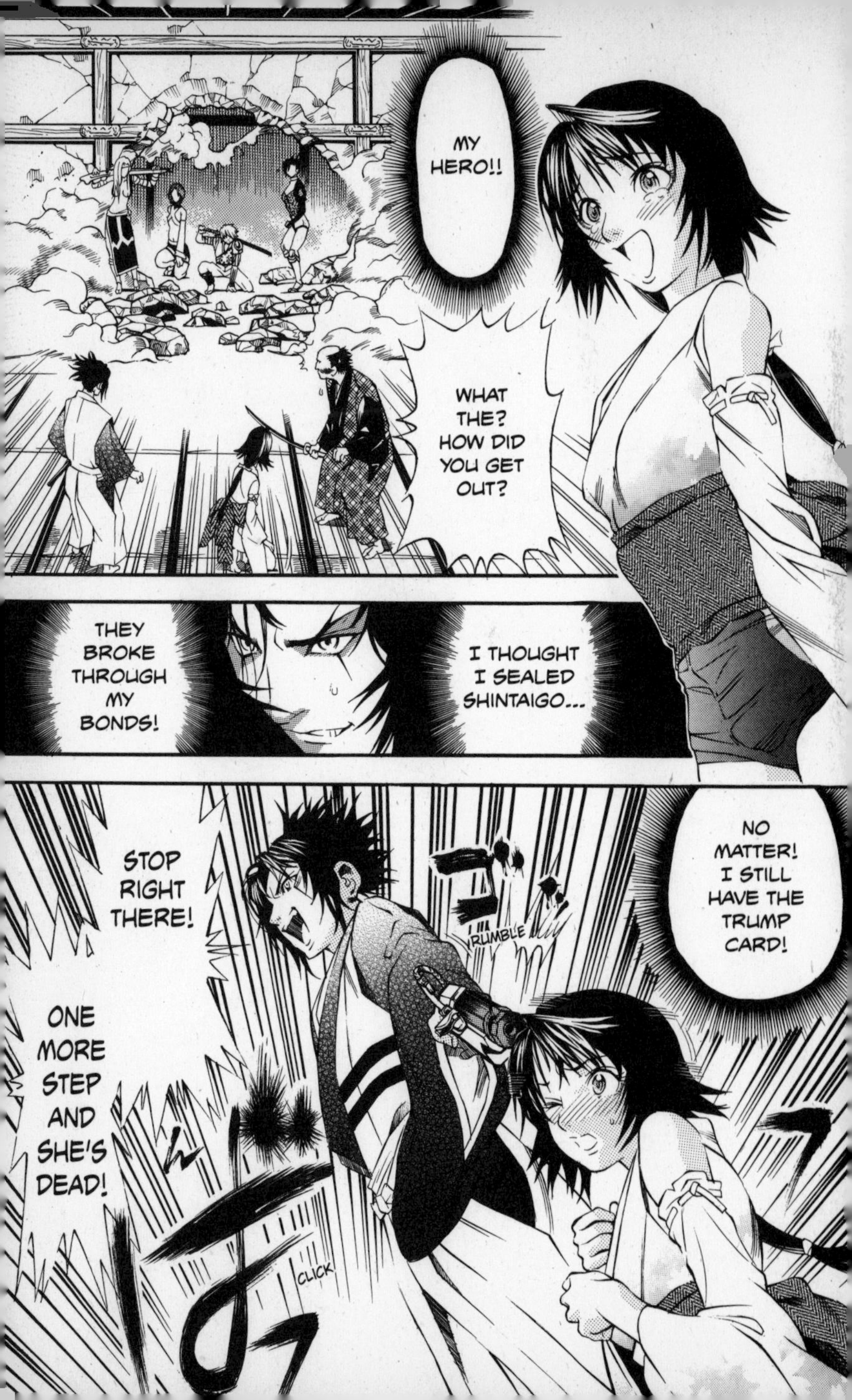
MY HERO!!
WHAT THE? HOW DID YOU GET OUT?
I THOUGHT I SEALED SHINTAIGO...
THEY BROKE THROUGH MY BONDS!
NO MATTER! I STILL HAVE THE TRUMP CARD!
RUMBLE
STOP RIGHT THERE!
ONE MORE STEP AND SHE'S DEAD!
CLICK

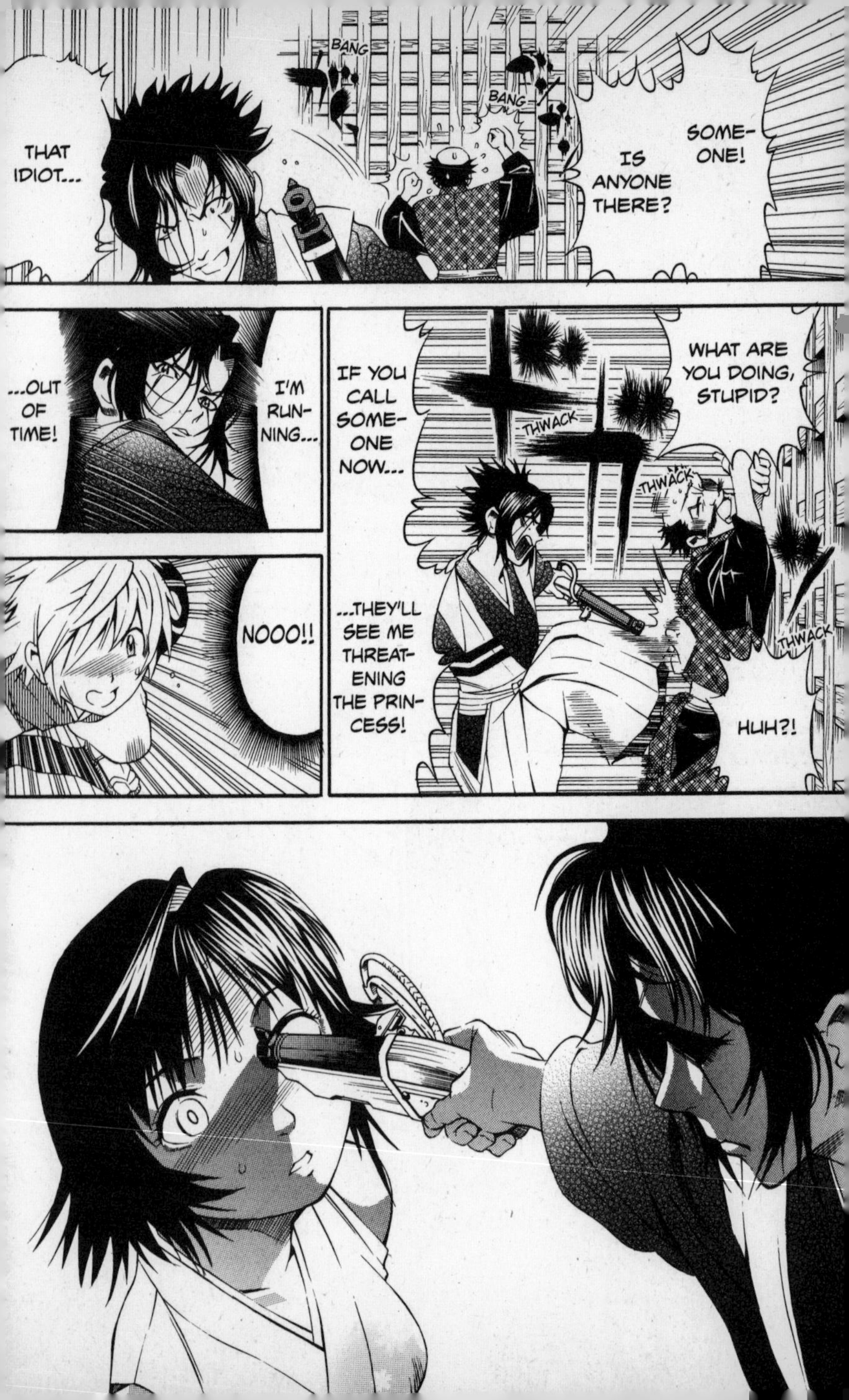
SOMEONE!
IS ANYONE THERE?
BANG
BANG
THAT IDIOT...
WHAT ARE YOU DOING, STUPID?
IF YOU CALL SOMEONE NOW...
THWACK
THWACK
...THEY'LL SEE ME THREATENING THE PRINCESS!
THWACK
HUH?!
I'M RUNNING...
...OUT OF TIME!
NOOO!!

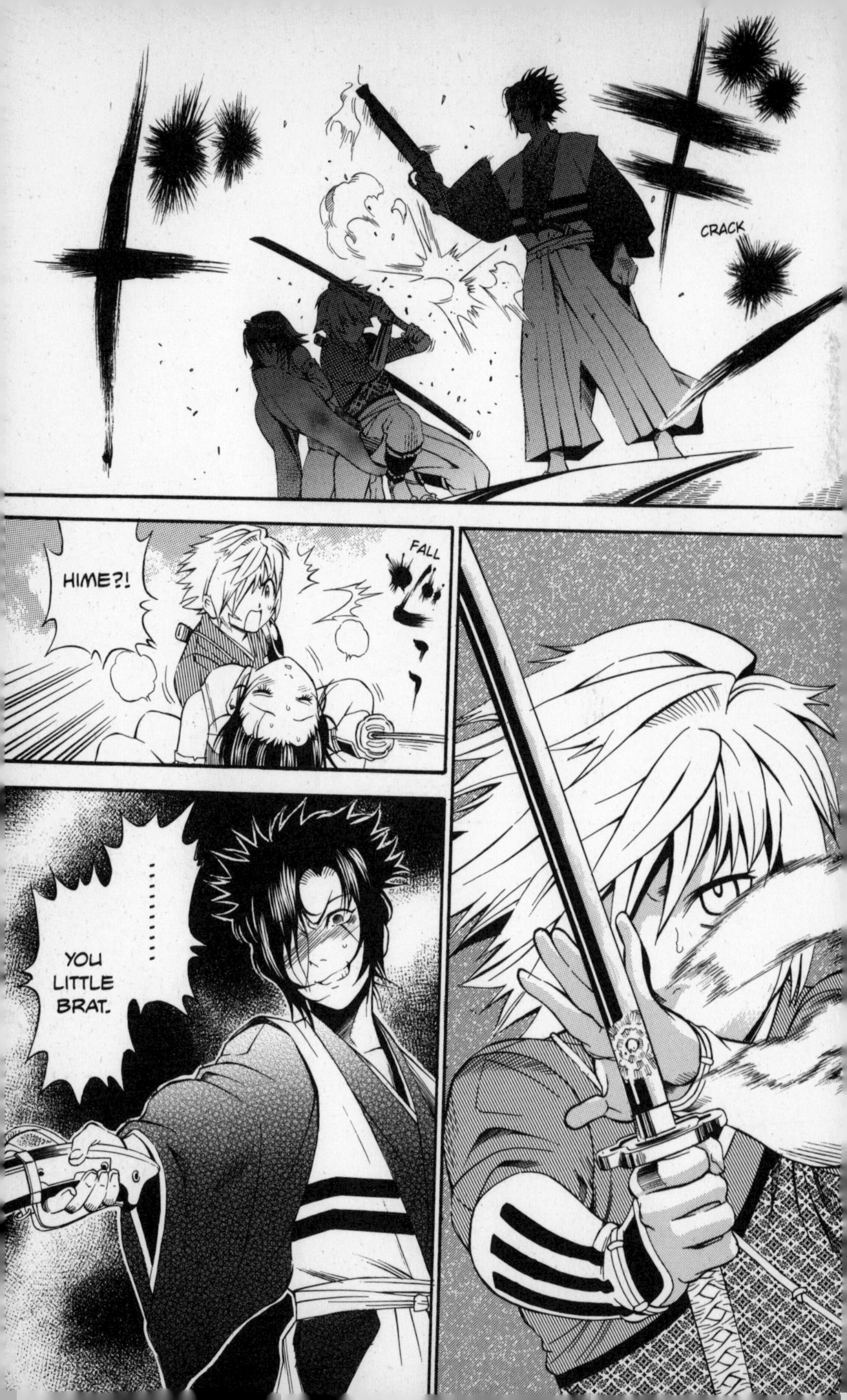
CRACK
FALL
HIME?!
......
YOU LITTLE BRAT.

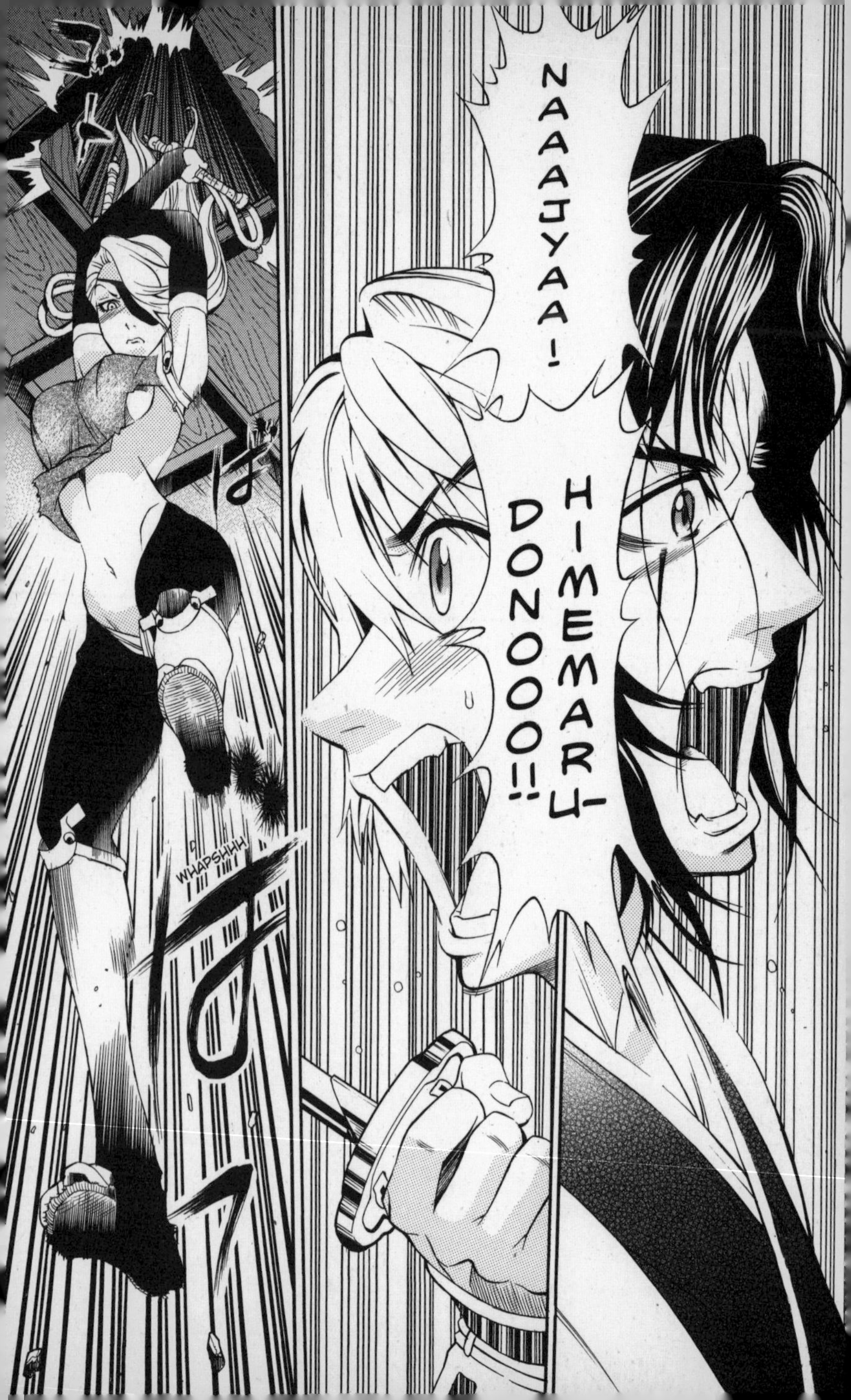
NAAAJYAAA!
HIMEMARU-DONOOOO!!
WHAPSHHH

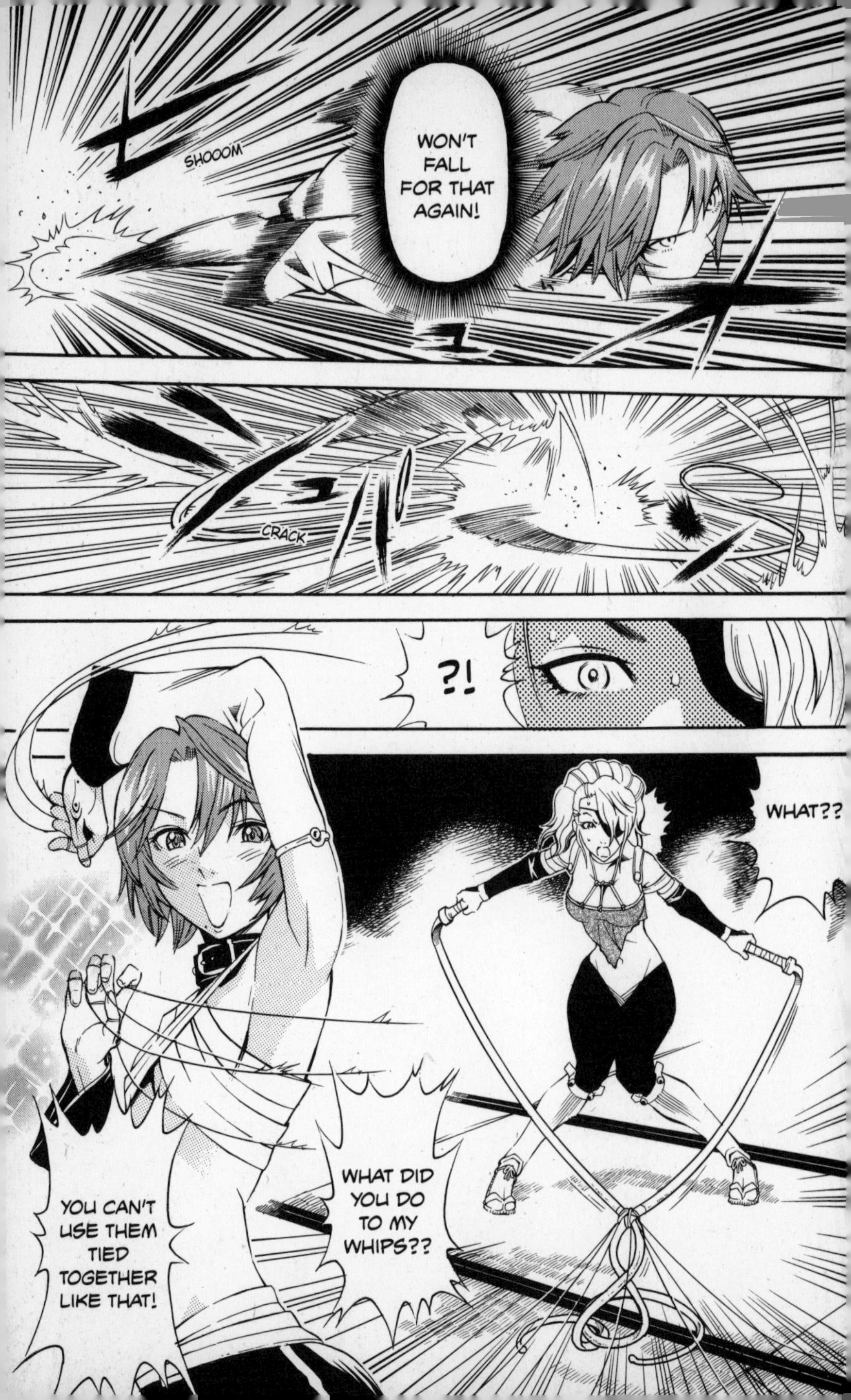
WON'T FALL FOR THAT AGAIN!
SHOOOM
CRACK
?!
WHAT??
WHAT DID YOU DO TO MY WHIPS??
YOU CAN'T USE THEM TIED TOGETHER LIKE THAT!

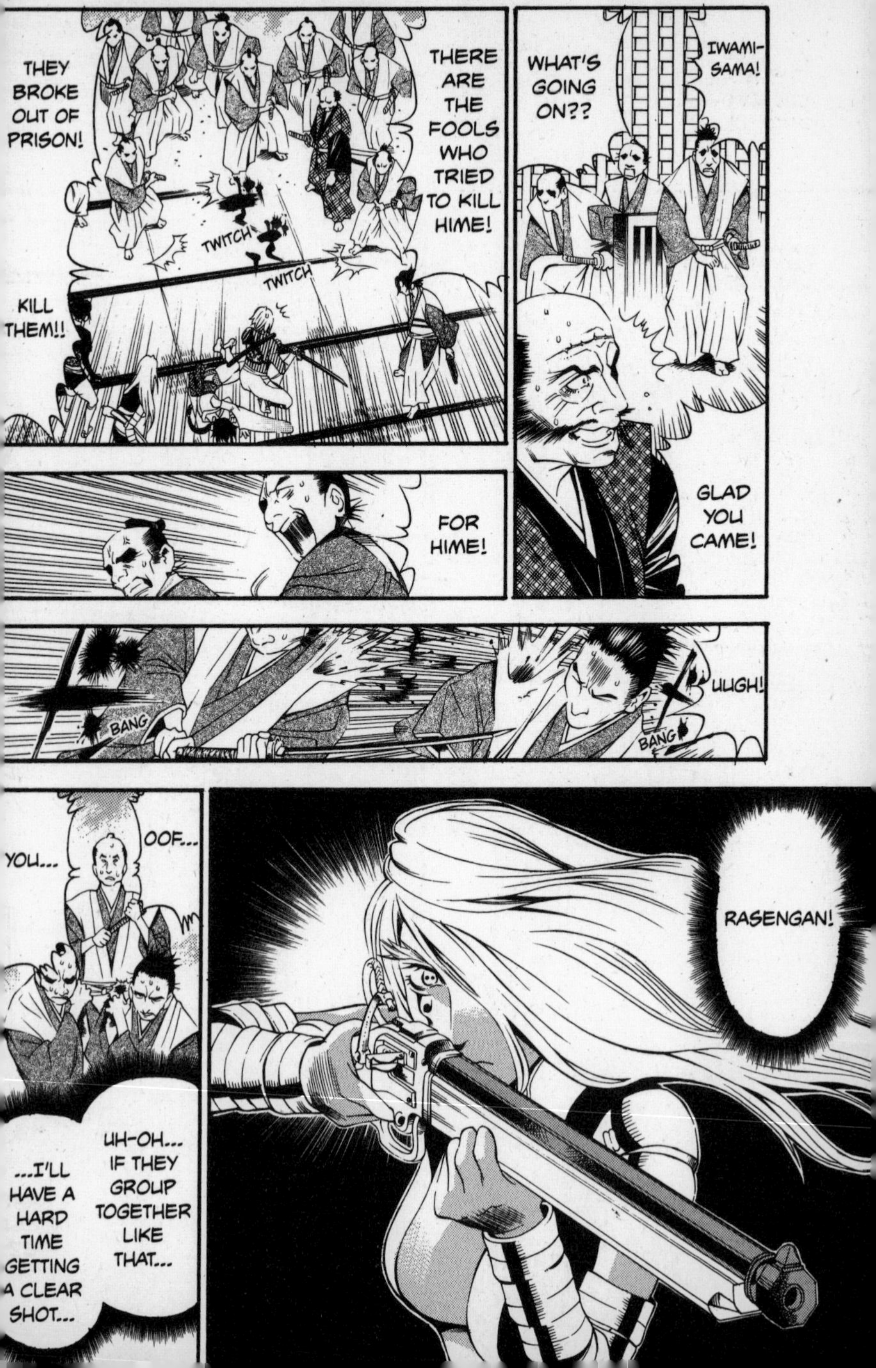
IWAMI-SAMA!
WHAT'S GOING ON??
GLAD YOU CAME!
THERE ARE THE FOOLS WHO TRIED TO KILL HIME!
THEY BROKE OUT OF PRISON!
TWITCH
TWITCH
KILL THEM!!
FOR HIME!
UUGH!
BANG
BANG
RASENGAN!
OOF...
YOU...
UH-OH... IF THEY GROUP TOGETHER LIKE THAT...
...I'LL HAVE A HARD TIME GETTING A CLEAR SHOT...

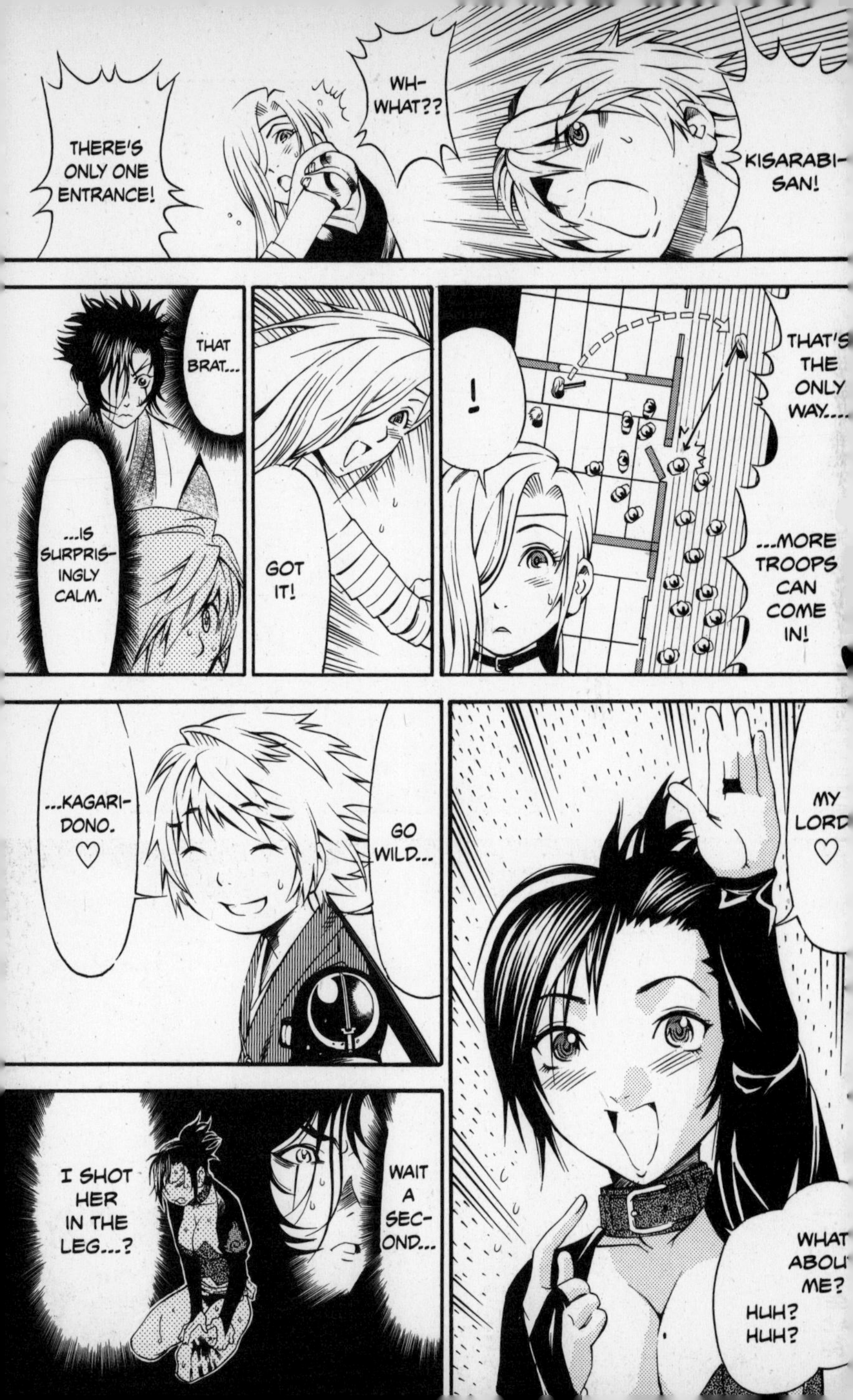
KISARABI-SAN!
WH-WHAT??
THERE'S ONLY ONE ENTRANCE!
THAT'S THE ONLY WAY....
!
...MORE TROOPS CAN COME IN!
GOT IT!
THAT BRAT...
...IS SURPRISINGLY CALM.
MY LORD ♡
WHAT ABOU ME? HUH? HUH?
GO WILD...
...KAGARI-DONO. ♡
WAIT A SECOND...
I SHOT HER IN THE LEG...?

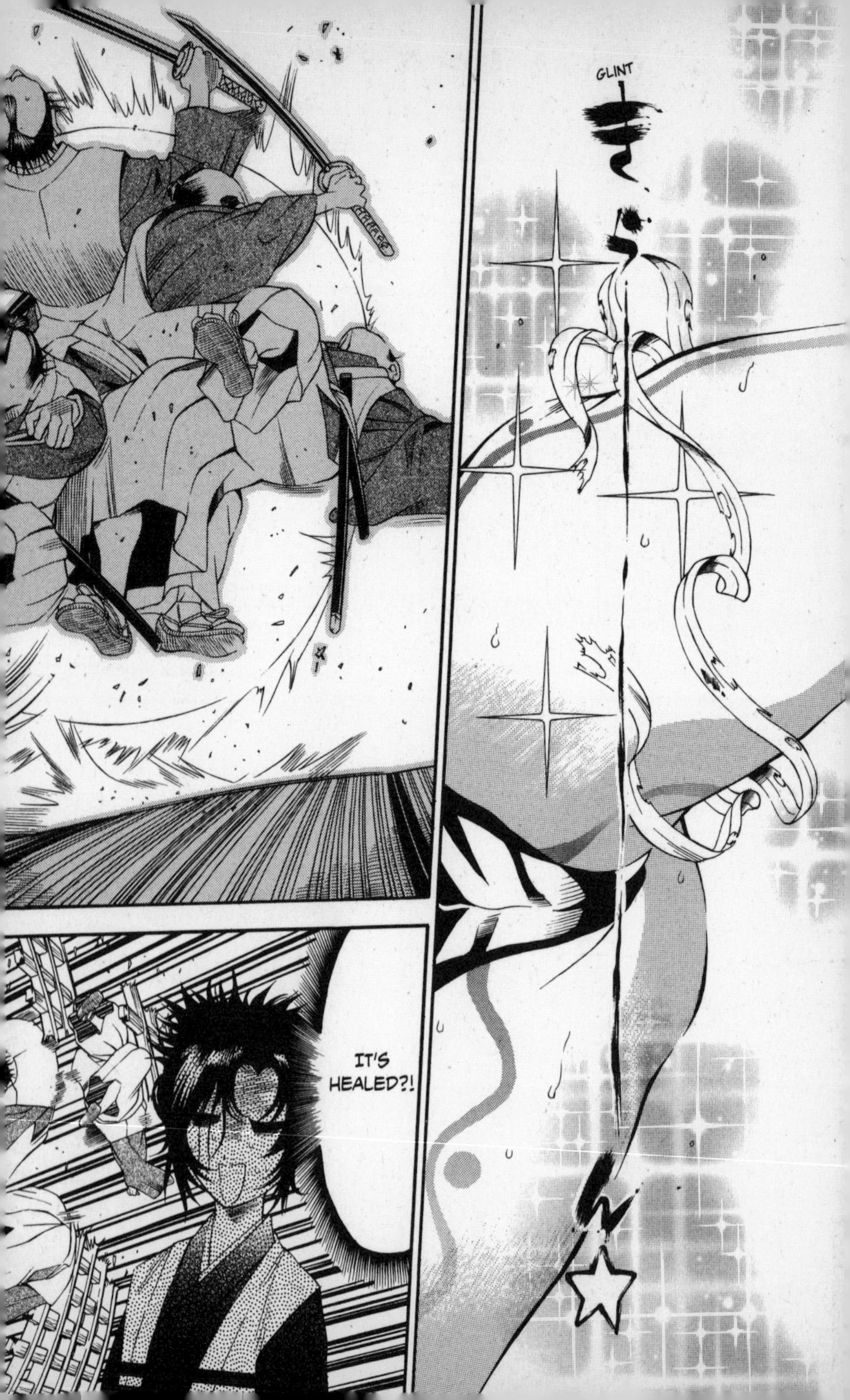
GLINT
IT'S HEALED?!

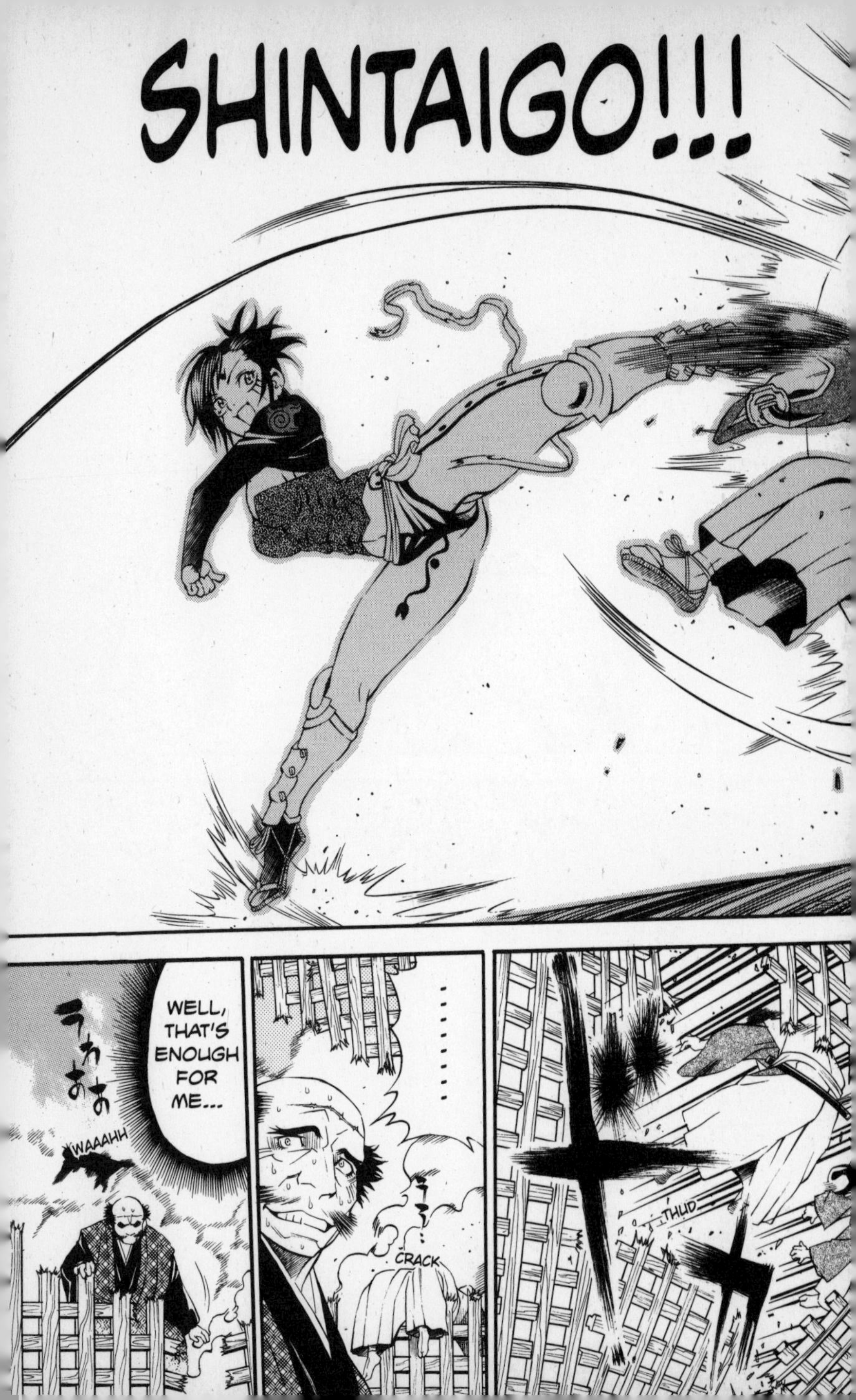
SHINTAIGO!!!
THUD
......
CRACK
WELL, THAT'S ENOUGH FOR ME...
WAAAHH

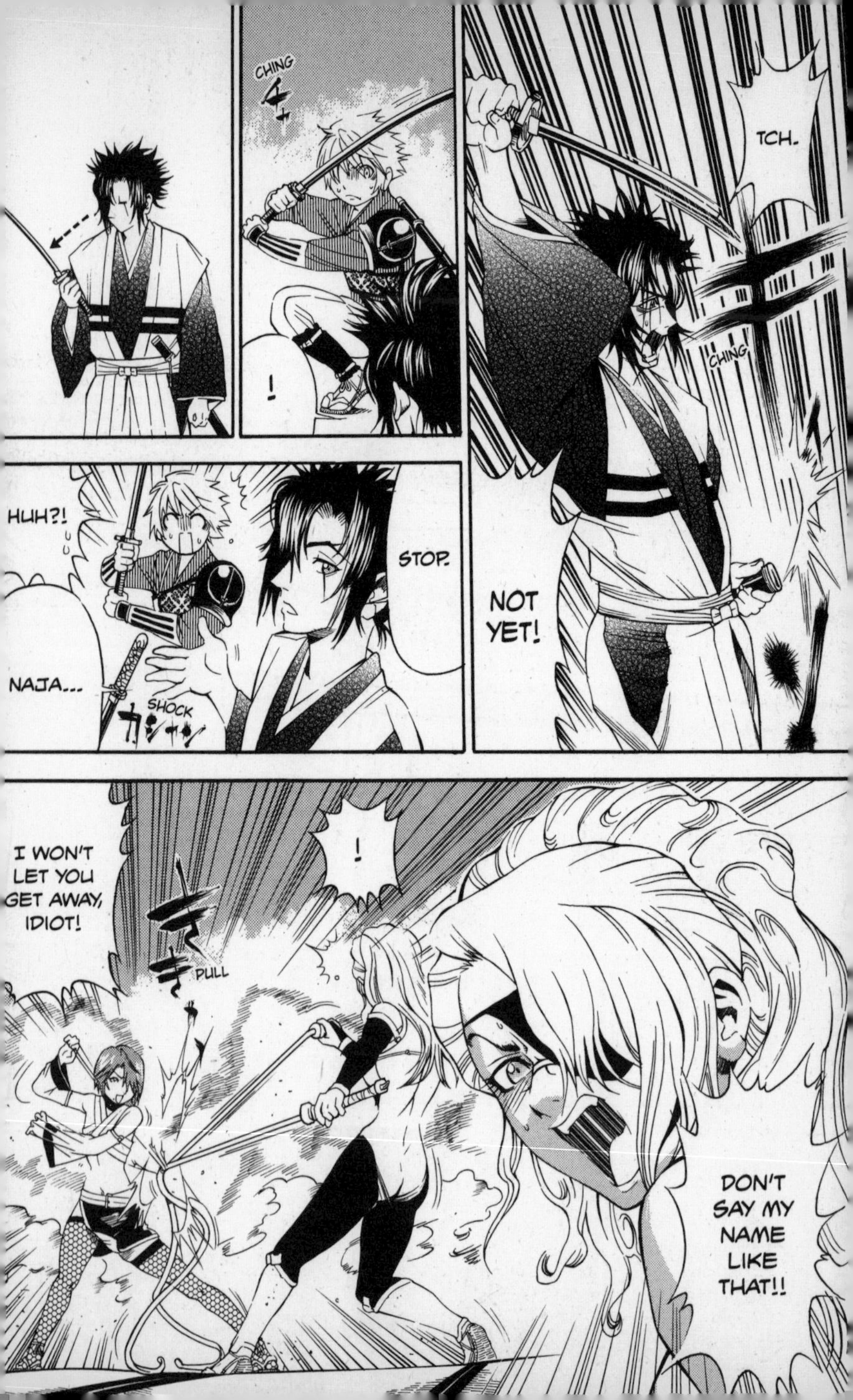
TCH.
CHING
NOT YET!
CHING
!
STOP.
HUH?!
NAJA...
SHOCK
!
I WON'T LET YOU GET AWAY, IDIOT!
PULL
DON'T SAY MY NAME LIKE THAT!!

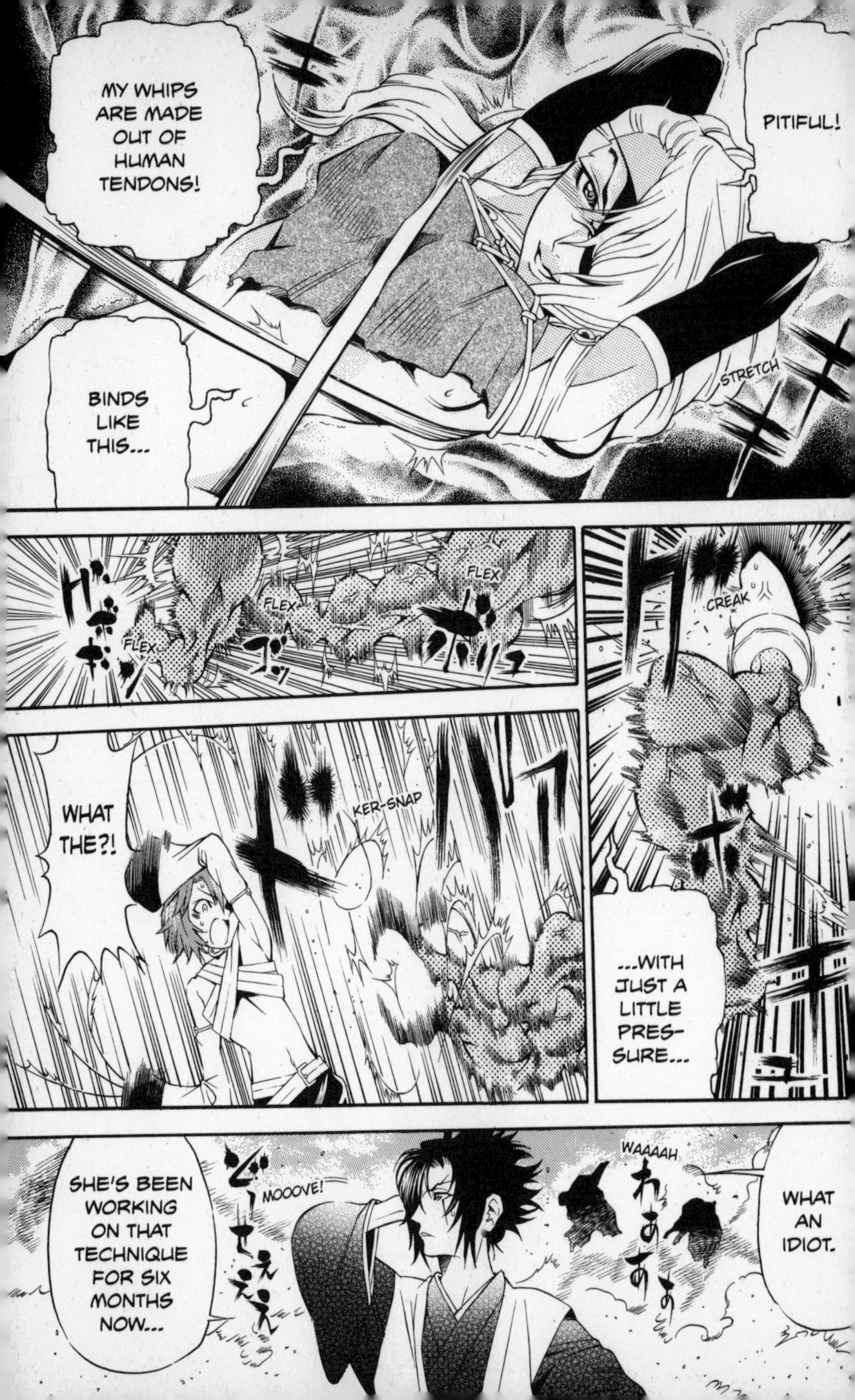
PITIFUL!
MY WHIPS ARE MADE OUT OF HUMAN TENDONS!
STRETCH
BINDS LIKE THIS...
CREAK
...WITH JUST A LITTLE PRES-SURE...
FLEX
FLEX
FLEX
KER-SNAP
WHAT THE?!
WHAT AN IDIOT.
WAAAAH
MOOOVE!
SHE'S BEEN WORKING ON THAT TECHNIQUE FOR SIX MONTHS NOW...

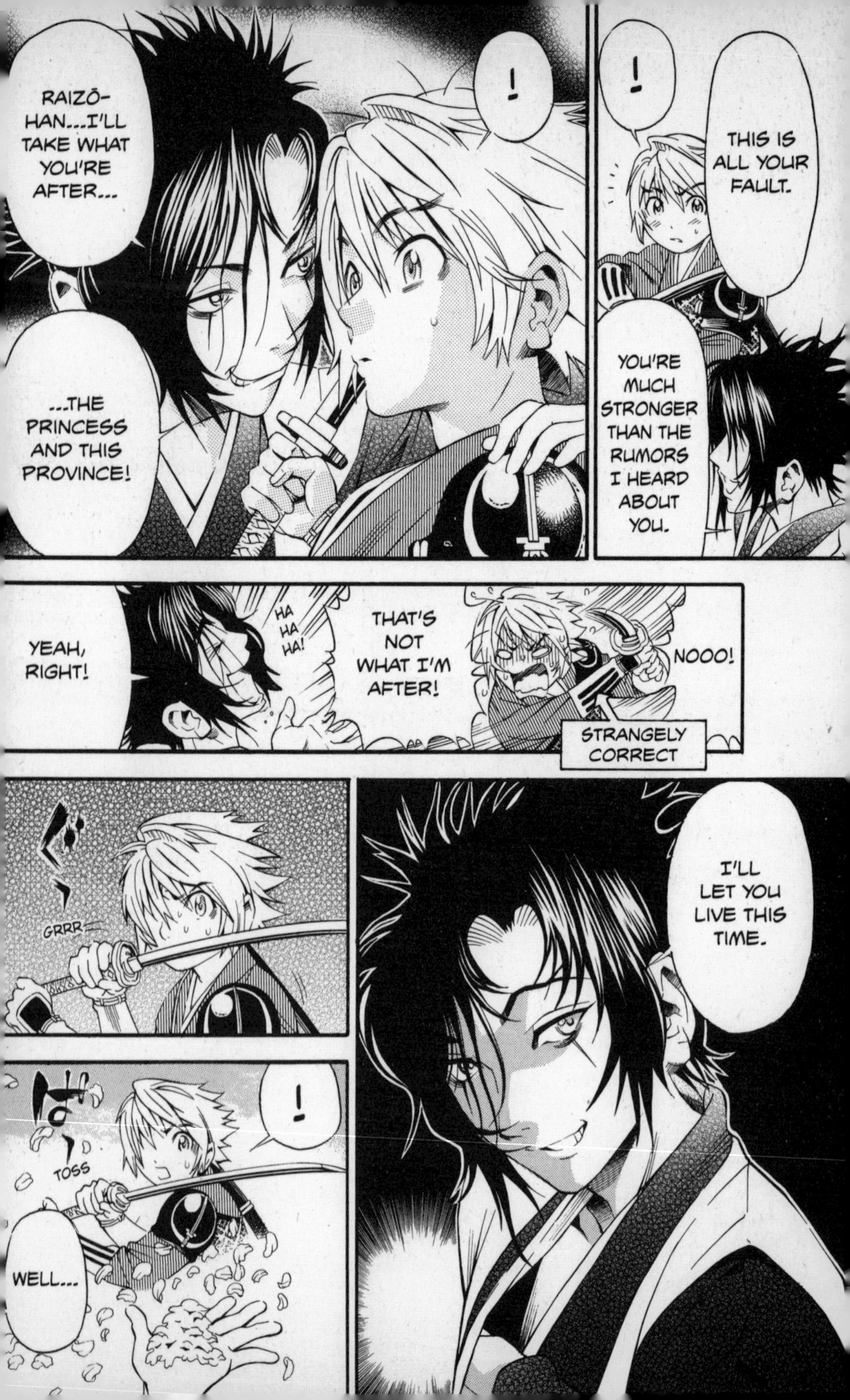
THIS IS ALL YOUR FAULT.
!
YOU'RE MUCH STRONGER THAN THE RUMORS I HEARD ABOUT YOU.
!
RAIZŌ-HAN...I'LL TAKE WHAT YOU'RE AFTER...
...THE PRINCESS AND THIS PROVINCE!
NOOO!
STRANGELY CORRECT
THAT'S NOT WHAT I'M AFTER!
HA HA HA!
YEAH, RIGHT!
I'LL LET YOU LIVE THIS TIME.
GRRR
!
TOSS
WELL...

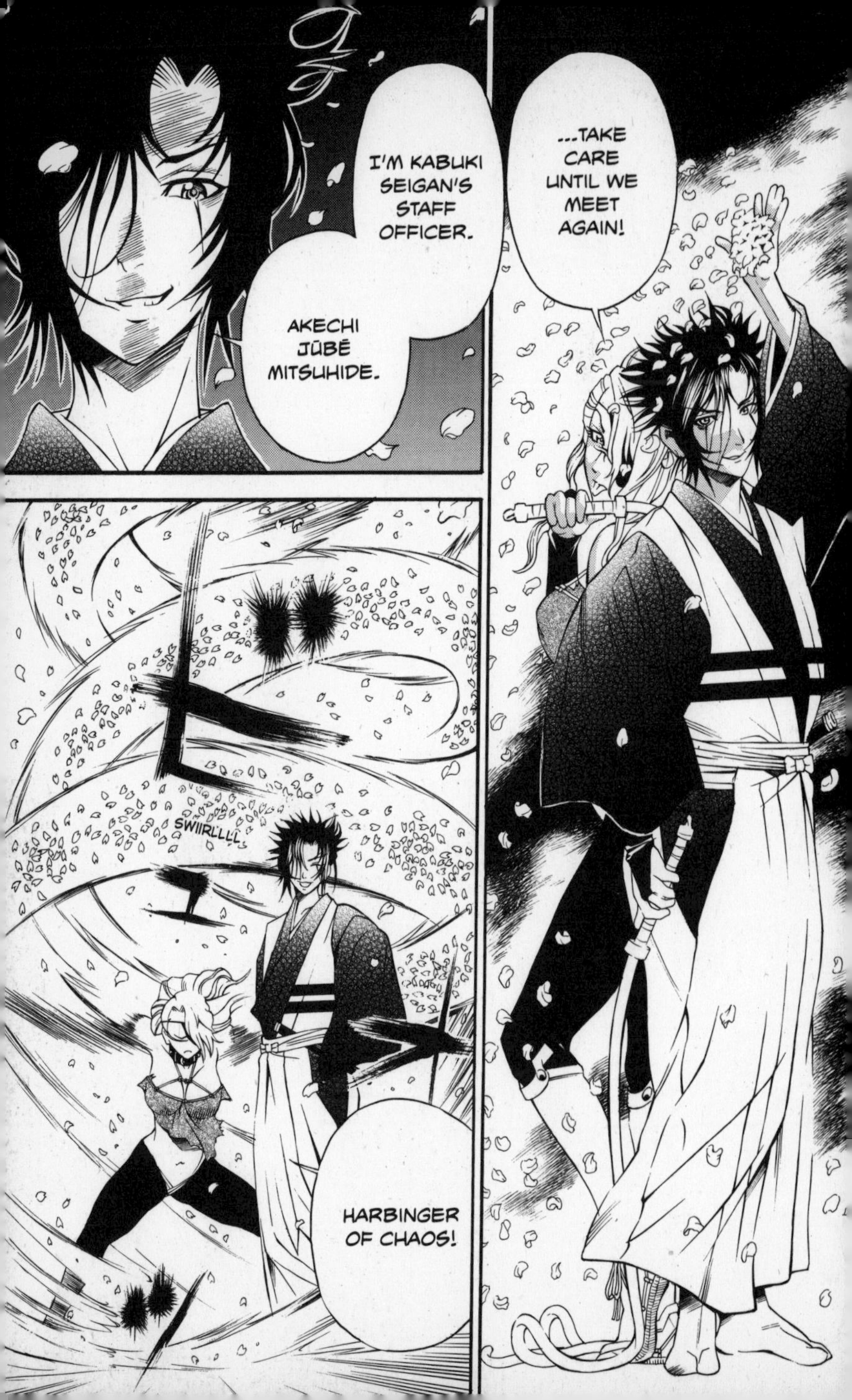
...TAKE CARE UNTIL WE MEET AGAIN!
I'M KABUKI SEIGAN'S STAFF OFFICER.
AKECHI JŪBĒ MITSUHIDE.
SWIIRLLLL
HARBINGER OF CHAOS!

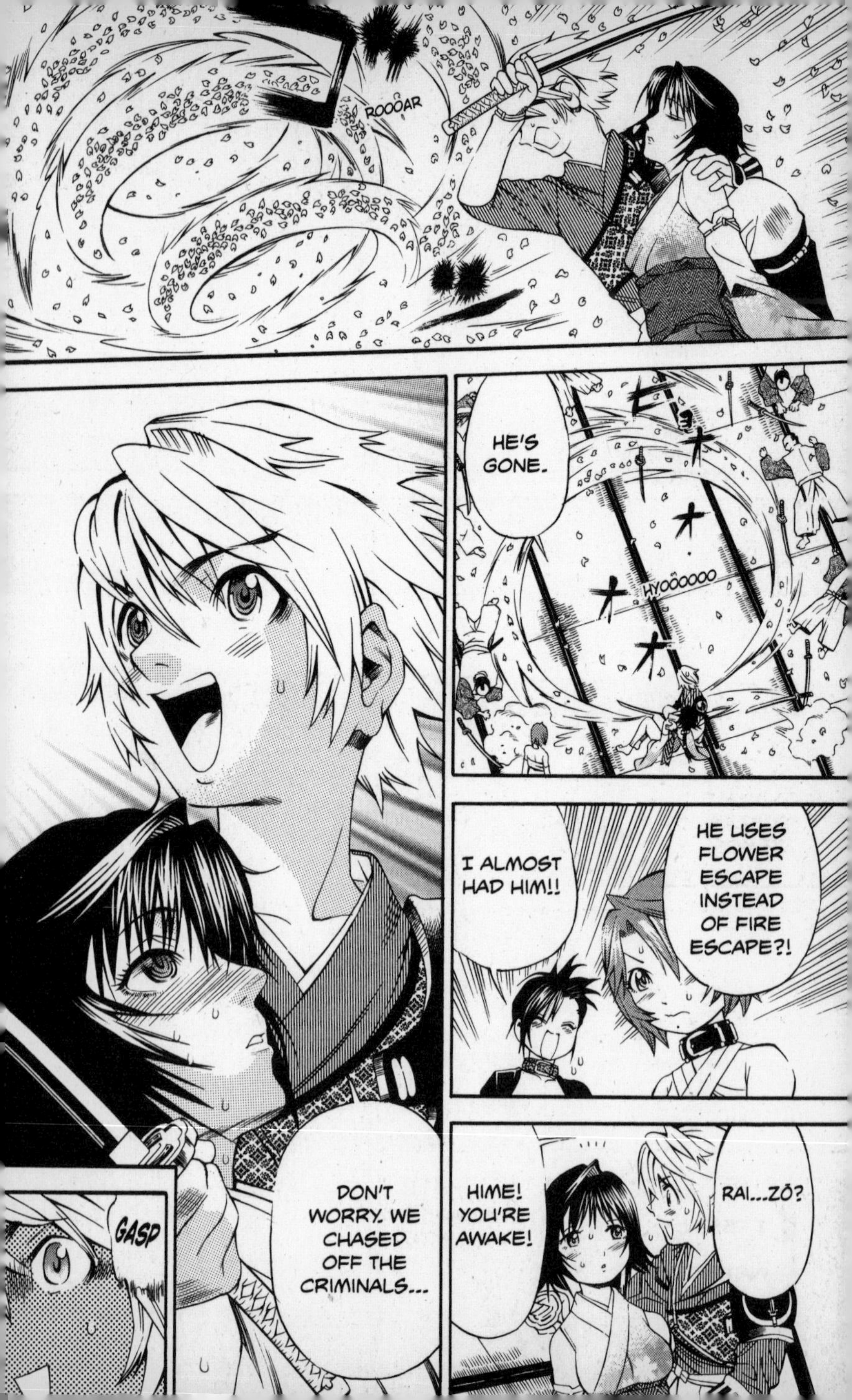

ROOOAR
HE'S GONE.
HYŌOOOOO
HE USES FLOWER ESCAPE INSTEAD OF FIRE ESCAPE?!
I ALMOST HAD HIM!!
RAI...ZŌ?
HIME! YOU'RE AWAKE!
DON'T WORRY. WE CHASED OFF THE CRIMINALS...
GASP

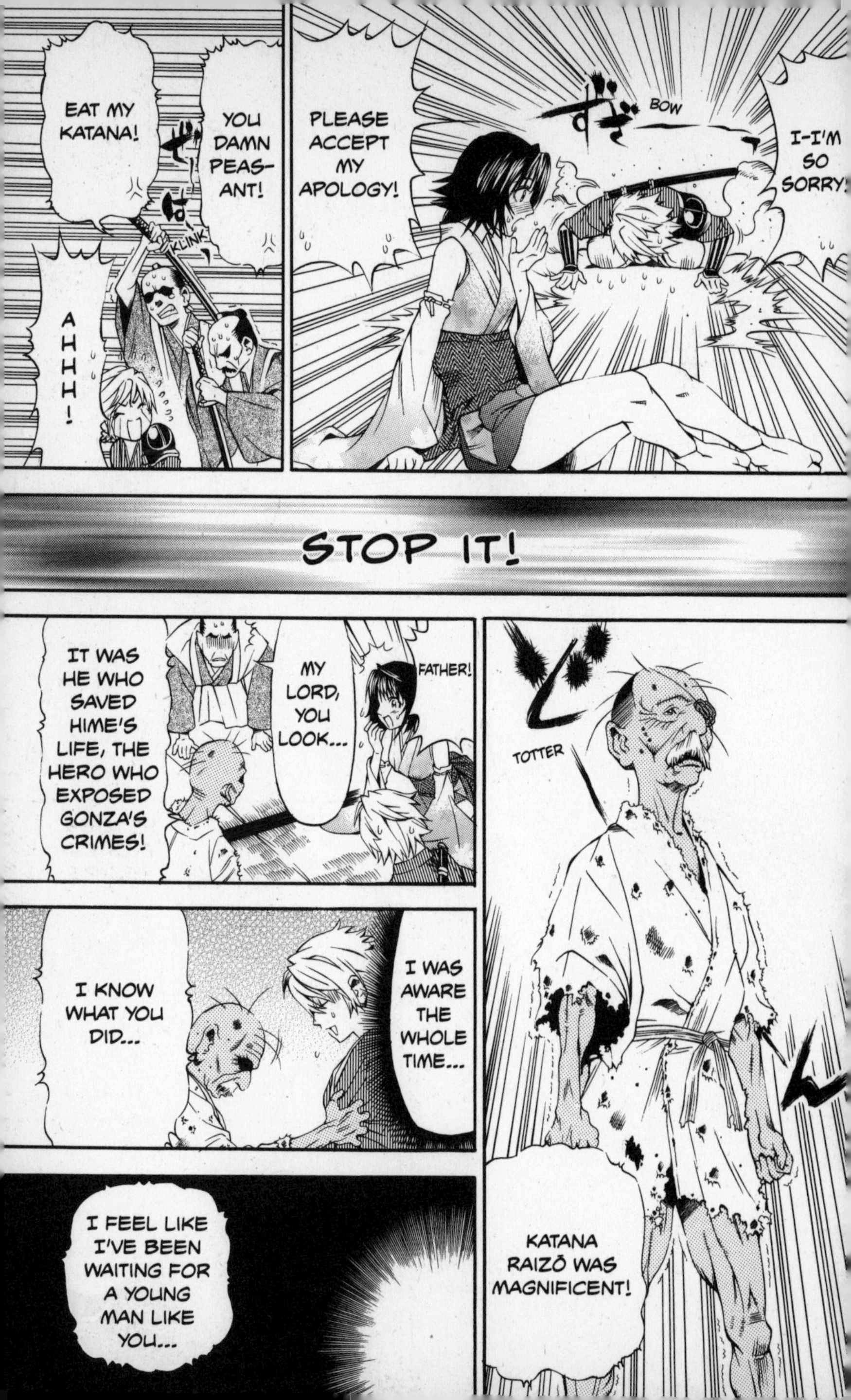
BOW
I-I'M SO SORRY!
PLEASE ACCEPT MY APOLOGY!
YOU DAMN PEAS-ANT!
EAT MY KATANA!
KLINK
AHHH!
STOP IT!
TOTTER
KATANA RAIZŌ WAS MAGNIFICENT!
FATHER!
MY LORD, YOU LOOK...
IT WAS HE WHO SAVED HIME'S LIFE, THE HERO WHO EXPOSED GONZA'S CRIMES!
I WAS AWARE THE WHOLE TIME...
I KNOW WHAT YOU DID...
I FEEL LIKE I'VE BEEN WAITING FOR A YOUNG MAN LIKE YOU...

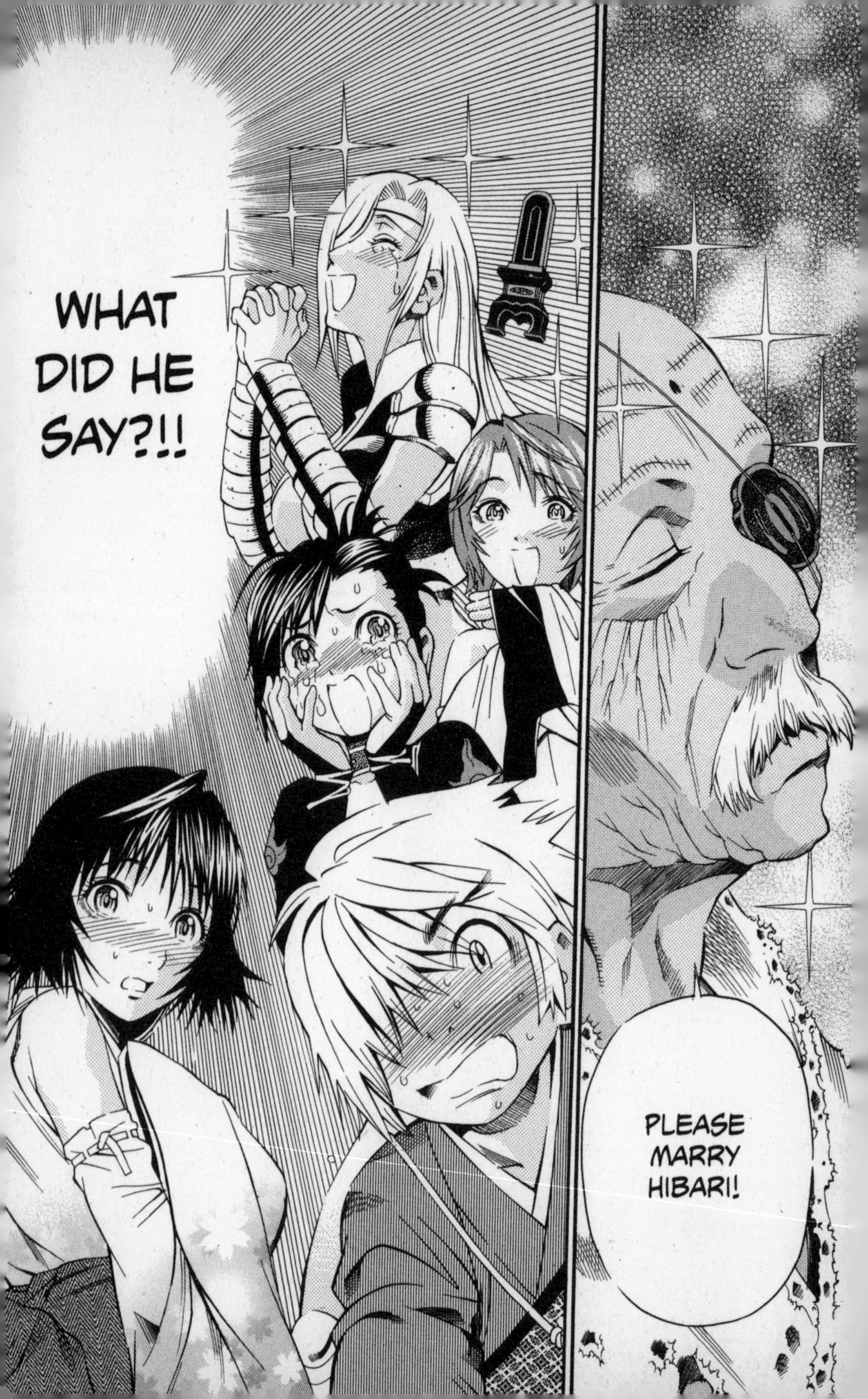
PLEASE MARRY HIBARI!
WHAT DID HE SAY?!!

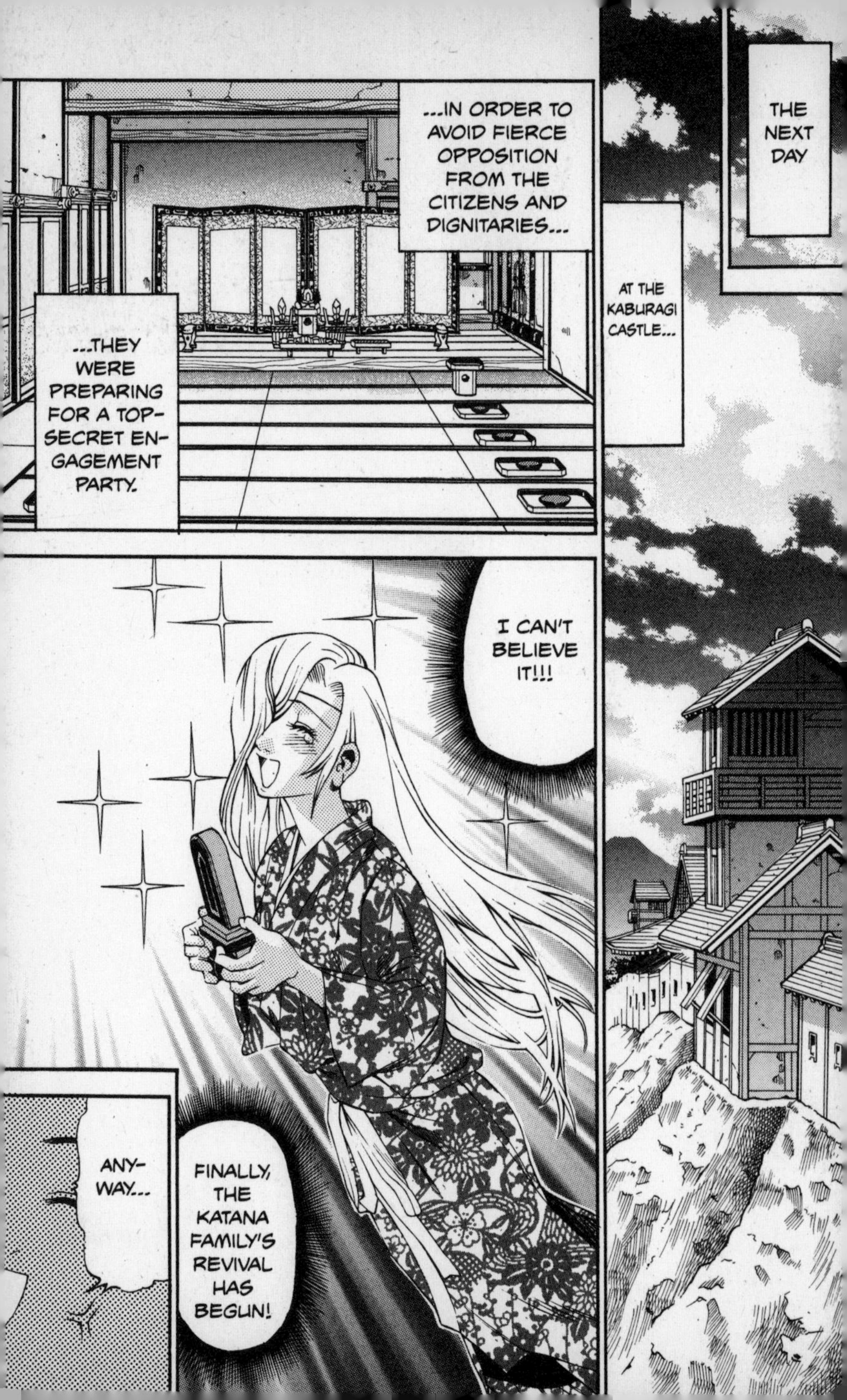
THE NEXT DAY
AT THE KABURAGI CASTLE...
...IN ORDER TO AVOID FIERCE OPPOSITION FROM THE CITIZENS AND DIGNITARIES...
...THEY WERE PREPARING FOR A TOP-SECRET EN-GAGEMENT PARTY.
I CAN'T BELIEVE IT!!!
FINALLY, THE KATANA FAMILY'S REVIVAL HAS BEGUN!
ANY-WAY...

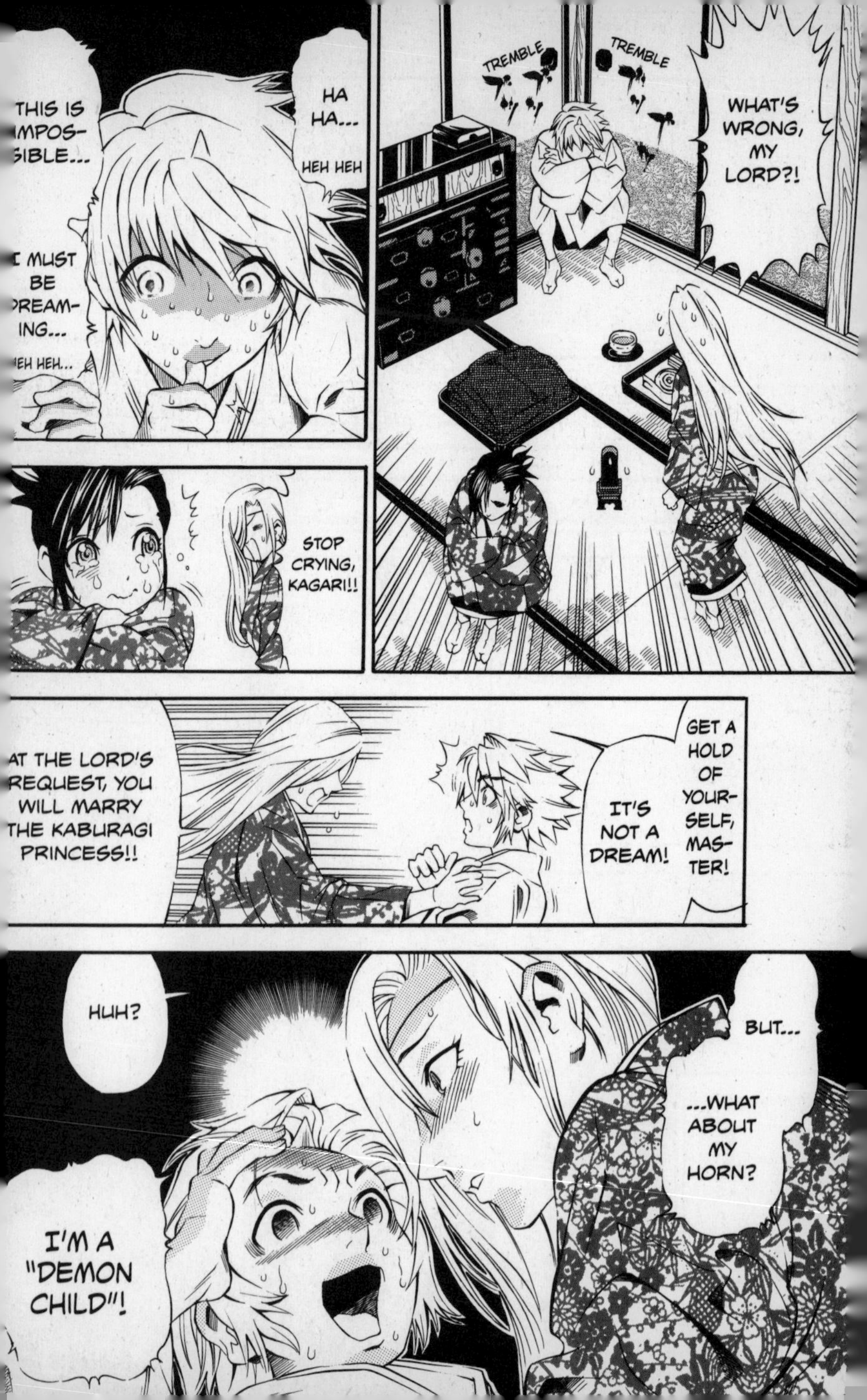
TREMBLE
TREMBLE
WHAT'S WRONG, MY LORD?!
HA HA...
HEH HEH
THIS IS IMPOSSIBLE...
I MUST BE DREAMING...
HEH HEH...
STOP CRYING, KAGARI!!
GET A HOLD OF YOURSELF, MASTER!
IT'S NOT A DREAM!
AT THE LORD'S REQUEST, YOU WILL MARRY THE KABURAGI PRINCESS!!
BUT...
...WHAT ABOUT MY HORN?
HUH?
I'M A "DEMON CHILD"!

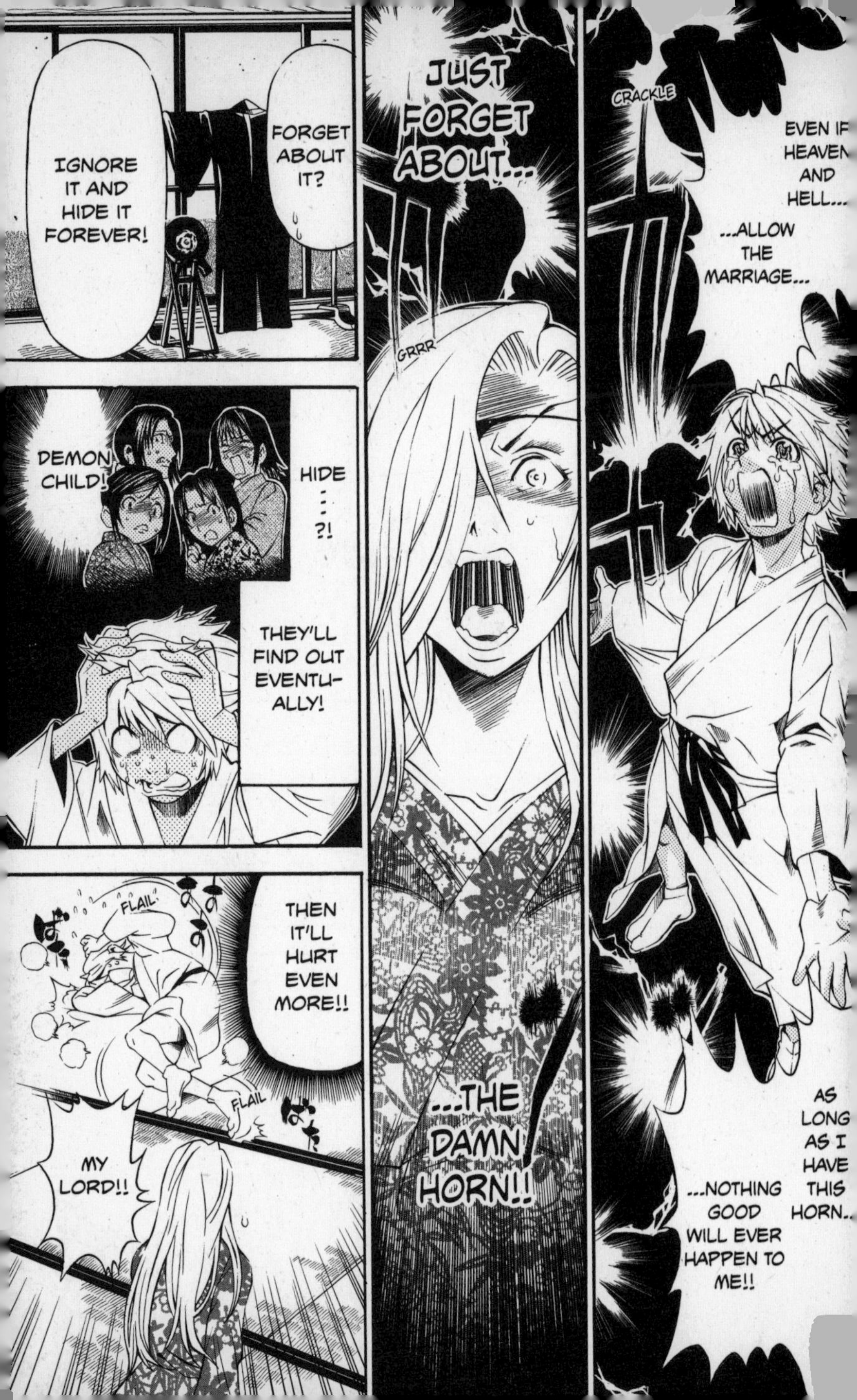
CRACKLE
EVEN IF HEAVEN AND HELL...
...ALLOW THE MARRIAGE...
AS LONG AS I HAVE THIS HORN...
...NOTHING GOOD WILL EVER HAPPEN TO ME!!
JUST FORGET ABOUT...
GRRR
...THE DAMN HORN!!
FORGET ABOUT IT?
IGNORE IT AND HIDE IT FOREVER!
HIDE...?!
DEMON CHILD!
THEY'LL FIND OUT EVENTU-ALLY!
THEN IT'LL HURT EVEN MORE!!
FLAIL
FLAIL
MY LORD!!

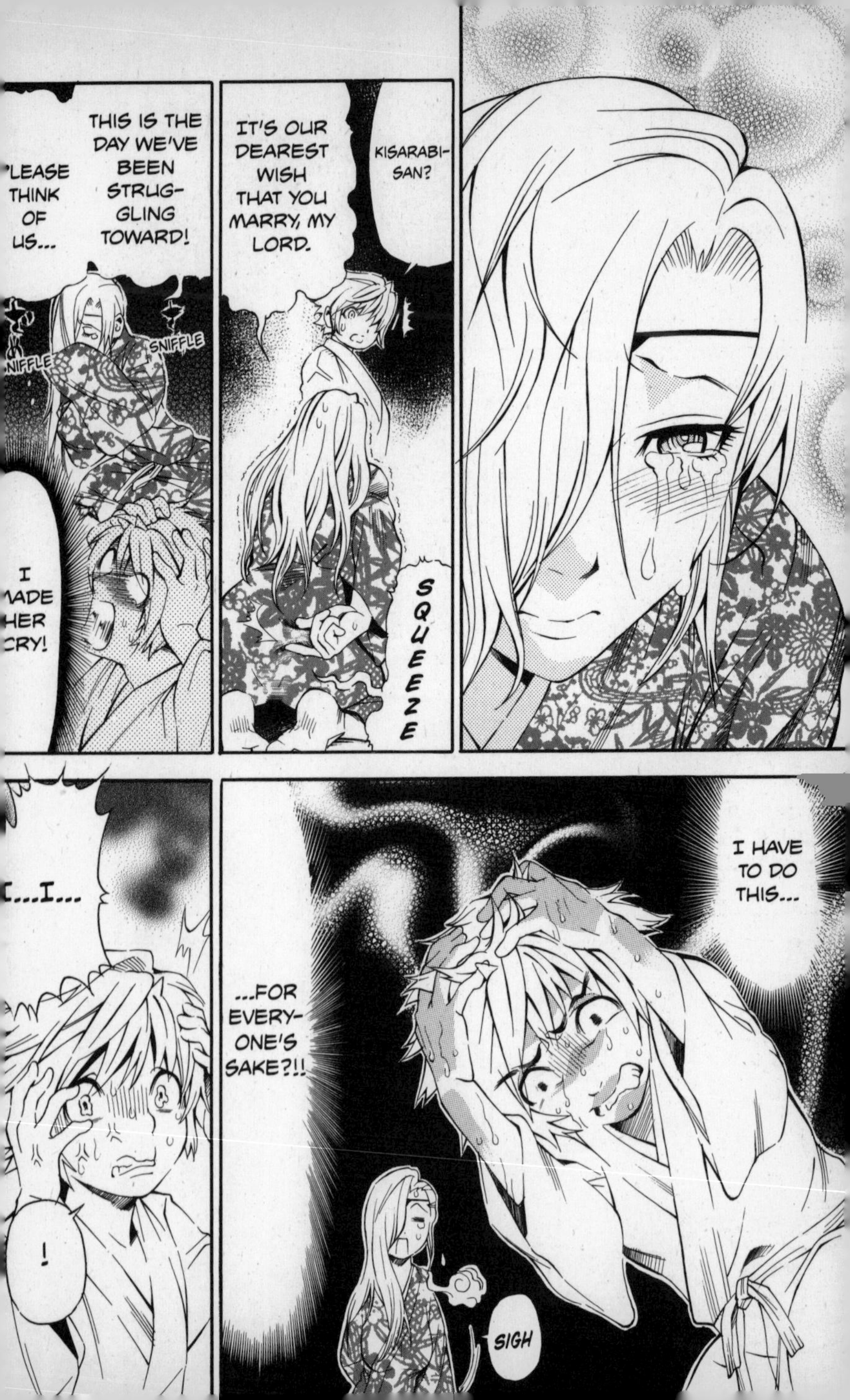
KISARABI-SAN?
IT'S OUR DEAREST WISH THAT YOU MARRY, MY LORD.
SQUEEZE
THIS IS THE DAY WE'VE BEEN STRUG-GLING TOWARD!
'LEASE THINK OF US...
SNIFFLE
SNIFFLE
I MADE HER CRY!
I HAVE TO DO THIS...
...FOR EVERY-ONE'S SAKE?!!
SIGH
I...I...
!

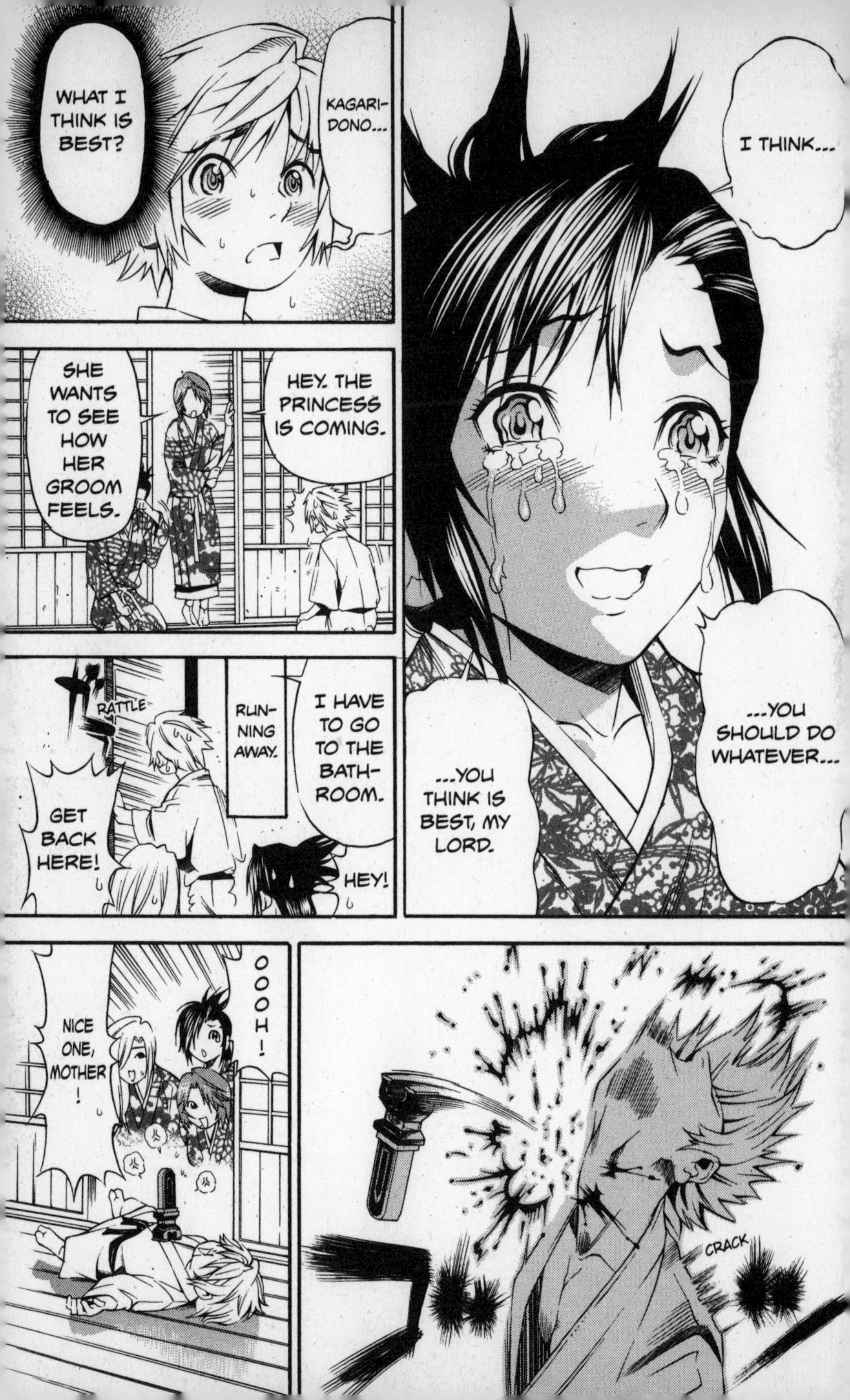
I THINK...
...YOU SHOULD DO WHATEVER...
...YOU THINK IS BEST, MY LORD.
KAGARI-DONO...
WHAT I THINK IS BEST?
HEY. THE PRINCESS IS COMING.
SHE WANTS TO SEE HOW HER GROOM FEELS.
I HAVE TO GO TO THE BATHROOM.
RUNNING AWAY.
HEY!
RATTLE
GET BACK HERE!
CRACK
OOOOH!
NICE ONE, MOTHER!

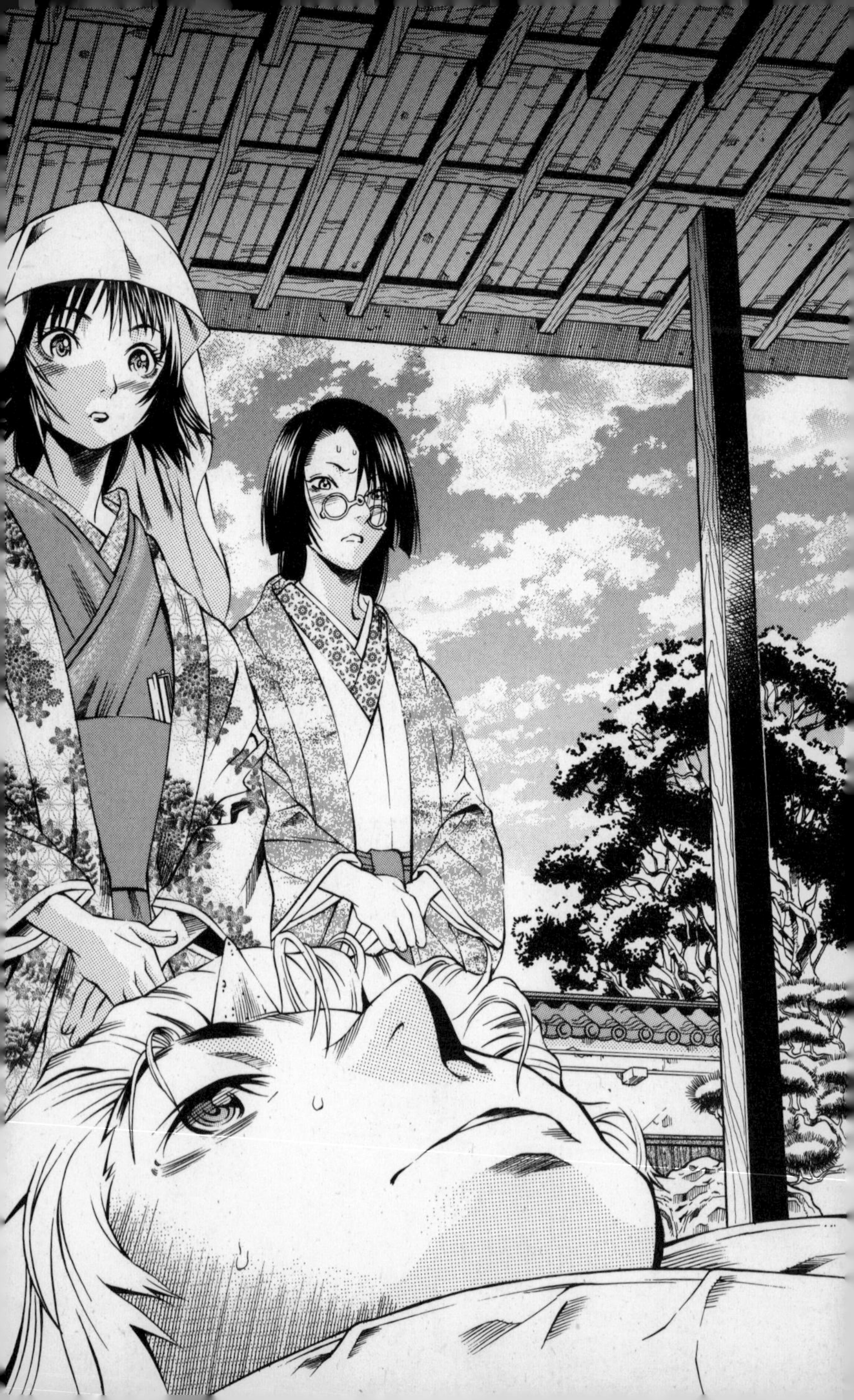

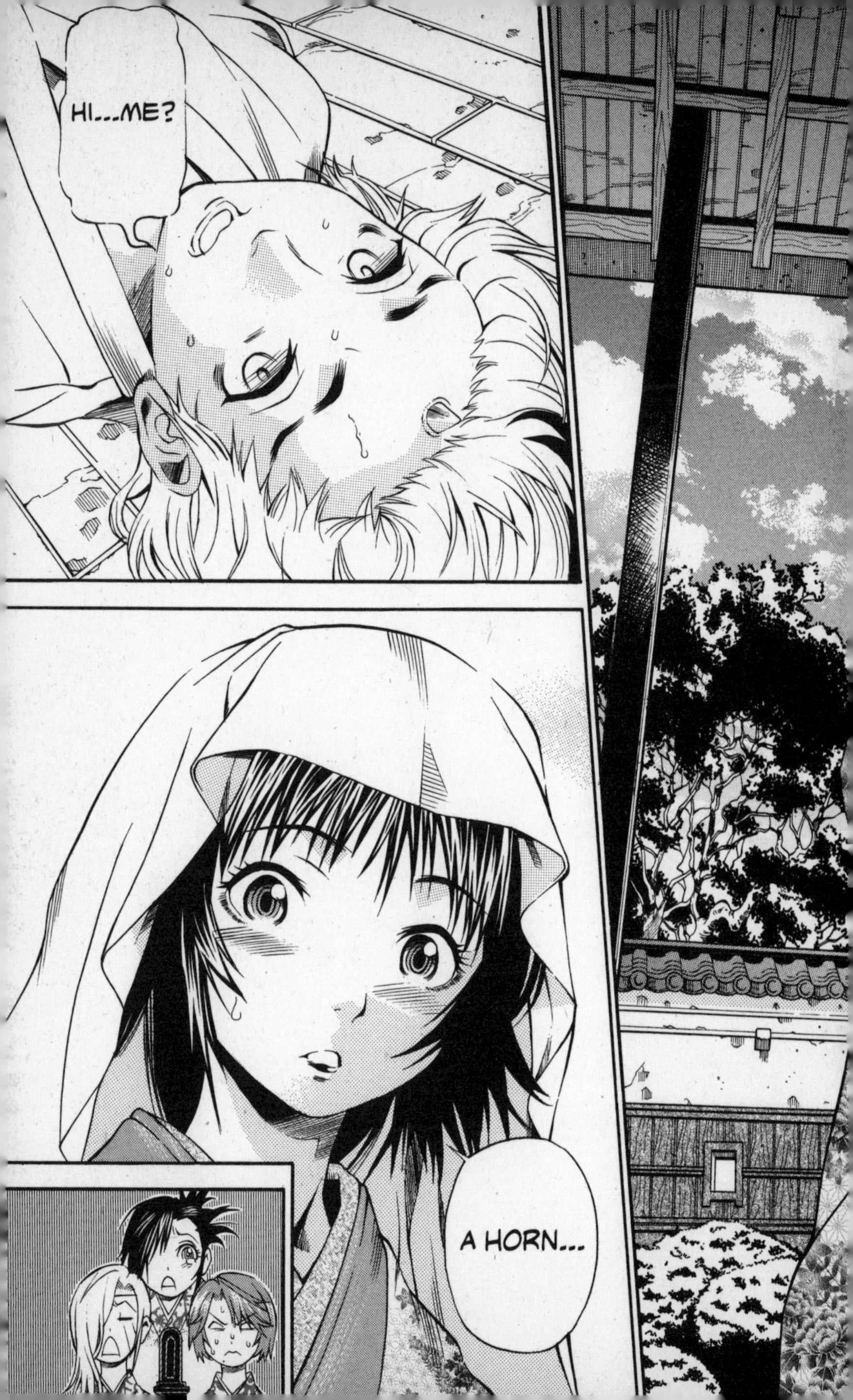
HI...ME?
A HORN...

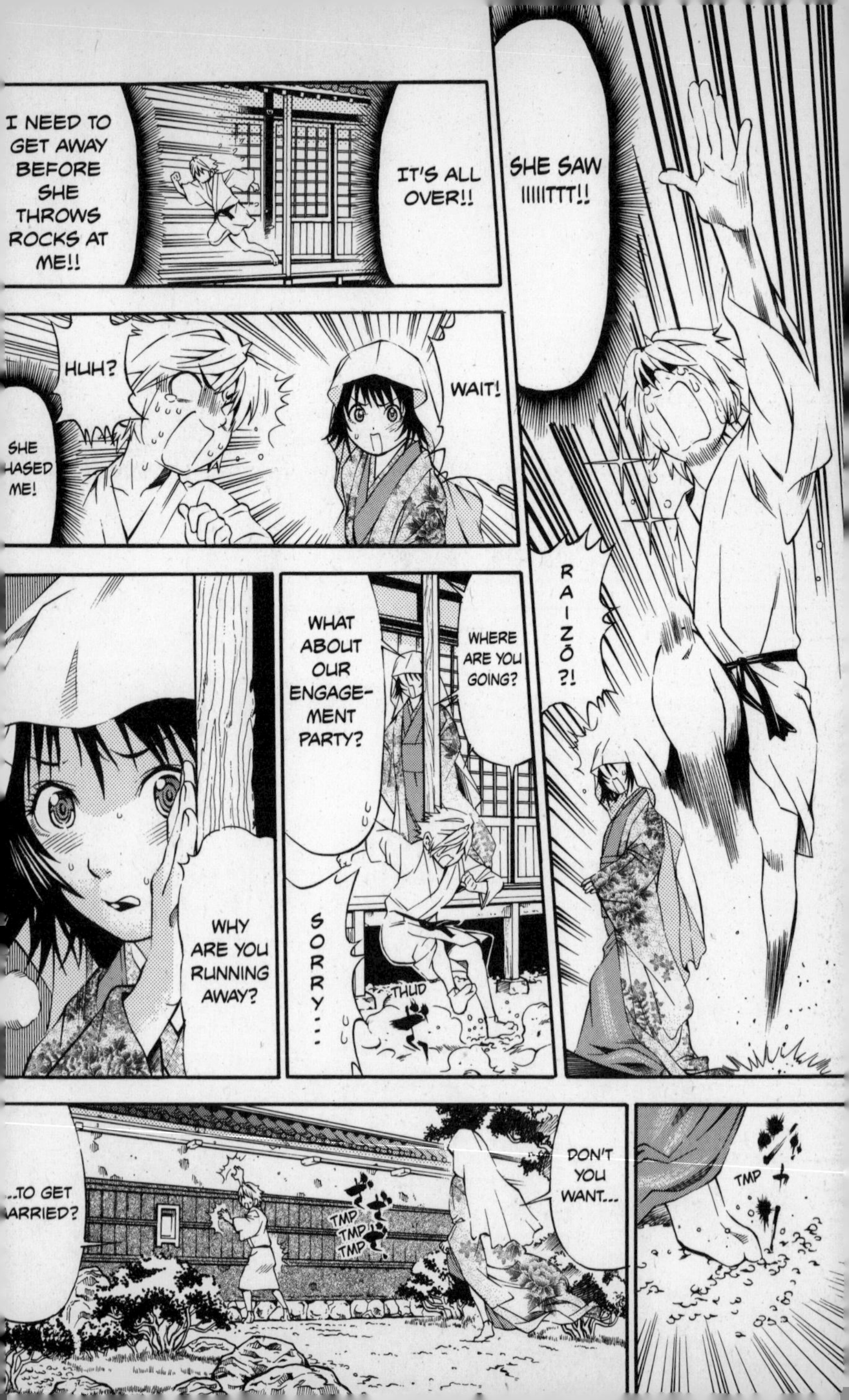
SHE SAW IIIIITTT!!
RAIZŌ?!
IT'S ALL OVER!!
I NEED TO GET AWAY BEFORE SHE THROWS ROCKS AT ME!!
WAIT!
HUH?
SHE HASED ME!
WHERE ARE YOU GOING?
WHAT ABOUT OUR ENGAGEMENT PARTY?
SORRY...
THUD
WHY ARE YOU RUNNING AWAY?
TMP
DON'T YOU WANT...
...TO GET ARRIED?
TMP TMP TMP

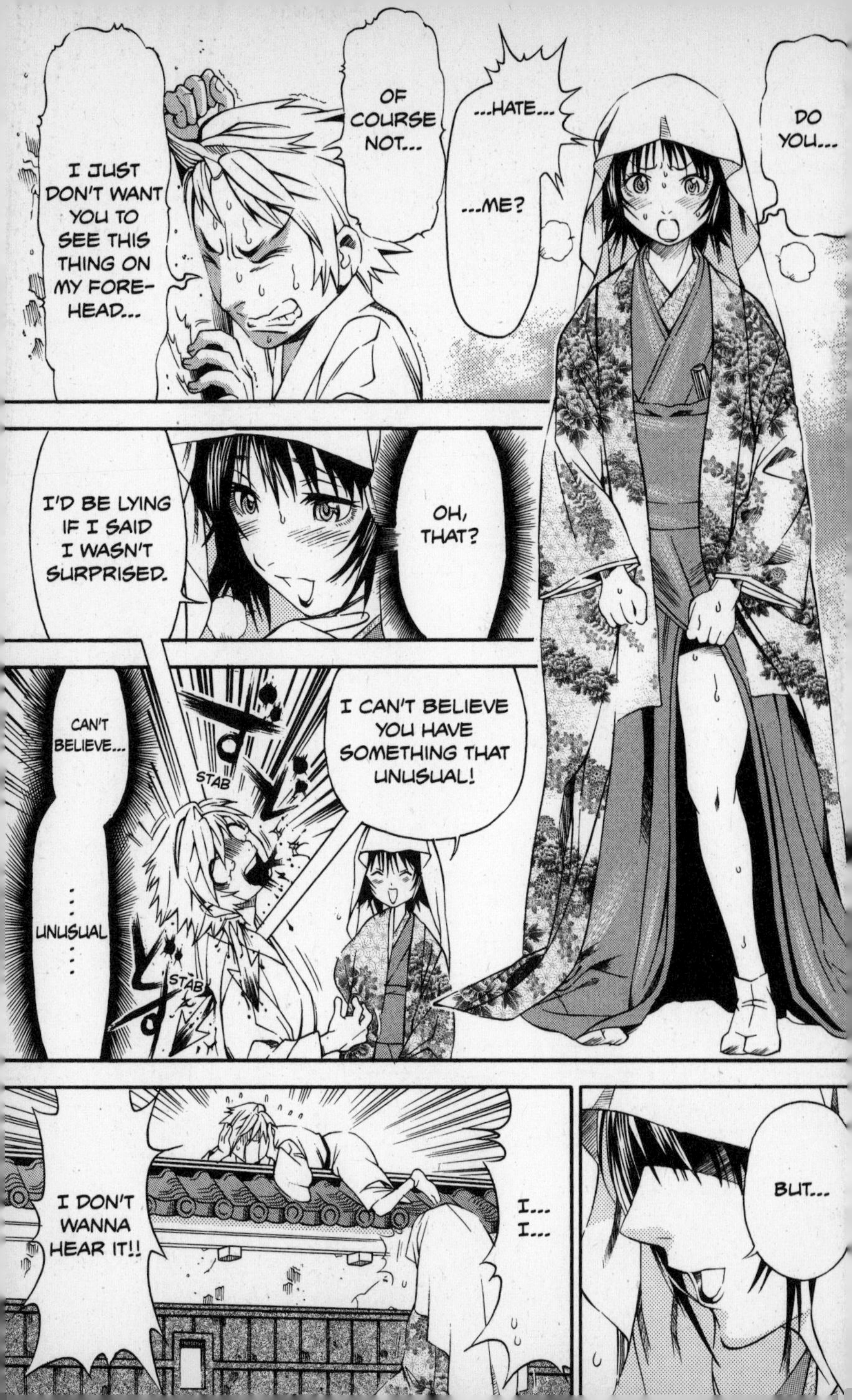
DO YOU...
...HATE...
...ME?
OF COURSE NOT...
I JUST DON'T WANT YOU TO SEE THIS THING ON MY FOREHEAD...
OH, THAT?
I'D BE LYING IF I SAID I WASN'T SURPRISED.
I CAN'T BELIEVE YOU HAVE SOMETHING THAT UNUSUAL!
STAB
STAB
CAN'T BELIEVE...
...UNUSUAL...
BUT...
I... I...
I DON'T WANNA HEAR IT!!

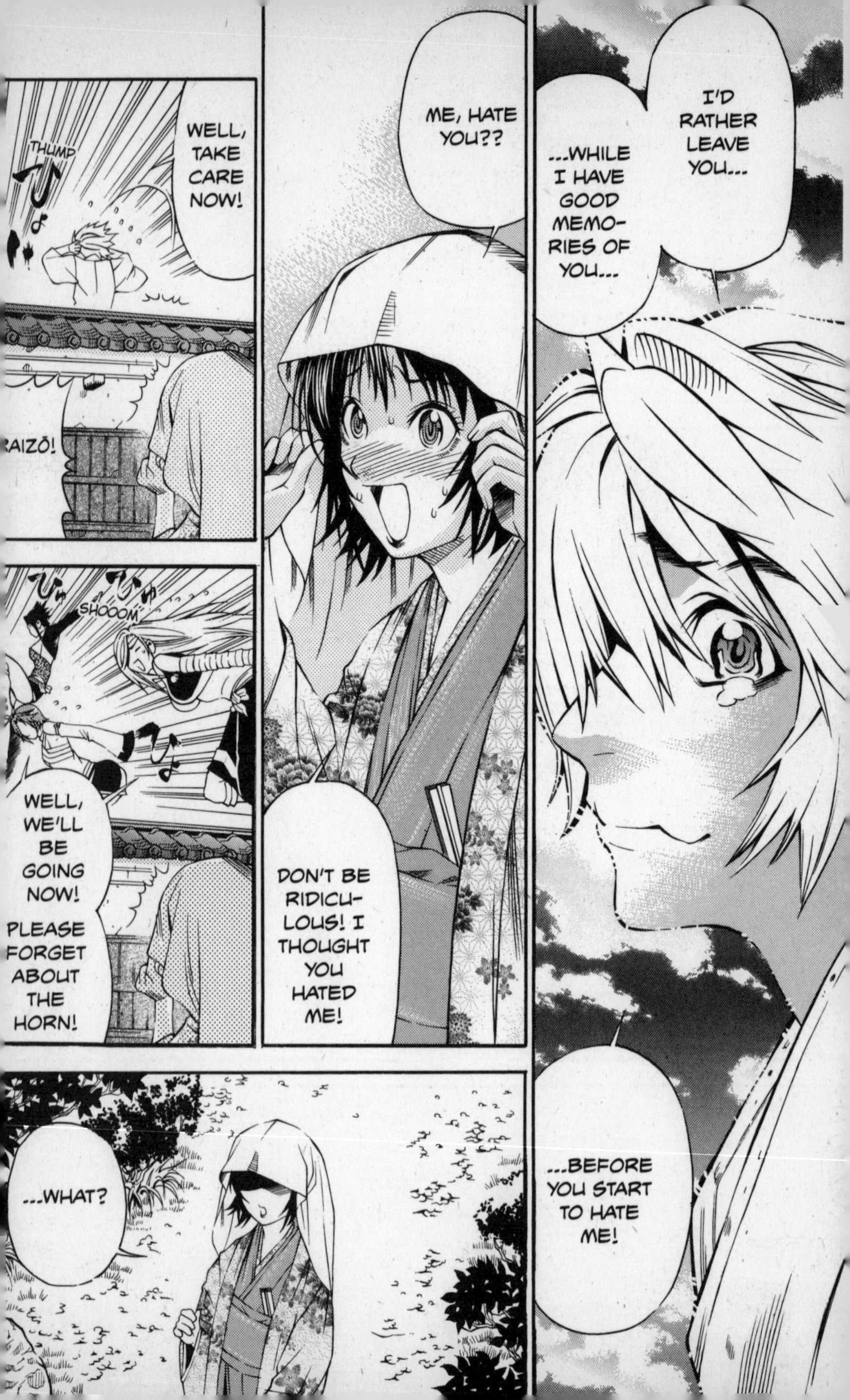
I'D RATHER LEAVE YOU...
...WHILE I HAVE GOOD MEMORIES OF YOU...
...BEFORE YOU START TO HATE ME!
ME, HATE YOU??
DON'T BE RIDICULOUS! I THOUGHT YOU HATED ME!
WELL, TAKE CARE NOW!
THUMP
RAIZŌ!
SHOOOM
WELL, WE'LL BE GOING NOW!
PLEASE FORGET ABOUT THE HORN!
...WHAT?

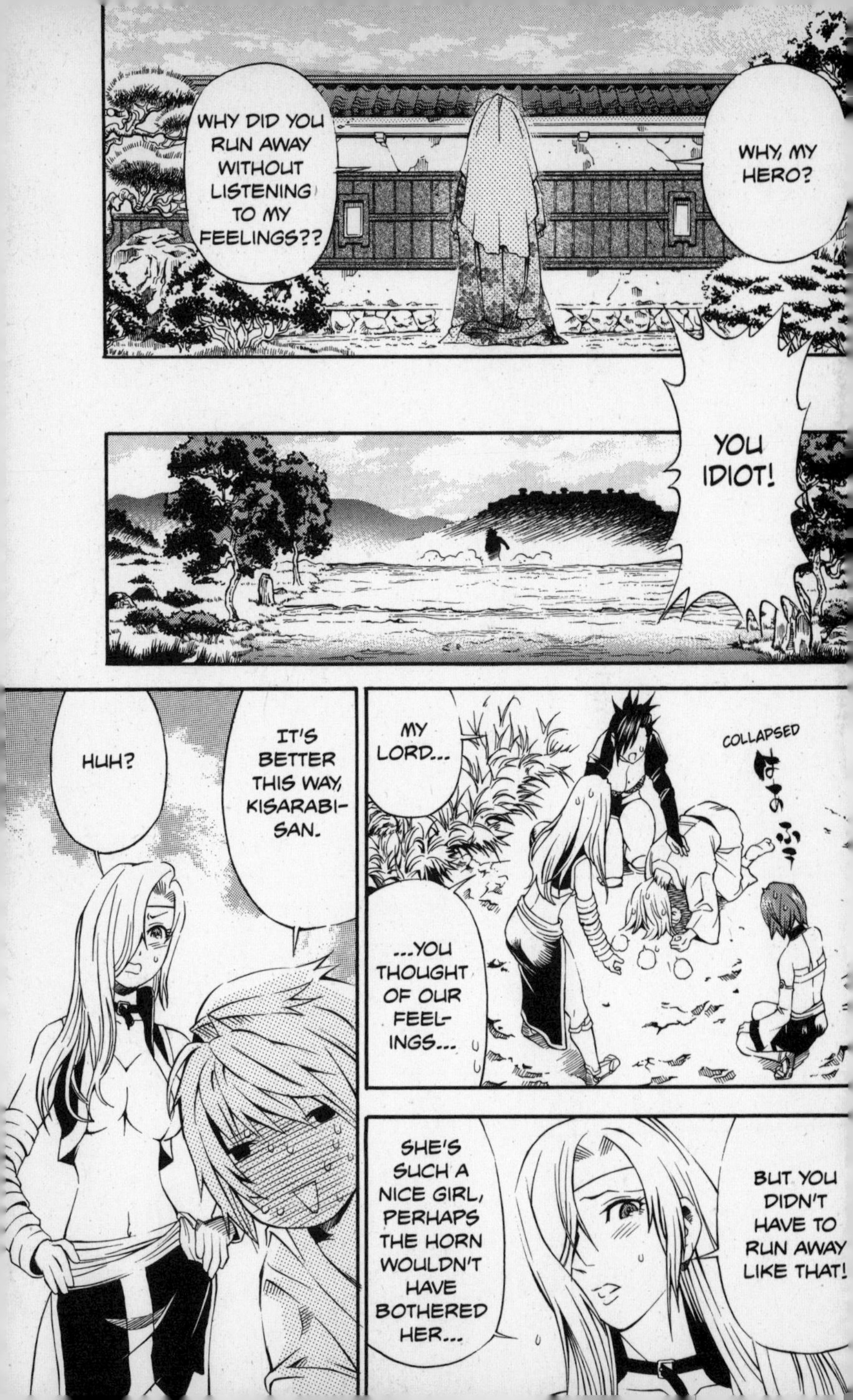
WHY, MY HERO?
WHY DID YOU RUN AWAY WITHOUT LISTENING TO MY FEELINGS??
YOU IDIOT!
COLLAPSED
MY LORD...
...YOU THOUGHT OF OUR FEEL-INGS...
BUT YOU DIDN'T HAVE TO RUN AWAY LIKE THAT!
SHE'S SUCH A NICE GIRL, PERHAPS THE HORN WOULDN'T HAVE BOTHERED HER...
IT'S BETTER THIS WAY, KISARABI-SAN.
HUH?

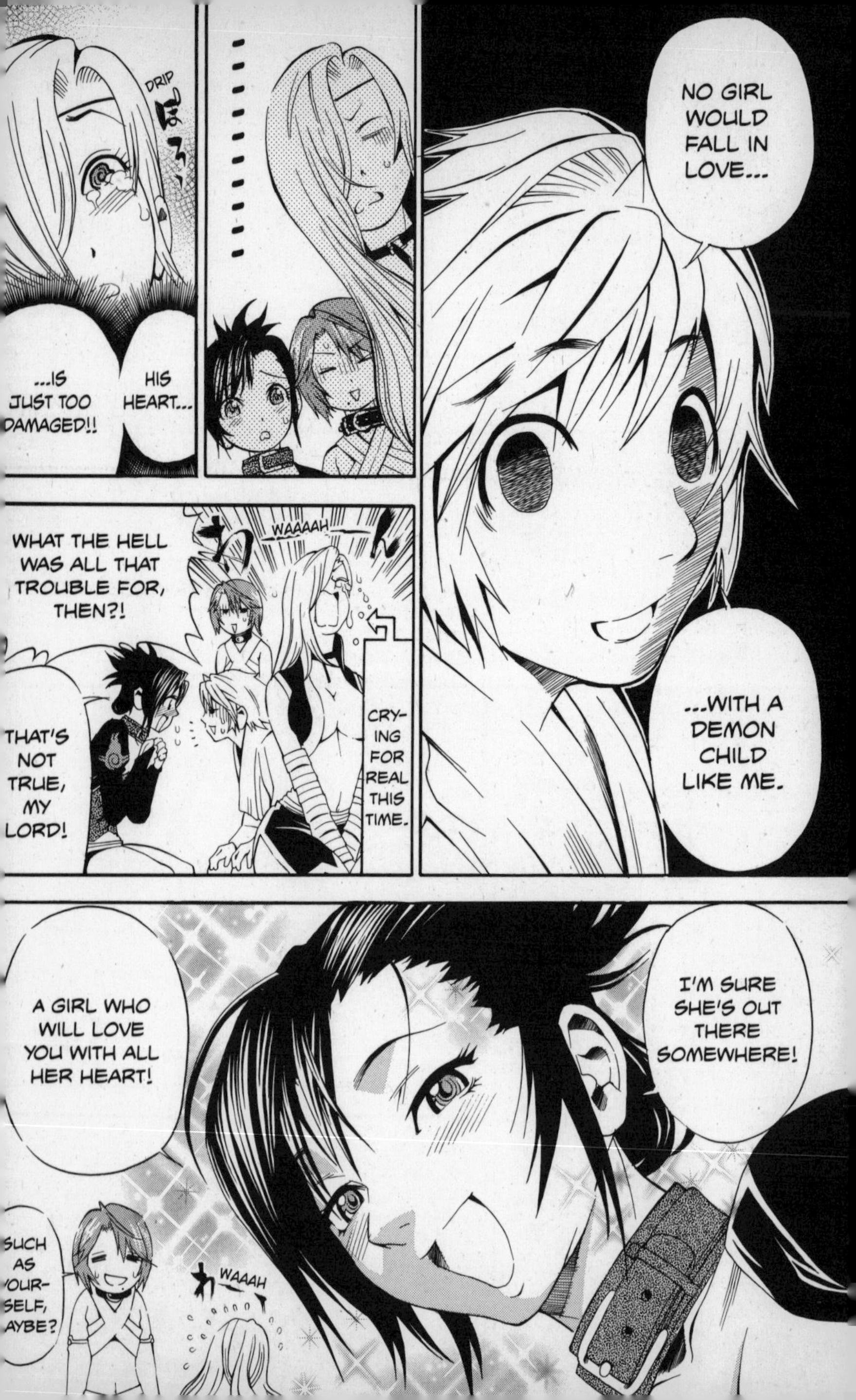
NO GIRL WOULD FALL IN LOVE...
...WITH A DEMON CHILD LIKE ME.
......
DRIP
HIS HEART...
...IS JUST TOO DAMAGED!!
WAAAAH
WHAT THE HELL WAS ALL THAT TROUBLE FOR, THEN?!
CRYING FOR REAL THIS TIME.
THAT'S NOT TRUE, MY LORD!
I'M SURE SHE'S OUT THERE SOMEWHERE!
A GIRL WHO WILL LOVE YOU WITH ALL HER HEART!
WAAAH
SUCH AS OUR-SELF, AYBE?

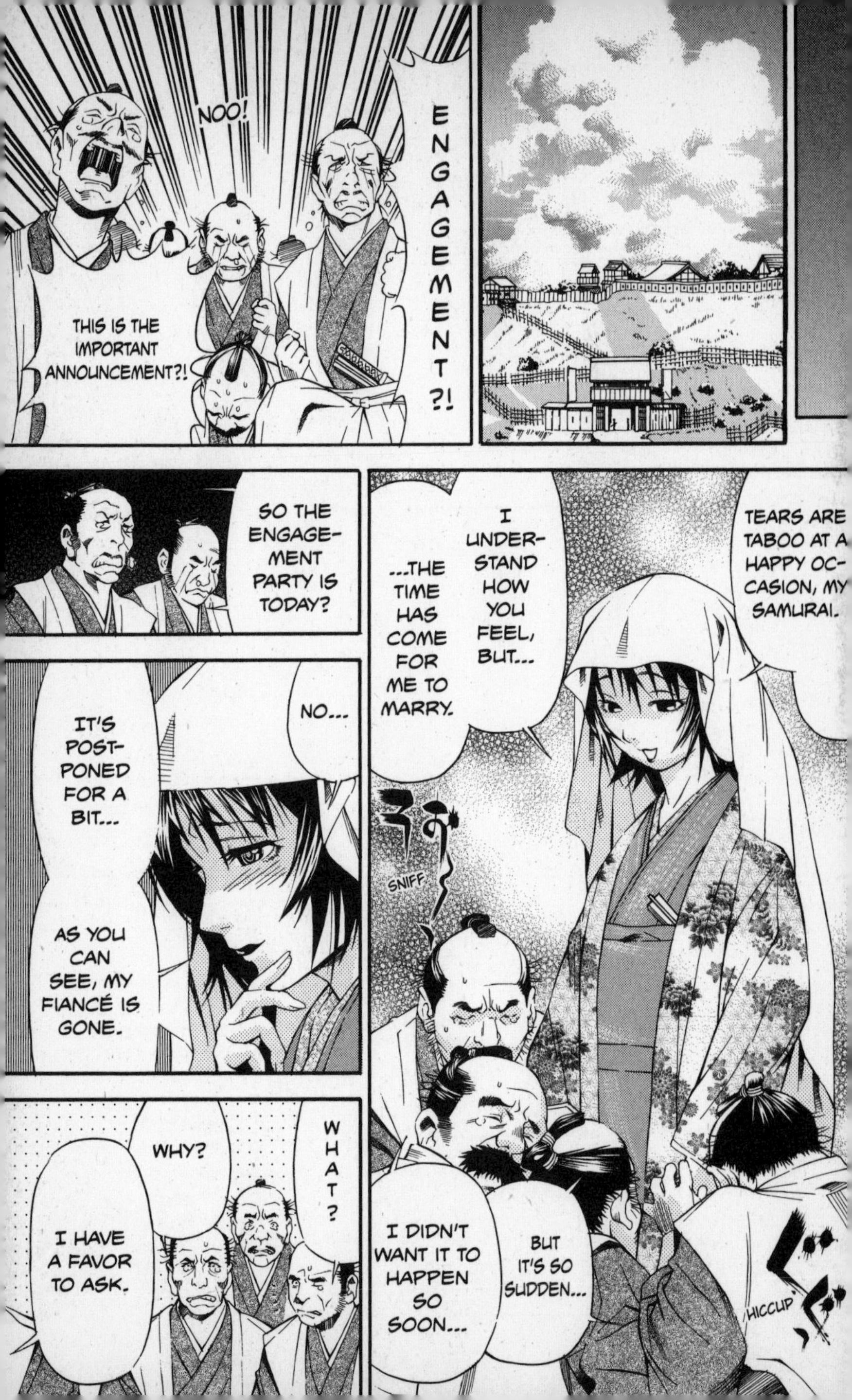
ENGAGEMENT?!
NOO!
THIS IS THE IMPORTANT ANNOUNCEMENT?!
TEARS ARE TABOO AT A HAPPY OCCASION, MY SAMURAI.
I UNDERSTAND HOW YOU FEEL, BUT...
...THE TIME HAS COME FOR ME TO MARRY.
SNIFF
HICCUP
BUT IT'S SO SUDDEN...
I DIDN'T WANT IT TO HAPPEN SO SOON...
SO THE ENGAGEMENT PARTY IS TODAY?
NO...
IT'S POSTPONED FOR A BIT...
AS YOU CAN SEE, MY FIANCÉ IS GONE.
WHAT?
WHY?
I HAVE A FAVOR TO ASK.

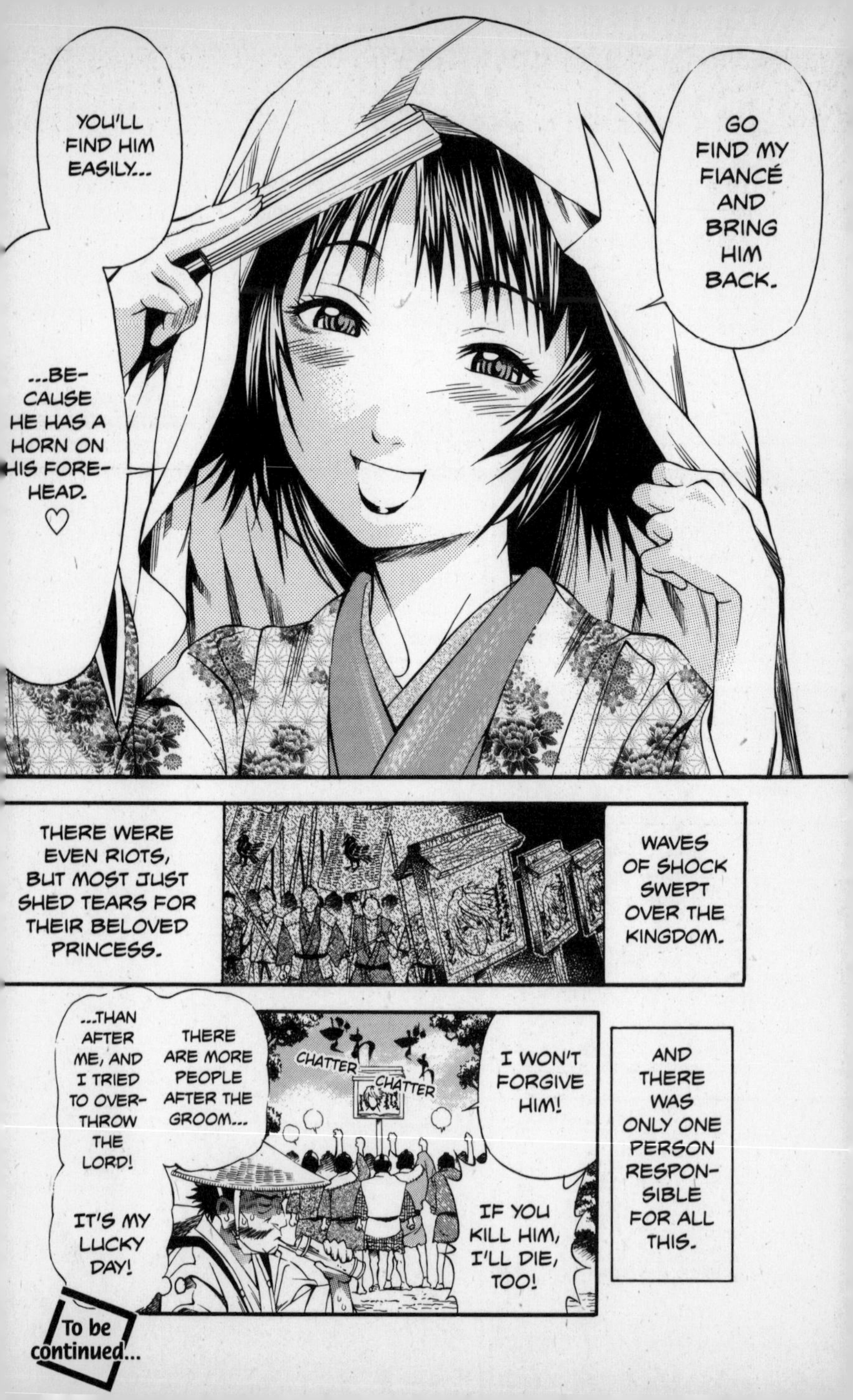
GO FIND MY FIANCÉ AND BRING HIM BACK.
YOU'LL FIND HIM EASILY...
...BECAUSE HE HAS A HORN ON HIS FOREHEAD. ♡
WAVES OF SHOCK SWEPT OVER THE KINGDOM.
THERE WERE EVEN RIOTS, BUT MOST JUST SHED TEARS FOR THEIR BELOVED PRINCESS.
AND THERE WAS ONLY ONE PERSON RESPONSIBLE FOR ALL THIS.
I WON'T FORGIVE HIM!
IF YOU KILL HIM, I'LL DIE, TOO!
CHATTER
CHATTER
THERE ARE MORE PEOPLE AFTER THE GROOM...
...THAN AFTER ME, AND I TRIED TO OVERTHROW THE LORD!
IT'S MY LUCKY DAY!
To be continued...

TRANSLATION NOTES

Japanese is a tricky language for most Westerners, and translation is often more art than science. For your edification and reading pleasure, here are notes on some of the places where we could have gone in a different direction in our translation of the work, or where a Japanese cultural reference is used.

Sengoku era

Sengoku jidai (Warring States Era) lasted from the mid-fifteenth century to the beginning of the seventeenth century. As its name suggests, it was a time of civil war in Japan, with regional lords (*daimyo*) taking control because of a weak central government. The most famous *daimyo* were Oda Nobunaga, known for his military prowess, and Tokugawa Ieyasu, who went on to become the first shogun of Japan's final shogunate.

-nee

-nee is a shortened version of "Oneesan" or "Oneechan"—"sister." It can also be used as a term of endearment toward older girls who aren't necessarily related to the speaker, as when Mizuchi calls Kagari "Kagari-nee."

Hime

Hime means "princess."

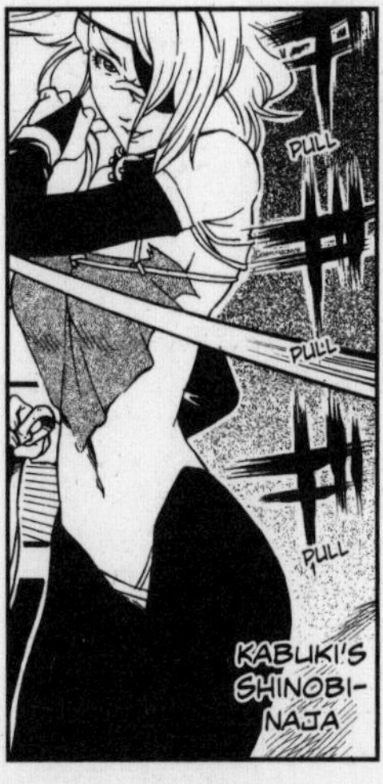
PULL
PULL
PULL
KABUKI'S SHINOBI-NAJA

shinobi, page 9

Another word for ninja. *Shinobi* was the more commonly used term for ninja until its usage declined in popularity post-World War II.

***kunoichi*, page 11**

A *kunoichi* is a female ninja. The kanji for the word resembles the kanji of the word for "woman."

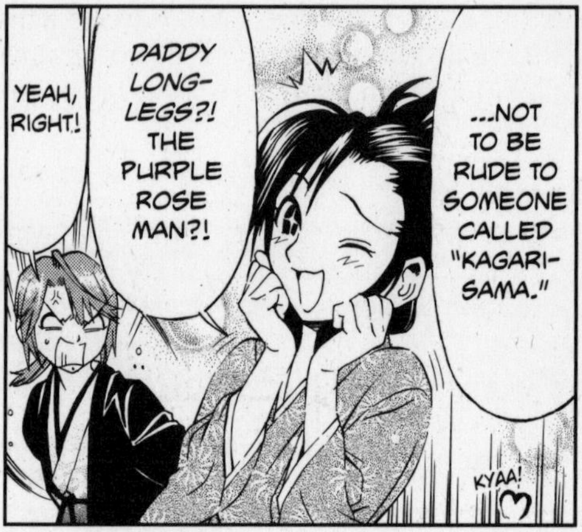
...NOT TO BE RUDE TO SOMEONE CALLED "KAGARI-SAMA."
DADDY LONG-LEGS?! THE PURPLE ROSE MAN?!
YEAH, RIGHT!
KYAA!

***Daddy Long-Legs*, page 13**

A novel by Jean Webster published in 1912 about a girl who writes letters to her benefactor, a rich man whom she has never met.

***Purple Rose Man*, page 13**

This refers to a character from *Garasu no Kamen* (*Glass Mask*)—a manga by Suzue Miuchi. The protagonist, aspiring actress Maya, is encouraged by the support of an anonymous fan whom she calls "The Purple Rose Man" because of the trademark purple roses he sends her. He pays for her tuition and takes care of her much like Daddy Long-Legs from Webster's novel does.

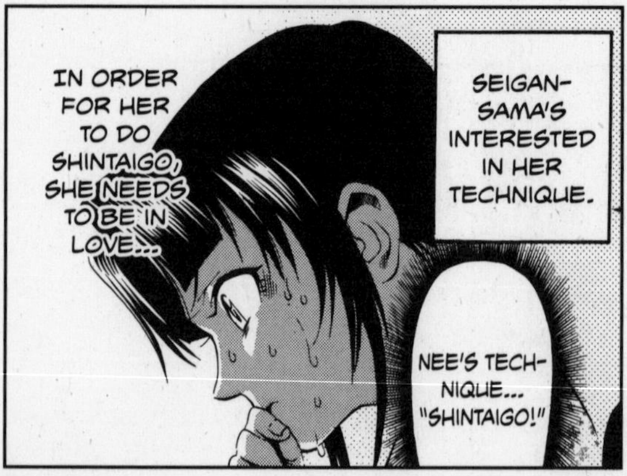
SEIGAN-SAMA'S INTERESTED IN HER TECHNIQUE.
IN ORDER FOR HER TO DO SHINTAIGO, SHE NEEDS TO BE IN LOVE...
NEE'S TECHNIQUE... "SHINTAIGO!"

***Shintaigo*, page 21**

Kagari's special *ninpo* attack. It's written with the characters for "god," "body," and "conjuction."

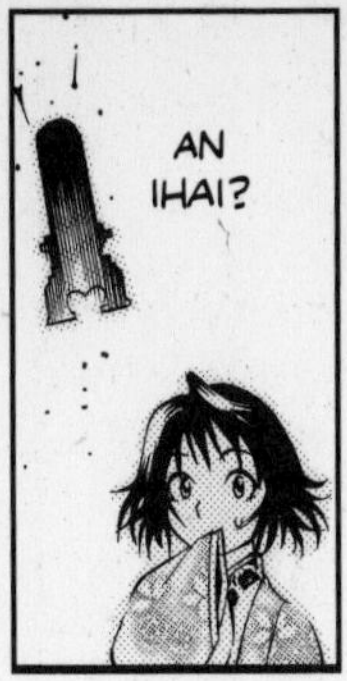
AN IHAI?

ihai, page 52
An *ihai* is a mortuary tablet that's often placed on a Buddhist altar to honor a deceased loved one. It's usually a wood or stone tablet that's engraved with the deceased person's posthumous name, which is given to them by the Buddhist priest who performed their funerary rites.

Marishi-ten, page 56
Goddess of light and heaven, patron deity of warriors. Samurai would invoke Marishi-ten before battle for protection and some believed she would make them invisible to their enemies.

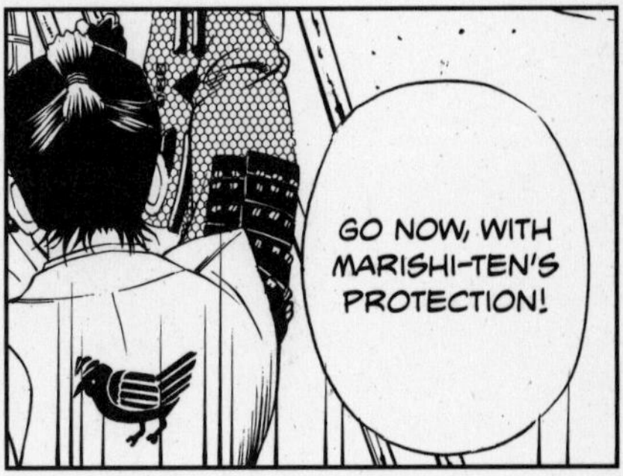
GO NOW, WITH MARISHI-TEN'S PROTECTION!

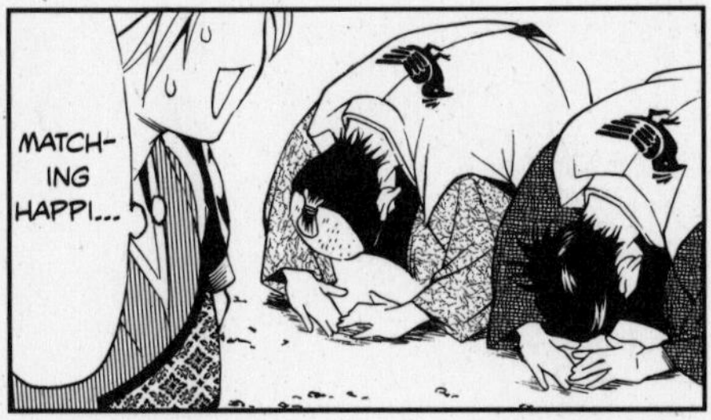
MATCHING HAPPI...

Happi, page 58
A *Happi* is a traditional Japanese coat, usually worn by servants in this time period.

kemari, page 72
A type of game played by courtiers in ancient Japan, *kemari* resembles hacky sack except it uses a ball instead of a beanbag.

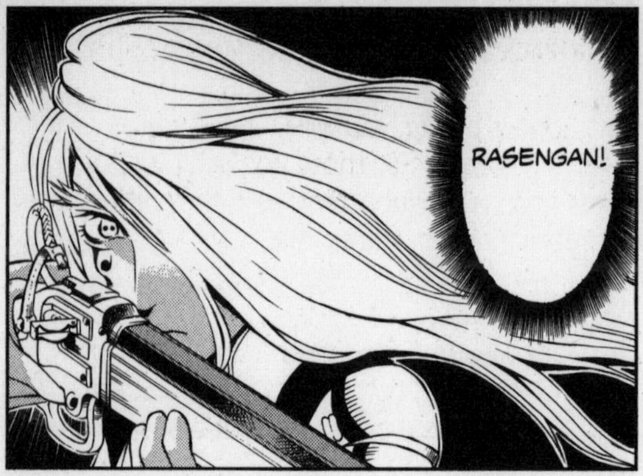
RASENGAN!

***rasengan*, page 166**

Kisarabi's special *ninpo* attack. It's written with the characters for "wizard" and "eye."

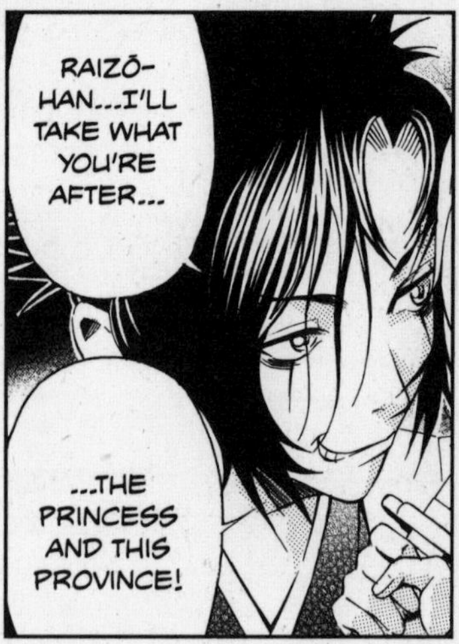
RAIZŌ-HAN...I'LL TAKE WHAT YOU'RE AFTER...
...THE PRINCESS AND THIS PROVINCE!

***-han*, page 172**

-han is an honorific that means roughly the same thing as –san. It's largely outdated, but is still used today in some parts of Japan, particularly in Kyoto.

HONORIFICS EXPLAINED

Throughout the Kodansha Comics books, you will find Japanese honorifics left intact in the translations. For those not familiar with how the Japanese use honorifics and, more important, how they differ from American honorifics, we present this brief overview.

Politeness has always been a critical facet of Japanese culture. Ever since the feudal era, when Japan was a highly stratified society, use of honorifics—which can be defined as polite speech that indicates relationship or status—has played an essential role in the Japanese language. When addressing someone in Japanese, an honorific usually takes the form of a suffix attached to one's name (example: "Asuna-san"), is used as a title at the end of one's name, or appears in place of the name itself (example: "Negi-sensei," or simply "Sensei!").

Honorifics can be expressions of respect or endearment. In the context of manga and anime, honorifics give insight into the nature of the relationship between characters. Many English translations leave out these important honorifics and therefore distort the feel of the original Japanese. Because Japanese honorifics contain nuances that English honorifics lack, it is our policy at Kodansha not to translate them. Here, instead, is a guide to some of the honorifics you may encounter in Kodansha Comics.

-san: This is the most common honorific and is equivalent to Mr., Miss, Ms., or Mrs. It is the all-purpose honorific and can be used in any situation where politeness is required.

-sama: This is one level higher than "-san" and is used to confer great respect.

-dono: This comes from the word "tono," which means "lord." It is an even higher level than "-sama" and confers utmost respect.

-kun: This suffix is used at the end of boys' names to express familiarity or endearment. It is also sometimes used by men among friends, or when addressing someone younger or of a lower station.

-chan: This is used to express endearment, mostly toward girls. It is also used for little boys, pets, and even among lovers. It gives a sense of childish cuteness.

Bozu: This is an informal way to refer to a boy, similar to the English terms "kid" and "squirt."

**Sempai/
Senpai:** This title suggests that the addressee is one's senior in a group or organization. It is most often used in a school setting, where underclassmen refer to their upperclassmen as "sempai." It can also be used in the workplace, such as when a newer employee addresses an employee who has seniority in the company.

Kohai: This is the opposite of "sempai" and is used toward underclassmen in school or newcomers in the workplace. It connotes that the addressee is of a lower station.

Sensei: Literally meaning "one who has come before," this title is used for teachers, doctors, or masters of any profession or art.

-[blank]: This is usually forgotten in these lists, but it is perhaps the most significant difference between Japanese and English. The lack of honorific means that the speaker has permission to address the person in a very intimate way. Usually, only family, spouses, or very close friends have this kind of permission. Known as *yobisute*, it can be gratifying when someone who has earned the intimacy starts to call one by one's name without an honorific. But when that intimacy hasn't been earned, it can be very insulting.

Preview of Volume 3

We're pleased to present you a preview from volume 3, now available from Kodansha Comics. Please check our Web site (www.kodanshacomics.com) for more details!

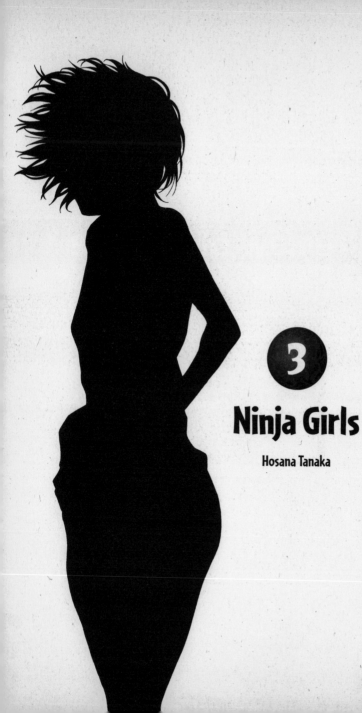

3

Ninja Girls

Hosana Tanaka

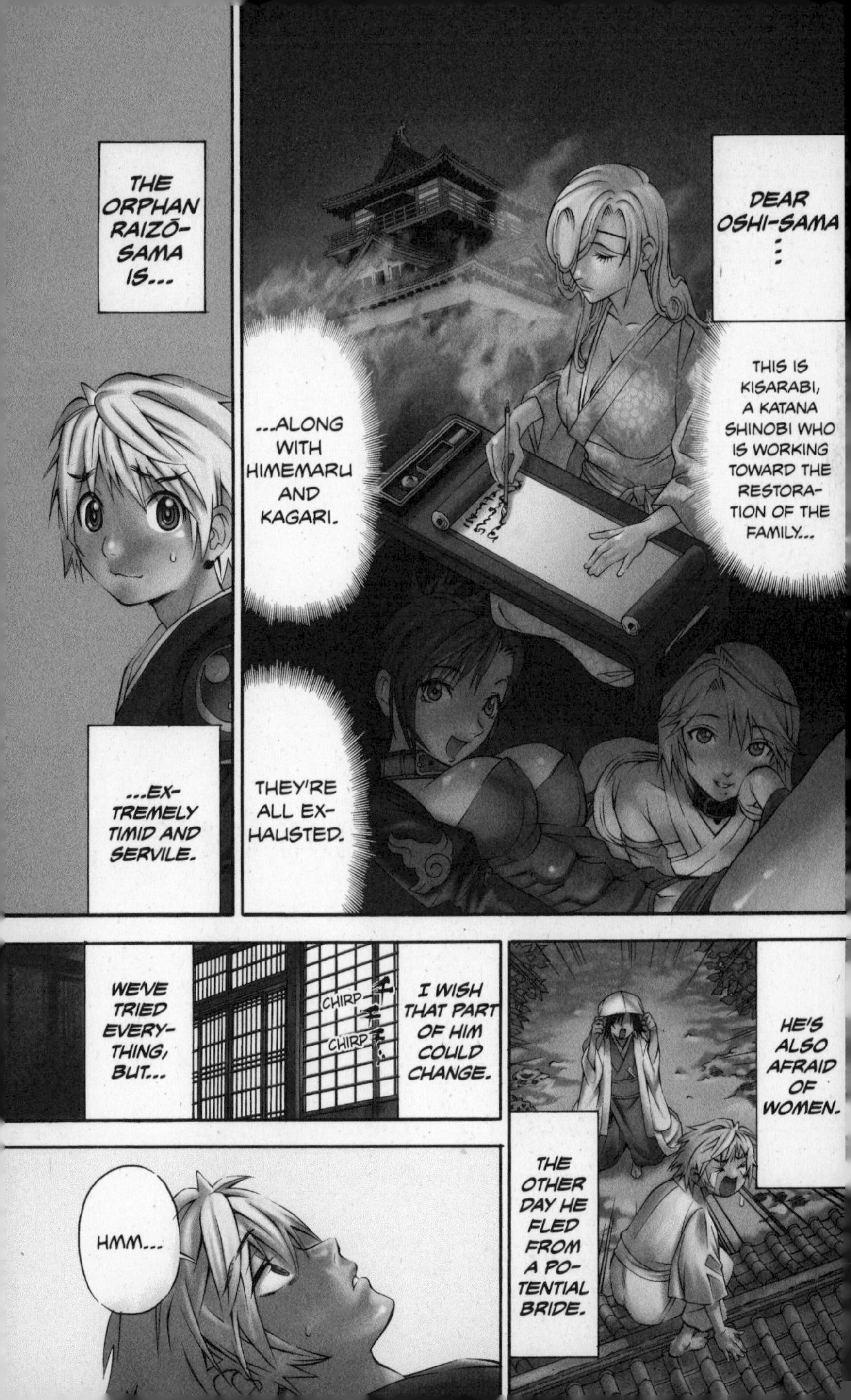
DEAR OSHI-SAMA...
THIS IS KISARABI, A KATANA SHINOBI WHO IS WORKING TOWARD THE RESTORATION OF THE FAMILY...
...ALONG WITH HIMEMARU AND KAGARI.
THEY'RE ALL EXHAUSTED.
THE ORPHAN RAIZŌ-SAMA IS...
...EXTREMELY TIMID AND SERVILE.
HE'S ALSO AFRAID OF WOMEN.
THE OTHER DAY HE FLED FROM A POTENTIAL BRIDE.
I WISH THAT PART OF HIM COULD CHANGE.
CHIRP CHIRP
WE'VE TRIED EVERYTHING, BUT...
HMM...

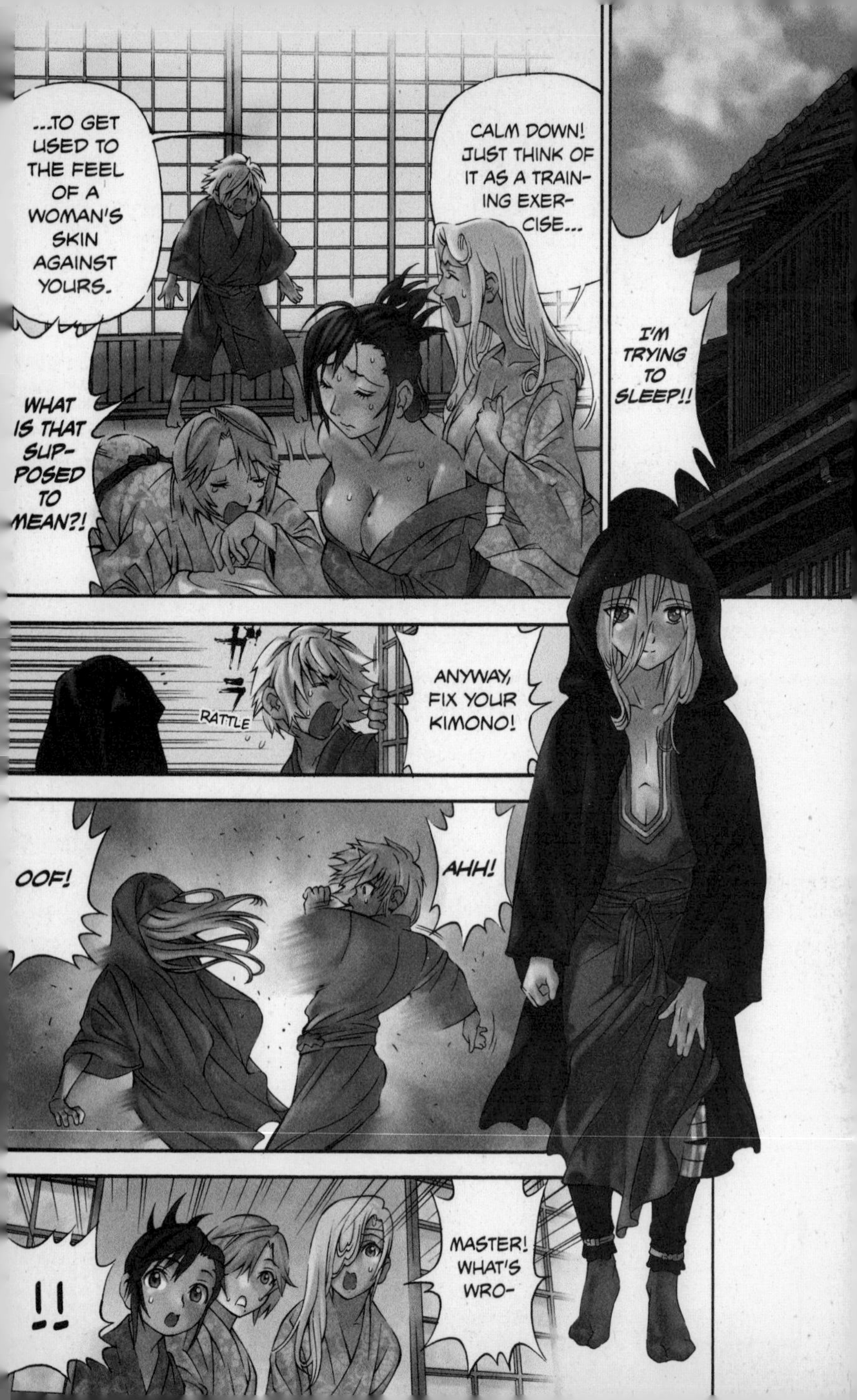
I'M TRYING TO SLEEP!!
CALM DOWN! JUST THINK OF IT AS A TRAINING EXERCISE...
...TO GET USED TO THE FEEL OF A WOMAN'S SKIN AGAINST YOURS.
WHAT IS THAT SUPPOSED TO MEAN?!
ANYWAY, FIX YOUR KIMONO!
RATTLE
AHH!
OOF!
MASTER! WHAT'S WRO-
!!

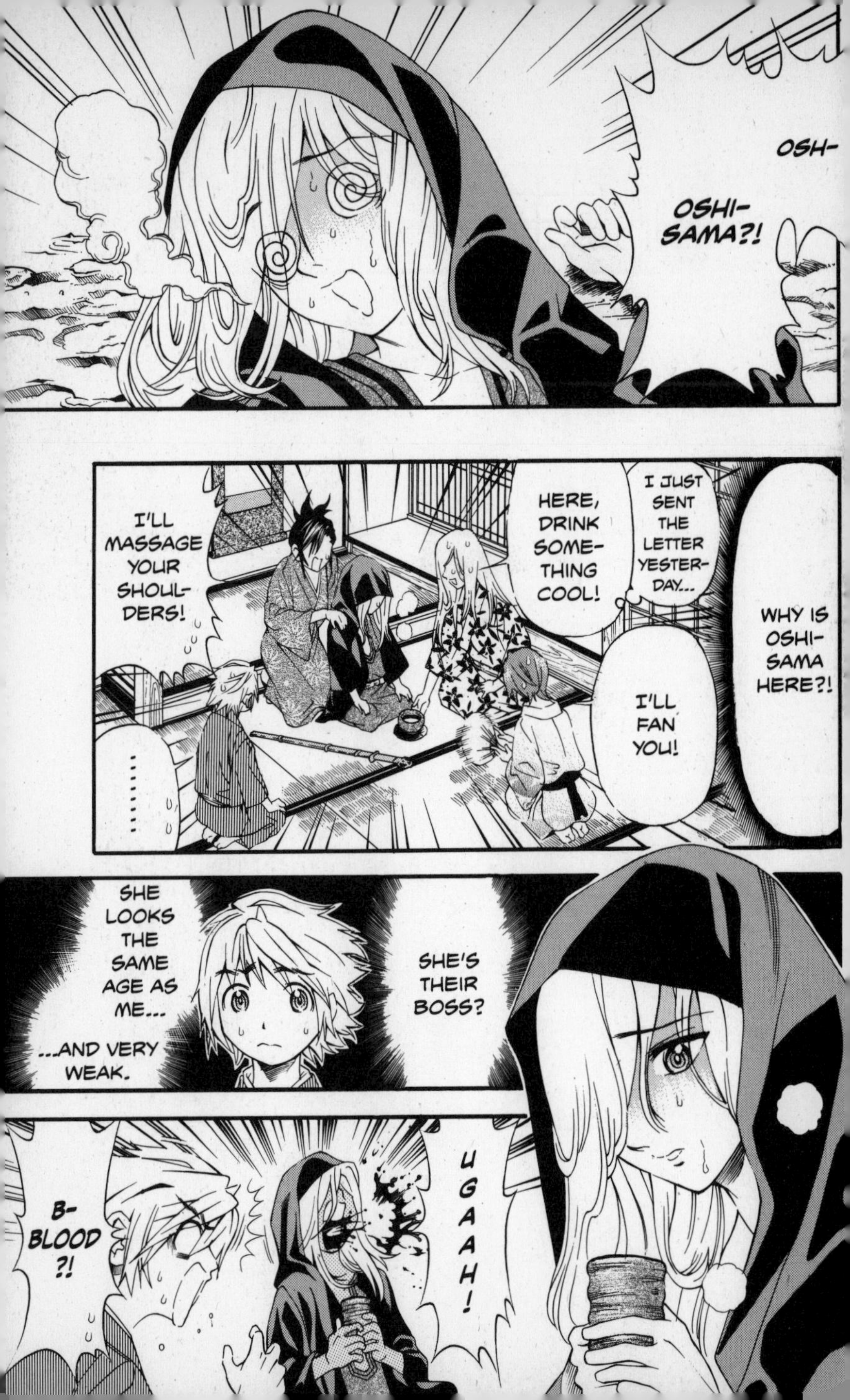
OSH-
OSHI-SAMA?!
WHY IS OSHI-SAMA HERE?!
I JUST SENT THE LETTER YESTERDAY...
HERE, DRINK SOMETHING COOL!
I'LL FAN YOU!
I'LL MASSAGE YOUR SHOULDERS!
....
SHE'S THEIR BOSS?
SHE LOOKS THE SAME AGE AS ME...
...AND VERY WEAK.
UGAAAH!
B-BLOOD?!

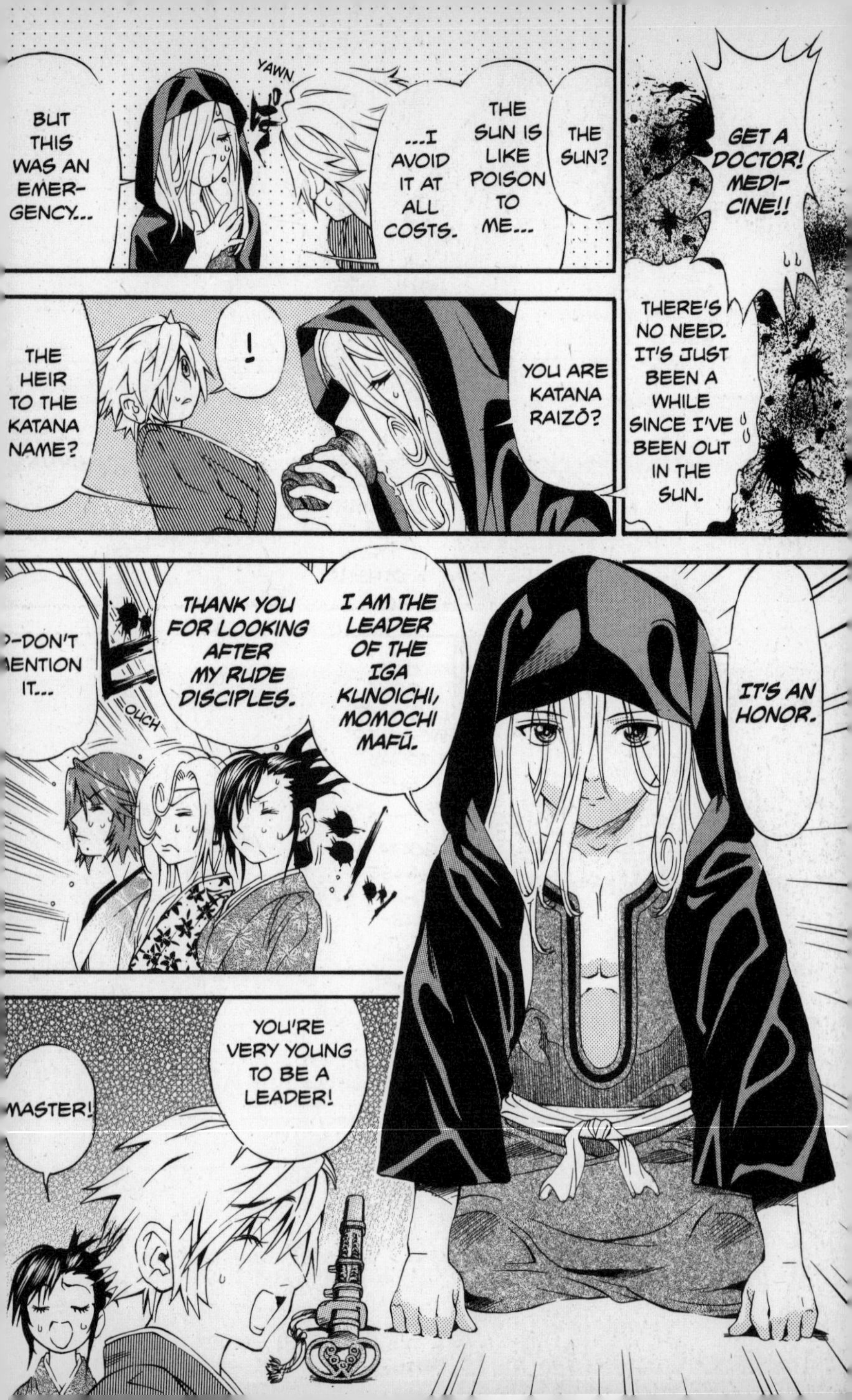
GET A DOCTOR! MEDICINE!!
THERE'S NO NEED. IT'S JUST BEEN A WHILE SINCE I'VE BEEN OUT IN THE SUN.
THE SUN?
THE SUN IS LIKE POISON TO ME...
...I AVOID IT AT ALL COSTS.
YAWN
BUT THIS WAS AN EMERGENCY...
YOU ARE KATANA RAIZŌ?
!
THE HEIR TO THE KATANA NAME?
IT'S AN HONOR.
I AM THE LEADER OF THE IGA KUNOICHI, MOMOCHI MAFŪ.
THANK YOU FOR LOOKING AFTER MY RUDE DISCIPLES.
OUCH
-DON'T ENTION IT...
YOU'RE VERY YOUNG TO BE A LEADER!
MASTER!

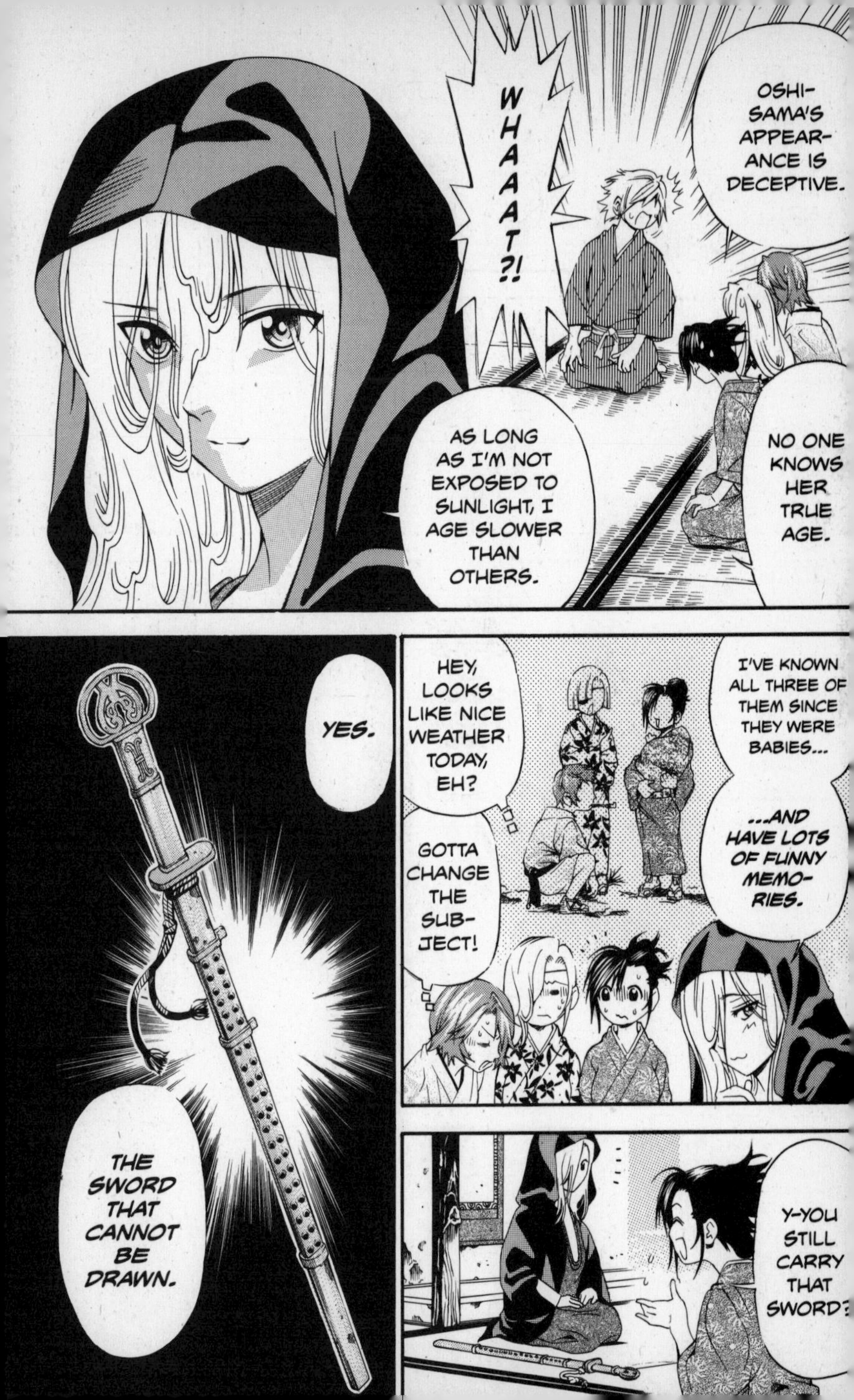
OSHI-SAMA'S APPEARANCE IS DECEPTIVE.
WHAAAAT?!
NO ONE KNOWS HER TRUE AGE.
AS LONG AS I'M NOT EXPOSED TO SUNLIGHT, I AGE SLOWER THAN OTHERS.
I'VE KNOWN ALL THREE OF THEM SINCE THEY WERE BABIES...
...AND HAVE LOTS OF FUNNY MEMORIES.
HEY, LOOKS LIKE NICE WEATHER TODAY, EH?
GOTTA CHANGE THE SUBJECT!
Y-YOU STILL CARRY THAT SWORD?
...
YES.
THE SWORD THAT CANNOT BE DRAWN.

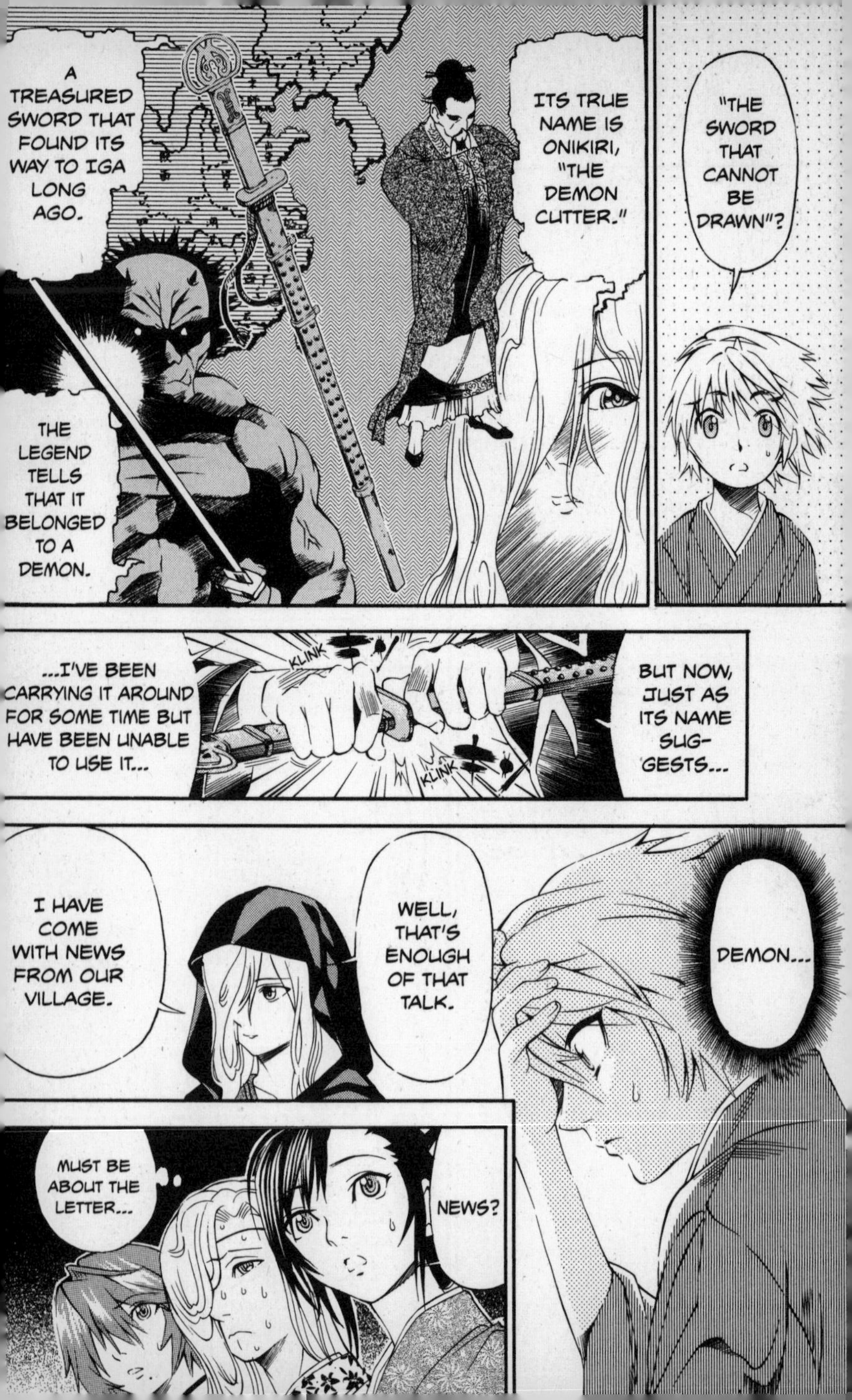
"THE SWORD THAT CANNOT BE DRAWN"?
ITS TRUE NAME IS ONIKIRI, "THE DEMON CUTTER."
A TREASURED SWORD THAT FOUND ITS WAY TO IGA LONG AGO.
THE LEGEND TELLS THAT IT BELONGED TO A DEMON.
BUT NOW, JUST AS ITS NAME SUG-GESTS...
KLINK
KLINK
...I'VE BEEN CARRYING IT AROUND FOR SOME TIME BUT HAVE BEEN UNABLE TO USE IT...
DEMON...
WELL, THAT'S ENOUGH OF THAT TALK.
I HAVE COME WITH NEWS FROM OUR VILLAGE.
NEWS?
MUST BE ABOUT THE LETTER...

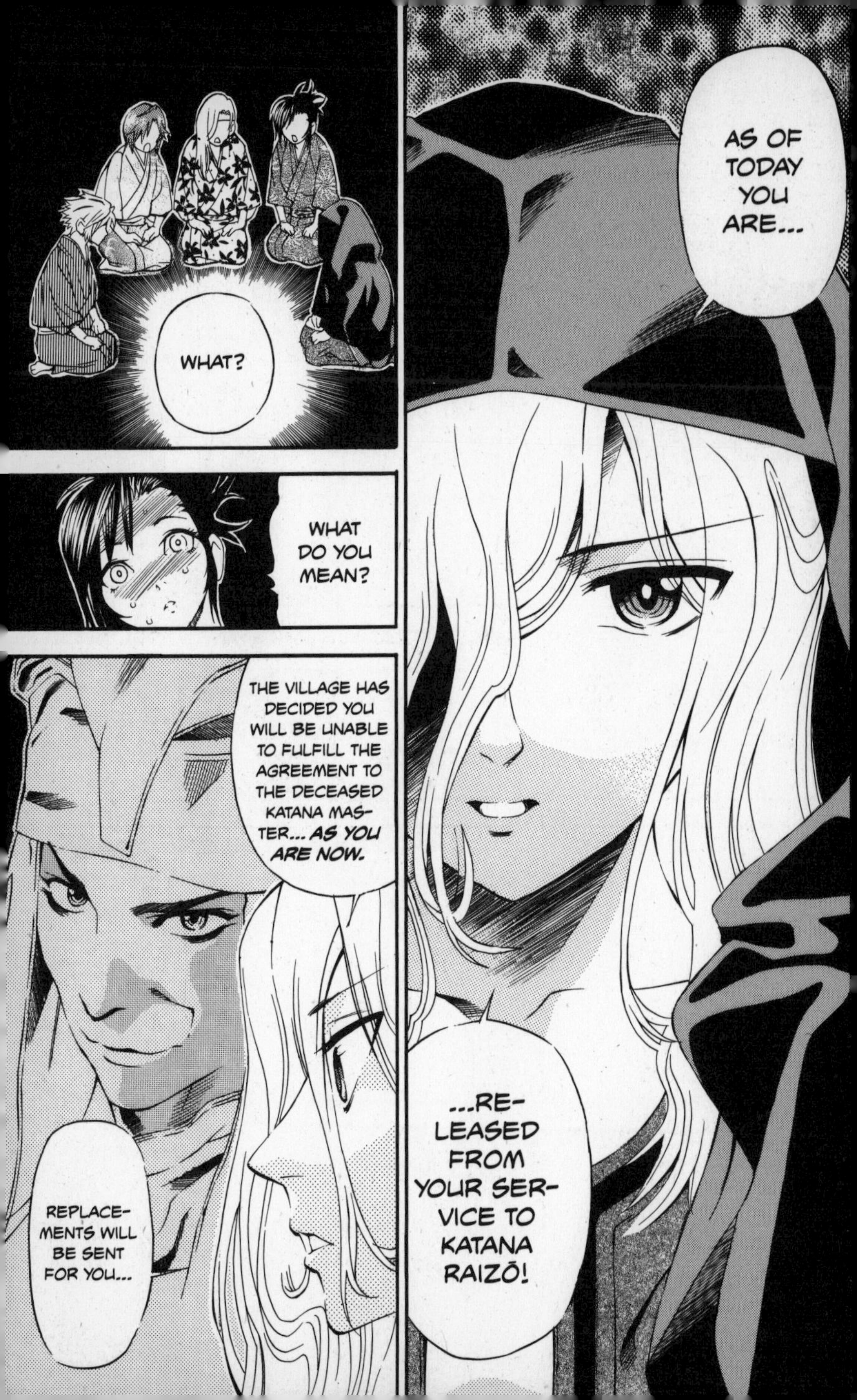
AS OF TODAY YOU ARE...
...RE-LEASED FROM YOUR SER-VICE TO KATANA RAIZŌ!
WHAT?
WHAT DO YOU MEAN?
THE VILLAGE HAS DECIDED YOU WILL BE UNABLE TO FULFILL THE AGREEMENT TO THE DECEASED KATANA MAS-TER... *AS YOU ARE NOW.*
REPLACE-MENTS WILL BE SENT FOR YOU...

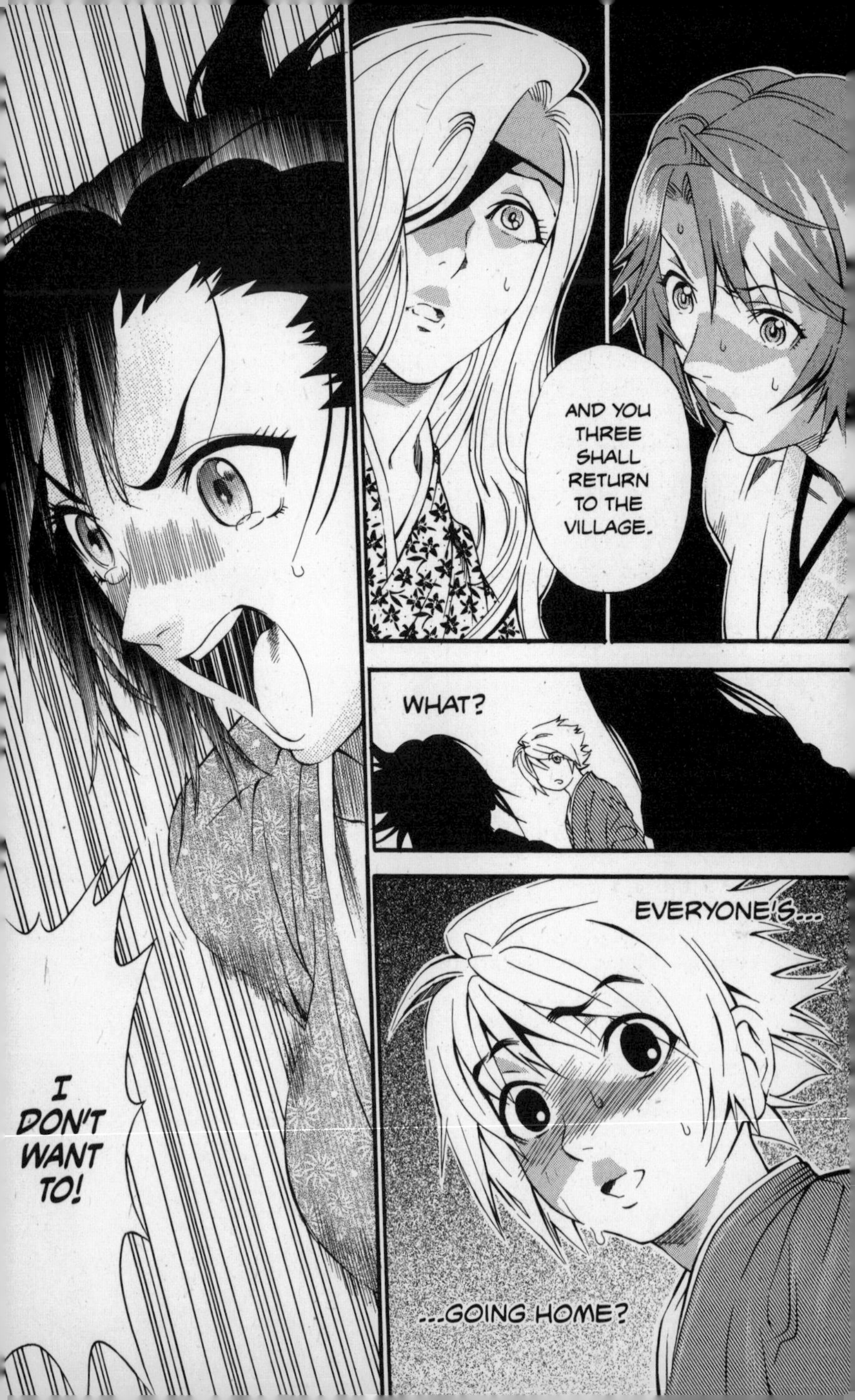
AND YOU THREE SHALL RETURN TO THE VILLAGE.
WHAT?
EVERYONE'S...
...GOING HOME?
I DON'T WANT TO!

Ninja Girls volume 2 is a work of fiction. Names, characters, places, and incidents are the products of the author's imagination or are used fictitiously. Any resemblance to actual events, locales, or persons, living or dead, is entirely coincidental.

A Kodansha Comics Trade Paperback Original.

Published in the United States by Kodansha Comics, an imprint of Kodansha USA Publishing, LLC., New York.

Publication rights for this English edition arranged through Kodansha Ltd., Tokyo.

First published in Japan in 2006 by Kodansha Ltd., Tokyo, as *Rappi Rangai,* volume 2.

ISBN 978-1-61262-338-2

Printed in the United States of America.

www.kodanshacomics.com

9 8 7 6 5 4 3 2

Translator/Adapter—Andria Cheng
Lettering—North Market Street Graphics

TOMARE!

[STOP!]

You are going the wrong way!

Manga is a completely different type of reading experience.

To start at the *beginning*, go to the *end*!

That's right! Authentic manga is read the traditional Japanese way—from right to left, exactly the opposite of how American books are read. It's easy to follow: Just go to the other end of the book, and read each page—and each panel—from the right side to the left side, starting at the top right. Now you're experiencing manga as it was meant to be.